Clas

Berlusconi's Shadow

DAVID LANE

Berlusconi's Shadow

Crime, Justice and the
Pursuit of Power

ALLEN LANE
an imprint of
PENGUIN BOOKS

ALLEN LANE

Published by the Penguin Group
Penguin Books Ltd, 80 Strand, London WC2R ORL, England
Penguin Group (USA) Inc., 375 Hudson Street, New York, New York 10014, USA
Penguin Books Australia Ltd, 250 Camberwell Road, Camberwell, Victoria 3124, Australia
Penguin Books Canada Ltd, 10 Alcorn Avenue, Toronto, Ontario, Canada M4V 3B2
Penguin Books India (P) Ltd, 11 Community Centre, Panchsheel Park, New Delhi – 110 017, India
Penguin Group (NZ), cnr Rosedale and Airborne Roads, Albany, Auckland 1310, New Zealand
Penguin Books (South Africa) (Pty) Ltd, 24 Sturdee Avenue, Rosebank 2196, South Africa

Penguin Books Ltd, Registered Offices: 80 Strand, London WC2R ORL, England

www.penguin.com

First published 2004
1

Typeset in 10.5/14 pt Linotype Sabon by Palimpsest Book Production Limited, Polmont, Stirlingshire
Printed in England by Clays Ltd, St Ives plc

ISBN 0–713–99787–7

For my parents

Contents

List of Illustrations

Photographic acknowledgements are given in parentheses.

1. (i) Berlusconi at high school (Ansa): (ii) around 1970 (Ansa); (iii) around 1950 (Ansa).
2. (i) at the funeral of Bettino Craxi (Ansa/Fethi Belaid); (ii) visitors' book comment (Ansa/KRZ).
3. (i) Forza Italia supporters (Ansa); (ii) saluting the party faithful (Ansa/Farinacci); (iii) in Venice, April 2000 (Ansa/Farinacci).
4 & 5. (i) holiday home on Sardinia (Ansa); (ii) Villa Belvedere (Agenzia Sintesi); (iii) Villa San Martino (Agenzia Sintesi); (iv) with Veronica Lario (Ansa).
6 & 7. (i) Cesare Previti (Ansa/Carlo Ferraro); (ii) Marcello Dell'Utri (Ansa/Michele Naccari); (iii) Bettino Craxi (Ansa); (iv) Giulio Andreotti (Ansa/Mike Palazzotto).
8. (i) with Marcello Dell'Utri (Ansa); (ii) with Cesare Previti (Ansa).
9. (i) Francesco Saverio Borrelli and Gian Carlo Caselli (Ansa/Vincenzo Bianchi); (ii) Franzo Grande Stevens (Ansa).
10 & 11. (i) the death of Giovanni Falcone (Ansa); (ii) Falcone with Paolo Borsellino (Ansa); (iii) the death of Borsellino (Ansa); (iv) Anna Maria Palma (Ansa); (v) Domenico Gozzo and Antonio Ingroia (Ansa); (vi) Ilda Boccassini and Armando Spataro (Ansa/KLD/Matteo Bazzi); (vii) Gherardo Colombo, Antonio Di Pietro and Piercamillo Davigo (Ansa).
12 & 13. (i–v) demonstration against the Cirami Law, September 2002 (Agenzia Sintesi).
14. (i) at AC Milan (Ansa); (ii) at Mediaset, with Fedele Confalonieri and Ubaldo Livolso (Ansa).
15. (i–ii) on magazines and television (Agenzia Sintesi).
16. (i–iii) on trial, June 2003 (Ansa/Daniel Dal Zennaro).

Author's Note

Corruption, the Mafia and justice make a potent mixture. Add Silvio Berlusconi, his huge wealth, enormous media-power, highly individual approach to politics and singular way of looking at the past, and that cocktail becomes even stronger. Yet although Berlusconi is at its heart, as the title suggests, this book is more than the story of the man. Berlusconi's Italy is the heir of *tangentopoli* (bribesville) that exploded in 1992 and the atrocious mafia murders of magistrates Giovanni Falcone and Paolo Borsellino that same year. And it is saddled with the legacy of a criminal justice system that was a mess long before Berlusconi turned to politics in 1993.

Many people helped while I was researching and writing. I owe a particular debt to Anne Engel, my agent, who encouraged me to tackle the project and then helped me wrestle with the tricky question of how the book should be structured. Conventional biography would have had the reader starting in distant times and often being taken to places with which Berlusconi has little or no connection, so I decided that the work should be thematic rather than chronological. My brother Michael read the typescript from start to finish and made helpful comments. I am grateful to Bela Cunha for her care and attention in editing, and to Stuart Proffitt at Penguin, my British publisher, and Giuseppe Laterza of Editori Laterza, my Italian publisher, for providing valuable support for the writing of a book that might be considered critical of a wealthy and powerful public figure.

Early during the two and a half years – from February 2001 to July 2003 – during which we followed these absorbing subjects for *The Economist*, I came to appreciate the tenacity of my colleague Tim Laxton in seeking out the facts and his precision when putting them on paper. My thanks are also owed to a small group of Italian journalists that I came to know after *The Economist* published a special feature on Berlusconi in April 2001: Gianni Barbacetto, Peter Gomez and Giovanni Ruggeri in Milan, Marco Travaglio in Turin, Mario Guarino in Rome, and Lirio Abbate, Enrico Bellavia and Salvo Palazzolo in Palermo. The lawyers Roberto Avellone, Alessandro Benedetti, Vittorio Grevi, Bruno Guardascione, Marisa Pappalardo, Giuliano Pisapia, Virginia and Vittorio Ripa Di Meana, Elisabetta Rubini, Gaetano Cappellano Seminara, Carlo Smuraglia and Ennio Tinaglia helped me understand Italian law and Italy's legal system, although any inaccuracies in how I have described them are clearly my own. Franzo Grande Stevens, whom I am privileged to have known for twenty-five years, also told me about himself as well as about the law.

Elio Collova, an accountant who administers assets confiscated from the Mafia and is now a friend, and a mutual friend through whom we met, showed me a side of Palermo and its citizens that was very different from the stereotypes. Through Francesco Giambrone, a music-loving doctor, I learned about both the scandal of Palermo's Teatro Massimo and the fine opera that is performed there. In the Sicilian capital I also discovered good food and agreeable company in a small trattoria, the Sant'Andrea, close to the Vucciria market, and was intrigued and pleased that this was where Peter Robb found sustenance when writing his excellent study of Sicily, Giulio Andreotti and the Mafia, *Midnight in Sicily*. If there were a model for my book, it would be Robb's work.

I found in Milan people representing the best of that city and an almost vanished rectitude who were horrified by the deep corruption that infected business and political life there; the writer Corrado Stajano, whose book on the murdered lawyer Giorgio Ambrosoli was a tribute to a Milanese bourgeois morality that had disappeared even before *tangentopoli* worked its corrosive effects; the former investigator Silvio Novembre, who was a colleague of Ambrosoli; and Salvatore Bragantini, a banker and watchdog of ethical values in business. I owe special thanks to my old Milanese friend Pierleone Ottolenghi, without whom the book would not have been started.

In some ways, the book has turned out to be a tale of two cities,

Palermo and Milan, with Rome appearing sometimes in the middle. But the academic spires of Oxford made an appearance too when Professor Alan Ryan of New College kindly gave me a half-day tutorial on ethics, the rule of law, rights, duties and the limits on government in democracies to help me clarify my ideas. If they still seem cloudy, the fault is entirely mine.

I do not intend to thank individually the many Italian magistrates who generously gave me their time to explain the magistrature's work. This book is about them, and about the assault to which they have been subject, as much as about Berlusconi and the trials in which he and his friends have stood accused of serious criminal offences. In any case, many of the magistrates' names are in the book and so are some of their experiences, often way beyond what magistrates in other western democracies have to cope with. I hope that I have done justice – in a work partly triggered by surprise at how many Italians have short memories about the sacrifices made by magistrates and other servants of the state who fight crime – to the magistrature's sense of duty and service. Under Berlusconi's government, Italians have also been encouraged to forget or to play down fascism and I understood the unease of Harry Shindler, representative of the veterans of the Italy Star Association 1943–1945, and his indignation about attempts to tamper with history.

Finally, I would like to thank the two Italian women in my life. My daughter Clara, who grew up in Rome and then became accustomed to a much faster pace on the trading floor of an investment bank in London, could not understand why the book took so long. She was always ready to ask reprovingly why progress was three, six or twelve months behind schedule. My wife Franca, never other than a great source of cheerful encouragement, will now be spared my frequent expressions of amazement at what had happened and what was going on.

Prologue

Standing on a hill above the town and overlooking the sea, the Anzio War Cemetery holds the graves of almost 1,100 British and Commonwealth sailors, soldiers and airmen who died during bitter fighting on the beaches below and in the surrounding countryside in January and February 1944. That winter was among the coldest in Italian memory, which added to the terrible suffering of soldiers bivouacked in foxholes and trenches.[1] The campaign at Anzio was one of the most brutal of the Second World War and the ferocious fighting for the beachhead shocked even the toughest, most experienced front-line officers.

Anzio and the neigbouring town of Nettuno lie on the coast about 40 miles south of Rome, on the edge of the Pontine marshes, the drainage of which was one of the few achievements of Italy's twenty-year fascist dictatorship. Early on 22 January 1944, the towns were shattered by a massive barrage of rockets fired from warships supporting an invasion fleet that carried American and British troops. The aim was to outflank the Germans' defensive Gustav line between Naples and Rome and break the stalemate that had developed there. The landings at Anzio and Nettuno went smoothly and surprised the German defenders; only a light swell was running when the ships arrived off the two towns and the allies were able to put more than 36,000 men ashore by evening.[2] But the generals failed to exploit their advantage and the shallow beachhead, on a plain overlooked by German positions in the Alban Hills, became a bloody battleground until the allied armies broke out four months later.

Just over a week after the landings, on the last day of January, an 800-strong battalion of Britain's Sherwood Foresters launched an unsuccessful assault on the German defences. Fewer than 300 from the battalion mustered that evening after the battle.[3] Captain Williamson was killed, and beside him in the cemetery lie Private Clamp and Corporal Belton of the same regiment, who died the same day. Four days later, Privates John and Thomas Cairncross, nineteen-year-old twin brothers in the London Scottish Regiment, were killed. They were the sons of Hugh and Elizabeth Cairncross of Newburgh, a small town in Fife, Scotland. About two miles inland, there are more than 2,000 British and Commonwealth graves in the Beach Head War Cemetery and, like those in the Anzio War Cemetery, the gravestones carry the crests of the regiments of the soldiers buried beneath them. The regiments engaged at Anzio had written chapters of British history across the centuries and around the world: the Buffs, Green Howards, Irish Guards, Scots Guards, Seaforth Highlanders, Black Watch, Royal Fusiliers. As well as the two in Anzio, the Commonwealth War Graves Commission tends thirty-five other war cemeteries in Italy. Almost 40,000 British and Commonwealth servicemen of the Second World War who died in the struggle to defeat the fascist regime and return Italy to democracy are buried there.

One mile inland from the sea at Nettuno, carefully manicured lawns cover the graves of almost 8,000 American sailors, soldiers and airmen who were killed helping to liberate Italy from fascism. Some had died during the landings in Sicily in July 1943 and during the fighting across the island. Others had been killed as they fought northwards through Calabria, during the landings at Salerno in September 1943 or in the fighting on the Gustav line.

America's military dead had been interred in temporary cemeteries along the line of advance. Some next-of-kin asked that the bodies should be reburied in Italy, the country where the soldiers had fallen in action. Two days after they landed at Anzio, the US Sixth Corps established a temporary cemetery at Nettuno. Twelve years later, on a 77-acre site there, the American Battle Monuments Commission completed a permanent cemetery, bringing together the bodies of those who had died at Anzio and those who had been buried further south. Evergreen holly oaks and cypress trees frame the burial area and umbrella pines give shade. A large memorial made of travertine stone from Tivoli near Rome overlooks the lawns and the rows of simple crosses.

Many soldiers buried in the American cemetery at Nettuno have Italian names. William Rosati, a private first class from New York, died on the day of the landings. Severino Caprini from Illinois, another private first class, was killed three days later. Dominic and Joseph Di Blasio, brothers from Vermont, were killed within a week of each other in early summer 1944. A private with the 15th Infantry, Pio Chiarlitti was only eighteen when he died on 24 January 1944. His parents had emigrated to New York from Monte San Giovanni Campano, a village about 50 miles southeast of Nettuno where his grandmother continued to live. Chiarlitti had written to her to say that he expected to see her soon, and got his letter across the German lines using a service provided by the Red Cross. Sixty years later, Pio Chiarlitti's niece still kept this letter and members of the family visited his grave.[4] Tens of thousands of American, British and Commonwealth lives were given between 1943 and 1945 in liberating Italy and freeing continental Europe from Nazi–Fascist dictatorship.

Silvio Berlusconi, who became Italian prime minister for the second time after elections in May 2001, had his own thoughts on the matter. He believed that Italians had had to wait until three years after the end of the Second World War before they could enjoy freedom and democracy. For Berlusconi, liberation arrived with the defeat in 1948's elections of the Italian left, many of whom had been brothers-in-arms of the American GIs and British tommies who had given their lives in the war against Nazi–Fascism.[5] Berlusconi was the Italian politician who, on becoming prime minister for the first time in 1994, invited into his government the political heirs of Benito Mussolini and the twenty years of fascism that the allied forces had battled against.

Berlusconi gave Italians a singular reading of their country's recent history. Carlo Azeglio Ciampi, Italy's president, reassured Italians that they were no longer divided by the past. They were rediscovering the deep sources of a shared memory, Ciampi told them on the day of national unity at the beginning of November 2002.[6] His remarks were welcomed by Gianfranco Fini, deputy prime minister and leader of the National Alliance, as the right-wing party whose lineage could be traced directly to Mussolini was called.

Some who had fought for democracy and liberty in the war against fascism were shocked. Armando Cossutta who had been elected eight times to parliament, either as a senator or a deputy, thought that Ciampi was mistaken. As a seventeen-year-old, Cossutta had joined the underground Italian Communist Party, fought with the 128th Garibaldi Brigade in the partisans' war against Nazi–Fascism, been captured and imprisoned in Milan's San Vittore prison.[7] Italy's day of national unity coincided with the day on which British forces success-fully broke out from El Alamein in Egypt in 1942. At El Alamein, said Cossutta, a battle was fought between the forces of democracy on one side and those of Nazi–Fascist dictatorship on the other.[8]

In March 1949, when the conflict was still very fresh in people's minds, Piero Calamandrei, a lawyer who had practised during the two decades of fascism, fought with the partisans and then been a member of the post-war constituent assembly, had spoken in parlia-ment of how democracy returned to Italy. A founding father of the Italian republic, Calamandrei held clear views of right and wrong and about how the country's recent history should be interpreted. This grand figure of twentieth-century Italy, who had experienced dictatorship at first hand, knew well that liberty and democracy had arrived in Italy with the allied forces and not in 1948. Italians owed their regained freedom to the miraculous Russian victory at Stalingrad, the heroic British resistance in August 1940 and the crush-ing weight of American armaments, said Calamandrei.[9]

Even Italians far too young to have been involved in the liberation struggle between 1943 and 1945 had doubts about what Ciampi, an octogenarian who had served as an officer in the Italian army during the war, had said. They had difficulty in understanding how Italians who had fought with the resistance could be put on the same plane as those who had supported Mussolini's regime and the Republic of Salo that the dictator established after Italy had signed an armistice with the Anglo-American allies in September 1943.[10]

A radically different view of history also threatened Italy's text-books, creating a stir among intellectuals and liberal professionals about where Berlusconi's government was heading. One group of concerned Italians, which included Gae Aulenti, a well-known archi-tect, Umberto Eco, the writer, Guido Rossi, a top corporate lawyer and former chairman of the stock market watchdog, and Umberto

Veronesi, a highly regarded cancer specialist, issued a warning and an appeal in December 2002.[11] The group was troubled by a proposal put forward in a parliamentary commission that the ministry of education should become involved in vetting the history books used in schools. Such a step, they thought, was unworthy of a democratic country. The task of producing textbooks belonged to authors and publishers, said the group, and the responsibility for their use lay with the teachers. It was for teachers to help students analyse sources critically; this was the only control that should exist in a free country. The fact that ministerial control over history books had been proposed aroused serious worries about the health of democracy in Italy. That the government should control the ideas expressed in textbooks was reminiscent of times in a not-yet-distant past when the fascist regime had exercised these powers of censorship.[12]

Franzo Grande Stevens, for many years the chairman of the Italian bar association, was among those who signed the appeal and expressed concern about the way that Berlusconi's government and its friends sought to tamper with history. Grande Stevens's uncle was Colonel Stevens, known to Italians of the Second World War as *Colonnello Buona Sera*, the newsreader at the British Broadcasting Corporation in London who, in perfect Italian with an unmistakable Neapolitan accent, told Italians the real news of the war that their fascist leaders wanted hidden.[13]

Yet the threat was there even before Berlusconi won power for the second time in May 2001. The Lazio regional government in Rome, headed by a member of the National Alliance, had voted in November 2000 to establish a commission to examine school textbooks. This example was quickly followed by the Lombardy regional government in Milan which adopted a motion proposed by the National Alliance and the xenophobic Northern League, another ally in the coalition government that Berlusconi formed in 2001.[14] Censorship of textbooks and the rewriting of history seemed close to the hearts of members of Berlusconi's party and other parties in his right-wing coalition. Some wanted to forget or deny the evil that stained their country's past, while others held that the two decades of fascism was a period of which to be proud.

On 31 July 2003, the senate met for its final session before breaking for the summer recess. The last item to which the politicians turned before the speaker wished them *buone vacanze* was the institution of a new national day.[15] At first sight, the proposal by Sergio Travaglia, an eighty-year-old lawyer and senator in Berlusconi's Forza Italia party, was uncontroversial but the bill he presented was provocative. Travaglia was born in Fiume, a city on the eastern coast of the Adriatic that Croats called Rijeka and which had been an early target for Mussolini's international aggression,[16] fascist thugs helping to overthrow Rijeka's autonomous assembly in 1922 and open the way for annexation by Italy.[17] Travaglia wanted Italy to have a day of freedom to mark the fall of the Berlin Wall. Why Italy should celebrate an event in Germany was a mystery to many, other than the fact that the fall of the Berlin Wall on 9 November 1989 also marked the demise of communism and was thus a cause for celebration in the ranks of Berlusconi's coalition. Because the Italian republic already celebrated liberation on 25 April, national unity on 4 November and the republic itself on 2 June, the need for another national day was in any case perplexing, not least because Italian communists had been important participants in the country's liberation and the establishment of the republic, as well as holding firm to the principle of national unity.

Moreover, the date put forward by Travaglia seemed a strange choice. In November 1926, Mussolini had taken the steps that would lead Italy to dictatorship and into a disastrous war, his government introducing measures that would bring to an end the freedom of both political association and the press. After publication in the official gazette, the measures had become effective on 9 November. This day, that the senator of Berlusconi's Forza Italia party thought suitable as freedom day for Italy, had also brought the reintroduction of the death sentence and the abolition of parliamentary opposition.[18] On 9 November 1926, seventeen communist members of parliament had been arrested and the fascist-controlled parliament had taken measures to establish special tribunals.[19]

History was one field where Italy's politicians formed their battle-lines but most Italians were mainly concerned with the present and the future which, as they looked into it, offered murky prospects and was fraught with uncertainty. Fascism and the disaster that it had brought was a very distant matter. Even the ever-present Mafia was far from the minds of most Italians when Berlusconi returned to power in 2001. Horrific violence and ghastly crimes had not made the headlines for many years; the war against the Mafia was a forgotten war, or even a phoney war. The situation was very different in the spring of 2001 from what it had been in the autumn of 1993 when Berlusconi entered politics. Then the memories of the appalling murders of magistrates in Sicily the previous year and the bomb attacks in Italian cities earlier in 1993 were still vivid. Italy was subject to a mafia cycle of peaks and troughs, in violence and in the authorities' attention to the problem and determination to tackle it. By the early years of the twenty-first century, the cycle had sunk into a deep, quiet trough.

I

Mafia

DECADES OF INDIFFERENCE

Notoriously, the Mafia owed a debt to America for the strong position that it established after the Second World War. The Americans had dispatched the gangster Lucky Luciano to help prepare for the sea and airborne assault before the allied landings in Sicily in July 1943. Michele Sindona, who would later combine the role of top banker with that of *mafioso*, and Gaetano Badalamenti, who would later become a mafia boss, were among the Sicilians whom Luciano met and both were thought to have had close contacts with the American secret service.[1] In recognition of the Mafia's help, the Americans endorsed *mafiosi* who had assisted with the invasion and the American military command installed *mafiosi* as mayors in many Sicilian towns.[2] America's clandestine involvement with one of Italy's obscure sides in Sicily during 1943 was the start of decades of meddling in the country's affairs. The Central Intelligence Agency would fund the Christian Democrat Party, considered a bastion against communism, and would be involved in encouraging deviant, extreme right-wing elements in Italy's own secret services.[3]

After the two decades of fascist dictatorship during which the authorities seemed to want to repress it, the Mafia, thanks partly to the helping American hand, was able to make a comeback. Yet, for years following the Second World War, Italy's leaders stubbornly ignored the problem. Blind eyes and deaf ears, or plain complicity, allowed the Mafia to grow stronger and weave itself deeper into Sicily's economic, social and political fabric but only a handful of national politicians acknowledged or seemed to understand what was happening.

Indeed, many politicians in Sicily were in the Mafia's pocket and the Christian Democrat Party, which had been founded in September 1942 and then played a marginal role in the struggle against fascism, owed its strength in the island to its relations with Cosa Nostra. On the evening of 4 January 1947 in the small *piazza* outside the elegant seventeenth-century Palazzo Graffeo in the centre of Sciacca, a town on Sicily's southern coast, the Mafia killed Accursio Miraglia, a leader of the agricultural labourers and one of those in the vanguard of the movement for land reform. A thorn in the side of the local bigwigs, Miraglia was a victim of the sinister alliance between the Mafia and Sicilian landowners who supported and were backed by the Christian Democrats. His murder was a disturbing signal, but worse was to come.

Few people remembered Portella delle Ginestre when, in 1992 and 1993, the Mafia set off bombs on the highway at Capaci and in Via D'Amelio in Palermo, and in Florence, Milan and Rome. The awful slaughter at Portella delle Ginestre, in the countryside south of the Sicilian capital, had taken place more than forty years earlier, on May Day 1947, when farm-workers and their families gathered for a rural *festa*. In a ruthless, ferocious display of force, the Mafia murdered eleven people 'to remind the peasants of who really held power in the province' and the communist leader Li Causi accused the landowners of being behind the massacre.[4] This crime was one of the matters behind the first question on the Mafia put to an Italian government, an opposition politician in Rome asking in 1948 what the government intended to do about the criminals. Not much, according to the internal affairs minister, a Sicilian who thought that the Mafia was simply an age-old, insoluble problem.[5]

At the end of 1958, more than a decade after the mass murder at Portella delle Ginestre, some members of parliament demanded an inquiry into what was going on in western Sicily. They were concerned about the Mafia's involvement in public works contracts, social security bodies and banks, and the patronage system it had created to put its people into jobs. The Mafia and politics were intertwined, said one of those members of parliament, the Mafia insinuating itself to become an ally of governments, governing parties and the organs of the state. He was sure that the problem was national rather than just Sicilian because the Mafia could go freely about its business, as it did, only with connivance from Rome.[6]

Such warnings went unheeded. Successive governments had other priorities and official indifference and complicity partnered the Mafia's development, but parliament eventually set up a commission to look into the problem. Reporting in 1963, fifteen years after the first question had been asked, the commission recommended that the fight against the Mafia should be managed better. The work of Italy's three police forces required coordination, said the commission, suggesting also that staff hired by state and regional bodies in Sicily should be carefully vetted before being taken on and that strict controls over public works contracts, town planning and building licences were needed.[7] Yet, the commission came up with only one proposal that led anywhere, that the criminal code should treat the Mafia more harshly. But the law enacted as a result of the commission's proposal, which allowed judges to compel *mafiosi* to live in cities and towns in the centre and north of Italy, probably did more harm than good.

Parliament's pace was slow but, over the years, the commission was able to point a preoccupied finger at several areas of the Mafia's influence. The Mafia had a hold over the credit system, and there was clear evidence of this in the large loans that banks granted to customers who were unable to provide collateral for the money they borrowed. Mafia bosses also had a say in how the courts worked. Judges and juries seemed to lack objectivity, and prosecutors and investigating magistrates were often short on initiative.[8] As for local government, public-sector bodies in western Sicily frequently bowed to the Mafia's wishes in choosing senior managers, recruiting staff and awarding contracts.

The parliamentary commission made large strides in 1971 and 1972 when, chaired by a Genoese lawyer, it finally recognized what its predecessors had preferred to ignore: that the Mafia systematically used violence and exploited its political links in order to make money. By the beginning of the 1970s, the Mafia's power was such that the police, the judiciary and the organs of the state had been revealed as impotent against it. Political blind eyes could no longer be turned to the problem as the fundamental characteristics of the Mafia's expansion were beyond denial even for the government. The Mafia had pushed into numerous businesses other than drug-trafficking and had developed strong links with the public sector and politicians.[9] It had spread beyond Sicily and taken root in the centre and north of the country, in big cities such as Rome, Milan and Genoa, but the authorities still did not want to take it on.

THE MURDER OF TWO MAGISTRATES

However, the cohabitation between the Mafia and the authorities, generally hidden but sometimes breaking to the surface in crimes of outrageous violence, was ruptured in November 1983 with the arrival of Antonino Caponnetto, who had volunteered to be transferred to Palermo following the murder of Rocco Chinnici, the head of the investigative office in the Sicilian capital. Caponnetto was sixty-three when he left his comfortable position as a prosecutor in Florence's appeal court for the harsh conditions of a room in a tightly guarded military barracks that would be his home for the next four and a half years. It was Caponnetto who established the anti-Mafia pool of magistrates that would scythe through Cosa Nostra's ranks. He gathered around himself a team of public servants and inspired them with his own courage and grit. Giovanni Falcone and Paolo Borsellino were members of that team.

Just before Christmas 1987, after almost two years of hearings in the bunker-court that had been specially built beside the Ucciardone prison in Palermo, the prosecutors scored an important victory over the Mafia. The year ended well for Italy's criminal justice system: verdicts of guilty were handed down on 344 defendants in the first so-called maxi-trial that had begun on 10 February 1986. Among the nineteen who received life sentences were Salvatore Riina, the boss who headed the Mafia in the area around the notorious town of Corleone, and his deputy Bernardo Provenzano, both sentenced *in absentia*. Falcone and Borsellino, who had been in the forefront of efforts to bring the *capi* (bosses) and lesser members of Cosa Nostra to book[10] and had spearheaded the prosecution, were in their late forties. They were both from La Kalsa, a run-down district in the old heart of Palermo, where they had grown up side-by-side with young-sters who would later become *mafiosi*. Less than five years after winning their cases in the maxi-trial, Falcone and Borsellino were dead, the victims of murder.

Yet the courtroom victory in 1987 had promised much: the forces of the law appeared to have gained the upper hand and got the Mafia on the run at last. The satisfaction of winning that battle in court was to be short-lived, however. Caponnetto left in March 1988 after unsuccessfully putting forward Falcone as his successor; intrigue, incompetence and ill-will in Rome and among magistrates in Palermo's court then combined fatally to undermine the work of those magistrates and other officials who were heavily engaged in the fight against the Mafia.

Despite the success of the prosecution in the maxi-trial in 1987, the Mafia had not been badly dented. The *capi* and their *gregari* (foot-soldiers) continued to oversee their districts, applying their own rules, disregarding the law of the state and carrying on unchecked with their campaign of slaughter. That bloodshed reached its zenith with the murder of Falcone and his wife and three bodyguards at Capaci, on the highway between Palermo and the city's airport on 23 May 1992, and of Borsellino and five members of his escort outside his mother's apartment in the Sicilian capital less than two months later.

Behind the murders were Riina and Provenzano. In September or October 1991, a small group of leading *mafiosi* had met in a house belonging to Riina in the countryside near Castelvetrano, in the southwest corner of Sicily, not far from the ruined Greek temples at Selinunte. Vincenzo Sinacori, who was soon to become the *capo mandamento* (district boss) of the Mafia in Mazara del Vallo, a sprawling, dusty, sun-baked coastal town near Castelvetrano, was there. At this meeting, Riina apparently suggested that they needed to think about how to deal with Falcone and Claudio Martelli, the min-ister of justice. 'Falcone had been a target of Cosa Nostra for a long time,' said Sinacori, who began cooperating with the authorities in September 1996.[11]

Riina and Provenzano put forward to Cosa Nostra's governing body, the *commissione*, the idea that Falcone should be physically eliminated. The magistrate who was to be killed had acquired a great deal of experience working in Palermo's court and in the broad swathe of countryside, villages and towns across southwest Sicily, the Mafia's heartland. He also held a key post in Rome at the time of his murder: as director-general of penal affairs at the ministry of justice, he was in a position to put the survival of the Mafia in real danger. This threat convinced the other members of the *commissione* to go along with the bloody scheme that Riina and Provenzano put to them.

The photographs of the huge crater in the highway, above the drainage tunnel where the *mafiosi* had placed the explosives they set off by remote control, recorded for ever the terrible scene late on that Saturday afternoon in May 1992. The immense shock of the explosion, a few minutes before six o'clock, was such that it registered on seismographs at Monte Cammarata in the province of Agrigento in the far south of Sicily.[12] Initially, the investigators thought that the advance car of Falcone's escort had escaped and gone ahead, but it was found later in the evening, completely destroyed, in a field by the highway.[13] Debris covered the wreckage of the vehicle in which the magistrate, his wife and driver had been travelling. Above the devastation was an overhead gantry, one arrow pointing ahead for Palermo, another to the right for the slip-road to the town of Capaci.

Paolo Borsellino had expected to be a target and had told a captain in the *carabinieri* military police that he was certain he would be the next to be murdered by the Mafia.[14] Wary and fearful members of the service that provided escorts to the magistrates tried to keep their distance and did not want to travel with him.

'He felt much safer when he was away from Palermo than in the city. He was very worried for his safety and for ours,' said Agnese Piraino Borsellino, the victim's wife, in reply to questions by a prosecutor conducting the case against her husband's killers.[15] The murdered magistrate had said to his wife that as long as Falcone was alive, Falcone would shield him. Borsellino had felt that he was racing against time in the last two months of his life but, he told his wife, he already understood everything about his colleague's murder.

The Mafia chose the place and the moment to strike at Borsellino after keeping him under close observation. The magistrate was a man of habit, usually attending mass on Sunday at a church in front of his home and regularly visiting his mother in Via D'Amelio on Sunday mornings as well, generally between nine and ten o'clock. The murderers followed Borsellino's moves closely and deployed patrols in the area around his home to find out exactly what he was doing. They thought that it was very likely that the magistrate would visit his mother on 19 July, a Sunday, and that day they were particularly watchful. The *mafiosi* involved in the reconnaissance were from the Noce *mandamento*, the area of Palermo where Borsellino lived, and two other *mandamenti* in the centre of the city.

That Sunday morning Borsellino did not follow his usual routine. The killers planning his death were not fazed, however, when he left home around half past nine and did not go to his mother's apartment. Instead, accompanied by his daughter, Borsellino joined the rest of his family in Villagrazia di Carini, to the west of the city. About half an hour after arriving there, and having changed, he went for a boat-trip with a friend.

He had retired to the bedroom to rest after lunch but had been very fretful, the numerous cigarette butts in an ashtray beside the bed showing that he had smoked heavily while there. He left Villagrazia di Carini to return to Palermo at around four o'clock that afternoon. His car joined the highway linking Palermo to the airport at the Carini slip-road and a few minutes later he passed the spot where his colleague Giovanni Falcone had been murdered two months before. With his escort cars, the magistrate had continued at high speed to the city's by-pass. The journey then took the convoy through suburban streets flanked with ten- to twelve-storey apartment blocks to the short cul-de-sac of Via D'Amelio.

Unlike the street outside Borsellino's own apartment in Palermo, where parking was strictly forbidden, the area beneath the block in Via D'Amelio where his mother lived was full of cars. Their presence made the only surviving member of the magistrate's escort, who had never before accompanied Borsellino to Via D'Amelio, very nervous. He turned his car in readiness to leave and watched as Borsellino approached number 19. He was struck by a hot blast and thrown around inside the vehicle. The magistrate had been about to ring the doorbell. Then came the explosion.

One resident in the street saw a flash and heard a terrifying noise that he thought would never end. There were bodies and cars in flames, he said, when he gave evidence in court in the trial of Borsellino's killers. 'Did you see anyone alive among all those broken bodies?' the prosecutor asked him. 'No,' he replied.

A MAGISTRATE REMEMBERS

That prosecutor was Anna Maria Palma. At boarding school in Palermo she had been a keen volleyball player. Her team played in the top division and the experience had instilled in the tall teenager a determination to succeed, to beat the competition whatever it might be.[16] Thirty years later she was a deputy chief prosecutor in the anti-Mafia team in the Sicilian capital.

The combative spirit that Palma had taken on to the volleyball court found a special outlet in the mid-1990s when she joined the team of prosecutors in Caltanissetta, a small city in central Sicily. Initially, she was assigned to the case of a young magistrate in Agrigento who had been murdered by the Mafia in 1990. Meanwhile, the first trial of the murderers of Paolo Borsellino was reaching its end. Palma joined the prosecution team on this big case as well. Her work in Caltanissetta's court put her in the front line against the Mafia. She was a prosecutor in all three trials of the *mafiosi* involved in Borsellino's murder.

Several years earlier in Palermo, Giovanni Falcone had tried to persuade Palma to join his investigative team but her husband had spoken against the move; such a post would be bound to complicate family life considerably. Yet, life at home had been badly disrupted even before she became involved in anti-Mafia work. Threats had begun when she was dealing with crimes concerning public-sector organizations. Her car had been damaged. 'A very worrying sign was opening the car and finding the logbook ripped and on the floor, a clear message that they could get into my car whenever they wanted. On another occasion it was stolen and abandoned where it would be found immediately,' remembered Palma.[17]

She received death threats and from 1993 onwards never moved without an escort of armed police. Bodyguards surrounded her everywhere she went and at all hours of the day; this had been a great sacrifice for her family. Her husband and son, who was eleven when Borsellino was murdered, were caused enormous worry because of her job. Being an anti-Mafia magistrate meant abandoning the routines of normal life, such as shopping, going to the cinema or eating out with her husband and son.

A photograph of Borsellino and Falcone hung on the wall behind her desk in her office in Palermo's court building. Anna Maria Palma was more than the prosecutor of Borsellino's killers, however. She had been close to him. He had been a friend of her family and she had got to know him while preparing for the oral examinations to enter the magistrature, having already passed the written examinations at the young age of twenty-three. Before she was admitted to the magistrates' roll, Borsellino had allowed her to follow his cases in Palermo's investigative office, giving her an unofficial pupillage that new magistrates rarely enjoyed. He had been her first teacher.

Her official pupillage began with Falcone in 1978. He had just returned to Palermo from Trapani in southwest Sicily to be a judge in the criminal court during the summer session from June to August, and she had sat in on his trials and drafted his sentences. She still kept them twenty-five years later, with the corrections and comments written in his hand. Another figure who had watched over Palma's start in the magistrature was Rocco Chinnici, the head of the investigative office murdered by the Mafia in July 1983.

Caltanissetta, where she returned to tackle the mafia cases in the 1990s, was the young magistrate's first post. The president of the court there needed someone to deal with bankruptcy cases and this was the area of her focused pupillage so it brought Palma under Falcone's wing again. Though he had been a judge for the summer session in Palermo, his usual work was in the field of bankruptcy and he taught his young colleague the practicalities of bankruptcy work. Palma remembered travelling with him in his car, before he had to accept the tight restrictions of a bodyguarded lifestyle, to seal the doors and gates of firms that had gone bust.

When Palma returned to Palermo in 1983 after trying, as a judge, civil cases that ranged from agricultural to labour matters, she spent a year in the juvenile court in the Sicilian capital, again as a judge. There, she struck up a friendship with a prosecutor who would later become Falcone's wife and die with him in the bomb-blast on the highway at Capaci.

Paolo Borsellino continued to help her. Between 1984 and 1990, Palma was a *pretore* in Palermo's criminal court, a post that involved both investigating and preparing cases for trial, and then judging them. Borsellino had been a *pretore* and knew the ropes, so Palma had often spoken with him, and she sought his advice again at the end of 1991 when she was looking for a complete change from bank- ruptcy work to which she had returned. She wanted to transfer to the prosecutors' department in Palermo but had not yet achieved the seniority that was needed; Borsellino backed her request.

With long fair hair, Palma did not fit the usual picture of a Sicilian. In fact, although her father was from Palma di Montechiaro in the province of Agrigento, her mother was from the Veneto region in northeast Italy. 'The most *mafioso* place in Sicily and one of the island's most bloody towns,' she said about her father's birthplace.[18] By becoming a magistrate, she had followed him. She had seen her father at work and, even when very small, had wanted to do the job he did.

Anna Maria Palma arrived in the Palermo prosecutors' department to start her new job on 11 May 1992, less than two weeks before the murder of Falcone, his wife and their escorts. 'The murders happened on 23 May. From that moment onwards, my life changed.'[19]

THE SEASON OF SLAUGHTER

Italians were stunned and outraged by the atrocities at Capaci and Via D'Amelio. The murders of Falcone and Borsellino made defeat- ing the Mafia more important than ever. There had never been much political will to tackle the problem before but now, it seemed, the authorities might be shamed into action. Public opinion was behind them. Horrified by the bloodshed as much as by the fact that public servants had been killed for doing their jobs, Italians appeared to want the Mafia beaten.

Public pressure for something to be done increased the following year when the Mafia targeted Rome, Florence and Milan in a campaign of terror to show its enormous strength and its ability to do whatever it wanted. Cosa Nostra had decided to launch an outright attack on Italian society itself, aimed at destabilizing the state by challenging its very power. The Mafia reckoned that this was the way to force the authorities into negotiations in which it could cut a deal. The deal Cosa Nostra wanted was softer conditions for jailed *mafiosi* and a relaxation of the authorities' anti-Mafia efforts.

Towards the end of 1991, representatives of the Mafia from all Sicily's provinces had met in Enna, a city in the centre of the island. At that meeting, Riina, the bloodiest of the bosses, had said that the Mafia should make war to be able to make peace later. When the shape of the Mafia's war-to-come was discussed in summer 1992 at a meeting of *capi* in a small villa near Mazara del Vallo, one of those present expressed concern that innocent bystanders might be hurt. Civil war was tearing Yugoslavia apart at the time and news programmes on Italian television showed the awful bloodshed. Many children had died in Sarajevo, said Riina, who saw no problem in killing indiscriminately in Italy.[20] Whatever the consequences, he was determined to push ahead with what he thought would further the interests of Cosa Nostra. The Mafia had used car-bombs to murder Falcone and Borsellino and it would employ the same means in the campaign launched in Rome in May 1993.

Maurizio Costanzo, a well-known television presenter with a much watched chat show, was the first target. The Mafia wanted him dead because he had denounced the Mafia strongly and publicly. On one of his shows he said that he was pleased that Riina had been caught. The arrest, in January 1993, was a major coup for the authorities as Riina had been on the run for twenty-three years. During one programme, Costanzo burned a T-shirt bearing the slogan *Viva la Mafia*. On yet another occasion, he spoke out against the ease with which *mafiosi* dodged harsh prison life by getting transferred to hospital and told viewers he hoped that the *mafiosi* really would be struck by incurable diseases.[21]

Mafia bosses from Catania in eastern Sicily believed that they could kill Costanzo using the Mafia's traditional method of hand-arms. Instead, explosives were used in the attempt. For several days, a group of mafia killers reconnoitred the area around the Teatro

Parioli, the studio where Costanzo hosted his show, searching for the best place to park a stolen Fiat Uno packed with around 250 lbs of a murderous explosive mixture that included TNT and T4.

On the evening of 14 May, Costanzo left the Teatro Parioli after his programme, and was driven along Via Fauro, his escorts following in the car behind. The killers knew that the television presenter had to pass that way and the bomb was set off by remote control at about half past nine. Fortunately the attempt failed. The killers had expected Costanzo to be in a large Alfa Romeo; instead, he travelled that evening in a Mercedes as the driver of the Alfa Romeo had been unwell. More than twenty people were injured, apartments and other buildings were damaged, and the force of the explosion catapulted one car into a shirt-maker's shop.

Less than two weeks later, the Mafia achieved its aim by causing death as well as destruction. The place on this occasion was Florence where, at one o'clock in the morning of 27 May, a car-bomb was triggered in Via dei Georgofili, in the heart of a city that more than any other was the symbol of the country's enormous cultural and artistic heritage. The killers used a Fiat Fiorino van packed with between 550 and 650 lbs of an explosive cocktail whose ingredients included nitroglycerine and TNT. Among the five people who died was a baby girl barely six months old. Both her parents and her sister were also killed. Almost forty people were injured.

The Torre del Pulci was brought down and the Galleria degli Uffizi was rocked by the blast. After the dust had cleared, the curators at Italy's principal art gallery found that Gherardo delle Notti's *Adoration of the Shepherds* and Manfredi's *Card-players* and *Concerto* were beyond restoration. The explosion, which blasted a crater over 5 feet deep and 12 feet wide in the street, damaged about one quarter of the Uffizi's works of art. The artistic casualty list included paintings by Rubens, Titian and Van der Weyden.

Milan was the next city hit by the Mafia's strategy of terror. Again the target was both cultural and human. For the failed attempt on Maurizio Costanzo in Rome, the mafia killers had stolen an anonymous Fiat Uno and they used the same type of car again and the same mixture of explosives as that used in Florence. The car was parked in Via Palestro near the entrance to the Pavilion of Contemporary Art.

The bomb exploded at a quarter past eleven in the evening on 27 July, killing four young firemen, called because smoke had been seen in the car, and a 54-year-old Moroccan in a park nearby. The explosion rocked property in several streets including Via della Spiga, a stylish pedestrian precinct with chic shops. The Pavilion of Contemporary Art was badly damaged by the explosion of a bubble of gas that had collected beneath it when the car-bomb fractured gas pipes. The five dead and many injured in Milan showed that the campaign of slaughter was being successfully accomplished, noted a court in Florence five years later.

Italy did not have to wait long for the next attacks. Just after midnight, on 28 July, car-bombs exploded in central Rome. Again the ubiquitous Fiat Uno was the car used for the bombings. The targets were the basilica of San Giovanni in Laterano and the neighbouring Lateran Palace, and the church of San Giorgio al Velabro.

Built at the beginning of the fourth century, San Giovanni in Laterano was the cathedral of Rome, the pope's own diocese, and a church of great religious significance for Roman Catholics throughout the world. Its most recent reconstruction, in the middle of the seventeenth century, was the work of Francesco Borromini, one of the best-known baroque architects. The Lateran Palace had been the papal residence until the popes moved to Avignon in France in the fourteenth century. Like the pope's summer residence at Castelgandolfo, it became an integral part of the Vatican City under the Lateran Pact, the treaty signed by Benito Mussolini in February 1929 that put an end to the dispute with the Church that had simmered ever since the newly created Italian state had expropriated the huge area of central Italy that had belonged to the pope. Through the Lateran Pact, the Vatican became a fully independent state and vehicles registered there carried number plates with the letters SCV – Stato Citta del Vaticano (Vatican City State).

By exploding their car-bomb in the square outside the Lateran Palace, the Mafia had gone for an important religious, historic, political and artistic symbol. The blast caused considerable damage to buildings that were part of the pope's own cathedral. Frescoes crumbled and marble floors and carved wooden ceilings were badly affected. Several people were injured and only a lucky combination of circumstances prevented mass murder.

Pisa's leaning tower had been in the Mafia's sights too, as it sought to force the authorities to come to its terms. The introduction of *carcere duro* (hard jail-time) for those convicted of mafia crimes, under a provision called Article 41bis, and news that *uomini d'onore* (men of honour) were being badly treated by prison guards were grave affronts to people used to being above and beyond the law. 'Until Article 41bis was introduced, murders were decided by people in prison, mafia wars were decided by people in prison and the smallest details of every possible criminal activity were decided by people in prison and communicated to accomplices outside,' explained Gabriele Chelazzi, a prosecutor in Florence. The trial was held in Florence because the first death from the bombing campaign occurred there. Chelazzi recalled how there had been opposition to the proposal for a tighter regime for certain categories of prisoner. Falcone's murder swept away that opposition. 'Article 41bis became law in early June 1992 and 300 *mafiosi* were put under its restrictions within a week of the implementation decrees,' he added.[22]

The state's reaction to the killings of 1992, particularly those of Capaci and Via D'Amelio in which Falcone and Borsellino were murdered, had brought serious problems for the Mafia. Mafia bosses wanted the state and Italians to learn to live and let live. Cosa Nostra sought an end to the conditions of isolation imposed on those of its members who were in prison and the closure of special prisons where some *mafiosi* were held, and it wanted legislative changes to reduce the effectiveness of *mafiosi* who decided to cooperate with the authorities as well as the discouragement of anti-Mafia comment in the media.

Cosa Nostra possessed a relentless and determined criminal imagination that never stopped producing ideas and plans, said the court in Florence that, between November 1996 and June 1998, tried those responsible for the bombing campaign. It had decided that it would go to any length in its attempt to bend the state to its will. The enormity of such an aim and of the schemes to reach it seemed beyond belief. Yet, the *mafiosi* thought up initiatives to raise the stakes in the confrontation and plans were well advanced for several projects. The Mafia had started to draw up an index of prison guards. They had access to large quantities of explosives. One idea, designed to hit

Italy's tourism industry, was to scatter used syringes infected with terrible diseases on the beach at Rimini, a large resort on the Adriatic. Giovanni Brusca, a *capo mafioso*, had taken steps to acquire infected blood.[23] Another idea was to poison food in supermarket chains. Aiming to provoke panic and widespread terror, the Mafia had prepared itself for every type of crime against public safety.

We decided we would show them who was in charge in Italy, one *mafioso* said in court. We would place so many bombs that the authorities would have to do what we wanted, said another. We would blow up the monuments unless Pianosa and Asinara (two high-security prisons built on small, isolated islands) were closed and the Article 41bis restrictions ended, said another.

All that had happened so far was just a prologue, warned letters sent to daily newspapers after the car-bombs in Milan and Rome. The Mafia's message after those explosions was that Italy should expect the next bombs to go off in daytime and in public places; Riina and his killers were out to take life randomly.

Italy's criminal justice system scored an important result in dealing with the Mafia's campaign of terror when magistrates laid charges in March and May 1996 and the judge responsible for the preliminary investigations completed his work in June. Those indicted were sent for trial. Brusca, who had activated, from the hillside above the high-way at Capaci, the remote control that set off the explosives that killed Falcone, had been caught in May 1996 in the south of Sicily and had soon decided to cooperate with the authorities. Testifying to the court in Florence in January 1998 about the bombing campaign in the cities in mainland Italy, Brusca said that its aim had been 'to get the state to crap itself'. In addition to the testimony of Brusca himself, the investigations benefited from the testimony of a further twelve *mafiosi* who had decided to cooperate with the authorities. 'All of these people made long and detailed statements about their lives, their places in the world of crime and about their involvement in the *stragi*,' said the court's judgement.[24] Between November 1996 and June 1998, two judges and a jury in a lower assize court in Florence had sat for 190 hearings. Their judgement ran to more than 1,700 pages. The crimes of which the defendants were charged included *strage* (slaughter) and *devastazione* (devastation). Under Article 422 of Italy's criminal code which deals with slaughter, 'whosoever commits acts that jeopardize public safety, with the aim of killing, is punished by life imprisonment, should those acts lead to the death of more than one person'.

Pietro Carra, a lorry driver, who had hung around the edge of the mafia underworld until April 1993, occasionally doing illicit runs for the bosses of the Brancaccio district of Palermo, had been arrested on 6 July 1995 and had agreed to cooperate with the magistrates at the end of August. He was a key witness, identifying those who committed the crimes and describing how they were committed. All the *mafiosi* who had decided to cooperate with the authorities talked of how the idea of the bombings was born, the discussions that took place around that idea and the execution of the plot.

Charges against two of the accused had been withdrawn to allow them to be brought to trial separately. The court did not find even one of the defendants innocent, said Chelazzi. The prosecutors had sought exemplary punishment, including sentences that combined life imprisonment with three-year terms of solitary confinement. The court handed down fourteen life sentences, while setting long terms, in prison, for another ten of the accused, and the verdicts of the assize court were confirmed at both levels of appeal in 2001 and 2002.[25] Seeking what it called the moral authors of the crimes, the court noted that the decision to commit those crimes had not been spontaneous but the result of careful planning that had started in July 1992, immediately after the bloody episodes in which Giovanni Falcone and Paolo Borsellino had died.

Not all the bosses of Cosa Nostra were involved, however, and those that took part did so in different ways. Consultations about the campaign of slaughter did not concern the Mafia's so-called institutional bodies, but certain leading members of the organization. The court decided that responsibility fell on Salvatore Riina, Bernardo Provenzano, Leoluca Bagarella, Matteo Messina Denaro, Giovanni Brusca, and Giuseppe and Filippo Graviano. Riina and Giuseppe Graviano, against whom the charges had been withdrawn, were found guilty by another court in January 2000 and received sentences of life imprisonment. Like Provenzano, a long-standing fugitive, Messina Denaro was also on the run when the court in Florence gave its verdict. He was high on the authorities' wanted list and had been sought since 1993, when he was just over thirty, for a range of serious crimes that began with murder. Riina had been captured in January 1993 and Leoluca Bagarella, his brother-in-law, who had been on the run since 1991, had been caught in Palermo in June 1995.

While the trials of the *mafiosi* involved in 1993's campaign of terror with car-bombs were being heard in Florence, the trials were underway in Caltanissetta of those suspected of planning and executing the murders of Giovanni Falcone and Paolo Borsellino in 1992. Central to the prosecution's case was the responsibility of the bosses, *figure di vertice* (figures at the top) as Chelazzi described them.

Forty-two people were tried for the massacre at Capaci in which Falcone, his wife and three escorts died in May 1992. The assize court delivered its verdicts in September 1997, handing down twenty-four life sentences. By then two of the accused were dead. Eight of those on trial were found not guilty. When the appeal court gave its verdicts in April 2000, the number of life sentences had risen to twenty-nine. In May 2002, the supreme court upheld fourteen of these sentences, referring back the others for retrial. It also upheld long terms in prison for another six accused. Salvatore Riina, Bernardo Provenzano, Leoluca Bagarella, and Filippo and Giuseppe Graviano, who had all been found guilty of being behind the car-bombings in Rome, Florence and Milan, were among those given life sentences in Caltanissetta.[26]

Anna Maria Palma was a prosecutor in all three trials of the murderers of her friend Borsellino and his escorts. Just four people stood trial in the first. All four were found guilty in January 1996, although after the appeal process had been exhausted only one of the three life sentences and one sentence of eighteen years' imprisonment were confirmed.[27] Eighteen people were tried in Borsellino Bis, the second of the three trials. The first appeal process, which ended in March 2002, resulted in thirteen life sentences: one was for Riina, another for Giuseppe Graviano.[28] The third of the trials in Caltanissetta concerning the massacre in Via D'Amelio, known as Borsellino Ter, was the biggest. There were twenty-seven defendants, among them Giovanni Brusca and Bernardo Provenzano, who had been found guilty in Florence of the 1993 car-bombings. All the accused were found guilty[29] and the lightest of the sentences when these were read in December 1999 was twelve years' imprisonment. Seventeen of the accused were sentenced to life in jail. Ten life sentences stood even after the final appeals had been heard during 2002; three had been reduced to twenty years' imprisonment and three had been referred back for retrial at appeal level. One of the accused had died.

The long list of *mafiosi* found guilty of murdering Falcone, his wife, Borsellino and their escorts was a tribute to the work of the prosecution team in Caltanissetta. They had had a hard task, however. Winning convictions had required much more than simply laying out the evidence to the court.

Defence lawyers made serious accusations against the prosecutors, claiming that they were guilty of falsification, suppression of the truth and abuse of office.[30] Formal charges were laid by Palermo's Camere Penali, the criminal bar association. The chairman of the Camere Penali, a lawyer who defended people accused of mafia offences, was Nino Mormino, who in 2001 was elected to parliament in the ranks of Berlusconi's Forza Italia party.[31]

In Sicily, where even looks or gestures carry messages, there were no doubts about the meaning and the aims of these accusations – they were unequivocal and full of menace. Prosecutors believed they were part of a strategy thought up by the *mafiosi*'s lawyers to expose them to even greater danger than they already usually faced. 'As the trials were evidently not going the way that the defending lawyers hoped, they used these accusations as a weapon,' said Palma.[32] The atmosphere in the court in Caltanissetta had been heavy with threat. During almost every hearing, the defending lawyers had aggressively bombarded the prosecutors with abuse and objections. The trials had taken place before video-conferencing had become part of procedures in criminal trials in Italy, so the defendants had been in court and perhaps their lawyers had felt they had to make a particularly tough show.

Magistrates in Catania investigated the charges that Palermo's criminal bar association had laid against the prosecutors but found the accusations groundless.

The final outcome of the Caltanissetta trials continued the run of good results in the fight against the Mafia. By 2004, Italy's police forces and anti-Mafia prosecutors had a string of successes to their credit. Hundreds of *mafiosi* had been caught, tried and jailed during the two decades since Antonino Caponnetto had moved from Florence to Palermo.

CONSPIRACY OF SILENCE

Yet, the Mafia was far from beaten. In the years following the terror campaign of car-bombings, it had kept a low profile, adapting itself to continue its challenge to the state. Prosecutors and investigators in Palermo warned that the Mafia continued to thrive in western and southern Sicily.

Cosa Nostra was flourishing more than ever in the province of Agrigento, Palma told a meeting of magistrates in the great hall of Palermo's court in December 2002.[33] Her responsibilities in the prosecutors' department in the Sicilian capital included dealing with Cosa Nostra in the city of Agrigento, famous for its valley of Greek temples, and the surrounding province. There, helped by a powerful, all-embracing omertà (conspiracy of silence) that appeared to be in the local population's genes, the Mafia exerted total control over business and the economy in its territory.

Ignazio De Francisci had no preconceptions when he was appointed to the post of chief prosecutor in Agrigento in August 1999. He knew a lot about the Mafia, however. A Sicilian from Palermo, he had joined Caponnetto's investigative office and anti-Mafia pool at the end of 1985. Working with Falcone and Borsellino had been a formative experience for him. He continued in the anti-Mafia prosecution service in Palermo until he moved to Agrigento. De Francisci knew that the situation there would be difficult but what he found was far worse even than his expectations.[34]

Agrigento's magistrature had not enjoyed a good name before De Francisci arrived, being disrupted by disputes and coming under heavy criticism. De Francisci put the prosecutors' department back on track but sorting it out had been just one of the problems. Tackling rampant crime in Agrigento city and the province was an enormous challenge. There was a poisonous climate of which verbal violence was only a part. There was widespread physical violence too, many cases of arson, intimidation and malicious damage.

Whether violence was cause or effect, the Mafia, not just Cosa Nostra but a local version called the *Stidde*, was deeply rooted in Agrigento. Some members of the *Stidde* had been affiliated with or close to families of Cosa Nostra. For many years, these particularly vicious criminal groups had waged war for supremacy in the area, leaving hundreds dead. The feud between the *Stidde* and Cosa Nostra reached a climax between 1991 and 1994.

Dealing with the Mafia was probably even harder in Agrigento than in other parts of Sicily, but police, investigating magistrates and prosecutors were able to score some successes. In one case in 1996, the court in Sciacca, about 30 miles west along the coast from Agrigento, dealt with twenty-four *mafiosi*. They had been brought to trial as a result of an operation that had thrown light on an especially violent association affiliated with the hardest fringe of the Corleonese and their boss, Riina, and with Messina Denaro, the boss in Trapani. In 1999, in another case, forty-nine people were brought to trial on charges that included thirty-one murders. Of those accused, forty-one were found guilty and the court passed twenty-one life sentences in July 2001.[35]

Despite the arrests and trials, murder and attempted murder continued to be part of Cosa Nostra's activities in and around Agrigento at the beginning of the twenty-first century. However, its real business was making money, which it did mostly through drug-trafficking (but not pushing), money-laundering, rigging public works tenders and extortion rackets.

Major drug-traffickers, whose relationships spread overseas to gangs in Colombia, Venezuela and Morocco, as well as across the European continent to Spain, the Netherlands and Belgium, were based in the province of Agrigento. The Cuntrera and Caruana families in the town of Siculiana, about 12 miles along the coast west of Agrigento, had played a central role in international drug-trafficking in the past, with their interests extending from Venezuela to Canada. Magistrates believed that the Cuntrera and Caruana clans continued to be active despite the convictions of senior members of the two families.

Almost every firm involved in public works and services in Agrigento paid off the Mafia, said Palma at the end of 2002, at a going rate of 2 per cent or 3 per cent of the contract value. Cosa Nostra was invariably behind the frequent cases of damage to plant at construction sites and it was responsible for acts of intimidation as well.[36] Placing a cigarette lighter and a bottle of petrol beside an excavator on a construction site was a clear threat that protection money had to be paid or that sub-contracts were expected.

For obvious reasons, many acts of intimidation and of malicious damage went unreported. Even so, official statistics revealed that over 300 cases were notified in 2002. Businesses in Palma di Montechiaro and Licata, on the coast about 25 miles east of Agrigento, were the worst hit.[37] Prosecutors found that Cosa Nostra had been intensifying its efforts in extorting money from businesses in order to cover its heavy outgoings, above all payment of the legal fees of lawyers defending *uomini d'onore* who were in jail.[38]

In some areas the Mafia's grip went even further: it had taken over from the state. Its word was the one that counted. In Canicatti, a large town about 20 miles northeast of Agrigento, the Mafia appeared to exercise total control.[39] With at least thirty-two families of Cosa Nostra grouped in eight *mandamenti*, the Mafia had spread its tentacles everywhere in the province of Agrigento. Magistrates and the police had been able to ascertain that it had close connections with Cosa Nostra in Palermo and Trapani – confirmation of Falcone's intuition about how the Mafia worked.[40] With his vast knowledge of the Mafia, it had been clear to him in the 1980s that Cosa Nostra was not compartmentalized but acted and gave mutual support across the whole of Sicily.

The public's reluctance to assist the authorities was a big handicap in the fight against the Mafia everywhere but in Agrigento cooperation was almost completely absent. This boosted the standing of *mafiosi* and allowed them to go undisturbed about their criminal activities. Rather than help investigators, businessmen preferred to deny that they had paid protection money or that they had been the targets of intimidation. This climate of *omertà* that discouraged victims of extortion from reporting the crime in Agrigento was also powerful in Palermo itself. Some cases did come to light, however. Magistrates looked into 183 new cases in Palermo during the 2002 judicial year and 104 in Agrigento.[41] During the five years between

1997 and 2002, an average of about 450 cases of extortion was ascertained each year by prosecutors in the judicial district overseen by the Palermo court: Palermo itself, Agrigento and five other courts.

Extortion was not piecemeal; the Mafia aimed to squeeze protection money from everyone. It cosied up to victims, using its helpers to present a friendly face and pretend to act as go-betweens to obtain large, but artificial, reductions in the amounts that the Mafia had initially sought. This way, victims were disinclined to lay charges and, even after a crime had been ascertained and the criminals responsible for it identified, to confirm that it had taken place. 'In other words, the victim's silence, originally caused by fear of retaliation, turns into a kind of enforced connivance, fed by the calculation that the costs could be borne and by the hope of being able to live with the Mafia,' said Palermo's chief prosecutor in January 2003.[42] That was what control of the ground meant to Cosa Nostra.

At the end of 2001, the Direzione Nazionale Antimafia (DNA), a central Rome-based body, issued a report on how the war against the Mafia was progressing. It offered little cause for celebration. The Mafia was everywhere, but nowhere more firmly entrenched than in western Sicily. In Palermo, its presence and power of control had always been so deep and widespread that Cosa Nostra was involved in almost every wealth-producing activity, licit or illicit.[43] Whatever crimes investigators dug into, the Mafia was likely to be behind them. It had systematically infiltrated civil society, the professions, politics and the institutions.

The magistrature and the police forces had achieved important successes during recent years, said Palermo's chief prosecutor at the beginning of 2003. He pointed to trials in courts in Palermo that had ended with many *mafiosi* being found guilty and facing severe sentences. Like the trials in Agrigento, those in Palermo involved large numbers of defendants: sixty-one in one trial, thirty-five in another, fifty-nine in another. And the charges were those typical of mafia cases: murder, kidnapping, extortion and drug-trafficking.

Gian Carlo Caselli, who had transferred to be chief prosecutor in Palermo after the murders of Falcone and Borsellino and was there for almost seven years, thought that the 251 life sentences confirmed or passed by the district appeal court of Palermo in the two-year

period of 2000 to 2001 said much about the commitment of the prosecutors to tackle the Mafia[44] and showed that they had been able to
get some results.

However, despite the large numbers of *mafiosi* and alleged *mafiosi*
involved and the gruesome crimes of which they were accused, the
Italian media was not much interested in what was happening in
Palermo and other Sicilian cities. These trials were covered by local
newspapers, and so were the arrests of *mafiosi*, but such news rarely
got space in the national press or time on national television. And,
though mass killing and outrageous crimes, such as the murders of
Falcone and Borsellino and the terror campaign of car-bombings, and
the capture of important mafia bosses forced themselves into the
national news, such events were reported nationally when they had
happened but interest soon waned, and it served Italy's politicians to
let the public believe that the Mafia was losing and in retreat.

'There was an opportunity to beat the Mafia after the murders on
the highway at Capaci and outside the apartment block in Via
D'Amelio,' said Antonio Ingroia, a magistrate in the anti-Mafia team
in Palermo who had worked closely with Borsellino.[45] That opportunity had come with the great surge of public indignation at the
murders of Falcone and Borsellino but it had been let slip. Indeed, ten
years after those terrible crimes, Cosa Nostra was far from beaten. It
maintained a deep and widespread presence in business and politics.
Investigations had revealed a vast network of supporters in many
parts of society, underlining Cosa Nostra's extraordinary capacity to
weave itself inextricably into Sicily's economic and social fabric.

THE CONFESSION OF A KILLER

Just before one in the afternoon of 11 September 1996, Francesco
Onorato, a 35-year-old *mafioso* from Palermo who had belonged to
the *mandamento* of Partanna-Mondello, on the western edge of the
Sicilian capital, started speaking to Gioacchino Natoli, a magistrate
with the anti-Mafia pool. Natoli had received a note, apparently
signed by Onorato, in which the *mafioso* urgently sought a meeting.
He had decided to tell the magistrate about his life of crime. The note

had been written by Onorato's wife, because he was in jail and, had its contents become known, the note would have put his life at risk. In prison, explained Onorato, there were people who knew even what he was dreaming about when he was asleep.

The *mafioso* had seen and done terrible things. 'I want to free myself of everything that I have inside me. I want a new life. I want to be born again. I want to create a new future for my children,' Onorato told Natoli.[46] He had been *combinato*, initiated into Cosa Nostra, in November 1980 and there was much he could tell the magistrate. Three weeks later, with his lawyer Roberto Avellone present, Onorato revealed how he had murdered Salvo Lima, a leading Christian Democrat politician.

He had first heard about the plan to kill Lima around the beginning of March 1992. He had attended a meeting at a house in Sferracavallo, a district between Partanna and Capaci, called by Salvatore Biondino, one of the killers of Giovanni Falcone whose life sentence was confirmed by the supreme court in May 2002. On hearing that Lima was a target, one of those present had exclaimed, 'Are you crazy? Do you want to wage war on the state?'[47] That, indeed, had been the aim.

One of the *mafiosi* – later to receive sentences of fifteen years eleven months for his part in the murder of Falcone and sixteen years and ten months for the murder of Paolo Borsellino – would use binoculars to observe Lima's villa from Monte Pellegrino, the mountain to the west of Palermo that looms over the city, and keep in touch with the other members of the gang via a mobile telephone. Onorato's partner in the killing of Lima was Giovanni D'Angelo.

Lima had not been seen at first. Then, one morning, Onorato and D'Angelo saw the politician's driver arrive in front of the villa. 'After a few days of observation, we realized that Lima always left between half past nine and a quarter to ten, accompanied by two or three people,' Onorato told the magistrate. Initially, the killers had planned to use three cars and pump shotguns but this idea was abandoned after their car was spotted.

Onorato had an alternative. The killers should use a motorbike, he suggested to Biondino. D'Angelo would drive a stolen 500cc or 600cc Enduro, with Onorato as pillion passenger with the job of doing the shooting. On 12 March, they rode around Mondello, like any pair of normal young men out to enjoy a spin on a fine morning. Then, when the lookout's call arrived, they returned to the street where Lima lived and saw him in an Opel Vectra car with two other people heading for Viale delle Palme, a boulevard of elegant villas at one end of Mondello's sweeping seafront.

'I told D'Angelo to draw alongside. Perhaps because of the emotion, as it was his first murder with firearms, he overtook the car and I had to swing round to shoot at a tyre and the windscreen. The car stopped and I saw Lima get out and start running. D'Angelo turned the motorbike round. I jumped off and chased after Lima, firing a first shot at his back and a second to his head after he had fallen to the ground. I was armed with two long-barrelled revolvers, a calibre .38 and a calibre .357 Magnum. I do not remember which I fired,' Onorato confessed to Natoli four and a half years after committing the crime.[48]

Onorato had spared the two people who had been with Lima. They had got out of the car and cowered down near a large refuse container. Biondino had given instructions that all were to die and Onorato had pointed a gun at one of them, but then decided that he had no reason to kill more people. He climbed back on to the motorbike behind D'Angelo and they rode away.[49] After abandoning the motorbike, they got into a small Fiat Uno car to travel clear of the scene of the crime and, while in the car, removed the crash helmets and outer clothes that they had been wearing. These and the firearms used for the murder were put in a rubbish bag for disposal.

When Francesco Onorato decided to talk, he joined the ranks of *pentiti*, repentant *mafiosi*.

PENTITI

Domenico Gozzo entered the prosecution service in Palermo in 1992. There had been seven vacant posts for assistant prosecutor, but nobody was interested after Lima's murder. Although Gozzo did not have the seniority to apply, he had said that he was available. The Consiglio Superiore della Magistratura, the magistrates' governing body, leapt eagerly at the 32-year-old's unofficial bid.

Announcing the appointment, the Consiglio's members had risen to their feet and applauded. 'At that moment,' said Gozzo, 'I thought I might have made a mistake.' Following the murder of the politician in Mondello, everyone felt that something awful was brewing. 'After Lima was killed anything could have happened,' Gozzo remembered eleven years later.[50] Indeed, it did.

Pentiti or *collaboratori di giustizia*, repentants or collaborators with justice, were the labels that *mafiosi* like Onorato were given. But it was wrong to call them *pentiti*, thought Gozzo, as real repentance was rare. He could remember just two or three cases that he believed were truly acts of repentance, when *mafiosi* had broken down as they began revealing their secrets. Collaboration with the magistrates was a rational choice, often stemming from the fact that a *mafioso* had been definitively sentenced after final appeals had been heard or sentences for murder passed in the lower assize courts. Instead of a life behind bars, cooperation with the magistrates offered an alternative for the future, perhaps distant, almost certainly more than ten years away, but a future all the same.

Even if collaboration was a reasoned and opportunistic choice for the *mafioso*, accepting such collaboration made sense for the state as well. Bugging, telephone taps and intercepts were not enough on their own to provide the investigators with the information they required on the Mafia. The authorities needed the kind of deep, inside knowledge that only the insiders of the mafia world possessed.

Magistrates had been gathering evidence from *mafiosi* for many years. *Collaboratori* played an important part in anti-Mafia efforts. In switching sides, *collaboratori* were a huge threat to their former partners in crime. Above all, they showed that Cosa Nostra was not invulnerable. Giovanni Falcone had been helped enormously by the confessions of Tommaso Buscetta and Salvatore Contorno in the first maxi-trial that had begun in Palermo in February 1986. The pair had started to give evidence in 1984 and had provided valuable information on the Mafia's organization in Sicily.[51] Many of the 475 accused in the maxi-trial had also contributed to the authorities' knowledge of Cosa Nostra's criminal activities, throwing light on numerous brutal murders. 'Until recently, getting suspects in Mafia trials to cooperate with justice was considered impossible. Such cooperation is one of the main successes in the battle against organized crime, as it broke the myth of *omertà*, the so-called culture of silence that made the Mafia impenetrable to investigations,' Falcone had told a meeting of Canadian criminal investigators in Ottawa in May 1986.[52]

Falcone attributed his success in getting the cooperation of *mafiosi* to patient investigative effort rather than luck. 'It was also the result of an untiring work of persuasion that kept in mind the characteristics of the mafia mentality and exploited the tensions existing within the Mafia,' he had told his Canadian audience.[53] Colleagues said that Falcone had a special way of handling *collaboratori di giustizia*. Whatever the reasons for the breakthrough, after Buscetta and Contorno started to talk, the authorities found themselves with a new weapon in their fight against the Mafia. Cooperation stopped being an exception.

Great care was needed in dealing with *collaboratori*. A process that was, in any case, tricky and fraught with risk had been made worse by confusion over how *collaboratori* should be used. There had been difficulties in coordination and different ideas on the acceptability of the evidence they provided. There had been cases in which magistrates in one city had been satisfied with the evidence they had obtained from a *collaboratore di giustizia*, while those in another city had not. Unified management of such witnesses was clearly needed.[54]

The question of *collaboratori* returned with a vengeance in mid-April 2002 when Antonino Giuffre was captured in the countryside near Caccamo, a village about 25 miles east of the Sicilian capital. Giuffre was the *capo mandamento* in Caccamo, a *mafioso* of the highest level and a close associate of Bernardo Provenzano whom he had last met one month before being arrested. Giuffre had taken on the delicate task of rebuilding Cosa Nostra after the damage that the police and the courts had inflicted on it with the capture and trials of many *mafiosi*.[55] Two months after his arrest, Giuffre told the magistrates in Palermo that he wished to cooperate with them. On the afternoon of 20 January 2003, he gave evidence in the trial of Marcello Dell'Utri, a Sicilian senator of Forza Italia who was accused of association with the Mafia. Long-standing close friends, Berlusconi and Dell'Utri had met at university, and Dell'Utri subsequently worked for Berlusconi and became the driving force behind his push into politics.

Giuffre was not in Palermo when he gave evidence. He was in a prison in northern Italy; his testimony from a secret location was heard thanks to modern communications. The large screen in the courtroom in Palermo showed the rounded shoulders of a balding man wearing an off-white jacket. Giuffre spoke slowly, sometimes running his fingers along a table's edge, other times twiddling a pen in his left hand.[56] That morning, Dell'Utri, dressed in a blue suit and wearing gold-rimmed spectacles, sat impassively with his arms crossed. He had heard his lawyers object that Giuffre's testimony was inadmissible, but the court had rejected the submission and decided that it would hear Giuffre.

Dell'Utri's lawyers had objected because a law had been passed in 2001 that set a time limit of six months during which *collaboratori* had to tell the magistrates everything they knew. From the moment that *collaboratori* decided to spill the beans they had just six months to spill them – all of them. After that period had passed, any facts or information they gave to investigators were inadmissible as evidence. Giuffre had started to cooperate in mid-June 2002, so his time for talking ended in mid-December that year.

'The six-months limit shows that the state is not interested in what *collaboratori* have to say,' observed Gozzo, who was one of the team prosecuting Dell'Utri.[57] Giuffre had spent thirty years as a criminal and the period of six months was not enough. It was impossible for Giuffre to tell everything by mid-December 2002. One of the problems was arranging meetings for all the magistrates, not only in courts in Sicily but in courts throughout Italy, who wanted to question Giuffre. There were also many blank days when, for one reason or another, he was not questioned at all.

As important, however, was the time that was needed to lead Giuffre into a frame of mind in which he would tell the magistrates all he knew. *Mafiosi* had so many reservations that prevented them talking about the Mafia, not least the *omertà* conspiracy of silence that bound them together, that they did not cooperate fully at the start. There was a psychological path along which *collaboratori* had to travel and the limit of six months did not recognize this. Moreover, *collaboratori* were prevented from telling more later, after the time limit expired. As the law stood, *collaboratori* and their families would be removed from the witness protection programme if the *collaboratori* subsequently remembered more things from their past, so they had to pretend to forget and that made a mockery of the system.

'Convincing a *mafioso* to talk about his criminal past is like asking him to speak about the most intimate facts of his life. He talks easily about normal things but has reservations about the intimate details,' said Palma.[58] The *mafioso* who decided to cooperate did not immediately become a *non-mafioso*; the path back from crime to legality was painfully hard and slow. American prosecutors and FBI investigators sympathized with their Italian counterparts. Such restrictions as those imposed on the anti-Mafia magistrates in Italy would have prevented the Americans from being able to work.[59] Indeed, if magistrates in Italy had been handicapped by the limit during the 1990s, they would not have been given crucial items of information that led to the successful prosecution of *mafiosi*.[60] Yet, the government did nothing in autumn 2002 as the six months that Giuffre was allowed for confession were about to run out. The government was deaf to loud calls for the period to be extended.

Just one week after Caponnetto died, on 6 December 2002, his eighty-year-old widow, Elisabetta, wrote to Berlusconi's justice minister to ask him to extend that damaging six-month limit. 'It seems strange once again to be bringing out the typewriter on which I wrote so many letters and messages for Nino, but reading your words in yesterday's newspapers added a further enormous weight to the pain of his death,' she said.[61] Despite the unanimous vote of parliament's anti-Mafia commission and appeals from the head of the DNA national anti-Mafia body and the magistrates in Palermo, the minister had stubbornly refused to extend the six-month period. The minister said that the pros and cons of an extension balanced each other out. 'I would be grateful if you would help me reply to a question that troubles me: what, Minister, are the cons?' asked Elisabetta Baldi Caponnetto. Berlusconi's minister did not budge, but she had experienced the warmth and solidarity of thousands of decent Italians, magistrates and ordinary people, who had travelled to Florence to pay tribute at her husband's funeral. Not only had Berlusconi's government been noticeably absent that day but it seemed to want to limit Giuffre's revelations.

In another act of terror, an epilogue to the car-bombs of 1993, the Mafia targeted Salvatore Contorno who, with Buscetta, had helped to make possible the authorities' victory in the maxi-trial at the end of 1987. The Mafia had discovered that Contorno lived at Formello, a small town on the outskirts of Rome. In April 1994, they had placed a large quantity of explosives in a drainage channel by a road that Contorno used but the explosives were found by chance and the attempt failed.[62] Contorno was an emblem of *pentitismo*, as the process of a *mafioso*'s cooperation with magistrates was called, and the Mafia needed to destroy such symbols, to discourage *mafiosi* from becoming *collaboratori*, to show that the state was unable to protect those who changed sides and to undermine the legislative and administrative provisions that encouraged them to do so.

THE MAFIA'S SILENT RESURGENCE

The strategy of terror thought up by Riina had been self-defeating. He himself had been arrested and was in prison, serving numerous life sentences; many other *mafiosi* were also behind bars. With Riina in jail, Bernardo Provenzano, who had disappeared from Corleone in 1963 and was still a fugitive forty years later, had become the undisputed head of Cosa Nostra. He had built a restricted circle of associates around himself at the top of the organization.

Provenzano's aim was to lead the Mafia out of the state of emergency into which it had been driven during the 1990s. Rebuilding Cosa Nostra had meant appointing temporary *capi* to the various families and *mandamenti* whose bosses had been jailed or had decided to cooperate with the authorities. The families would run the everyday business such as extortion while the small group at the top would devise and implement overall strategy. This small group would resolve any problems within Cosa Nostra itself and be responsible for relations between the Mafia and the world outside.[63]

In August 2000, the police eavesdropped on a conversation between *mafiosi* in a house at San Vito Lo Capo, a village at the end of a mountainous headland about 60 miles west of Palermo. The *mafiosi* talked about a meeting of Cosa Nostra's top group at which both Provenzano and Giuffre had been present. 'The picture that emerged was of a Cosa Nostra headed by Provenzano, fully operational and vertically managed,' said Palermo's chief prosecutor at the beginning of 2003.[64] Shaken by the consequences of the decisions that had been taken in the recent past, Cosa Nostra's leaders had sought to repair the damage, to put the organization back on its feet by living alongside the state rather than attacking it frontally. This was the way forward and essential if the Mafia was to prosper and expand.

Giuffre confirmed what the authorities had heard and suspected. The reorganization of Cosa Nostra was well advanced following the crisis that had struck in the immediate aftermath of the *stragi*, the season of slaughter. There were discussions within Cosa Nostra to reach agreement over the interests of those *capi mandamenti* who were in jail and those who were still free and running the organization. In some areas, however, there was antagonism between emergent groups who were seeking to win power and a consequent risk of a sudden fracturing of the delicate equilibrium inside the organization. It was impossible to predict whether peaceful coexistence between rival groups would be consolidated, said Palermo's chief prosecutor, or whether the disagreements between them would be the dominant factor, something that might lead to a return to violent action against representatives of the state's institutions.[65] The Mafia might start feuding again and killing its own and there was a real danger that some *mafiosi* might even decide to return to attacking the state and its servants.

Yet, the Mafia had profited from keeping its head down and its voice low. In the ferocious internecine war that the Corleonese began in 1978 and in the murders of magistrates and policemen, the Mafia had broken with its silent ways and had attracted an unwelcome spotlight of attention and public demands for effective anti-Mafia action.

'Under Provenzano, Cosa Nostra has returned to its traditional modus operandi,' explained Antonio Ingroia.[66] It had become more elastic and shown its capacity to adapt. Cosa Nostra had changed its structure and significantly tightened the way it recruited. For ordinary criminal jobs such as extortion it increasingly used affiliates, people who had not been subjected to rigorous selection and initiation and who were kept in the dark about the organization. It had created cells similar to those used by terrorists. Most *mafiosi* knew only members of their own mafia families and news no longer circulated freely within Cosa Nostra as it had once done.

Despite the arrest of Giuffre in 2002 and his decision to become a *collaboratore di giustizia*, the task faced by anti-Mafia magistrates had become tougher. Fewer bullets and bombs and less bloodshed meant that an increasingly large part of the public started to think that the Mafia had ceased to be a problem. And it was not in the government's interest to admit that Cosa Nostra continued to be a huge threat.

Moreover, Silvio Berlusconi's government failed to give anti-Mafia forces the resources that they needed to carry out their duties. Dealing with illegal immigrants had become a priority in the south of Sicily and many policemen were engaged in this and not in tackling the resurgent Mafia. Fingerprint experts were kept busy with boat-people rather than *mafiosi*. The number of magistrates and police in Agrigento province, for example, was wholly insufficient when set against the number of investigations to be carried out and the number of trials to be held.[67] Good results in the courtroom around 2000 were owed to efforts in the field five to ten years before.

In the province of Agrigento, the authorities were having difficulty in implementing plans to combat extortion and intimidation because of lack of resources. The anti-Mafia magistrates were handicapped by a shortage of manpower and equipment that had significantly worsened over recent years. 'We have reached the paradoxical situation of having to choose which of the numerous investigations we should put in hand,' said Palma.[68] There were just not enough policemen to deal with telephone taps and monitor listening devices.

Some magistrates spoke about a slackening of effort, less commitment, a relaxation in the fight against Cosa Nostra. Perhaps that was not surprising. Many of the armour-plated cars in which anti-Mafia magistrates travelled were old and prone to break down. There were problems in finding the money to pay for the petrol of the vehicles of the escorts who put their lives on the line. Magistrates thought that many Italians, and members of the government, did not care if the

Mafia was beaten or not. 'It is very sad, but most people have forgotten the sacrifices made by Falcone and Borsellino,' said Palma.[69] Moreover, in a vicious campaign of denigration of the magistrature, Berlusconi and his allies had adopted those very arguments that criminals had used for years against the magistrature, that judges were prejudiced and that prosecutors hid or invented evidence. While anti-Mafia forces in Sicily struggled, the government in Rome appeared unconcerned that it was giving comfort to Cosa Nostra.

2

Success

GROWING UP IN MILAN

In the 1930s, the Mafia was a strictly Sicilian problem, a sore on Italian society but a distant issue for the upright Lombard citizens of Milan. Such Sicilian matters would not have been among the worries in Berlusconi's modest, Milanese middle-class family. Their main concerns would have revolved around the everyday struggles of jobs and making ends meet, and the threatening clouds of war. Berlusconi was almost four in 1940 when Mussolini allied fascist Italy's forces with those that Nazi Germany had aggressively unleashed against its European neighbours, tying his fortune to Hitler's in their so-called 'pact of steel'.

Silvio Berlusconi was born in Milan on 29 September 1936, the son of a bank employee; there was little in his background to suggest big things for his future. Life was difficult and his family shared the hardships that most Italians suffered, the war disastrously intruding into daily life in 1942, he remembers.[1] That was the year the tide of the war turned. At the beginning of November 1942, the British army won a great victory at El Alamein in Egypt that drove the armies of Italy and Germany into a retreat from which they would never recover. Conditions worsened in northern Italy after 8 September 1943 when Italy signed an armistice with the Anglo-American allies. This was the great crisis for Italy, the fall of fascism. Although not yet finally beaten, the forces that Mussolini and Hitler had put together were well and truly on the run.

The carpet-bombing that had flattened large swathes of Milan in 1943 had been a taste of what was to come. Three weeks before the armistice, on the night of 15/16 August, during the fourth big raid by allied air forces, the city's famous La Scala opera house had been hit by an incendiary bomb and gutted. When, after the armistice, the Germans started to round up Italian soldiers, Berlusconi's father, Luigi, slipped over the nearby border into Switzerland to escape from them. 'He made the right choice,' said Berlusconi, 'saving his own life and the future of all of us.'[2]

While Luigi Berlusconi was in Swizerland, Berlusconi's mother, Rosa, worked as a secretary at the Pirelli tyre company to support two children, her mother-in-law and her father. The family was living outside Milan, between the city and Como. She had to be at work early and got up at five in the morning to catch the bus that went to the station at Lomazzo. There she would take the Ferrovie Nord train for Milan and then, in the evening, she faced that same exhausting journey home.[3]

Severe, determined and a fighter, Rosa had a steely character that helped form Berlusconi's own during that crucial, uncertain and worrying war-time period while his father was away. But there was great affection and tenderness also. Many years later, Berlusconi was in Paris on her seventieth birthday and arranged for seventy roses to be delivered. But the surprise arrived when he rang her doorbell at midnight with a special present, a sculpture of the Madonna with the child offering a rose. 'He told me that it was carved in 1936, the year that he was born, and it was because of this that he wanted to give it to me,' recalls Rosa Berlusconi. 'I am proud of everything that my children have done and thank the Lord for this. But I am especially proud of their concern and love for me.'[4] She clearly doted on Silvio and Silvio adored her.

Berlusconi missed his father greatly during his absence in Switzerland. Fathers, uncles and brothers who had gone away to avoid capture by the Germans returned when the war ended, he recalled, but for him the worrying and waiting continued. He went to the railway station to wait for the trains coming from Como because Italians who had fled to Switzerland arrived from there. 'So many were coming back, but not my father. I went there every day for a month,' he remembered. Then, at last, his father returned. 'I recognized him from way off and my heart leapt.' Berlusconi thought himself fortunate as many children never saw their fathers again.[5]

Back in Milan, Berlusconi's father returned to his job in the Banca Rasini, a small, family-owned credit institution. The bank's owner later remembered Luigi Berlusconi's dedication and trustworthiness, such commitment to the bank and such honesty that he even made subordinates give back the stubs of old pencils before handing out new ones.[6]

The Salesian Fathers, an order approved in 1868 by Pope Pius IX, a famously conservative pontiff who proclaimed the dogma of papal infallibility, saw to Berlusconi's high school education at the strict Liceo Sant'Ambrogio boarding school in Milan. Latin and Greek were on the curriculum. He excelled in these ancient languages and in Italian, recalled Guido Possa, a school friend who later became a member of parliament in the ranks of Berlusconi's Forza Italia party. According to Possa, Berlusconi was the centre of attention in class, thanks to a bubbling and extrovert vitality. His taste in clothes, easy way with words and success with girls aroused some envy.[7] One of the high school's teaching fathers remembered Berlusconi's self-confidence, capacity to communicate and ability to speak off-the-cuff. When the school had official visitors, said Father Erminio Furlotti, Berlusconi was given the job of making the welcome speech.[8] Of the stories about Berlusconi's youth, one shows that he caught the entrepreneurial bug early: he finished his homework quickly and then made a few lire by selling his services to classmates who were not as bright as him. Moreover, ran the tale, he gave back the fees if the work he had done for others failed to earn good marks from teachers.[9]

Another story is that his musical prowess helped pay for his legal studies at Milan University, where he graduated with top marks, writing a dissertation on advertising contracts that won him a prize. It is certainly true that with his friend Fedele Confalonieri, who would later take over the running of the Fininvest group, Berlusconi formed a musical duo. They went to sea to entertain holidaymakers on cruise-ships, Confalonieri at the keyboard and his future boss on the guitar or double bass. Berlusconi would also sing from his repertoire of dozens of songs crooned by Charles Trenet, Gilbert Becaud and Charles Aznavour.[10] According to employees who knew him many years later, he continued to let his hair down in the late 1980s, entertaining staff at their social gatherings with his singing.

Foreign diplomats in Rome spoke about Berlusconi's enthusiasm for sing-songs too, about how he would invite well-known singers to international gatherings and then add his voice to the show. But he was not just a performer; he had pretensions as a songwriter too.

In 2002 he found time, while combining the jobs of prime minister and foreign minister, to collaborate with Mariano Apicella, a Neapolitan popular musician, in writing songs for a compact disc. One of these ended: *Comme si bella, bella, bella tu si a chiù bella e nun c'è bella ch'è chiù bella e te.* (How beautiful you are, nobody is more beautiful than you.) They worked late at night in Berlusconi's villa in Sardinia. 'He has a powerful and warm voice that he uses often, particularly in Edith Piaf's French repertoire. Yes, he has got music in his blood,' gushed Apicella.[11] At high school, Berlusconi had dreamed of becoming an orchestral conductor.[12]

PROPERTY DEVELOPER

Instead, he went into business, tackling his first real estate development project in Milan in 1960. Berlusconi's arrival in property could hardly have been better timed. Italy was recovering strongly from the devastating effects of the Second World War. The country's factories were turning out an increasing range of goods that were finding willing buyers at home and abroad. The post-war economic miracle was underway. During the 1950s, Italy's economy grew rapidly, its average annual rate of growth almost 6 per cent – higher than all other European countries except Germany. Italy made up for the industrial revolution it had missed during the nineteenth century and the opening years of the twentieth century, enjoying an extraordinary economic expansion that reached its climax in the five years following 1958.[13]

Milan was at the front of this surge in activity. Although economists spoke about Italy's industrial triangle of Milan, Turin and Genoa, the Lombard city was much more than just one of three major industrial centres. It took on the role of economic capital for the whole country. Companies and institutions throughout Italy looked to Milan for financial leadership. Moreover, the kind of development that took place in the 1950s was responsible for the idea that Milan was rather more than simply a city of bankers and industrialists. It was Italy's moral capital as well, setting an example by doing things by the book, although that morality in the Lombard capital was soon lost. When the corruption and tacky dealings that corroded values so thoroughly in the 1980s were exposed in the 1990s by the *mani pulite* (clean hands) prosecutors, Milan would be labelled *tangentopoli*, bribesville.

Construction boomed as the Milanese busily set about repairing bomb damage, building apartments and erecting high-rise office blocks. Two of these still towered above the city's skyline forty years later. One was the hammer-shaped Torre Velasca, put up between 1956 and 1958. The other was Gio Ponti's slender Pirelli tower, completed in 1960 and representing the flowering of 1950s optimism and the solid achievement of Italy's post-war economic miracle. Not only did they rise high; the Torre Velasca and the Pirelli tower were two fine pieces of architecture, admired long after they were built.

Large numbers of migrants from the *mezzogiorno*, Italy's poor south, were attracted by Milan's booming economy, and the need for housing increased. Many of the arriving mass of workers found themselves at its metropolitan fringes as Milan grew through an urban sprawl that ate into the countryside. Planning controls were often absent, abused or ignored in a post-war reconstruction of the city and its hinterland that generally left much to be desired. These were the surroundings in which Berlusconi, an aspiring property developer, embarked on his business career.

While at university, Berlusconi had worked in a small construction company owned by Pietro Canali, a client of the Banca Rasini to whom he had been introduced by his father and the bank's owner. Berlusconi had noticed a plot of land in Via Alciati, west of the city's centre and close to the Pio Albergo Trivulzio, the old people's hospital that just over thirty years later would be the starting point for the *tangentopoli* scandals. The district around Via Alciati was being built up and the sharp-eyed Berlusconi, in a hurry to make his mark, saw the opportunity that the land offered for development. They should set up a new company for the project, on a 50:50 basis, he suggested to a surprised Canali. And that is what they did, Canali and Berlusconi in partnership establishing a company, Cantieri Riuniti Milanesi, to develop the site. Berlusconi put in half of its share capital, the money coming partly from his father and partly from savings that he himself had put aside from his earnings as a musician.[14]

A mortgage loan from the Banca Rasini allowed Cantieri Riuniti Milanesi to buy the land. The costs of construction were met by money received from buyers as work progressed at the site. Apartments were sold on the basis of plans for the development, this technique of selling off-plan being possible in a market driven by strong demand. One story says that Berlusconi sold the first apartment in Via Alciati to Fedele Confalonieri's mother, taking her to the site and showing her the layout for the apartment that he was trying to sell her. Berlusconi was the mind and the force behind the development of Via Alciati. He had found the site, organized the finance and tackled the many bureaucratic procedures for obtaining building licences. Canali later said that Berlusconi had a great capacity for work and learned quickly. One of his strengths lay in arriving five minutes before the crowd, another in being a convincing salesman. As well as looking for clients inside his own circle of friends and acquaintances, he also tried to charm them into selling on his behalf.[15]

After tasting success in his first venture, Berlusconi turned to bigger projects. He had become a rising star in Milanese property development. In 1963, he boldly took on a project to build a substantial new residential district for about 4,000 inhabitants. This was at Brugherio, outside Milan's city limits to the northeast, just beyond the neighbouring steel-making town of Sesto San Giovanni and south of Monza, famous for its motor-racing circuit and royal palace. In the future, Berlusconi would continue to be attracted to this area north of Milan, called the Brianza and noted for its hard-headed businessmen, hard-working people and elegant villas. His own family properties later included the Villa San Martino and the Villa Belvedere in the typical Brianza towns of Arcore and Macherio.

The Banca Rasini and Canali were again involved, although Berlusconi had brought in new partners for the Brugherio project. The vehicle for the development was a limited partnership called Edilnord in which Berlusconi was working partner, the capital being put up by a private Swiss company, Finanzierungsgesellschaft fur

Residenzen, registered in Lugano with a nominee director and bearer shares of which the ownership was unknown. It was this Swiss company that owned Edilnord.[16] Brugherio was not the success that its promoters had hoped for, however, due partly to the fact that the district was poorly served by public transport. Berlusconi had almost bitten off more than he could chew; the scheme turned out to be a challenge that forced him to be even more creative and tenacious than usual. He worked day and night, seven days a week, to boost the slow sales. Berlusconi's gift of the gab, his ability to invent new forms of advertising, direct promotion and sales, were needed to get the development off his and his partners' hands.[17]

While building was underway at Brugherio, the up-and-coming property developer launched into a more personal project; Berlusconi married. He had to draw on his charm and skills of persuasion. Carla Dell'Oglio was waiting for a bus outside Milan's main railway station and had caught Berlusconi's eye as he passed in his car. He stopped, introduced himself, made a joke and offered her a lift. They married in March 1965 and Maria Elvira was born a year later. Two years after the birth of Marina, as she was known, Pier Silvio was born.[18] Both children would later take top positions in their father's business empire.

Property development was becoming more challenging by the mid-1960s, however, as the conditions under which land was developed were tightened, land prices rose and interest rates moved higher. Developers found that some tax breaks were phased out, and they faced the prospect of having to contribute to the cost of roads, water supplies and drains in areas where they were building. Moreover, planning regulations became stricter. But the changes did not deter Berlusconi who plunged into a bigger scheme than he had ever ventured before, the one of which he would be most proud.

Milano 2 was a residential project in the town of Segrate, neighbouring Milan's eastern boundary and a few miles from Linate airport. Berlusconi's idea was to build an Italian garden city that would rise on about 7 million square feet of land that had previously belonged to Conte Bonzi, a local aristocrat.[19] Bonzi had reached an agreement with Segrate's town authorities in the first half of the 1960s for the land's development and the development agreement was transferred to Edilnord when it bought the land in 1968.

Edilnord obtained its first building licence in spring 1969. Although difficulties cropped up with Milan's provincial authorities over the building plan, these were eventually sorted out and Edilnord and the authorities in Segrate signed a new agreement three years later. Planning consents and the like were not the only obstacles that Edilnord had to overcome, however. Milano 2 was underneath the path of aircraft taking off from Linate, at that time Milan's main airport, making a nonsense of the notion that the new development was an island of tranquillity for those hoping to escape from the city's noise. An astutely orchestrated campaign got the flight path altered to benefit residents in Milano 2, controversially so because the new flight path disturbed the peace of residents elsewhere in Segrate.[20]

Milano 2 was completed in 1979, apartments in the development appealing particularly to buyers from Milan's upwardly mobile professional classes. The project provided residents with plenty of trees and greenery and, with a concept new to Italy, it kept cars and pedestrians separate. The brown-red apartment blocks weathered well during the following years, but Milano 2 continued to be a dormitory district, a long way from the centre of Milan and connected to the city by an infrequent suburban bus service.

Twenty years after the fanfare of the project's inauguration had been forgotten, lack of business had forced many shops in the development's arcades to lower their shutters for good. An oasis for apartment-owners; perhaps, but a desert with spooky overtones for visitors. Antennae sprouting from the roof, Berlusconi's Mediaset television company had located its offices in Milano 2. Video cameras mounted high above the pavements and *piazze* spied constantly and officious security guards in civilian clothes stopped and grilled passers-by.

Berlusconi would later claim that Milano 2 was absolutely innovatory and that it offered a futuristic urban model. 'Milano 2 became a reference point. There was a flow of developers and architects, above all from abroad. Its model was examined by many foreign universities. Everyone tried to grasp the secrets of a success created from a thousand ingredients cleverly brought together,' he claimed.[21] Reality was rather different. The development copied examples of urban planning that were already well known in northern Europe.

As with Berlusconi's Brugherio development, capital for the company that was the vehicle for the Milano 2 project, Edilnord Centri Residenziali sas di Lidia Borsani e C, came from Switzerland. (Borsani was Berlusconi's cousin.) The limited partnership's initial capital and successive increases in capital were provided by Aktiengesellschaft fur Immobilienanlagen in Residenzzentren, a private Swiss company in Lugano whose owners were unknown.[22] A singularity of Milano 2, a project for which Berlusconi proudly claimed the parentage, was that his name did not appear in the official records of the business that was responsible for it. Neither did Berlusconi's name appear in the official documents concerning Societa Generale Atrezzature (Sogeat), another company involved in the development of Milano 2, where the managing partner was an elderly Milanese accountant, a long-standing friend of Berlusconi whose offices were used as Sogeat's address.[23]

An inspection by the Guardia di Finanza financial police in October and November 1979 concluded that Berlusconi could not be identified as the owner of the Lugano-based companies that owned Edilnord Centri Residenziali and Sogeat.[24] The team for that inspection had been headed by Massimo Berruti, an officer in the corps who would soon resign, become one of Berlusconi's lawyers and later be elected to parliament in Forza Italia's ranks.[25]

Yet one Italian bank that had lent money for Milano 2's development considered that Berlusconi was the beneficial owner of Edilnord Centri Residenziali and Sogeat, and the Ufficio Italiano dei Cambi (UIC, the Bank of Italy's foreign exchange service) believed that Edilnord Centri Residenziali had previously been called Edilnord sas di Silvio Berlusconi & C, which had been liquidated in November 1976. In the letter to the Guardia di Finanza that triggered the inspection in October and November 1979, UIC had noted that Berlusconi had guaranteed loans to Edilnord Centri Residenziali.[26] He and his father had given guarantees for large loans to Sogeat as well. This was a way of acquiring credit with his main clients for whom he was simply a consultant, Berlusconi explained to the Guardia di Finanza officer who would become his lawyer.[27]

With the lira under severe pressure throughout the 1960s and 1970s, UIC tried to keep tight control over capital flows into and out of Italy and the law backed up UIC's work by imposing very severe penalties on exchange-control violations. Undeclared and unauthorized ownership or partial ownership of two secretive Lugano-based companies would probably have brought serious trouble and perhaps even prison. The two Italian companies engaged on Milano 2 benefited from inflows of capital from Switzerland amounting to 4 billion lire during the first half of the 1970s but their two Swiss parent companies had been scrupulous in asking the Bank of Italy to authorize them.[28]

Berlusconi's involvement in property development did not stop with Milano 2, where work had earned him, at the early age of forty, recognition in the title of *cavaliere* (knight). He turned his attention to the south of Milan and the neighbouring town of Basiglio. There, in 1978, work started on Milano 3, a mixed development of residential property for around 14,000 inhabitants combined with offices.[29] Located less conveniently than the earlier development, it did less well commercially. But Berlusconi was already diversifying into the business for which he would later be best known. He was pushing aggressively into television.

VILLA CASATI, ARCORE

Born in Milan, 29 September 1936, resident at Villa San Martino in Arcore, province of Milan – Silvio Berlusconi's residence was there for all to read in the judgement given in November 1999 by Alessandro Rossato, a judge in Milan's court responsible for preliminary investigations, that sent Berlusconi for trial on charges of judicial corruption in Rome.

Villa San Martino, a former Benedictine monastery, was where Berlusconi liked to entertain and display his wealth. Even before becoming prime minister, he had been host there to Valery Giscard d'Estaing, a former French president, and Mikhail Gorbachev, a former Soviet leader, and his wife.[30] The villa was also a place for doing business and impressing visiting businessmen with how much he had achieved. When the car-maker, Fiat, Italy's biggest industrial concern, ran into difficulties, his residence at Arcore rather than the prime minister's offices was where Berlusconi chose to meet its top managers in October 2002 to discuss the future of the troubled group.[31] Some people thought that this was his way of showing the Agnelli family, Fiat's founders and biggest shareholders of a company that was holding out a begging bowl, that he had become the power that counted and that the old aristocracy of Italian industry needed to keep this in mind.

Despite his connections with Milan and Rome, and his holiday villa in Sardinia, Arcore is associated more than any other place with Berlusconi. Yet, on the map the town council gave visitors long after Berlusconi had bought the property, the Villa San Martino was still called Villa Casati – the name of the family who owned it before Berlusconi. It had been bought by Count Giorgio Giulini, a member of a patrician Milanese family, at the beginning of the eighteenth century, passing by marriage to the Casati family in 1849.[32]

Villa Casati became famous as a meeting place of the liberal intelligentsia. Alessandro Casati was a close friend of Benedetto Croce, the Neapolitan philosopher, historian and critic. Internationally the most noted of Italy's anti-fascists, Croce wrote the Manifesto that expressed the firm opposition of Italian intellectuals to Mussolini's regime. Croce had been minister of education in the government of Giovanni Giolitti in 1920 and 1921 and was never far from the political stage, but he was better known as a thinker and writer. During a friendship with Casati that lasted almost half a century, Croce spent long periods at the Villa Casati. Other guests were surprised by this olympian intellectual who was so approachable and never pompous. He was an amazing source of anecdotes that spanned centuries and covered every kind of writing. While walking in the gardens at Villa Casati, spectacles balanced on his nose, Croce loved to talk with his companions, avoiding the deep issues, however, and preferring to chat about the minor weaknesses of men.[33] The two black decades of fascism provided abundant material to engage his mind and entertain his friends.

Casati and Croce were of a kind. Both were thinkers, both liberals and determinedly anti-fascist. Casati helped re-establish the Liberal Party in 1925 after Mussolini had made clear his intentions to set up a dictatorship. He represented the party in the National Liberation

Committee and took part in the underground struggle against Nazi–Fascism after the armistice in September 1943. Casati had been considered a candidate to become Italy's head of state in 1948 and had enjoyed the support of the left despite being an aristocratic liberal and landowner.[34] He died in 1955, aged seventy-four, three years after his friend Croce. Casati was one of the last examples of loyalty to the ideals of the Risorgimento, wrote one historian, 'true to liberal patriotism, rich of spirit, a life that alternated study with healthy politics and the just war'.[35]

Despite being the town where Italy's right-wing prime minister had his official residence, and where Mussolini had taken his first flying lessons,[36] Arcore prides itself on its history of anti-fascism. During the Second World War, two of its parish priests had been active in helping Jews and allied servicemen who had escaped from prisoner-of-war camps. Resistance around Arcore was possible thanks to the solidarity and help of a large part of the population. Whenever he arrived by car in Arcore, shortly before driving through the gates of his villa Berlusconi passed close to two roads named after a pair of *partigiani* (patriots who fought against Nazi–Fascism) from Arcore who were murdered by the fascists, and to the town's large monument to the resistance.[37]

Berlusconi acquired Villa Casati after a drama involving Alessandro Casati's nephew and heir, Camillo Casati Stampa, played out in a torrid Roman summer in a luxurious attic apartment in Via Puccini, near the capital's Villa Borghese gardens. Camillo Casati Stampa had obtained an annulment of the marriage to his first wife and married again in 1961. He had returned to the apartment one day at the end of August 1970, shot his second wife and her young playboy lover, and then killed himself. By his first wife, Camillo Casati Stampa had a daughter, Anna Maria, who inherited the estate. Born in May 1951, Anna Maria was still a minor at the time of the multiple killing. Her dead stepmother's lawyer was Cesare Previti, and he became Anna Maria's lawyer after the terrible drama of Via Puccini. Anna Maria also had a guardian but he was elderly and a busy senator, so the management of the Casati Stampa inheritance was effectively in Previti's hands.[38]

That inheritance was enormous and encumbered with tax

problems. In October 1972, Anna Maria Casati Stampa, who had moved to Brazil, signed an agreement to sell a plot of land west of Milan to one of Berlusconi's companies. Generous terms for the buyer spread payment over several years, a condition that the heiress tried, unsuccessfully, to alter through her lawyer. In April 1974, Previti acted in the sale of Villa Casati to another of Berlusconi's companies for the modest sum of 750 million lire, with payment by instalments. A year later, Previti had become a member of Berlusconi's entourage. From then onwards, he was to be a close colleague and counsellor in Berlusconi's business and political adventures. Almost three decades later the two men were still side-by-side, in court in Milan facing charges of bribing judges.

Berlusconi's choice of Villa Casati as his residence ensured even tighter security in Arcore when he entered politics; cars of the *carabinieri* military police constantly prowled the streets after he became prime minister and two patrol vehicles were parked permanently outside the villa's high gates. Being Berlusconi's home town inevitably brought the spotlight of public attention and some disadvantages, said Antonio Nava, the town's mayor, and even the smallest things that went wrong had repercussions. Moreover, Nava, a representative of the centre-left elected as mayor by a substantial majority in June 2002, felt he had to be more careful when he spoke.[39]

TELEVISION TYCOON

Berlusconi's transformation from property mogul to television tycoon was more logical than might at first appear. In the garden city at Milano 2, he had sought to avoid the ugly jungles of television antennae and wires that often sprouted on the roofs of apartment blocks in Italian towns and cities by installing a central antenna linked by cable to homes in the development. This attention to appearances had a result that perhaps even Berlusconi did not expect: within a decade he would own three national channels and dominate commercial television in Italy.

During the mid-1970s businessmen were launching local channels and these were attracting viewers, so Berlusconi decided to offer a local service to the people who moved to Milano 2, and acquired the equipment needed to make transmissions. Telemilano was established in 1973 and started transmitting on a modest scale via cable in 1974.[40] Fininvest, the parent company of Berlusconi's business empire, said that the year Telemilano started was 1978.

Italy's constitutional court ruled in July 1976 that private channels could transmit legally at a local level and Telemilano – renamed Canale 5 in 1980 – began to spread beyond the boundaries of Milano 2. Berlusconi acquired other local stations in the region, installed transmitters and repeaters and began broadcasting on the airwaves to viewers in Lombardy. This soon gave him his first big breakthrough in the new business: live transmission in Lombardy of the Mundialito soccer tournament in South America for which he had bought the rights, and the taped transmission of the tournament's matches elsewhere in Italy.[41]

The law that limited private television to local broadcasting was, however, far too strict for Berlusconi's ambition to be as big in broadcasting as he had become in property development. 'One cannot really be in the television business without being linked directly with the whole of the country and with the world,' he argued in April 1981.[42] He got round the law's constraints through a clever stratagem.

Every day Berlusconi's budding Milanese television company recorded a master tape of all the programmes to be transmitted on the following day, including advertising slots. The master tape was then sent to the many local stations up and down Italy with which Berlusconi had agreements. Then, on the day following the recording, all the stations, including Berlusconi's own in Milan, ran the tape at the same time, creating the illusion of a national broadcasting channel. The Sunday afternoon programme *Buona Domenica*, for example, was recorded on Saturday. There was a big sign in the studio that said *oggi è domenica* (today is Sunday) and this gave the impression that the programme was live when it went on air at the same time from all the local television stations.[43] The appearance of transmitting live allowed Berlusconi to compete directly with RAI, the state-owned broadcasting company: for the first time, advertisers were able to check the national impact of their campaigns on commercial television.

An important part of Berlusconi's leverage over Italy's local channels was the films and serials in his packages – a major attraction to viewers. Part of his strategy was therefore to acquire a substantial film library which he started to do in summer 1979. He had thought up an arrangement that was a winner all round for himself: he controlled the content of programmes and earned the revenues of advertisers glad of an alternative to RAI. Initially, the advertising side of Berlusconi's television business was managed by his Rete Italia company itself. At the end of 1980, Rete Italia set up a specialist advertising subsidiary, Publitalia, a company that was later to make a crucial contribution to Berlusconi's entry into politics.

Winning advertising was one thing but, by signing up stars, Berlusconi's television business invaded what RAI had considered its own territory in another way. One such star was Mike Bongiorno, who was born in New York in 1924 and had been a leading quiz-show host with the state-owned broadcaster. 'Old and new personalities, who became real friends of the family, spoke to the Italians and smiled from the screens of Canale 5, Italia 1 and Retequattro. To make a full list of these personalities would be impossible. But wanting to remember some of them, the list begins with Mike Bongiorno, an authentic icon of national television.'[44] Bongiorno started with Berlusconi at the end of the 1970s; other big names followed him.

Its market under attack by the newcomer, RAI was poorly placed to fight back, above all because it was divided and failed to offer a united front to the interloper. The state-owned broadcaster had been partitioned by party bosses. The first of its three channels was in the hands of the Christian Democrat Party, Italy's biggest political party. The second was the fief of the Socialist Party, although the smaller centrist parties also had a say. The third leaned heavily towards the Communist Party. RAI was a swollen bureaucracy where jobs were filled through patronage and connections. Berlusconi's channels offered viewers large rations of televisual pap, but the state broadcaster's programmes too were far from being national assets in terms of cultural content or entertainment. Split, inefficient and politically compromised, RAI was unable to respond to Berlusconi's offensive.

Moreover, the state broadcaster was handicapped by the support given to Berlusconi by the Socialist Party and its leader, Bettino Craxi.

This threw a spanner in the delicate mechanism that governed relations between politics and television. Before Berlusconi's arrival, television had been shared between Italy's political parties. After his arrival, there was a new and powerful force against which there was no counter-balance and the way was opened for Berlusconi to control virtually all the country's television.

RAI was also affected by a process of consolidation that Italy's commercial television went through at the beginning of the 1980s. During the second half of the 1970s, after the ruling of the constitutional court allowing local transmission by private-sector broadcasters, small television stations had mushroomed. Consolidation among the commercial concerns meant that the state broadcaster was no longer up against just a fragmented group of small television operators. Instead, RAI faced one large and growing competitor as well. By 1982, RAI's share of audience had slipped to 63 per cent. With 13 per cent, Berlusconi's Canale 5 was the biggest of the private broadcasters. Italia 1, part of the privately owned Rusconi publishing group, had an audience share of almost 10 per cent and Retequattro, owned by the Mondadori publishing house, 8 per cent.[45]

Berlusconi acquired Italia 1 for 30 billion lire in September 1982 in a transaction that caught Mondadori, which had been expecting to merge its Retequattro with Italia 1, completely by surprise. By winning a battle for advertisers in 1983 – signing on attractive exclusive contracts the companies that were the biggest spenders on advertising in Italy[46] – Berlusconi dealt Mondadori another severe blow. It weakened Retequattro sufficiently that Mondadori was persuaded to sell it: Retequattro was added to Berlusconi's television empire in August 1984. The Berlusconi group was then able to boast almost total national coverage, an audience share that matched RAI's and advertising revenues on a par with the state broadcaster's.

The defenders of the old television order resisted bitterly through their friends in parliament who saw their control being eroded. The courts aimed at gagging Berlusconi's television, complained his supporters. It was a very difficult period for Berlusconi who felt that the survival of his television business was continually threatened. 'RAI, its powerful lobby and all the print publishers, jealous of our advertising revenues, wanted to throw us out of the market, annihilate us. But we were able to survive,' said Berlusconi.[47] That his television empire did survive was due to the work of Craxi, who enjoyed enormous and increasing power during the 1980s. Thanks to the politician's astute, behind-the-scenes manoeuvres, the aggressive newcomer was helped to elbow his way forward. Between 1983 and 1986, Italy's prime minister paralysed RAI by blocking the renewal of its board. Then, when a new board was appointed in October 1986, Enrico Manca, a leading figure in the Socialist Party and a former minister of foreign trade, was appointed chairman. RAI's chairman until 1992,[48] Manca was the appointee of Craxi, Berlusconi's political patron.

The upstart broadcaster was also able to go head-to-head with magistrates who thought that his way of broadcasting nationally broke the law. In October 1984, magistrates in Rome, Turin and Pescara ordered the blackout of Berlusconi's three channels. Within four days Craxi, who was then prime minister, promulgated a decree legalizing Berlusconi's television operations and allowing him to start transmitting again. The decree gave immediate effect to measures to save Berlusconi's television business: it said that until such time as an umbrella law was enacted to deal with broadcasting overall, all privately owned broadcasters who were operational on 1 October 1984 would be allowed to continue broadcasting. It also allowed the transmission of identical pre-recorded programmes by different broadcasters. One month later, parliament's lower house decided that the decree, by then known as the Berlusconi Decree, was unconstitutional and refused to ratify it.

Parliament's refusal to approve the measure did not deter stubborn Craxi. Threatening a government crisis, he presented the decree once more and bullied parliament into voting its assent, and the decree, which had temporary effectiveness lasting just sixty days, entered the statute book as a permanent law.[49] In July 1988, the constitutional court went into action, albeit feebly and inconsequentially. Craxi's law was adjudged unconstitutional. It was merely a transitional measure that should have been replaced quickly by legislation to regulate the television sector and provide real guarantees of pluralism in television broadcasting.

Legislation, fiercely contested both inside and outside parliament, eventually arrived at the end of July 1990. It was called the Mammi

Law, after Oscar Mammi, minister of posts at the time and, as such, the minister responsible for broadcasting. 'The fruit of innumerable disagreements and clashes, secret pressures, brokering and back-tracking, in substance it was conceived to guarantee Berlusconi the ownership of all three of his channels and leadership in winning advertising,' recounts one record of how the Mammi Law was enacted.[50] The constitutional court had warned that it would itself promulgate broadcasting rules if parliament did not pass legislation before the summer recess and this renewed the threat that Berlusconi's television channels would be blacked out.

Craxi did not let Berlusconi down. The Socialist Party leader's commitment to Berlusconi's cause drew an acid comment from Ciriaco De Mita, a former prime minister and a leading member of the Christian Democrat Party: 'I follow the rules, the Socialists follow Canale 5.'[51] Craxi was locked in a powerful political embrace with two other Christian Democrat leaders, Giulio Andreotti, prime minister at the time, and the party's secretary. Craxi threatened to pull the Socialist Party out of the governing coalition if his rich friend's television channels did not get preferential treatment. Andreotti resorted to a vote of confidence to force Mammi's bill through parliament, a move that caused a mutiny in his government. Five cabinet ministers and a platoon of junior ministers from the left wing of the Christian Democrat Party resigned in disgust and outrage at the legislation that parliament was being asked to enact. They were quickly replaced. Andreotti kept the prime ministership and Berlusconi his television channels.

The Mammi Law failed to ensure that Italy would have a pluralism of information and of television operators, instead sealing Berlusconi's complete dominance of private television and allowing him to continue his tight grip on television advertising. When Berlusconi's television business was floated on the stock market six years later, it was able to claim more than 60 per cent of the total of television advertising revenues in Italy.[52] Most of the remaining revenues went to RAI.

Less than three years after Mammi's defective and partial law was enacted it attracted the attention of the anti-corruption magistrates in Milan who thought there were grounds for investigation. One reason for their suspicion was that a member of Mammi's staff, after leaving the ministry, had been given a lucrative consultancy contract by Berlusconi's Fininvest company. After being arrested in May 1993, a civil servant at the ministry of posts admitted to having received bribes from suppliers to the ministry, for whom he had rigged tenders, and to having distributed money to political parties.[53] However, Milan's *mani pulite* team was pulled off the case which was transferred to Rome where magistrates claimed jurisdiction; like numerous investigations in Rome, it came to nothing.

INTO FINANCE

In 1990, the property tycoon had clearly won his struggle to become a television baron. Meanwhile, he had diversified into financial services, launching a company called Programma Italia in February 1982. Ennio Doris, Berlusconi's partner in this venture, had read an interview in which Berlusconi invited budding entrepreneurs to offer him ideas for new businesses. Bumping into Berlusconi in the *piazza* at Portofino, a fashionable resort on the Ligurian riviera, Doris sold his future partner the idea of establishing a network of agents selling financial products.[54] Four years Berlusconi's junior, Doris had worked for Italy's leader in this field and then spent ten years creating a network of 700 financial agents for a major insurer.[55]

In 1984, Programma Italia bought Mediolanum Assicurazioni, a minor insurance company. The business grew strongly, thanks to Doris's flair and deep knowledge of the financial services sector, to encompass not just mutual funds and insurance but banking and private pension funds. By the end of 2000, the Mediolanum group boasted a sales network of over 6,000 agents. Customers held 220,000 current accounts with the bank, a figure that grew to almost 300,000 in the following year. Funds managed by the group amounted to almost 18 billion euros at the end of 2000 and return on equity was 27 per cent.[56] Mediolanum expanded its operations into Spain, Germany and Austria.

Berlusconi had had to wait until June 2000 before he could say that he had really arrived on the financial stage. That was when

Mediolanum announced that it had acquired a 2 per cent stake in Mediobanca, a small but exceptionally well-connected Milanese investment bank. The financial services group controlled by Berlusconi and Doris had paid 476 million euros effectively for the privilege of sitting in Mediobanca's *salotto buono* (literally, good drawing room), and Doris had been given a seat on the board.

Although the large American investment banks had eaten into Mediobanca's franchise after they arrived in Italy during the 1990s, and the influence of the Milanese institution had waned, membership of its *salotto buono* still had a certain cachet. Mediobanca's shareholders included most of the country's notables and two of the biggest names in Italian business: Fiat, the automobile group controlled by the Agnelli family, and Pirelli, the family-controlled tyres and cables group.

From its discreet offices tucked away in a narrow street beside Milan's La Scala opera house, Mediobanca had once cooked up all the deals that mattered in Italy. It was the place where Italy's most important industrial families and firms traditionally met to decide what had to be done, who was to do it and how; no acquisition, merger, bond issue or increase in share capital of any importance took place without Mediobanca's approval. Often the small investment bank played an active part, having its fingers in many corporate pies and stakes in its own shareholders. It had been at the centre of the web of financial power in Italy for decades, and it had also been a very secretive institution.

Without doubt, the most important investment in its bulging portfolio was a stake of about 14 per cent – the largest single shareholding – in Assicurazioni Generali, by far Italy's biggest insurance company and a European leader. Generali – once the employer of Franz Kafka – was the ultimate in Italian blue chip stocks. Conservative and prudent, Generali was not the likeliest partner for the dynamic outsider, only recently admitted into the *salotto buono*. Less than half of the large insurer's revenues were sensitive to volatility in equity markets, compared with almost 90 per cent at Mediolanum, and its market capitalization was more than five times that of Mediolanum, whose shares had been listed in 1996.[57] Yet, Mediobanca tried to twist Generali's arm into a deal with Mediolanum in 2001.

Had this succeeded, Berlusconi, owning more than one third of Mediolanum's share capital, would have become the second biggest shareholder in Italy's insurance giant. Generali's management was cool towards the idea that it should merge with Mediolanum, however. The project was shelved, but some financial analysts expected that it would at some time in the future be taken down, dusted off and dressed up in an attempt to make it less of an affront to the market.

Berlusconi's ambitions to count in Italy's financial community were not new when Mediolanum bought its stake in Mediobanca, or even in 1982 when he launched Programma Italia. In 1980, after he had already made his name as a property developer but before he had elbowed his way to the top of commercial television, Berlusconi had had the audacity to propose himself for the chairmanship of the Cassa di Risparmio delle Province Lombarde (Cariplo). This bank, based in Milan, was one of Italy's biggest and strongest high street institutions and its catchment area covered Italy's wealthiest region.

Cariplo was then a public-sector institution, its board appointed by politicians with the treasury minister having a big say in deciding who would get the chairmanship. Berlusconi called on the minister to suggest that he was the right man for the job, only to learn that the minister thought that there would be a certain incompatibility of roles. The bank, after all, was heavily involved in property lending and a Milanese property developer would face an enormous conflict of interest; Cariplo already had links to Berlusconi's property business.[58] That would be no problem for Berlusconi who, never at a loss for words, had an answer ready. He would transfer all his business in the property sector to his brother, Paolo. The minister thought this an interesting example of the family firm at work.[59] Berlusconi's self-candidature to Cariplo got no further.

A SECOND FAMILY

Nevertheless, Berlusconi's star was rising inexorably. With Craxi's help, during the second half of the 1980s, Berlusconi moved closer to becoming Italy's wealthiest and most powerful man. There was more to the *cavaliere*, however, than the accretion of wealth and power. He had always had a profound respect for the family and gave his own all the time he was able to spare from work, his official record told Italians in the election campaign in spring 2001.[60] There was no stronger supporter of the family than Pope John Paul II and the Church and what they said was important for many Italians. Even the secular Forza Italia, the political party that Berlusconi had established, declared its belief in the family as the bedrock of Italian society.[61]

In 1978, Berlusconi had bought the Teatro Manzoni, one of the city's main theatres, which was in financial difficulties at the time, and the purchase may have contributed to the creation of his second, parallel family. In 1980, he met a Bolognese actress called Miriam Bartolini who was performing at the theatre. Her stage name was Veronica Lario. Away from the spotlight, their first child was born in Switzerland in July 1984, when Berlusconi was almost forty-eight. In October 1985, a court in Milan recorded the separation agreed between Berlusconi and his wife, Carla Dell'Oglio. 'One evening at the Teatro Manzoni in Milan, Berlusconi saw Veronica Lario on stage. It was immediately love. Some years later they married and Barbara (1984), Eleonora (1986) and Luigi (1988) were born,' recounts Berlusconi's official story.[62] In fact, the couple married in 1990.[63]

Veronica Lario would appear less and less by her husband's side after his first political victory in 1994. Her maternal grandfather had been murdered by the Nazis in a reprisal during the Second World War, in the countryside near Bologna. She would speak publicly against war in Iraq in a magazine with left-of-centre leanings in March 2003, and declared herself in favour of public demonstrations. She believed they served to wake people's conscience and that those who demonstrated did so in order to elicit answers to what rendered them uneasy. She thought demonstrations deserved respect.[64]

FROM FOOTBALL TO PUBLISHING

The early years of Berlusconi's relationship with Veronica Lario coincided with the consolidation of his position as the dominant force in commercial television in Italy and his diversification into finance. Property development, television and finance were not enough, however, to satisfy the energetic businessman. During the 1980s and 1990s, he extended his frontiers into football, print media, retailing and telecommunications. The move into soccer came at the end of 1985 when Berlusconi saved AC Milan, founded in 1899 and one of the city's two big clubs, which had fallen on hard times and was about to go bankrupt. He officially became a shareholder in March 1986.

Berlusconi had been a big soccer fan when he was a boy and his father had taken him to the stadium to watch AC Milan play. Matches were on Sunday afternoons and the family lunch could not pass quickly enough for the young supporter. 'I was always asking the time, impatient and scared of being late,' he remembered. Then hand-in-hand to the Arena or San Siro stadiums where, at the turnstile, Berlusconi would try to look small, to get in with his father for the price of just one ticket.[65] With his father as accomplice or teacher, Berlusconi learned to be *furbo* (street-wise) at a tender age – a snippet from his boyhood that he was willing to share with Italian voters many years later.

With the purchase of AC Milan, Berlusconi had realized what for many schoolboys was a dream. More than just the ownership of a major football club, it was ownership of the club keenly supported in childhood. To the boy, AC Milan had represented 'something wonderful, a wealth of affection to defend strenuously in heated discussions with school chums'.[66] As an adult, the passion of an armchair sportsman gave Berlusconi the touch of the common man, at ease standing in the corner of the bar debating team tactics and personalities. As a politician, he used sporting analogies; he liked to show how he was involved in men's business.

With an injection of cash from Fininvest to buy management and playing talent, AC Milan's results improved. It won a cupboard full of trophies over the next decade, the lengthy roll of successes beginning soon after Berlusconi took over. The club won the Italian league in the 1987–88 season and Europe's Champions Cup in the following season.

But when the club's accounts were subjected to the scrutiny of magistrates in Milan in 1994, they found evidence that AC Milan had made a large under-the-counter payment in 1992 to purchase a footballer from Torino, one of two important football teams in Turin.

(The other, better-known, team is Juventus.) As AC Milan's chairman, Berlusconi was sent for trial, accused of false accounting; with him were the club's managing director and Massimo Berruti, the lawyer who wrote the footballer's transfer contract. As well as the declared figure of 18.5 billion lire that AC Milan had paid for the footballer, offshore companies belonging to Fininvest had paid an undeclared sum of just over 10 billion lire to Torino's chairman in order to secure the footballer's transfer. Despite an admission of guilt by the chairman of the Turinese club, who had plea-bargained a lower sentence, Berlusconi and his fellow defendants were acquitted in November 2002.[67] Berlusconi's government had, soon after it came to power in May 2001 and amid great controversy, changed the law on false accounting, decriminalizing some types of the offence and reducing the period of the statute of limitations. The court ruled that the offence of which Berlusconi was accused was statute-barred. The prosecution had simply run out of time.

Legal problems aside, Berlusconi's acquisition of AC Milan increased his visibility and the team's victories boosted his standing in a football-mad country. At least, soccer was something that caused few misgivings among those concerned about Berlusconi's accumulation of interests.

His expansion into print media was another matter. After making his first move by acquiring a 12 per cent stake in the loss-making daily newspaper *Il Giornale* in 1977, Berlusconi grew much bolder, in step with his success in television. Two years later, he increased his interest to almost 38 per cent and soon after took full control.[68] In 1983, the equity in the company owning *Il Giornale* was split 51:49 between Berlusconi personally and Fininvest. At the end of 1986, the company changed its name to Silvio Berlusconi Editore.

Berlusconi later sold *Il Giornale* to his brother.[69] This move may have been inspired less by brotherly affection or fraternal generosity than by the need to satisfy a legal requirement imposed by the Mammì Law that limited the interests that television-owners could hold in daily newspapers. The sideways shift of ownership of *Il Giornale* within the Berlusconi family in 1992 showed how the tailor-made legislation, cooked up by Craxi and steamrollered through parliament, suited the Socialist Party leader's wealthy friend.

As well as continuing to exert an effective control over the newspaper, Berlusconi had added a major publishing house to Fininvest's portfolio in 1991. This was Arnoldo Mondadori, Italy's leading publisher of books and magazines. With around 30 per cent of the country's book market, Mondadori had twice the share of its nearest rival. In addition to the Mondadori imprint itself, the group's imprints included Einaudi, a highly prestigious name in Italian publishing, Electa, a publisher of coffee-table art books, and Sperling & Kupfer. That Mondadori was an important publisher of school textbooks and a major printer represented another source of conflict of interest when Berlusconi became prime minister. Mondadori's magazine division had fifty or so titles, including a widely read weekly news magazine called *Panorama* and other big-selling consumer magazines such as *Grazia* and *TV Sorrisi e Canzoni*. When Berlusconi won the elections in May 2001, Mondadori's magazines held almost 40 per cent of the Italian market.[70]

CORPORATE COMPLEXITY

Mondadori was acquired only after a bitter and controversial battle with Carlo De Benedetti, a leading entrepreneur who was then the principal shareholder of Olivetti, a computer and telecommunications group. The battle that De Benedetti and Berlusconi fought for the control of Mondadori attracted the attention of anti-corruption magistrates in Milan who later sought Berlusconi's indictment on charges of bribing judges. It was one of several serious legal cases arising from the dealings of Berlusconi's business empire that led to him being brought to trial in the Lombard capital during the 1990s.

The judicial authorities in Milan were not alone in their interest in Berlusconi and his business activities, however. At the other end of the country, on the island of Sicily, magistrates and investigators in Palermo's Direzione Investigativa Antimafia were trying to understand more about what this businessman-turned-politician had been doing before he entered politics. Their work threw light on Fininvest, the company that controlled Mondadori and Mediaset, and gave the public a glimpse of the shadowy structure that lay behind it.

When Finanziaria di Investimento Fininvest Srl, a limited liability company, was established in Rome on 21 March 1975, its sole director was Giancarlo Foscale, a cousin of Berlusconi. Foscale gave mandates to two trust companies owned by Banca Nazionale del Lavoro, a large bank that was state-owned at the time, to be the registered holder of the shares, a way of allowing Fininvest's beneficial owner, or owners, to remain anonymous. Cesare Previti and his father, Umberto, were on the board of Fininvest's statutory auditors. Berlusconi became openly associated with the company when a board of directors consisting of his cousin, his brother Paolo and himself as chairman was constituted towards the end of 1975.[71] Another piece in the intricate corporate puzzle that Berlusconi and his associates put together in the 1970s was a second limited liability company, Fininvest Roma, which was set up on 8 June 1978 by Umberto Previti. This merged with the earlier Fininvest at the beginning of 1979, based on the year-end accounts for 1978, after a series of operations in 1977 and 1978 that anti-Mafia investigators were unable to clarify twenty years later.[72]

How Fininvest had been funded with capital during the period when it was building up its television operations was a matter that interested the authorities. In June 1998, Domenico Gozzo and Antonio Ingroia, two magistrates in the Sicilian capital, issued a request for documentation held by the Banca Popolare di Lodi. This bank had taken over Banca Rasini, the small bank in Milan where Berlusconi's father had worked for decades and that had helped Berlusconi in his first property projects. Banca Rasini had cropped up in trials of money-launderers in the 1980s. (In an interview in 1985, Michele Sindona, a mafia banker, had pointed to Banca Rasini as a bank used by Cosa Nostra.)

The request from these magistrates in 1998 was connected to the criminal case in Palermo involving Marcello Dell'Utri. The anti-Mafia authorities wanted to learn about the relations that Banca Popolare di Lodi and Banca Rasini had had with two Swiss companies, named as Finanzierungs Gesellschaft fur Residenzen and Aktien Gesellschaft fur Immobilienanlagen in Residenzentren.[73] These were the Lugano-based private companies that had provided the capital for Edilnord's Brugherio project and Edilnord Centri Residenziali's Milano 2 scheme. Among the other names on the anti-Mafia magistrates' list were Fininvest, Mediaset, Publitalia, Canale 5, Retequattro, Italia 1, Edilnord, Silvio Berlusconi and his brother Paolo.

The investigators were curious about a group of companies called Holding Italiana, of which there were twenty-two separate concerns, Holding Italiana Prima, Holding Italiana Seconda, Holding Italiana Terza and so on up to Holding Italiana Ventiduesima. The information the investigation into these companies uncovered at Banca Popolare di Lodi had come from Banca Rasini's information system in 1992, following the takeover. The investigation found that Banca Rasini had had relations with these Holding Italiana companies between 1978 and 1983, and that they had been described as hair-dressers and beauty parlours.[74]

How a company called Holding Italiana could be classified as a hairdresser or beauty parlour was a mystery. And how twenty-two could be was even stranger. In fact, Holding Italiana was very different from *parrucchieri per donna* (ladies' hairdressers) or *istituti di bellezza* (beauty parlours): far from caring for the looks of Milanese women, the Holding Italiana were financial companies owned by Berlusconi and holding shares in Fininvest. Perhaps it was an inno-cent error of classification, but certainly the mushrooming of so many financial companies would have aroused interest while the anonymity of hairdressers or beauty parlours blended more easily into bank records.

Moreover, there were not just twenty-two of them. The investiga-tors eventually found even more companies called Holding Italiana; altogether there were thirty-eight. The first nineteen had opened accounts with Banca Rasini on 6 December 1978, signing powers being held by an uncle of Berlusconi.[75] Other Holding Italiana had opened their accounts with the bank in 1980 and 1981. Over the following years, some of these companies changed their names.

On 16 June 1998, the anti-Mafia prosecutors from Palermo asked the legal representatives of the first twenty-two Holding Italiana com-panies to make accounting and administrative documents available. Berlusconi did not cooperate, two of his lawyers objecting to the authorities' request.[76] The prosecutors then obtained an order to seize the documents they wanted. When the anti-Mafia team executed that order, they again ran into opposition from Berlusconi's lawyers. The order directly affected the person of Silvio Berlusconi, direct or indirect owner of the shares in the Holdings covered by the order, one of Berlusconi's lawyers told the officials who were executing it. It was an act of coercion, said the lawyer, in violation of the rights afforded to Berlusconi as a member of parliament by article 68 of the constitution.[77]

Faced with the order from the authorities in Palermo in 1998, the businessman-turned-politician seemed determined to prevent them and the public from learning how he had organized his affairs. Yet, just over two years later, shortly before the elections in 2001, he tried to justify the large clutch of companies called Holding Italiana. 'My father was advised by our trusted consultants to establish the holdings,' explained Berlusconi. 'Capital payments were made by bank and current account cheques,' he added.[78]

Whatever Berlusconi told the electorate, the anti-Mafia investigators had uncovered things that seemed unusual and were hard to understand. An accountant and auditor at Banca Rasini, Armando Minna, had been until his death one of those trusted consultants about whom Berlusconi spoke. Minna had a stake of 20 per cent in Holding Italiana Prima when this was established in June 1978 and his wife held the remaining 80 per cent of the share capital. Though a housewife by occupation, she had been appointed managing director and was said by the official documents to manage the company. In December that year, both shareholders transferred their shares to two trust companies, Minna to one called Parmafid and his wife to another, called SAF.[79] Silvio Berlusconi's name did not appear.

The other twenty-one Holding Italiana from Seconda to Ventiduesima began in the same way, with the same shareholders (Minna and his wife) and stakes in the 20 million lire capital of the limited liability companies. And the records showed similar stories of significant increases in share capital between the end of 1978 and the beginning of 1985 about which the anti-Mafia magistrates wanted to learn more. Various companies other than the trust companies, where shares were parked anonymously, became involved in some of the Holding Italiana. Berlusconi himself took open ownership of the shares of Holding Italiana Seconda on

16 March 1998.[80] The shares of another thirteen of the Holding Italiana (from Ottava to Ventesima) had been transferred to Berlusconi in October 1990.

Banca Popolare di Lodi was not the only credit institution visited by Palermo's anti-Mafia team. On 28 July 1998, they called at the head office in Rome of Banca Nazionale del Lavoro (BNL). The BNL was the parent of SAF and Servizio Italia, another trust company used by Berlusconi for keeping ownership of shares hidden. The bank immediately gave the investigators full cooperation. In July 1994, the bank's inspectorate had investigated the trust companies' relations with Berlusconi's companies. No sooner had that been completed than another inspector was given the job to do again.[81] The BNL's managers had clearly been worried that the first inspection at the trust companies had not been sufficiently exhaustive.

The BNL inspector who first delved into the trust companies' dealings with the Holding Italiana reported that his work had not revealed anomalies or picked up working methods that did not follow the rules. However, he had found that some operations had been undertaken without reference to the trust companies and registered without documentary evidence. The second inspection revealed rather more about operations undertaken without any documentation showing the movement of funds. One example was on 12 November 1992, when shares in Holding Italiana Terza were sold to one of the many companies within Berlusconi's group and the payment of 165 billion lire to him bypassed the trust companies.[82]

Palina was the name of one of the companies that the anti-Mafia investigators came across between July 1998 and the beginning of 1999. Then they obtained more information about Palina from a book-keeper called Amilcare Ardigo who had kept its books – not a hard job, as those books contained few entries and none that mattered. He told the investigators that Palina had been part of the Berlusconi group. It had been established on 19 October 1979 and was soon liquidated, in 1980. Palina had had a sole director, a front man who had died in 1986. 'Concerning this director, I would like to say that, at the time of his appointment, he was about seventy-five years old and was recovering from a stroke. Because of this I preferred to accompany him each time he came to Milan for business with the companies of the Berlusconi group of which he was a director,' Ardigo told the authorities from Palermo.[83]

After reading old documents, Ardigo subsequently told the investigators that he believed that Palina had been set up to book substantial capital gains on a share transaction. He said that shares in Cantieri Riuniti Milanesi had been bought for 2.6 billion lire and sold for 27.7 billion lire to Milano 3 (a company in Berlusconi's group) on 19 December 1979, this sum being credited to an account with the Banca Popolare di Abbiategrasso that Palina had opened one month before. 'On that same date, the whole amount was withdrawn and transferred to SAF's account with Banca Popolare di Abbiategrasso and available to Silvio Berlusconi,' said Ardigo.[84] The documents did not show how payment of the 2.6 billion lire to the original sellers of the shares in Cantieri Riuniti Milanesi might have been effected.

The Palina affair threw light on Berlusconi's business relations with Anna Maria Casati Stampa, who had sold him the Villa Casati at Arcore. She had also sold him land in Cusago, for which she had been paid in shares in Cantieri Riuniti Milanesi. The investigators discovered that she had sold those shares to Palina for 1.7 billion lire on 28 November 1979.[85] A week later, a trust company in Milan had sold other shares in the property company to Palina for 0.9 billion lire.

Equally intriguing was what apparently happened to the funds after they arrived at the Banca Popolare di Abbiategrasso. On 13 December 1979, Berlusconi had sent instructions to SAF and Parmafid, the two trust companies. They were to use 25.7 billion lire that would arrive in Palina's account on 19 December as shareholder financing for nine of the Holding Italiana companies.[86] A further two of the Holding Italiana (numbers eighteen and nineteen) received 2 billion lire to cover share capital increases. On that same day, the Holding Italiana together credited Fininvest with the 27.7 billion lire for a share capital increase and shareholder financing. Again on that day, Milano 3 was credited with 27.7 billion lire.

Money had gone round in circles. Or rather, it seems that there had been no movement of real money but just a trail of virtual money that had left one group company (Milano 3), transited through Palina, the trust companies, the Holding Italiana and Fininvest, and ended back where it had started at Milano 3. Yet some real money had been involved in this strange financial manoeuvring. Anna Maria Casati Stampa, who had wanted cash instead of shares in Cantieri Riuniti Milanesi, had been bought out and there had been another beneficiary who had received cash for shares in that company. But the anti-Mafia team was unable to discover where the money to pay Casati Stampa and the other beneficiary had come from, or who that other beneficiary was.

When Palina was liquidated, there was no entry in the company's accounts either for the purchase of shares in Cantieri Riuniti Milanesi for 2.6 billion lire or for the sale of those shares to Milano 3 for 27.7 billion lire.[87] Such a transaction would have led to taxable gains, albeit that somewhere within the group there would probably have been losses of the same amount that might have been offset against tax liabilities. The manager of the branch of the Banca Popolare di Abbiategrasso at the time told the anti-Mafia investigators, however, that he believed that it was not a matter of a real movement of money, but of operations that were accounting justifications for capital increases or shareholder financing. He remembered that Fininvest subsequently undertook similar operations.[88]

Whatever way Palina was looked at, it was unusual. Immobiliare Coriasco, a wholly-owned subsidiary of Fininvest with a paid-up share capital of 200 million lire, was also a vehicle for a matter that was hard to understand, a share capital increase of 2 billion lire in 1979 that bypassed SAF, the trust company registered as Coriasco's shareholder. Although an attempt was made to mask the operation by using bank cheques, this was really a cash transaction undertaken by a Sicilian book-keeper called Giovanni Del Santo in cooperation with the trust company. Del Santo had taken 2 billion lire in cash to SAF which had obtained two bank cheques from two high street banks and then endorsed them to Coriasco.[89] At the end of 1979, Fininvest's stake in Coriasco was just over 9 per cent. The increase in share capital had diluted Fininvest's stake, the remaining 91 per cent belonging to whoever had subscribed the 2 billion lire increase in share capital. Who had provided the cash that had been laundered by SAF and Del Santo was a mystery.

Del Santo himself was something of an enigma. The Sicilian book-keeper had been linked at crucial moments to companies in

Berlusconi's business empire. He had been the sole director of Milano 3 when it merged with Cantieri Riuniti Milanesi in July 1980, and then changed its name from Milano 3 to Cantieri Riuniti Milanesi, as well as of the company that bought the villa at Arcore. He had served on the boards of statutory auditors of the Holding Italiana companies and had also been the sole director of Istifi, the finance company that would become Fininvest's financial lung, holding that position from the company's acquisition in 1976 until the beginning of 1978.[90]

Operations like Palina and Coriasco interested the investigators; so did the use of transit accounts in which details of transactions were lost. And so also did the financing of the twenty-two Holding Italiana companies with cash or cash equivalents to the tune of 29.7 billion lire. (Cash equivalents can be bank cheques (not current account), uncrossed postal orders, bank passbooks, etc.) Moreover, the investigators were unable to find extant supporting documents for a total of 20.6 billion lire. Using every documentary and cross-referencing source available to them, from company accounts and bank statements to daily journals and shareholder records, the investigators found that the Holding Italiana companies had received almost 94 billion lire of funding between 1978 and 1985.[91] It was not possible, the report of the anti-Mafia team concluded starkly, to trace the origins of the capital used for all the operations that were undertaken.

QUESTIONS ABOUT THE PAST

Knowing about the birth of Fininvest was one thing; discovering exactly where it got its funds turned out to be quite another for the anti-Mafia team. Palermo's chief prosecutor had written to the Bank of Italy, the country's respected central bank, asking it to lend one of the experts among its staff to help in the investigations. The central bank had agreed and seconded Francesco Giuffrida, one of its senior officers in Sicily. On 6 May 2002, Giuffrida took the oath before giving evidence at the trial. 'Aware of the moral and legal responsibility that I bear with my testimony, I will tell the whole truth and will not hide anything that I know,' he said. He asked that cameras in the courtroom be turned away from him.[92] There had recently been threats to his life. 'It seems important to make public the attempts, deliberate or otherwise, that could have intimidated the witness who has given evidence today,' the prosecutor told the court after he had continued his examination of Giuffrida on the following day.[93]

In reply to the prosecutor's questions, Giuffrida guided the court through the maze of transactions undertaken by Berlusconi's companies with banks and trust companies and identified the fronts that Berlusconi employed to keep himself hidden in the background. The use of cash and cash equivalents that had funded the Holding Italiana was opaque. Some operations had been very anomalous, he said.[94]

Had the regulations that would later be introduced to combat money-laundering already been in force, there was no doubt that the Palina operation would have been considered suspicious and would have been investigated. There was no logic to the operation, explained Giuffrida, just a series of account movements, on the same day and with the same value-date, that did not transfer anything but ended with a zero balance for the companies concerned. 'It did not create a real financial flow, neither did it give rise to a cost or a revenue for anyone,' he said.[95] There were five parties, five account transfers made on the same day on which the bank charged nothing in interest and the client paid nothing in interest charges; the operation was worth absolutely nothing to the bank where the accounts were held.

Could the operations have been used to launder money, asked Ennio Tinaglia, the lawyer representing the province of Palermo, civil co-plaintiff in the trial. 'In theory, yes,' replied the central bank's officer.[96] Testifying on the previous day, he had described Coriasco's increase in share capital in 1979. He had uncovered solid evidence that this had been a huge cash transaction. A document even showed the denomination of the banknotes exchanged for one of the two bank cheques that the trust company obtained. 'There were 12,000 banknotes each worth 100,000 lire,' said Giuffrida. He added, 'From a banking point of view, turning 2 billion lire of cash into bank cheques was not a normal operation and would have caught the eye.'[97]

'Is it correct to say that it is not known where Berlusconi got the money?' asked Tinaglia. The defence counsel objected strongly several times that such a question should be put. He did not want it to be answered, but the court allowed it. 'On the basis of the documentation available at the Banca Rasini, it is not known where the funds came from for the issue of bank cheques, but certainly there had clearly been funds,' replied Giuffrida.[98] The anti-Mafia investigators, whose work had been triggered by an allegation from a *pentito* that 20 billion lire of mafia money had been used to build up Fininvest's television interests, had not been able to find out where all the financing for Berlusconi's companies had originally come from. For eighteen months, investigators had dug into the sources of funding for Berlusconi's business empire in the late 1970s and first half of the 1980s. They had found that documents had gone missing at a trust company through which many companies in Berlusconi's group had passed. They might have been able to find out more if they had been allowed an extension to the period of investigation, but they were not. They had run out of the time that judicial procedures allowed them. The origins of Berlusconi's wealth were still a mystery.

The prosecutors wanted to question Berlusconi as a witness. Matters on which they sought clarification were the Holding Italiana companies and their funding. Just where did Berlusconi's money come from? That was the question that kept being asked. The prosecutors were also curious about why the Italian prime minister had employed Vittorio Mangano, a *mafioso*, at his villa in Arcore. Tinaglia wondered why the Milanese Berlusconi turned to Sicily to recruit household help and not to somewhere closer to home.[99] The prosecutors and Tinaglia had a long list of questions that they wanted to ask and matters that they wanted to get to the bottom of. Berlusconi would be in a position to help them.

Since the trial had started, however, Berlusconi had won an election. His supporters in Sicily had achieved a clean sweep, giving his coalition sixty-one out of sixty-one first-past-the-post seats on the island. Berlusconi had become prime minister once again. He said he had commitments and affairs of state took precedence; Italy's prime minister was unable to keep appointments with the anti-Mafia prosecutors from Palermo. Eventually, after aborted appointments, the prosecutors were able to tie Berlusconi to a date and a time. The hearing was set for 26 November 2002. He would be given privileged treatment, however. The hearing would be at Palazzo Chigi, in the prime minister's offices in Rome, and the public would be kept out. The prosecutors would question the head of Italy's government away from the public's gaze.

When the day arrived, the hearing was very brief; it was over in a matter of minutes. Yet it was not an anti-climax. Berlusconi did not swear an oath to tell the truth. Instead, he availed himself of the right to silence. He had been advised not to answer questions.[100] Many people wondered why Berlusconi, famously loquacious on every possible occasion, was now so tight-lipped about the origins of his success.

3

Corruption

DEFEAT IN A LONDON COURT

The Queen's Bench Division of England's High Court sits in imposing white stone buildings at the top of London's Fleet Street, the Royal Courts of Justice that have been the stage for many legal dramas. It hears few cases: those it does are usually complex and important and often make news. Regina versus the Secretary of State for the Home Department, *ex parte* Fininvest SpA was one such case.

Silvio Berlusconi probably never imagined that he would be a party to wranglings in such august surroundings. Yet, there he was in October 1996, in name if not in person, together with his Fininvest holding company, through which he controlled his business empire. The name of Fedele Confalonieri, his long-standing friend from university and musical adventures on cruise-liners, who had become a colleague during Berlusconi's large property projects and been Fininvest's president since 1991, was also on the brief. Their lawyers were trying to convince Lord Justice Simon Brown and Mr Justice Gage that confidential documents relating to Berlusconi's businesses should not be transferred to Italy, as magistrates of the *mani pulite* anti-corruption team in Milan had asked.

Hard as his lawyers tried, however, the British judges could see no reason to lend a hand to the Italian businessman-turned-politician. For all its forensic expertise and advocatory skills, Berlusconi's legal team was unable to help its powerful client, Italy's richest man who had been prime minister in 1994 and was leader of the opposition in parliament in Rome at the time of the hearing in London. On 23 October 1996, Lord Justice Simon Brown gave his judgement against the

Italian applicants.[1] One week later the three law lords who formed the appeal committee of the House of Lords, Britain's highest court of appeal, refused Berlusconi, Confalonieri and Fininvest leave to take their case further. The documents sought by *mani pulite*'s magistrates were transferred to Italy.

The court in London heard that the applicants and others were alleged by the Italian judicial authorities to have been involved in a huge fraud whereby at least 100 billion lire had been surreptitiously removed from Fininvest and used for criminal purposes. Prosecutions were already afoot against Berlusconi for bribing revenue inspectors, said Lord Justice Brown, and for making illicit donations of 10 billion lire to Bettino Craxi, the former prime minister and leader of the Italian Socialist Party.

At the heart of the four days of hearings in London were documents held by CMM Corporate Services at an address in Regent Street. (CMM stood for Carnelutti, a Milanese law firm, and MacKenzie Mills, the surname of a British solicitor who was a partner of the London arm of the Milanese firm.[2]) The Serious Fraud Office, a special department of lawyers, accountants and police officers that investigated and prosecuted serious or complex fraud, had implemented a request for judicial assistance. A search warrant had been issued by the Bow Street Metropolitan Magistrate on 15 April 1996 and executed that same day.

The authorities in London believed that they needed to act quickly. They were concerned that the documents giving details of Fininvest's offshore empire would be concealed, destroyed or removed from Britain. Their fears were well-grounded. The documents at the centre of the legal battle had previously been kept in Switzerland and evidence had come to light that one of CMM's directors had required those responsible for holding them in Switzerland to transfer them to CMM in London. The director of CMM had given the instructions at the beginning of April 1995, shortly after letters requesting judicial assistance had been sent to Switzerland from Italy. If there was an innocent explanation for this, observed the British judge, none had ever been provided.

Fininvest, Berlusconi and Confalonieri had challenged the implementation of the Italian prosecutors' letter of request for judicial assistance. Their lawyers argued that both the Italian request for assistance and the British warrant were impermissibly wide. Plausible though these arguments appeared, ruled the judge, they proved unsustainable on closer examination. Another challenge concerned the contention that Britain's minister for home affairs was required, but failed, to consider whether there was dual criminality in respect of the alleged offences before referring the Italian request to the Serious Fraud Office. This seemed a wholly barren point to the judge. He also gave short shrift to the objection that the Italian magistrates and investigators who had travelled to London to inspect the documents had sent evidence back directly to Italy, when the law required that any evidence obtained by the Serious Fraud Office on the indications of the Italian team should have passed through Britain's ministry of home affairs before being sent to the Italian authorities.

Lord Justice Brown dwelt at length on the political issue. Throughout *mani pulite*'s investigations into his affairs, Berlusconi had insisted that he had been subject to persecution by a politically motivated magistrature. Towards the end of his judgement, the British judge said, 'It is a misuse of language to describe the magistrates' campaign as being for political ends, or their approach to Mr Berlusconi as one of political persecution. On the contrary, all that I have read in this case suggests rather that the magistracy are demonstrating both their proper independence from the executive and an even-handedness in dealing equally with the politicians of all political parties.'[3] The British judge could not see corrupt political contributors as today's Garibaldis, seekers after freedom or political prisoners. Berlusconi's assertion that he was politically persecuted by magistrates in Milan was groundless.

In London, the Italian tycoon had run up against judges who would not be bullied, cajoled or otherwise deterred from handing down judgements that were unpalatable to him. Moreover, the no-nonsense British justice system worked quickly. The judges in London would not have tolerated for a moment the ploys to which Berlusconi's lawyers resorted in Italy or the delaying tactics that served him so well in his *bel paese* (beautiful country).

His losing sally in London's High Court was just one act in a decade of continuous legal activity for Berlusconi and his large team of lawyers. Mostly, however, his legal lieutenants were kept busy at home, as lawyers in the court in Milan and as members of the Italian parliament in Rome, where they were behind the efforts to push through legislation aimed at nullifying the trials that affected their client and his friend Cesare Previti.

When Berlusconi took office as prime minister for the second time in June 2001, Italy was unique among western democracies. Nowhere else was a nation's richest man also its political head, and nowhere else did a country's political head effectively enjoy a monopoly of the country's television broadcasting, as Berlusconi did in Italy. Moreover, Italy was unique in another, more anomalous, respect. It had a prime minister who was on trial, accused of bribing judges, and a governing coalition whose first priority was the enactment of bespoke laws to get that prime minister off his legal hooks.

BEFORE BRIBESVILLE

The hearings in London's High Court were a small scene in the huge drama of Italian corruption on which the curtain rose at the beginning of 1992. Yet although *tangentopoli* (bribesville) opened in 1992, corruption was far from being a new problem. Several important cases had come to light and been investigated during the previous decade.

Piercamillo Davigo and Antonio Di Pietro were members of the original *mani pulite* team. It was a very small group, never numbering more than six magistrates. Davigo and Di Pietro had been involved in the case of the *carceri d'oro* (golden prisons) at the end of the 1980s which had started with a tip-off from a discontented public employee about bribes paid to win contracts for constructing prisons. The firm building the 'golden prisons' had been forced to pay off nearly everyone because, it claimed, crooked state employees took advantage of the fact that the government was the only customer to which it could offer its services for building prisons. 'This defence seemed reasonable at first sight but, looking deeper, the argument was complete nonsense. The firm was paying off civil servants even after they had retired and that did not seem like extortion at all,' said Davigo.[4]

There had been an even earlier case of corruption in 1984 that pointed clearly to what was happening in Italian public life, in Lombardy particularly. It concerned the building of the underground railway in Milan, the Metropolitana Milanese, a business owned by the city's authorities. During investigations into a fraudulent bankruptcy, a director of the bankrupt company said that money that was missing had gone to pay public officials, including Metropolitana Milanese's chairman.

Under arrest and in jail, the chairman of the underground railway company became ill. Davigo was intrigued that the Italian prime minister at that time asked to visit the sick prisoner, saying that he was a close friend and he needed to talk about party political matters with him. Just look at the situation from the point of view of someone called to give evidence against a defendant, suggested Davigo. 'Would a witness think that the state is represented by the magistrate who is questioning him,' he pondered, 'or by the defendant, given that the head of government is the defendant's friend and had visited and spoken with him in prison?'[5]

That Italian prime minister was Bettino Craxi, whose conviction in April 1996 in the Metropolitana Milanese case at the peak of the *tangentopoli* trials was one of the high points of *mani pulite*'s work. The magistrates had wondered why the Socialist prime minister wanted to talk with the prisoner. Eight years later they learned that Craxi himself was a major beneficiary of the money that had gone mising.[6] In April 1992, one of the firms involved in a case of corruption in Milan's hospitals admitted to having paid bribes to the Metropolitana Milanese. The chief executive of one of Italy's leading construction companies was arrested a few days later and other top managers followed. All of the country's main political parties, except for the Movimento Sociale Italiano (MSI), the neo-fascist party, had been taking money from the contractors who built Milan's underground railway.

Milan had a better underground railway than Rome. Milan's proud citizens thought that their *metro*, unlike the one in the Italian capital, was in keeping with a major European city; it was extensive, clean and efficient. But it was also much more expensive than most underground railways, thanks to the hidden 'taxes' that Italy's crooked politicians levied and thereby added considerably to the costs of building it. About 4 per cent of the value of construction contracts, and as much as 14 per cent of equipment contracts, was the premium hidden in the invoices and stolen by the politicians.

The trial heard evidence that Craxi's Socialist Party devoured the lion's share of the bribes, taking more than one third of the total. The Italian Communist Party and its successor, Partito Democratico della Sinistra (Democratic Party of the Left), shared a similar amount with the Christian Democrat Party, while the Social Democrat Party and the Republican Party split what remained. The bribes were collected by senior managers of the lead companies of consortia involved in building the underground railway. They distributed it among party bosses or gave it to one party boss for him to share among his accomplices in the way they had agreed.

On the surface, there were governing and opposition parties in Milan, but beneath it they all shared in a criminal conspiracy to steal from the taxpayer. 'They were like the thieves of Pisa, pretending to argue during the day but ganging up together at night to rob,' Davigo said.[7] 'If opposition parties are in bed with governing parties in accepting corrupt payments, what kind of opposition is it?' asked Gherardo Colombo, another magistrate in the original *mani pulite* team.[8] The politicians' criminal behaviour raised questions about the nature of Italian democracy. Yet, the argument that the politicians used to excuse the theft was that paying for democracy needed money, lots of it. But the crime was more than the illicit financing of political parties. It was blatant corruption and damaging to the democracy in whose interests the politicians claimed they were acting. More than that, many of Italy's politicians were gaily using those proceeds of crime to support their extravagant lifestyles.

THE BEGINNING OF *MANI PULITE*

Italians continued to be deeply attached to cash many years after credit and debit cards were introduced and were much less likely than other Europeans to use non-cash means of payment. Figures from Italy's central bank showed that Italians used non-cash operations only half as much as people in other countries in the euro area and that when Italians went to cash machines the average amount they withdrew was higher than in any other country of the European Union, more than half as much again as the average.[9]

Cash left few traces. Along with illegal offshore transfers, cash was the oil that kept *tangentopoli*'s wheels turning. Envelopes stuffed with banknotes, sometimes hidden in rolled-up newspapers, passed from businessmen to public officials and politicians.

Mario Chiesa, the president of the Pio Albergo Trivulzio, the biggest geriatric hospital in Milan, had just accepted 7 million lire in cash from the owner of a cleaning firm when he was arrested in the late afternoon of 17 February 1992. It was an instalment of a bribe for a contract worth 140 million lire.[10] Every contract that the hospital signed with its suppliers had a price; Chiesa and the Socialist Party made 5 per cent of the contract value on construction work, up to 10 per cent on materials supplies and as much as 15 per cent on cleaning.[11]

Antonio Di Pietro was the magistrate who arrested Chiesa, catching him in the act of taking the money in his office at the hospital. Luca Magni, the owner of the cleaning firm, was fed up with paying bribes in order to obtain contracts and had reported the matter to the *carabinieri* military police. They had equipped him with microphones to record his meeting with the hospital's president and the 7 million lire in banknotes that Magni gave to Chiesa had been marked.

For many Italians, *mani pulite* was personified by Di Pietro, a rough diamond and the protagonist in a real-life drama that made the headlines day after day, month after month, first with the arrests of people suspected of being involved in corruption and then with their trials. Di Pietro was an unusual figure in the magistrature. While there was no easy way into the profession, his route had been tougher than most. It had been very different from the usual path that his colleagues had taken through high school, university and then competitive examinations.

Di Pietro was born in 1950. His parents were modest farmers in a rural backwater of central Italy. His school studies ended with an electronic technician's diploma. After turning his hand to various jobs, he spent six years employed by the Italian defence ministry, studying in his spare time for a degree in law. He graduated in 1978 and worked in the police before passing the examinations for the magistrature. He spent a year as an assistant prosecutor in Bergamo, a town about 30 miles northeast of Milan, returning to the Lombard capital in 1986.

Although enjoying none of the advantages of wealth, culture and social class, Di Pietro brought wide experience, great capacity for work and a peasant intuition to the magistrate's job. During the second half of the 1980s, Di Pietro had been involved in several investigations of white-collar crime in the public sector and he had first heard of Chiesa in 1987.[12] A couple of years later, after a journalist had written about how the funeral business was managed at the hospital – a racket in which one undertaker had a monopoly and sub-contracted work to competitors at 100,000 lire for every corpse – Di Pietro had added this new snippet to his computer archive. The magistrate had been hot on the trail for some time when he arrested the crooked official at the hospital.

Chiesa's telephone had been tapped and his bank accounts identified, so the magistrate was at once able to lay his hands on the shares, government securities, bank passbooks and safe deposit boxes where the ill-gotten wealth had been stashed. With Chiesa in prison, the magistrate continued his investigations. At the end of February, he questioned Chiesa's wife, who was seeking a divorce and deeply resented her husband's suggestion that alimony should be calculated on his declared salary. She knew about fat Swiss bank accounts. Di Pietro dug into the larger contracts the hospital had awarded in the previous five years and called in the heads of the firms concerned for questioning. Some admitted to having paid bribes to get business. Eventually, more than a month after being arrested, Chiesa, whose partner was expecting a child, broke his silence and started talking.[13]

The president of the Pio Albergo Trivulzio gave the names of the many firms from which he had taken money: those that did painting and hospital maintenance, others that supplied equipment and materials, construction firms that had signed contracts to build new wings for the hospital. Chiesa described how cartels had been formed to avoid the risk of market competition interfering with how contracts were doled out. The disgraced hospital manager recounted how he had taken his first kickback in 1974, when he was head of technical services at another Milanese hospital. That had come from a maintenance firm. Chiesa's penultimate bribe, from that same maintenance firm, had been delivered shortly before Magni arrived at the Pio Albergo Trivulzio with the *carabinieri* close behind. After his arrest, Chiesa had used the excuse of visiting the lavatory to flush away banknotes worth 37 million lire.

THE PIO ALBERGO TRIVULZIO

Cellini's funeral parlour, offering round-the-clock burials and cremations, was sandwiched between Tubin's Chinese takeaway and the Minoyoshi Japanese restaurant. There was a choice of eating places and undertakers in that part of Milan. Down the road, L'Italica funeral parlour was on call twenty-four hours a day as well but Cellini's business had an edge by being right opposite the main entrance of the Pio Albergo Trivulzio. A five-minute walk from the De Angeli underground railway station, an area of modest medium- and high-rise apartment blocks, it seemed an unlikely place for the beginning of the *tangentopoli* corruption scandal that, when it burst in 1992, blew apart the political parties that had governed Italy for the previous forty years.

The fog of greed and corruption that swirled round the geriatric hospital at the end of the twentieth century was far removed from the charity and civic responsibility that lay behind its foundation in 1767. Prince Antonio Tolomeo Trivulzio, the hospital's founder and a member of one of Milan's leading noble families, died that year, bequeathing his large fortune to establish a hospice for the poor and powerless.

While the Borromeo and Visconti families were better known, Prince Antonio Tolomeo had some weighty ancestors. Around the beginning of the sixteenth century, the Trivulzio family became the local potentates in the town of Maleo, about 30 miles southeast of Milan. 'To remember the Trivulzio is to remember a lineage of *condottieri* who, serving the Sforza first and then the French, became a very rich and powerful family in the state of Milan,' recorded a history of Maleo.[14] Success in leading the bands of mercenaries that plundered the rich Lombard plains required political as well as military ability. Gian Giacomo and Teodoro Trivulzio displayed both skills during the first three decades of the sixteenth century.

Invaders and locals fought over and shared the booty of Milan and Lombardy for centuries. No surprise, perhaps, that *tangentopoli* was at its peak in the Lombard capital. And no surprise either that in the go-getting late 1980s and early 1990s, before the scandal broke, some leading businessmen were labelled *condottieri* (mercenary military commanders). 'New *condottieri*. Three names feature among the newcomers whose increasing importance during the 1980s poses a challenge to the power of the establishment,' said a business guide to Italy in 1989.[15] They were Carlo De Benedetti, Raul Gardini and Silvio Berlusconi.

De Benedetti, who faded from the scene after his Olivetti computer and telecommunications group ran into trouble in the mid-1990s, spontaneously admitted to the Milanese magistrates in May 1993 that his group had illicitly financed political parties. Olivetti had been an important supplier of equipment to the ministry of posts and the company's sales there had been at risk if the political parties were not paid. 'Several times I refused to pay but then I had to give way in order to ensure the company's survival and safeguard the interests of tens of thousands of employees and shareholders,' De Benedetti told the magistrates.[16] Gardini's Ferruzzi-Montedison agri-industry and chemicals empire crashed the next month, in June 1993. One month later, shortly before he was due to be arrested at his Milan apartment, Gardini shot himself. He was a flamboyant, hard-driven and hard-driving figure who had married the boss's daughter, taken over the family's empire, spent time on an enormous Argentinian ranch and huge sums of money on 12-metre yachts. Berlusconi always denied any wrongdoing.

In the fifteenth and sixteenth centuries there were powerful people in and around Milan, moved perhaps by an inescapable sense of mortality, who did good works for the poor and sick. Death was rarely far away. Codogno, a town near Maleo, had suffered a terrible plague in 1527 that continued into 1528 and killed almost two thirds of the population. Prince Antonio Tolomeo Trivulzio's ancestor Onofrio Bevilacqua made donations to the poor. In his will in 1484,

Onofrio's nephew Galeotto made bequests to the hospital in Milan. Nearly 300 years later, Prince Antonio Tolomeo's will left his furniture, jewellery, silver, money and all other goods to establish the Albergo de' Poveri in his palace.

At the beginning of the twentieth century, the Pio Albergo Trivulzio moved from the Palazzo Trivulzio in the Contrada della Signora, near Milan's cathedral, to a site on the road to Baggio, from which it took the familiar name Baggina. It ceased to be a private charitable institution and became part of the local health services. It accepted elderly patients, people over sixty, from throughout Lombardy. Some of its 1,000 beds were for rehabilitating cardiotherapy or physiotherapy patients. The hospital also took in the chronically sick, and treated and sheltered the sufferers of Alzheimer's disease. The calls for these services were increasing steadily.

Under the guidance of its crooked president, the hospital planned in the mid-1980s to build four new blocks to provide protected surroundings for patients. Only two were built before the Pio Albergo Trivulzio achieved its unwelcome notoriety. 'It does not seem right, when set against human poverty and suffering and the deep and constant attention that the Milanese have shown towards the most needy citizens, to allow recent events and the human error of an individual to cancel and sweep away centuries of history,' a history of the hospital noted sombrely.[17]

THE P2 MASONIC LODGE

For twenty years before his arrest, the president of the geriatric hospital had been a member of the Socialist Party. Being a party member was a way of getting ahead in public-sector employment, and being a public-sector manager was a way to increase a party's membership and capture more votes. In local elections in 1990, Chiesa supported Bobo Craxi, son of the Socialist Party leader, Bettino Craxi. Before that, Chiesa had hitched himself first to Carlo Tognoli, one of the most important figures in the party, and then to Paolo Pillitteri, Bettino Craxi's brother-in-law.[18] Both Tognoli and Pillitteri had terms as mayors of Milan, Bettino Craxi's birthplace and political base. The anti-corruption magistrates of *mani pulite* were successful in prosecuting cases against both those Socialist local bigwigs.[19]

With another colleague, Gherardo Colombo had come close to pinning charges on Bettino Craxi at the beginning of the 1980s. Examining papers seized in connection with investigations into the subversive P2 masonic lodge, Colombo found a typewritten note headed with the words: 'UBS-Lugano c/c 633369 Protezione'. The words referred to a bank account with a branch of the Unione Banche Svizzere (UBS) in the Swiss city of Lugano.

The account was in the name of Claudio Martelli, said the note, although its real beneficiary was Bettino Craxi.[20] Roberto Calvi, the chairman of the Banco Ambrosiano, had credited the account with 3.5 million dollars at the end of October 1980 after signing an agreement with the finance director of ENI (Ente Nazionale Idrocarburi, a large state-owned oil, gas and chemicals group). The note added that there would be a further payment of the same amount one month later. At that time a rising young star in the Socialist Party, Claudio Martelli was a member of parliament but there was no suggestion that he was a member of the P2 lodge. Neither was the name of ENI's finance director among those on the list of P2's members although ENI's deputy chairman, Leonardo Di Donna, was a member and so also were other senior managers of the group.[21]

Their fellow masons in the lodge had included Roberto Calvi himself, as well as numerous other senior bankers, politicians, magistrates, civil servants, generals and journalists who manoeuvred suspiciously behind the scenes. The P2's ranks also embraced shady figures such as the *mafioso* banker Michele Sindona. A parliamentary commission set up in the wake of the scandal that broke in 1981 spotlighted the threat that the lodge had posed to democracy in Italy. The commission was greatly worried by this secret association, a state within a state, with hidden centres of power able to influence economic activities, information, the life of political parties and the trade unions. In its report, the commission noted that the P2 lodge had effectively taken control of Rizzoli, a very important publishing group that owned the country's most influential newspaper, the *Corriere della Sera*, through lodge members who were the group's principal shareholder and chief executive. At the beginning of 1982, parliament passed a law dissolving the lodge and introducing a new crime of secret association aimed at influencing state institutions.

Berlusconi had also been initiated into the P2 lodge, taking the membership number 1816 when he joined at the beginning of 1978, although he later tried to play down his membership. Testifying in a libel case in Verona on 27 September 1988, he said, 'I do not remember the exact date of my initiation, but do remember that it was shortly before the scandal broke.'[22] He added that he had never paid a membership subscription. Two years after his appearance in court in Verona, an appeal court in Venice, where he was on trial for perjury, ruled that Berlusconi's evidence had been untruthful. He had been a member of the P2 lodge three years before the scandal broke and there was clear evidence that he had paid his subscription. Berlusconi had lied and had done so in his role as claimant in a libel action. Moreover, his evidence had been such as to influence the outcome of that libel action. In the meantime, however, there had been an amnesty and this meant that Berlusconi's crime was expunged.[23]

Membership of the P2 lodge may have offered advantages. The Banca Nazionale del Lavoro, the large state-owned bank that controlled the trust companies that Berlusconi's nascent group used to keep the ownership of his businesses anonymous, had more senior managers who were members of the P2 than any other bank, including the chief executive of one of those trust companies. Berlusconi's group enjoyed generous support from Italian banks during the 1970s; Monte dei Paschi di Siena, where the general manager was a member of P2, was one of the banks that lent to Berlusconi's group. Subsequently the bank's statutory auditors noted that the risk profile towards Berlusconi's group was wholly exceptional. Inspectors who had looked at the loan book had concluded that there had been significant favouritism in that lending.[24]

Certainly, favours – granted or called in – were part of the tangle that bound together Italian finance, business and politics and it was in that mouldering, murky undergrowth that the Socialist Party had borrowed heavily from the Banco Ambrosiano. At the end of January 1981, it owed the bank over 11 billion lire in Italy.[25] The Protezione account with the UBS into which the party's illicit funds flowed from the Banco Ambrosiano's offshore organization belonged neither to Craxi nor Martelli, but indirectly to Silvano Larini, a close friend of Craxi. The story of the bank account in Lugano became public in 1994 when the three were on trial with Licio Gelli, the P2's grand master and ENI's former deputy chairman, facing charges of complicity in Banco Ambrosiano's bankruptcy.

Colombo thought that if he and his colleagues had not investigated the P2 lodge and Michele Sindona more than ten years earlier, they might never have arrived at that obscure and distant, but crucial, part of *tangentopoli*.[26] While the *mani pulite* team was engaged on the Metropolitana Milanese trial, Larini returned to Italy after making himself scarce for a while. In February 1993 he admitted to having been involved in the transfer of bribes to politicians from companies involved in building Milan's underground railway.[27] Without being asked, Larini spoke about the Protezione account. One day in summer 1980, walking with Craxi and Martelli in the centre of Milan, the Socialist Party leader had confided that a Swiss bank account was needed for depositing some hidden financing. Could Larini help? Martelli had jotted down the account's details.[28]

The funds that had been illicitly obtained from the Banco Ambrosiano had not stayed long in the Protezione account. Larini moved swiftly to limit the damage when he heard in April 1981 that the Milan prosecutors had received documents that connected his account at UBS with Craxi and Martelli. He travelled to Lugano to break every connection with the big Swiss bank and made a withdrawal in cash to empty the account.[29] This amounted to almost 5 million dollars. Larini arranged to meet another Socialist politician near the bank, where he handed over the money in a canvas bag, advising his accomplice not to deposit the same amount that he had just withdrawn. He wanted to avoid such an obvious and risky coincidence.

In July 1994, the Milan court found Craxi, Di Donna, Gelli, Larini and Martelli guilty of complicity in the fraudulent bankruptcy of Banco Ambrosiano, although appeals and changes in the law led to retrials and to reductions and annulments of the sentences. Craxi faced eight years and six months in jail when the court of first instance in Milan delivered its verdict, but the Socialist Party's leader had skipped the country in May to settle in his villa in Hammamet on the Tunisian coast. (There, at the beginning of 2000, the former Italian prime minister would die, a figure disgraced by deep involvement in corruption, a fugitive from justice.[30]) The court of first instance had passed the same sentence on Martelli as on Craxi, while sentencing Di Donna to seven years' imprisonment, Gelli to six years six months and Larini to five years six months.[31] In 1997, the appeal court confirmed the verdicts but reduced the penalties. When the supreme court, the highest level of appeal, gave its judgement in June 1999, it had to take account of new legislation concerning the admissibility of evidence. It confirmed the appeal court's verdict for Larini but annulled those for the other defendants, referring the cases concerning Craxi, Di Donna and Martelli back to the appeal court for retrial there. The supreme court did, however, at the same time definitively quash Gelli's sentence. By the time the appeal court heard the cases again, in 2001, Craxi was dead and only two defendants remained. The appeal court found both Di Donna and Martelli guilty and reduced Martelli's sentence, although this was annulled once more by the supreme court and sent back to the appeal court. When the case was heard again by the appeal court, the crime of which Martelli stood accused was statute-barred and the politician had by then agreed to pay damages.[32]

BLACK FUNDS

The search for black funds, often used for paying bribes, and the reconstruction of bank transactions were two crucial aspects of *mani pulite*'s inquiries, said Gherardo Colombo, in a speech on the subject of global crime, corruption and accountability. He told his audience of experts in Boston, America in 1999 that looking for and discovering the systems used to mask the creation of black funds had been central to their investigations.[33] They often found false consultancy contracts and invoices that aimed to conceal the true reason behind financial transactions.

With a mop of shaggy hair, thick spectacles and a pipe in his mouth, Colombo looked more like an absent-minded professor than a sharp prosecutor tackling some of the country's most challenging cases. He had become a well-known, easily recognizable public figure. He was from a small town called Renate, about 20 miles northeast of Milan, and still enjoyed going there in summer to relax in the calm and simplicity of his family's old farmhouse.[34] There was nothing sophisticated or fashionable about Colombo's country home, a complex of unpretentious traditional buildings clustered around a courtyard where he was able to wind down from the stress of the courtroom. The town of Lecco, Lake Como and the Alps were not far up the single-track railway line from Renate. Down the line towards the Lombard capital were the towns of Macherio and Arcore. In each of them, Berlusconi owned a grand and elegant villa. The man who was prosecuting Berlusconi for bribing judges and the tycoon-turned-politician who faced that grave charge might have been neighbours, but they were on the same track in one sense only.

Colombo had joined the magistrature in 1974. One of his earliest big cases concerned the murder in 1979 of Giorgio Ambrosoli, the lawyer-liquidator of Michele Sindona's bankrupt Banca Privata Italiana. Colombo and a colleague had dug into Sindona's phoney kidnapping in New York and obtained a lead through a freemason doctor who had given Sindona hospitality in Sicily when he was supposedly in the hands of kidnappers in America. The doctor made frequent trips to Arezzo in Tuscany, central Italy, the home of Licio Gelli, grand master of the P2 masonic lodge, of which Sindona was also a member.

They ordered a swoop on all Gelli's known addresses. This uncovered a rich hoard of compromising documents at a clothing factory that Gelli managed at Castiglion Fibocchi, near Arezzo. 'There was a list of members, documents concerning the lodge's organization and about thirty sealed envelopes containing information that pointed towards illicit financing operations,' remembered Colombo.[35] He and his colleague uncovered the P2 lodge in March 1981 but the case was soon taken from the Milanese magistrates, transferred to Rome, sucked into the capital's judicial quicksands and not heard of again.

The investigations in which Colombo was engaged during the 1990s frequently uncovered international middle-men who were responsible for creating the funds from which bribes could be paid.

These middle-men supplied their clients with a full service in which funds were created and financial transactions undertaken; they concealed the funds and transactions by false invoicing and other tricks; they camouflaged banking relationships by using transit and trust accounts as well as trust companies.

As Italy began cleaning up its business and politics in the second half of the 1990s, the experience of the *mani pulite* team in tackling corruption caught the attention of the authorities in many other countries. Corruption and related crime became matters on which Italians were able to give advice to those who upheld the law rather than to those who broke it. Colombo was increasingly asked to share his knowledge and he was invited to address conferences, meetings, seminars and courses throughout the world. He spoke at the World Bank, the OECD, Europe's security organization, bar associations and universities. In Europe, he travelled to Switzerland, Belgium, France, Portugal, Hungary, the Czech Republic and Ukraine, while his speaking engagements further afield took him to South Africa, the USA, Peru, Brazil and Argentina. The subjects on which he spoke were those around which *tangentopoli* revolved: corruption, the illicit financing of political parties and money-laundering.

Authorities abroad were also interested in the question of international judicial assistance. This was another area in which Colombo and his colleagues in the *mani pulite* team had obtained a wealth of experience. Italian politicians and businessmen did not need to be financially sophisticated to know that it was safer to draw up false accounts, create black funds and be corrupt offshore than at home because the evidence was further away from the investigators and harder to get at. *Tangentopoli* was an Italian phenomenon but much of it was an international affair as well.

It happened frequently that the bribes were paid abroad or that the bank accounts of the corruptor or the corrupted, or both, were abroad, Colombo explained to one foreign audience. Or perhaps money paid in Italy had been transferred abroad. Whatever the case, the evidence of illicit financial transactions was often to be found outside Italy and Italian magistrates frequently had to seek assistance from foreign judicial authorities.[36] Indeed, between 1992, when *tangentopoli* exploded, and 1999, the *mani pulite* team made over

600 requests for assistance from foreign authorities, such requests being known as *rogatorie*.

Was the outcome satisfactory? Certainly, it could have been much better. Just over one half of *mani pulite*'s requests had been answered. In 1993, the magistrates had made 112 requests for international assistance and only forty-six of these had been satisfied six years later. The outcome for 1994 was better: foreign authorities had responded to sixty-seven of the 126 requests they had been sent. The figures for 1997 were similar, with 145 replies being given to the 236 requests made by the team in Milan.[37]

Requests for judicial assistance had been sent to countries inside and outside the European Union. Despite the fine words of partnership and cooperation, Italy's partners in the European Union had not been any more helpful than countries who were not members. In fact, it was a country outside the European Union that received more requests for *rogatorie* than any other. This country was Switzerland which, because of its geographical position, the know-how of its financial institutions and its laws on banking secrecy, was a natural haven for ill-gotten Italian wealth. Between 1992 and 1999, the magistrates in Milan made 442 requests for assistance to their counterparts in Switzerland. They received 252 replies, a better-than-average rate of success.

The problems were not so much those of formal refusal, however, but of delay. Procedures in some countries allowed those under investigation by the *mani pulite* team to obstruct the transfer of information. Years could go by in the bureaucratic paper-passing between judiciaries, ministries and embassies of both countries, and the banks or financial institutions where the proof of wrongdoing lay. But sometimes the procedures delivered the goods in time. When Colombo helped prepare the case in which Berlusconi was accused of bribing judges, he was able to draw on a mass of evidence along a Swiss money trail.

THE SWISS CONNECTION

Verdi, Tiziano, Canaletto. Some trains from Milan to Lugano, a Swiss city nestling under the southern side of the Alps, carried the names of famous Italians. Another was called Ticino, after the Italian-speaking canton of which Lugano was the capital and whose border lay half an hour from the Lombard capital. Other trains were called Riviera dei Fiori and Cinque Terre, two smart stretches of the Italian coast where well-off Milanese spent summer weekends. The Ceresio was one of the fastest trains on the Lugano run, leaving Milan's central station at a quarter past seven in the morning and arriving in the Swiss city in under an hour, to catch the banks as they opened. Diligent savers, a generation of Italians after the Second World War quietly beat a path across the border, looking for somewhere safe for their money. In the 1980s and 1990s, rich Italians spent conspicuously, but still accumulated wealth abroad. And even after exotic offshore fiscal paradises such as the Virgin Islands were discovered, Lugano was still a magnet.

For many years, checks at the Italian frontier were tight for travellers going into Switzerland and money-contraband was handled by specialists, *spalloni*, money-movers who carried bags stuffed with lira banknotes over the border and into the security that the Swiss banks offered. These clandestine operators in foreign exchange lost many clients in the 1970s when Italian businessmen realized that there were easier, less risky methods for shifting funds abroad. Over-invoiced imports or under-invoiced exports, the differences between the true amounts and those invoiced being credited to Swiss bank accounts, or phoney consultancy contracts awarded to foreign companies or individuals, were smarter ways of building up offshore wealth than unsophisticated cash transfers in suitcases. After businessmen cottoned on to such wheezes and to back-to-back operations, the customs controls at Como, on the Italian side of the border, became a *passeggiata* (stroll).

An official estimate put Italian holdings of undeclared offshore assets at around 500 billion euros in 2001. The amount of money Italians had salted away in Lugano was quite amazing, said an Italian private banker who worked in the Swiss city. Financial institutions in Switzerland benefited more than those in any other country from the illicit flight of wealth from Italy. Swiss banks were famed for secrecy and Swiss bankers for their discretion and investment nous. Add a common language and Italian enthusiasm for Lugano was understandable.

Soon after taking office in June 2001, Silvio Berlusconi's government dreamed up a scheme for getting offshore wealth home, a move that was clearly enormously beneficial to any businesman who had illegally accumulated assets abroad. For a very small penalty, Italians were allowed to repatriate their assets anonymously, protected by a *scudo fiscale* (tax shield). Some rich Italians took the opportunity, drawn by the end of an imagined communist threat to Italian democracy, a stable currency after the lira had entered the euro and, in some cases, the need to tackle inheritance matters. Almost 55 billion euros returned home, temporarily at least. About 60 per cent of this came from Switzerland, mostly from Lugano.[38]

Curving round Lake Lugano, where the pretty lakeside gardens were manicured with the attention for which the Swiss were famed, the city had things to offer after financial business had been done. Stylish shops lined the centre's main street. One claimed to have Europe's biggest selection of Rolex watches, as well as models from Baume & Mercier and Piaget. Italian fashion leaders had stores nearby. A large Cartier shop dominated one *piazza* in the centre. Since its gala opening at the end of 2002, visitors with a gambling streak were able to play the tables and feed the slot machines at Lugano's lakeside casino, an attraction fit to compete with the long-established casino in Campione d'Italia, an Italian enclave across the water.

Lugano catered to the spirit as well. An early sixteenth-century church, Santa Maria degli Angioli, contained a fresco of the crucifixion, Switzerland's biggest Renaissance masterpiece, painted in 1529 by a pupil of Leonardo da Vinci. In 2002, craftsmen completed the restoration of the baroque church of San Rocco, known for its stuccoes and octagonal lantern. The cantonal branch of the Swiss National Bank had its offices across the *piazza*, a reminder that money was rarely far away.

Lugano's commercial banks even got involved in culture. Credit Suisse had helped sponsor a summer jazz festival. BSI, which claimed to be the science of private banking, had supported the city's classical music festival and used its windows for art displays. The Banca del Gottardo ran its own gallery. In 2002 it held an exhibition of photographs by Ferdinando Scianna, a Sicilian. The stark images of

Bagheria, a town near Palermo with a bloody mafia history, brought a distant culture to Lugano's solid burghers. The words on one panel told of Sicily's water problem: *Controllare l'acqua era un grande potere; i mafiosi controllavano* (Controlling the water was a great power; the *mafiosi* controlled).

Italian ghosts haunted Banca del Gottardo's recent past; it had been a subsidiary of the Banco Ambrosiano. Under the burden of 1.3 billion dollars of unrecoverable loans made by its Latin American subsidiaries, the large Milanese institution had folded in June 1982, less than two years after it had paid millions of dollars into the Socialist Party's Protezione account with UBS in Lugano.[39] Italy's central bank stepped in on 17 June, the day before Roberto Calvi, the Banco Ambrosiano's chairman, was found hanging from scaffolding under Blackfriars Bridge in central London, his death probably murder, a settling of accounts by the Mafia.

The bank in Lugano had been at the centre of a web of fraud in which the Vatican's Istituto per le Opere di Religione (IOR) bank had been involved. Yet the signs of impending difficulties had been clear for some time. In 1978, four years before the crash, inspectors from the Bank of Italy had identified the Banca del Gottardo as the link between the Banco Ambrosiano and Cisalpine Overseas in Nassau, established by the Milanese bank in the Caribbean fiscal paradise in the early 1970s with the IOR as a founding shareholder.[40]

Even while Calvi was sealing the Banco Ambrosiano's fate through its Swiss and offshore empire, part of another Italian banking drama was being played out in Lugano. In September 1974, Giorgio Ambrosoli, a Milanese lawyer, had been appointed liquidator-commissioner of the Banca Privata Italiana, one of the Italian tentacles of a financial octopus created by Michele Sindona, a mafia banker. Ambrosoli travelled often to Lugano, trying to discover more about the bank and why it went bust, as well as to recover assets. He met Sindona's son-in-law there, believing that it was useful to keep contacts alive with Sindona, but the meetings got nowhere and were risky. The lawyer's diary showed two evening meetings with Sindona's son-in-law in the Swiss city in May 1977, another two months later. Ambrosoli was murdered on Sindona's instructions in July 1979, his murderer receiving an advance of 25,000 dollars and a further 90,000 dollars after the killing, paid into a bank in Lugano.[41] Extradited from America, Sindona died in Voghera prison in northern Italy in March 1986 after drinking a cup of coffee that had been laced with cyanide; the Mafia had dealt with him as it had probably done before with Calvi.

Its banks and private wealth management made Lugano tick and proved a powerful magnet for mafia money. In June 1989, a bag containing a bomb was found on the rocks outside the seaside home of Giovanni Falcone at Addaura, near Palermo. His guests at the time included Carla Del Ponte, a prosecutor from Lugano. Investigations subsequently concluded that she and her Swiss colleagues were in the Mafia's sights as well as Falcone.[42]

'Know-your-clients and due diligence are now the rule. Switzerland has a national interest in preventing criminals from exploiting the banking system and the penal consequences of money-laundering are severe,' said a private banker in July 2002.[43] With 30,000 inhabitants, Lugano was home to around 400 financial institutions. Despite the risks of their customers being unmasked during checks by inspectors from the Bank of Italy, about twenty Italian banks were present: Banca Monte Paschi (the world's oldest bank), Banca Commerciale Italiana and BPL Bank to name just three. Trust companies sprouted like fungi.

The Casa Airoldi, an early nineteenth-century villa in the Piazza Alessandro Manzoni, named after the nineteenth-century Milanese writer who went to school in Lugano, housed the Banca Arner. Giuseppe Mazzini, a leading political figure of the nineteenth century, stayed in the Casa Airoldi. The composer Franz Liszt performed there in 1838.

Casa Airoldi's connections with Mazzini belonged to a distant past but through its use as offices for Banca Arner the building had recent ties with Berlusconi. The dealings that Mediaset, Berlusconi's television company, had transacted through Banca Arner had caught the eye of investigating magistrates in Milan, although the company quickly said that the searches in Switzerland were part of old investigations when there were reports of checks being made at the bank. 'Mediaset repeats its absolute extraneousness to the facts under investigation. The recent search at the Banca Arner in Lugano is not the result of any new proceedings concerning Mediaset,' said the company in July 2002.[44]

Berlusconi's embryo business empire had also had links with the Swiss city. As we have seen, Edilnord and Edilnord Centri Residenziali, the firms he used for his Brugherio and Milano 2 construction projects in the 1960s and 1970s, had obtained their capital from private companies incorporated in Lugano. The city had been very different then. In the 1960s, Lugano was a tourist centre with old-fashioned trams and many small family hotels. Forty years later, its characteristic trams had disappeared for ever and the small hotels had been demolished to make way for large modern blocks or had been turned into offices for banks and other financial institutions. Many tourists were day-trippers from Italy visiting to check on their investments; even after the *scudo fiscale*, Italian-owned assets administered in Lugano were thought to be worth around 200 billion euros.

BRIBESVILLE

Bettino Craxi was among a host of political worthies from parties belonging to the coalitions that governed Italy until 1993 found guilty when Milan's fifth criminal court delivered its verdict in the Enimont bribes case in October 1995. It was the biggest single case infecting the rotten body of Italian business and politics uncovered by the *mani pulite* magistrates.

Enimont was an ill-fated, public–private joint venture between ENI and Montedison. State-owned ENI and the private-sector Ferruzzi agri-industry group had decided in 1988 to pool their chemicals businesses, Enichem (owned by ENI) and Montedison (owned by Ferruzzi), in a joint venture called Enimont. Each would own 40 per cent of what was planned to be Italy's national chemicals champion and 20 per cent would be sold to the market through a flotation.[45] Enimont's shares started trading in October 1989 but Raul Gardini, Ferruzzi's boss, soon clashed with ENI's management about who should be in charge of Enimont and the affair broke up acrimoniously, at least on the surface.[46]

Oiling the political wheels with slush funds of 153 billion lire created through funny deals, phoney transactions and false account-ing, Gardini was able to engineer the renationalization of the busi-ness.[47] In November 1990, with the government's blessing, ENI agreed to purchase Ferruzzi's stake in the joint venture for almost 3,000 billion lire. There was evidence of massive bribery. ENI's chair-man, Gabriele Cagliari, who committed suicide in July 1993 while in custody in Milan, had received almost 5 billion lire. Another member of ENI's executive board was paid off. But leaders of the Socialist Party and the Christian Democrat Party were the biggest beneficiar-ies of the hidden funds created by Montedison.

When the government floated ENI in autumn 1995, around the time that the court in Milan delivered its verdict in the Enimont bribes case, the prospectus dealt with the company's legal difficulties. 'Senior managers of ENI have been accused of various crimes, includ-ing illicit financing of political parties, corruption, false accounting and misappropriation (mainly in relation to payments to foreign intermediaries within the framework of contract negotiations with foreign entities),' ENI told its would-be investors.[48] The large state energy and chemicals group had taken action to recover losses caused by the illegal action of its managers, laid down procedures aimed at preventing recurrences of improper behaviour and replaced the boards of all its principal subsidiaries.

Soon after the scandal made the news, ENI's board had decided to set some standards and had issued a code of conduct to discourage unethical behaviour. Introducing the code, ENI's chairman said that integrity, transparency and commitment were to be the foundations on which the group would build success. When the government sold a third tranche of ENI's shares in June 1997, the appeal process had been exhausted for four of the group's senior managers who had been definitively found guilty of corruption.

Cooking the books was at the centre of *tangentopoli*. 'All the firms that we dealt with during our investigations had false accounts, including those listed on the stock market and those that had audi-tors,' noted Piercamillo Davigo.[49] That the magistrates of *mani pulite* did not find one set of accounts in which there was an item recording a payment to a public official was not surprising, however. To have made such an accounting entry would have been an admission of corruption. Then a serious criminal offence, false accounting offered an opening to the prosecutors. Nailing businessmen as they paid backhanders was rare and proving collusion in matters of corruption, whether bribery or extortion, was almost impossible. Instead, the *mani pulite* team dug into firms' accounts, searching for strange items and transactions and anomalies with which to confront the suspects. Bribes could have come only from black funds that had been created by false accounting.

The names that Chiesa mentioned when answering Di Pietro's questions about corruption at the Pio Albergo Trivulzio led the investigators to other public-sector bodies and top managers with powerful political connections. By the mid-1990s, the magistrates' scrutiny had revealed dirt almost everywhere. Milan's AEM electricity and gas municipal utility reported in 1997 that investigations were still underway concerning former directors and a former general manager. The utility had sought damages from people brought to trial and taken action against companies that had swindled it. By the end of 1996, it had recovered more than 8 billion lire.

Rome's ACEA electricity and water utility, whose board had been dismissed at the end of 1992, noted in 1999 that criminal proceedings for corruption were underway against former directors. Like AEM in Milan, Rome's utility had recovered some of the money that had been criminally diverted.

The huge investment programmes at Enel, the large state electricity corporation, were an appetizing target for corrupt politicians. Enel was central to the country's political spoils system, a crucial strand in a web through which industry, the world of finance, the labour market and the political parties were linked. Board and management positions were shared out by the political parties; lower level jobs were rewards doled out in an all-embracing patronage system. Plant purchase orders were made as much to keep Italy's engineering companies in work as to satisfy Enel's real needs. Heavily indebted and starved of capital, Enel had to rely on borrowings, thus providing large flows of interest income to the Italian banking system, most of which was then in public ownership and, like Enel, locked into the spoils system.

Whether in the public sector or privately owned, big or small, thousands of businesses found themselves caught up in *tangentopoli* and *mani pulite*'s investigations. Several top managers at Fiat, Italy's biggest industrial group, suffered the indignity of being remanded in custody while they were questioned. At a certain point, the group's management switched tack. 'I remember Fiat well. We ran into enormous resistance at first, but then they changed their approach significantly,' recalled Colombo.[50] The company came clean and admitted to misdemeanours. Expressing the hope of a political and moral rebirth in the country, Fiat said in 1993 that it had promulgated a set of rules for proper behaviour in business. They would form a code of ethics to which all the group's employees, as well as all companies and self-employed professionals who worked for companies within the group, would be expected to conform.

BRIBING JUDGES

Mani pulite was the name given to the investigations into corruption involving businessmen and politicians. *Toghe sporche* (dirty robes) was what the Italian press called the cases of corruption involving the judiciary. 'The public official who receives money or goods himself, or through a third party, or accepts the promise of them, in return for omitting or delaying an action of his office, or in return for undertaking or having undertaken an action contrary to the duties of office, is punishable with a term of imprisonment beween two and five years,' states article 319 of Italy's criminal code. The penalty is increased to between three and eight years where such acts or omissions were aimed at favouring or damaging one party in civil, criminal or administrative proceedings.

If there was one matter on which Italy's law professors, prosecutors and lawyers seemed to agree, it was that bribing judges was a heinous crime. 'Corruption of a public official is serious. Corruption of a judge is much worse. It is the violation of a fundamental principle of the rule of law,' commented Carlo Smuraglia, a law professor who served from 1986 to 1990 on the Consiglio Superiore della Magistratura (CSM, the magistrature's governing body).[51] 'Bribing judges is absolutely one of the most serious crimes. Not only does such corruption damage parties to trials where judges have been bribed, but it leads to a general loss of trust in the legal system,' said Giuliano Pisapia, a lawyer for a civil co-plaintiff in cases involving Berlusconi that began in 1999.[52]

On 29 April 2003, a criminal court in Milan delivered its verdict in two cases, tried in parallel, concerning the corruption of judges. Two judges in Rome – Vittorio Metta and Renato Squillante – were found to have accepted bribes. The former was sentenced to thirteen years in jail, the latter to eight and a half years. Cesare Previti, the lawyer who had been involved in business with Berlusconi since the purchase of the villa in Arcore and the setting up of Fininvest in the mid-1970s, and in politics from the very foundation of Forza Italia, was sentenced to eleven years in jail.[53] Previti had been re-elected to parliament as a deputy in May 2001. The court found that he had paid money to two judges in Rome in the early 1990s to obtain favourable sentences in cases concerning two clients. One of those clients was Berlusconi's Fininvest group.

Defence lawyers had used every possible ploy to avoid sentencing by the court. They had raised numerous objections, put forward a stream of reasons to get hearings postponed and invented new gambits. In parliament, Berlusconi's large majority enacted controversial laws on international judicial assistance and change of trial jurisdiction that aimed to get Previti off the hook but, despite all those Herculean efforts, the court reached its verdicts and announced the sentences. For the court in Milan, the 68-year-old Previti was corrupt and deserved a long spell in prison.

The two cases in which Previti was convicted were called the Lodo Mondadori (the Mondadori arbitration) and IMI-SIR. When Berlusconi was campaigning for election in spring 2001, his lawyers were busily engaged in Milan's court on case 11343/99, as the Lodo Mondadori proceedings were known to the court's administrators. As well as Previti, two other Rome lawyers stood accused of bribing judges. One was Attilio Pacifico, the other Giovanni Acampora. A former Rome judge, Vittorio Metta, was accused of accepting bribes. Until 12 May 2001, Silvio Berlusconi's name was on the list of people whom the magistrates wanted tried in the Lodo Mondadori case. On that day, the fifth criminal section of Milan's appeal court had delivered a judgement that sent Previti, Pacifico, Acampora and Metta for trial and ruled that the crime was statute-barred for Berlusconi.[54] But the court had not found Berlusconi innocent. It had applied the statute of limitations to remove his name from the list of those whom the prosecutors wanted to be sent for trial, because bribing judges indirectly through an intermediary was not considered an aggravation of the offence of corruption under the law existing between 1990 and 1992, in the way that direct payment was. Hence the statute of limitations came into effect earlier.

A network of private, personal and non-transparent relations between public functionaries working in the judicial field and independent professionals, interested in the judicial matters dealt with by the functionaries but without having formal roles in those matters, existed in the Italian capital. The fifth criminal section of Milan's appeal court expressed serious misgivings about what had been going on in Rome. It said that the situation there 'was not just compatible with cases of judicial corruption, it was strongly suspect and well-suited to generate such cases'.[55]

The judgement was one milestone in a contorted legal process that started at the beginning of November 1999 when prosecutors in Milan asked for eleven people to be sent for trial on charges that concerned the alleged bribing of the Rome judge Metta.[56] According to the prosecutors, money was paid to obtain a favourable verdict in a dispute over the ownership of Mondadori, Italy's biggest publishing group. At the end of the 1980s when the scrap over its ownership took place, Mondadori was Italy's largest publisher of periodicals and controlled *La Repubblica*, a leading national daily newspaper, and a chain of local newspapers. A major publisher of books as well, the Mondadori group was an appetizing prey on which both Carlo De Benedetti and Silvio Berlusconi had fixed their sights.

The Mondadori case was a typical story of Italian dynasties, about families, money, power, lawyers and courtrooms. Both Berlusconi and De Benedetti owned stakes in Mondadori and both wanted to be in charge. In December 1988, aiming to get control, De Benedetti reached an agreement with the Formenton family, who were among the heirs of Arnoldo Mondadori, the publisher's founder, that they would sell their interest to him before the end of January 1991. But in December 1989, the Formenton family tore up the agreement and decided to sell to Berlusconi instead. Lawyers got busy, the affair went to arbitration and the arbitrators decided in June 1990 that De Benedetti's agreement was valid. The Formenton family appealed against this and an appeal court in Rome overturned the arbitration decision in January 1991. Berlusconi's Fininvest holding company took part in the appeal as an interested party, and then acquired control of Mondadori. Vittorio Metta was one of the judges of that appeal court.

Berlusconi's name headed the list of the accused that Gherardo Colombo and Ilda Boccassini, the prosecutors in the case, asked the judge of the preliminary court to send for trial in November 1999. In a judgement running to almost 100 pages, Rosario Lupo, a *giudice per le indagini preliminari* (judge for the preliminary investigations) in Milan, ruled in June 2000 that there was no case against Berlusconi, Previti, Pacifico and Metta. The alleged fact did not exist, said Lupo. The prosecutors appealed, and the appeal court overturned the decision made by Lupo and ruled that Previti, Pacifico, Acampora and Metta should stand trial. The three appeal judges set the first hearing for October 2001.

Magistrates and investigators in Milan had focused on a Swiss money trail to gather evidence against the accused. They had dug into All Iberian, an offshore company domiciled in St Helier in the British Channel Islands and used by Fininvest for fronting operations so as to make them appear as if they were undertaken by third parties, and to hide the fact that Fininvest was involved. All Iberian was used as a transit treasury for secret operations through which funds passed on their way to their final destinations. In almost all the transactions, instructions were given to banks carrying a specific indication that the outward transfer should not mention the instructing party.[57] The transactions had to be cloaked in the maximum of secrecy. All Iberian's beneficial owner was Giancarlo Foscale, Fininvest's managing director and Berlusconi's cousin.

Another company in Fininvest's complex offshore empire that interested the magistrates was called Libra Communication. Various bank accounts proved helpful to investigators, including one belonging to All Iberian with Societa di Banca Svizzera in Lugano and a transit account with Credito Svizzero in Chiasso, used by Fininvest, that was called Ferrido.[58] With the cooperation of the Swiss authorities, the Milan magistrates obtained evidence of transfers of funds that they believed supported their case that Metta had received money from the Fininvest group.

On 12 February 1991, All Iberian's account in Lugano had received just over 4.5 million dollars from Libra Communication's account at the same bank. On the following day, All Iberian transferred just over 2.7 million dollars (about 3 billion lire) to the Ferrido account, the same amount being transferred on 15 February to an account called Mercier that Previti held with Darier Hentsch, a Swiss private bank in Geneva. On 27 February, the sum of 1.5 billion lire was transferred from the Mercier account to the account of Careliza Trade with the Banque Internationale du Luxembourg. This company was traced to Acampora.

Later that year, at the beginning of October, a sum of 425 million lire was debited from Careliza Trade's account and transferred to Previti's Mercier account. From there, payments were made on 11 and 16 October, the first for 225 million lire, the second for 200 million lire, to an account called Pavoncella that Pacifico held with Banca del Sempione in Lugano. Pacifico made two cash withdrawals, one for 225 million lire on 15 October, the other for 300 million lire on the next day.

According to the prosecutors, Pacifico gave 425 million lire to Metta who, around September or October 1991, had started negotiations for the purchase of an apartment for his daughter. But could the money to buy the flat have been a gift of Orlando Falco, a retired Rome judge who died in 1994 bequeathing a substantial inheritance to Metta? The appeal court said that money received from Falco could not have accounted for the cash payment of 400 million lire made by Metta in April 1992 when the contract for the apartment was signed.[59]

Lupo's judgement had provided some details of Falco's wealth. A Swiss lawyer gave evidence to the prosecutors that Falco had accumulated around 5 to 6 million Swiss francs in Switzerland before he retired there in 1982. 'There can be no doubt about the strangeness of a retired magistrate possessing enormous wealth about whose origin nothing is known,' commented Lupo.[60] He described Falco's relations with various people as unusual and suggested that the relationship between Metta and Falco merited further investigation.

The appeal court looked at Metta's relationships with his fellow defendants. The judge had a long-standing and confidential relationship with Acampora, dating from the early 1980s, but Metta declined to answer questions concerning Acampora's role in managing the foreign cash received from Falco.[61] The appeal court thought that this demonstrated the great trust existing between the two men in financial matters.

In June 1998, replying to questions from the magistrates, Metta said that he had had no contact with Previti in 1991 and 1992. His relationship with Previti had effectively started when he agreed to work with Previti's law firm in 1995. Yet, the prosecutors had telephone records that belied Metta's affirmation. Fifteen phone calls were recorded between numbers used by Metta and Previti in 1992 and 1993, including calls early in the morning and late in the evening.[62] Contrary to Metta's claims of only sporadic and occasional relations with Pacifico, the prosecutors produced records showing almost 130 calls since 1991.

While Previti, Pacifico, Acampora and Metta were sent for trial, the appeal court ruled that the case against Berlusconi should not proceed because, as we have seen, the crime of which he was accused was statute-barred. This judgement in Berlusconi's favour arose from a fortunate legal nicety that stemmed from a legislative oversight. 'When dealing with events in 1991 that concern money received that year, or in any case before April 1992, then the statute of limitations would come into effect before 14 October 1999 if general extenuating factors are granted to the private corruptor, and cause the crime to be expunged,' said the judgement.[63] That time-gap provided the key to the judgement. The court then only needed to find those general extenuating circumstances that would allow Berlusconi to avoid an indictment. It was able to do so, although some Italians considered that the reasons the judges put forward for letting Berlusconi off the hook were deplorable.

Just what were those extenuating factors that closed the case against Berlusconi? First, people choose their lawyers to get the results they want and are willing to spend large sums of money for this, said the judgement, as if to condone the use of intermediaries for corruption. Second, because there had been a trade in court sentences in the Rome area, any businessman might have got caught up in that dirty business. Third, following the verdict in Berlusconi's favour in 1991, the television magnate had generously agreed to split Mondadori and allow De Benedetti to own *La Repubblica* and the weekly magazine *L'Espresso*. Fourth, in his monopoly of commercial television, Berlusconi had a business and economic activity of national importance. Lastly, the fact that Berlusconi had an important public position, the leadership of a large political party, at the time of the court's deliberations also helped the judges look less severely on any part he might have had in the affair.

'Those factors are aggravating not extenuating. The fact that the judicial system in Rome was easily corrupted and that Berlusconi was leader of the opposition ought to have added to, not lessened, the gravity of the charges,' said Giuliano Pisapia, the lawyer representing De Benedetti.[64] The timing could not have been better for the businessman who had turned to politics: the judges reached their decision on the day before Berlusconi won a big election victory.

At the end of July 2002, just over a year after the appeal court ruled that Berlusconi should not go for trial, judges, prosecutors and defence lawyers in Milan were still working on the Lodo Mondadori case. Most Milanese had left for their holidays and the few who remained in the city had to endure strength-sapping days of high temperatures and soaring humidity. A handful of legal people and journalists were in the almost empty Palazzo di Giustizia court building for a hearing that had started at ten in the morning. It had dragged on, a mind-numbing wait as the panel of three judges discussed the defence's procedural procrastinations. At last, at seven thirty in the evening, the presiding judge brought the day to an end. He set the next hearing for 19 September, after the summer break, and wished everyone *buone vacanze*. The thermometer still registered 28 degrees Celsius, but even the muggy evening heat was a welcome escape.

Taped to the courtroom door in Milan was the list of defendants. Heading it was Primarosa Battistella, an unknown figure, born in the

Lombard capital but a Swiss resident in Lugano. The others were much more in the public eye, including Cesare Previti and the three former senior Rome judges – Vittorio Metta, Renato Squillante and Filippo Verde – who were alleged to have accepted bribes in exchange for handing down bent verdicts. Because some of the accused were involved in two trials (the IMI-SIR case was being heard in parallel with the Lodo Mondadori case), the two cases had been rolled into one. The IMI-SIR case had its origins in a dispute over damages following the collapse of a large chemicals group.

While Battistella was little known, Nino Rovelli, her husband, who died in 1990, had been in the news for many years. Thanks to his looks, Rovelli was called the Clark Gable of the Brianza, the area north of Milan with which Berlusconi had ties.[65] Rovelli was more than a Hollywood look-alike, however. He was a powerful, politically connected and buccaneering industrialist until his SIR chemicals empire crashed at the end of the 1970s, weighed down by debts of more than 3,000 billion lire (about £1.3 billion or $2 billion at the time).

In 1982, Rovelli had started a legal action against Istituto Mobiliare Italiano (IMI), a leading investment bank that was then state-owned, alleging that it had caused SIR's downfall by refusing to disburse loans that it had already agreed. In 1986, a Rome court presided over by Filippo Verde ruled in Rovelli's favour and transferred the decision concerning the amount that IMI should pay SIR to another court. This decided in 1989 that Rovelli was owed around 650 billion lire. Then, in November 1990, the appeal court in Rome confirmed the judgement in SIR's favour, setting the amount at around 1,000 billion lire, including costs and interest. Vittorio Metta presented the judgement. In July 1993, the final appeal court also found in SIR's favour, on a technical objection raised by the company's lawyers after a document had mysteriously gone missing.[66]

IMI had to pay and did so six months later. According to the prosecutors, however, the IMI-SIR case gave rise to other, hidden and criminal, transfers of money. On 15 November 1999, Alessandro Rossato, the *giudice per le indagini preliminari*, delivered the judgement in Milan that sent Rovelli's wife and son, the three former Rome judges, Previti and two other lawyers – Attilio Pacifico and Giovanni Acampora – for trial. The preliminary hearing was the moment of the final check on investigations, to ascertain whether the charge formulated by the prosecutor was supported by the body of evidence needed to justify indictment. Fixing the first hearing for 11 May 2000 in the Milan court's fourth criminal section, Rossato summarized that evidence in his judgement.

On 24 June 1991, Rovelli's wife and son transferred 1 billion lire from a bank account in Zurich to the Pavoncella account at the Banca del Sempione in Lugano of Attilio Pacifico.[67] Pacifico withdrew 450 million lire in cash on 2 July. He had already transferred 133 million lire to an account in the name of Rowena Finance, a Panamanian company, with the Societa Bancaria Ticinese (SBT) in Bellinzona on 26 June, the day that the payment from the Rovellis was credited to his account. Rowena Finance belonged to Renato Squillante. On 2 July, Pacifico also transferred 133 million lire to Previti's Mercier account with Darier Hentsch in Geneva.

Three years later, the Rovellis were again transferring money to the lawyers. Between 21 March and 24 June 1994, Pacifico's accounts with banks in Switzerland and Liechtenstein were credited with a total of almost 29 million Swiss francs. A single transfer of 18 million Swiss francs was made to Previti's account with Societa di Banca Svizzera in Geneva on 21 March.[68] Questioned in 1997 about that transfer, Previti said that the money from Rovelli was not meant for him personally but for him to pay other beneficiaries, whom he refused to name. Under cross-examination in Milan in September 2002, the former defence minister changed his story. That offshore payment was money due to him as professional fees, he claimed, implicitly admitting to large-scale tax evasion.[69]

The Rovellis sent almost 11 million Swiss francs to various accounts of Giovanni Acampora on 24 June 1994. Altogether Nino Rovelli's widow and son paid just under 58 million Swiss francs to the three lawyers between March and June 1994, an amount equivalent to about 67 billion lire at the exchange rates at the time of the transfers.[70]

During the course of questioning, the Rovellis said that they did not know the reason for Nino Rovelli's debt towards the three Rome lawyers. They had instructed Rubino Mensch, a lawyer in Lugano, to make the payments.[71] The preliminary court heard a statement by Mensch that these payments were made in accordance with the amounts and methods indicated by the beneficiaries. The prosecution submitted documents concerning the Master 811 account opened with the Societa Bancaria Ticinese on 30 April 1991 of which Verde and his wife were beneficiaries and for which Pacifico had power of attorney.

Judge Rossato also noted that evidence showed the existence of contacts between the defendants and that there had been telephone traffic between them, particularly around the times that the court in Rome was dealing with the case.[72] In his judgement, Rossato wrote that all the accused made statements, except Squillante, who availed himself of his right to silence. A year and a half later, a Milan court found Acampora guilty of corruption in judicial acts and sentenced him to six years in prison. He had opted for a shortened trial procedure that reduced sentences where the defendant was found guilty, and the judges had found solid proof against him. On 10 May 2004, the appeal court in Milan would confirm the verdict of guilty that had been passed on Acampora by the lower court, although it would reduce the prison sentence to five years.[73]

Soon after eleven in the evening of 29 April 2003, the presiding judge and his two fellow judges in the Lodo Mondadori and IMI-SIR cases entered the packed courtroom to announce their verdict. They had retired at three in the afternoon. The trial had taken two weeks under three years and the court had sat eighty-eight times to hear evidence.[74] IMI, the bank that had suffered from the corrupt sentence in SIR's favour, was awarded damages of 516 million euros and De Benedetti's CIR company was awarded damages of 380 million euros. The court ruled that the prime minister's department should receive more than 1 million euros of damages from the defendants who had been found guilty.[75]

Public attention focused more on the prison sentences read by the presiding judge, however, than on the sums that the court awarded in damages to the civil co-plaintiffs. Only one defendant escaped the verdict of guilty: Filippo Verde, one of the three judges on trial. 'It remains a fact that judge Verde received from his fellow defendant, without reason, a considerable sum of money that certainly originated from the Rovellis,' stated the court's judgement. Moreover, Verde was one of the judges who moved in Previti's circle. All things considered, the description of the defendant as 'a judge on the payroll' did not seem completely out of place, the judgement added. However, looking at the specific matter in the indictment, 'there is insufficient proof to rule that the payment of money, even though made for no reason, was linked to the role of judge Verde in the IMI-SIR case'.[76] Vittorio Metta was sentenced to thirteen years in jail and Renato Squillante, whose long experience as a judge had included being judicial counsellor to Craxi when the Socialist politician was prime minister, received eight years and six months. Rovelli's widow was sentenced to four years and six months in jail and her son to six years. Attilio Pacifico's sentence was eleven years in jail, while Giovanni Acampora's, for the Lodo Mondadori case only, was five years and six months. No sentence attracted more comment, however, than the term of eleven years' imprisonment that the court deemed suitable for Cesare Previti, Berlusconi's close friend and the defendant most in the news.[77]

LEGAL CORRESPONDENCE

On 27 January 1998, Franzo Grande Stevens testified in Milan. Trusted lawyer of the Agnelli family (the founders of Fiat), secretary of Fiat's board and a director of numerous important companies, Grande Stevens had been chairman of the Italian bar association from 1984 until 1991. The magistrates wanted to ask the silver-haired doyen of the Italian bar about Previti, the Rome lawyer who was accused of bribing judges.

'He has never participated in conventions, debates, round tables, legal conferences, negotiations, important appeal cases. I have not met him and never heard him named, even though I consider I know a very large number of civil lawyers throughout Italy,' said Grande Stevens whose legal career had started in 1954. He had represented the counter-parties to Fininvest in various cases but had never encountered Previti.

Writing to Grande Stevens on 15 December 1998, Previti complained that the testimony made false insinuations about his work and denigrated him personally. Previti wrote that Grande Stevens should note that his professional activity was documented 'by brilliant scholarship, forty years of activity, the prestige of clients and colleagues who have admired me and who admire me from time immemorial, as well as by declared income much higher than the average of the profession, the exclusive fruit of my professional activity'. Previti threatened to sue Grande Stevens. Unfazed, Grande Stevens fired back a firm riposte to the Rome lawyer, 'I confirm that I told the magistrate the truth, as should be the duty and habit of everyone.[78]

MORE JUDICIAL CORRUPTION

Previti's trials were far from over when the court handed down its sentences at the end of April 2003. Apart from appeals against the verdicts in the Lodo Mondadori and IMI-SIR cases, he was still on trial in a third case involving the bribing of judges in Rome. Two judges, Filippo Verde and Renato Squillante, who had been found guilty in the IMI-SIR case, were on trial with him and so was Attilio Pacifico, one of the two lawyers who had been found guilty with Previti in the Lodo Mondadori and IMI-SIR cases. There were another five defendants in this third case and one of them was Silvio Berlusconi. Since May 2001, when the charge of corruption of which he stood accused was ruled to be statute-barred, Berlusconi had not been further involved in the Lodo Mondadori trial. Yet, Italy's prime minister still faced charges of corrupting judges. One part of the case against him also involved the takeover of a large company and the civil co-plaintiff in the criminal trial who claimed to have been wronged by Berlusconi was again De Benedetti.

The nine accused had been committed for trial in November 1999 by Alessandro Rossato, the judge responsible for the preliminary investigations who had also been involved in the IMI-SIR case. Rossato set the first hearing for 9 March 2000.[79] This case's origins lay essentially in a bid by De Benedetti, owner at that time of the Buitoni food group, for a conglomerate called SME which was owned by the Istituto per la Ricostruzione Industriale (IRI, a giant state holding corporation) and whose portfolio included several major

Italian food brands. IRI's chairman when De Benedetti made his bid was Romano Prodi, who became Italy's prime minister in 1996 and would subsequently become president of the commission of the European Union.

Prodi and De Benedetti signed a contract in April 1985 under which IRI would sell a controlling interest in SME, but under political pressure, Prodi reopened the deal. Bettino Craxi, then prime minister, wanted to block De Benedetti, ostensibly because the government considered SME to be a strategic state asset; in any case, the price was too low and the conditions of the contract too favourable to the buyer.[80] It was also said that Craxi was angry at having heard of SME's sale from newspaper reports and because he thought that bribes were being paid to the Christian Democrat Party while his Socialist Party was being ignored.

So Craxi asked his friend Berlusconi, in defence of whose television channels he had recently forced decrees through parliament, to get involved. With the aim of derailing De Benedetti's proposed acquisition, Berlusconi assembled a bidding vehicle called IAR, roping in two well-known food companies, that made an offer that scuppered De Benedetti's deal.[81] Stymied by IAR, Buitoni took legal action in Rome in June 1985, asking the court to sequester the shares that IRI held in SME, but the court turned down the request. In January 1986, IRI declared that only the IAR offer was valid. Six months later another Rome court, presided by Verde, annulled the operation altogether, with a two-pronged judgement that allowed IAR to avoid buying the company, while stopping De Benedetti from buying it.[82]

The magistrates arrived at Berlusconi, Pacifico and Previti indirectly while looking into dealings by Pietro Barilla, the owner of Italy's leading pasta-maker and one of the partners in IAR. They found that on 2 May 1988, immediately after the highest appeal court had rejected Buitoni's case, 750 million lire was transferred from Barilla's account with the InterAllianz Bank in Zurich to the account of Pacifico's Quasar Business with Societa Bancaria Ticinese in Bellinzona, a city in the Italian-speaking Swiss canton of Ticino.[83] Pacifico withdrew this sum in cash one week later and, according to the prosecutors, he gave about 200 million lire to Verde who deposited it in his account with Banco di Roma.

On 27 July 1988, immediately after the highest appeal court's judgement was published, 1 billion lire left Barilla's account in Zurich, again to feed Quasar Business's account. Two days later, Previti's Mercier account with Darier Hentsch in Geneva was credited with 850 million lire and the Iberica account with Banca Commerciale in Lugano, to which Squillante had access, with 100 million lire by Quasar Business.[84] Why Barilla might have wished to pay these lawyers raised questions.

One of the most telling pieces of evidence the prosecutors offered concerned 434,404 dollars that arrived in Previti's Mercier account in March 1991. Among *mani pulite*'s mountains of papers were bank documents concerning this money which showed that it originated in the account with Credito Svizzero in Chiasso that belonged to All Iberian, the offshore company that Berlusconi's Fininvest group had set up for secret deals. The funds had then passed through two transit accounts called Polifemo and Ferrido, which acted as cut-outs to hide the real origins of the money, before their transfer to the Mercier account. On the same day, the same amount was transferred from Previti's Mercier account to the account of Rowena Finance, the company belonging to Squillante.[85]

When the court gave its verdict on 22 November 2003, the prosecution's case was upheld on one of the two charges of corruption and the presiding judge read out sentences of eight years' imprisonment for Squillante, four years for Pacifico and five years for Previti. However, the prosecutors had failed to make their case stick regarding the specific matter of SME and Pacifico, Previti and Verde were found not guilty on that charge.[86] Money had gone from accounts of Berlusconi's companies to pay a judge, the court decided, but the prosecution had not convinced the court that money had been paid to swing decisions concerning SME. The case concerning Berlusconi had been spun off and proceedings against the prime minister had been suspended thanks to legislation that his government rushed through parliament, but he still stood accused of paying money to corrupt judges.

Strangely, a case that took its name from a food group threw some light on a leading figure in Italian television during the 1980s. One of the witnesses who was called to give evidence was Enrico Manca,

. Before fame, wealth and power
ut Silvio Berlusconi in the public
ye

above) Showing style in his final
ear at high school.

above right) Sporting a fashionable
noustache – probably around 1970.

ight) Oldest son with mother,
oung sister and father – probably
round 1950.

2. Death of a sponsor
(*above*) Berlusconi sheds tears in Tunis at the funeral of Bettino Craxi, the corrupt former Italian prime minister who died there, a fugitive from justice, in January 2000.
(*below*) 'To remember an intense friendship', Berlusconi wrote of his political patron in the visitors' book in the cemetery at Hammamet where Craxi is buried.

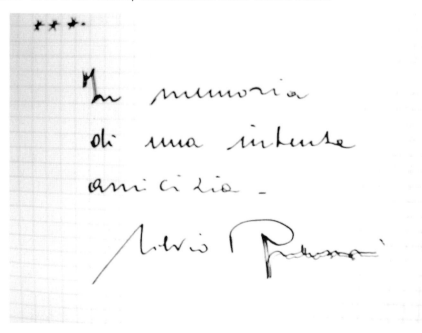

3. Charismatic party leader
(*above*) A group of Forza Italia's supporters.
(*right*) Saluting an audience of party faithful in Milan, March 1996.
(*below*) In line with majorettes in Venice, April 2000.

4 & 5 Berlusconi's villas and second wife
(*above*) Sardinia, a favoured holiday retreat.
(*below*) Villa Belvedere at Macherio, northeast of Milan.

(*above*) Villa San Martino (also known as Villa Casati) at Arcore, not far from Macherio. (*below*) Berlusconi with his wife Veronica Lario.

6 & 7 Public figures on trial
(*above*) Lawyer and former defence minister Cesare Previti, found guilty of bribing judges and sentenced to jail, in court in Milan.
(*below*) Marcello Dell'Utri (*left*) with lawyer (*right*) in court, Palermo, January 2003, facing charges of complicity with the Mafia.

(*above*) Bettino Craxi, in court in Milan, where he was found guilty of corruption. (*below*) Giulio Andreotti, seven times prime minister and innocent of complicity with the Mafia, in court in Palermo. Andreotti's faction had benefited from his friendly relations with mafia figures.

8 Berlusconi and friends
(*right*) With Marcello
Dell'Utri (*right*), business
associate in Fininvest and
co-founder of Forza Italia.
(*below*) With Cesare Previti
(*right*), business associate in
Fininvest and Forza Italia's
first national coordinator.

the Socialist politician who had been planted in the chairmanship of RAI by Craxi in 1986, and who had then headed the state television corporation during six years in which Craxi helped Berlusconi's television empire to sink deep roots. In 1985, Manca had brought a case for defamation and Filippo Verde had been president of the court in Rome that heard the case.[87] Manca's name had been found in the list of members of the P2 masonic lodge, a membership that Manca had denied, and he had sought damages over an article that had suggested that this made him unsuitable for the chairmanship of parliament's industry commission. Verde had given judgement in Manca's favour.

Manca and Previti had been friends since the mid-1970s and Previti had represented Manca in the case heard by Verde. But the relationship between Manca and Previti went beyond friendship and legal business. Until he became a member of parliament in 1994, Previti had been involved in transferring large sums of money to and from Switzerland on Manca's behalf, operations that also involved Pacifico, and he had managed an account with Darier Hentsch for Manca. 'At a certain moment towards the end of the 1970s, I asked Previti for special help as my mother, who was worried about the economic situation and inflation, wanted to transfer money to Switzerland,' Manca explained to the court.[88] From 1994 until 18 March 1996, when he closed his account immediately after learning that the Milanese magistrates had arrested Pacifico and Squillante, the former president of RAI had managed his financial affairs in Switzerland directly. For Manca, his close relationship and clandestine financial dealings with Previti, an intimate of Berlusconi, the owner of RAI's burgeoning competitor, surprisingly did not represent a conflict of interest.

MANI PULITE'S RESULTS

Tangentopoli was a revelation for many Italians. Most knew that corruption infected business and public life but few guessed the vast extent of that infection. Construction companies, public officials, plant engineering concerns, listed corporations and private companies, politicians, materials suppliers, small contractors and big insurers were all revealed to have fallen way short on ethical standards and to have been involved in serious criminal activity.

Searching for something emblematic of cleansing, the board of ACEA, the municipal electricity and water company in Rome, decided to spend money that it had been able to recover from those involved in graft to build some new fountains for the Italian capital. A few new fountains in Rome, codes of behaviour regulating Italy's large groups, especially those with international exposure, and lip-service to accounting transparency lower down the corporate scale were, however, slender results from what promised in 1992 to be a thorough clean-up.

Ten years after the arrest *in flagrante* of the president of the Pio Albergo Trivulzio in Milan, the *mani pulite* team reviewed the record of its work. 'It certainly does not make me happy that the results in the courtroom are so much less than we could have expected, but there is a positive side. We now have enormous knowledge about the crime of corruption that was completely hidden before,' said Gherardo Colombo.[89] During the decade after *tangentopoli*'s first, explosive revelations, the small group of dedicated magistrates – just three and their chief at the start and never more than six – asked for 3,200 people to be sent for trial.

About one third of those were dealt with by judges at preliminary hearings in Milan; just over 600 were sentenced, either through short-ened procedures or plea-bargains, and fewer than 300 cases were dis-missed by the judges on the evidence presented by the prosecutors. The judges at the preliminary hearings sent over 1,300 people for trial and about 430 to other jurisdictions. Just over 650 people were sentenced by higher courts, more than one half through plea-bargains. Higher courts dismissed only 166 cases on the evidence presented by the prosecution.[90]

Francesco Saverio Borrelli, who had headed the *mani pulite* magis-trates, said that the significant moments in the team's work were at the beginning, during the first two years. 'Most of the results were obtained from investigations in that period, thanks to the cooperation that many of the accused gave to magistrates and investigators. The period was also important because public opinion was behind us then.'[91] Why did Italians, who so enthusiastically cheered and encouraged Borrelli and his team then turn against them? Partly, the switch in loyalty was due to an unrelenting media campaign aimed at helping those who felt threatened or were among those accused of crimes. Partly, the explanation for the increasing public indifference to the work of *mani pulite* was sheer boredom. 'Psychological fatigue was a factor. Italian public opinion is fickle, easily tired and cares little about ethics,' remarked Borrelli.[92]

Ten years after *tangentopoli* burst open, Piercamillo Davigo expressed surprise at how Italy's political system had been unable to purge itself. 'As an Italian, one of the worst moments in my life was when Craxi addressed parliament,' observed Davigo, 'and said that he had only done what everyone else had done.'[93] The anti-corruption magistrate remembered that nobody had leapt up in protest and thought that it was tragic that Italians lacked the capacity to be indignant.

Colombo offered another view. Almost everyone was in favour at the start because the targets of the investigations were so distant; few people could see themselves as the mayor of Milan or the head of a political party. 'Little by little, however, the investigations involved ordinary people, like town policemen or non-commissioned officers in the Guardia di Finanza [financial police]. People could identify with these,' he said.[94] Minor local businessmen, who had paid a few million lire to the Guardia di Finanza, labour inspectors or town policemen to encourage them to turn a blind eye to small errors in documents or permits, started to worry that they were about to be lined up in the prosecutors' sights.

Italy was a country of two worlds and two sets of rules, said Colombo. The first was that of the constitution in which the cardinal principle was that of equality. This was a theoretical world, a world on paper, a world of appearances. The other world was real, where the rules were different for people who were able and wanted to make them different. Italian intolerance towards rules over recent years had been due to a culture in which prerogatives and advantages could be gained through violence, cheating or subterfuge.[95] It was a culture that was spreading because it often produced results.

Losing public support, facing fierce opposition from government politicians and struggling to win convictions in the courtroom, it was hardly surprising that Italy's fight against corruption had run out of steam. That the country had again won a reputation as a safe place in which to be corrupt came out in the findings of the world's watchdog on corruption, Transparency International. This non-governmental organization, devoted solely to curbing corruption, publishes an annual corruption perceptions index, which reflects perceived levels of corruption among politicians and public officials. Italy ranked thirty-first in 2002, its score of just over five out of ten placing it below Chile, Botswana, Estonia and Taiwan; of its partners in the European Union, only Greece, scoring just over four, was perceived as more corrupt. The nation of *tangentopoli* was rated little better than Malaysia, Belarus, Lithuania and Tunisia, and a long way off the standards set by Finland and Denmark at the top. Transparency International's chairman noted that Slovenia, a country in transition from communism, had a cleaner score than Italy.[96] Politicians increasingly paid lip-service to the fight against corruption throughout the world, while political elites and their cronies continued to take kickbacks at every opportunity. A year later, Italy had slipped to thirty-fifth place in Transparency International's ranking.

The forces of the law may have become better equipped to deal with corruption but the forces of corruption in Italy had not stood still. Davigo described the institutions responsible for repressing crime as having the same relationship with criminals that predators have with their prey. 'They help to improve the species. We have taken the slowest, but the fast ones have escaped. Of course, in the long term, improvements in the prey also improve the predators' performance.'[97] The prosecutors had helped create strains of corrupt people that were resistant to the investigative techniques or procedures used in the past and simply could not be tackled with them.

Davigo would have wished to live in a country where courage was needed to be a crook, where courage was not needed to be honest. This bleak thought had disturbed him for over twenty years. He had been one of the original *mani pulite* team in the Lombard capital, but ten years later, in 2002, he had left the prosecution service to sit as a judge in criminal cases in Milan's appeal court. He still clearly remembered his first case of corruption in 1979, a year after joining the magistrature and thirteen years before the scandal of *mani pulite* broke open.

Davigo was then an examining magistrate in Vigevano, a medieval town about 25 miles southwest of Milan, working with prosecutors and the police to prepare cases for trial. His first encounter with corruption concerned a group of employees at the local office that dealt with value added tax. They had offered a painless tax inspection to a jeweller, the tariff for going easy in the inspection being 5 million lire and a gold watch.

Never having seen a corrupt person, Davigo did not know what to expect. The defendant, who had already confessed to the prosecutors, was a young man just like himself. He might have been a fellow student at university or one of the crowd at the disco. Davigo was amazed by how normal the tax official was, and he put aside the long list of questions he had prepared and asked just one. He wanted to learn why a young man of twenty-seven would sell himself for 250,000 lire, an amount equal to about the monthly salary for a junior civil servant at that time.

The reply had troubled Davigo ever since. 'You are part of a world where these are personal choices. To be honest or dishonest depends on you,' the tax official told the magistrate.[98] The young man described how, soon after he joined the tax office, he had seen the way the wind blew and he had understood that his colleagues would not have tolerated someone honest in the group because it would have meant danger for them all. He was on probation as a new employee and did not have the courage to refuse when the head of department handed him the money because he was scared of being sacked. Nobody would have believed him if he had blown the whistle. 'You cannot understand because this courage is not asked of you,' he told Davigo.[99]

Only one of the thirty employees in the tax office escaped being found guilty, the case against the thirtieth being dismissed for insufficient proof. Davigo was full of illusions in 1979, convinced that the case of the tax office was a rare exception. Later, the magistrate drew two bitter conclusions about the crime of corruption. First, it was infectious. Where there was one corrupt person, there would soon be others. Second, it was a serial crime. Offences were never isolated. Those who were corrupt would continue to be so.

The investigations of Milan's *mani pulite* team and the vast scandal of *tangentopoli* they started to unearth in 1992 had only confirmed that a diffuse and deep-rooted corruption infected the country. Francesco Saverio Borrelli, who retired from the post of state prosecutor early in 2002, was not optimistic. Despite the efforts of his team and magistrates in other cities, Italy had not made much progress in extirpating graft and Italians had not changed their views on that crime.

Dishonesty and swindling continued to come to light as unscrupulous business dealings made a comeback, particularly in local administrations. Politics and corruption continued to be linked. 'I have the sensation that not much has changed,' said the man who led the operation that most promised to alter the Italian way of thinking about corruption and doing business.[100] Unfortunately, the government Silvio Berlusconi headed from June 2001 considered that corruption was not an issue that should be tackled. The cleansing of Italian public life, which had already slowed, came to a halt.

4

Power

THE BIRTH OF FORZA ITALIA

Everyone knew Berlusconi was extremely rich, but nobody was able to say just how rich. Putting a value on his business empire when he diversified into politics at the beginning of 1994 was difficult; more a matter of guesswork than calculation. The job was much easier in 2001 when he fought parliamentary elections for the third time. Both Mediaset and Mediolanum had been floated on Milan's stock market in 1996 and Berlusconi's private Fininvest holding company's stakes in them were publicly known, as was the interest in Mondadori, a listed company. Calculated on market capitalization – the way the stock market values companies – Berlusconi's investments were worth the huge figure of 22,500 billion lire (about £7.5 billion or $13 billion) in the three listed businesses alone.[1]

The bursting of the stock market bubble and the collapse of media stocks in 2001 hit the Italian tycoon badly. Even so, *Forbes*, the American business magazine, estimated Berlusconi's wealth at 7.2 billion dollars in 2002 and said that he was still Italy's richest man.[2] He was also the thirty-fifth richest man in the world; only eight Europeans stood ahead of him. *Forbes*'s list of the world's hundred wealthiest people contained the names of only two other Italians: Leonardo Del Vecchio, the founder of Luxottica, the eyeware company, and Luciano Benetton, the clothing manufacturer. According to the magazine, Berlusconi was far richer than Rupert Murdoch, another media mogul.

However much Berlusconi spoke in the election campaign in spring 1994 about his mission to save Italy, his mission to secure the future of his businesses seemed paramount. His group was in a sticky position when, on 26 January that year, Fininvest's boss announced his decision to plunge into politics, *scendere in campo* (literally, to get on to the pitch).[3] His taped speech announcing the move was transmitted first on the afternoon news programme of his Retequattro television channel. With the reputation of Bettino Craxi, Berlusconi's political patron and the person who had made possible the growth of the television company, blackened by the *tangentopoli* corruption scandals, Berlusconi was vulnerable. Italy's political system had been thrown into turmoil by the dirt exposed by investigators and magistrates in Milan, and positions that had appeared invulnerable had crumbled.

Berlusconi's monopoly of private commercial television was in the spotlight and the laws enacted to legitimize his position were being closely scrutinized. Electoral victory for political parties determined to tackle Berlusconi's dominance in television might have threatened his ability to use the medium for personal gain and to help his political allies. Moreover, the business empire that Berlusconi had built with the aid of powerful political friends was mired in debt and its prospects were uncertain at best.

A report by the Rome-based investment bank Efibanca had noted in January 1985 that the consolidated accounts of the Fininvest group for 1983, audited for the first time, by Arthur Andersen, showed a financial structure 'characterized by high indebtedness of 840 billion lire, an unbalanced short-term liquidity ratio and by negative net working capital, despite including work in progress and buildings for sale among the liquid assets'.[4] Expanding the television business and diversification had required huge investment and by the early 1990s Fininvest was deep in hock to the banks. Berlusconi's lenders were so concerned, especially after *mani pulite*'s investigations began, that they demanded that a tough, professional manager should be appointed to run Fininvest, where debt had rocketed to 4,500 billion lire in 1992. Some observers thought that the group was on the brink of collapse.

Of course, Berlusconi had great wealth. Massive liabilities weighing down corporate balance sheets did not stop owners from becoming immensely rich themselves, and Fininvest's financial fragility had not prevented Berlusconi from doing so, but corporate catastrophe and personal eclipse seriously threatened Fininvest's founder. He decided in summer 1993 that politics offered a way to counter the threats to his business. In a newspaper interview that July, he spoke about his ideas on the country's political situation and revealed that he had been meeting businessmen and interest groups around Italy. He did not intend to establish a party or to enter politics himself, he said.[5] Events were to turn out differently: Berlusconi had been testing the water.

Despite the popular notion that Berlusconi drew a political party out of a hat and was at once crowned with electoral success, reality was far more mundane. He did win Italy's parliamentary elections in March 1994, just two months after announcing his decision to go into politics, but he had been hard at work on his political project for some time. 'Berlusconi had had politics in mind for months. It would have been impossible to create a political party in just a few days,' remarked Vittorio Dotti, a leading corporate lawyer in Milan, who was Fininvest's lawyer between 1980 and 1995 and became the leader of Berlusconi's party in parliament after the elections in 1994.[6]

As early as July 1993, Fininvest's owner was trying to understand Italian politics, in the way that any businessman would tackle a new market and launch a new product, through research and opinion polls. The first piece of research told Berlusconi that over three quarters of the electorate wanted a new liberal-democratic movement with fresh faces.[7] *Tangentopoli* had left its mark on Italians who then seemed determined that those old political figures who had been, or were being, shown up as flawed and corrupt should give way to others who were new and untainted. Italians appeared to want politicians who were morally and judicially above suspicion. That seemed important in the frenzied political climate at the end of 1993 when the *mani pulite* prosecutors were hard at work exposing the breadth and depth of corruption in Italian politics and business.

Berlusconi used the techniques and methods of modern marketing to discover the public's preferences for political 'products'. Focus groups, soundings and interviews bared the Italian state of mind to the media magnate. Ownership of a large group that included a major retail chain as well as a television company that dominated commercial broadcasting, sectors whose business centred around mass communication, gave Berlusconi an immense advantage in developing his political interests rapidly. A former marketing manager of Fininvest, whose job had included analysing the preferences of television viewers, and a former senior manager of Standa, a large food, clothing and household goods supermarket chain that Fininvest had acquired in 1988, headed the research and polling efforts. By the end of 1993, their company employed 150 telephone researchers and twenty marketing experts, one half of whom were from Fininvest.[8] A team of advisers was able to provide Berlusconi with information on the electorate's thinking day by day. Madison Avenue had arrived in Milan to devise and drive his communications strategy.

Berlusconi was making a huge effort to launch himself into politics. He joined forces with Giuliano Urbani, a professor of political science who had been a consultant to the Liberal Party, a small centre-right party that was submerged by the tidal wave of *tangentopoli*. In September 1993, Urbani had founded a group called Alla Ricerca del Buongoverno (in the search for good government) that brought together intellectuals and businessmen with liberal leanings.

At the same time, Berlusconi was pushing ahead with finding parliamentary candidates. He was helped in this by his Publitalia advertising company, whose management had been recruited to the campaign in September 1993. Around sixty of Publitalia's senior and middle managers contributed to building the political party, attending an intensive politics course that the company's training service organized every Monday and Tuesday morning in October and November. Among the subjects they studied were political history, economics, party organization and constitutional law.[9]

Publitalia had an extensive national network and its managers, particularly the twenty-six regional heads, had accumulated deep knowledge of the regions where they worked and had formed solid contacts with leading local businessmen in more than a decade of dealings with them. These senior associates of Berlusconi were well placed to know who would be suitable to stand for election. He gave them the job of identifying candidates both for parliament's lower house and the senate in each of the seats where the winner would be chosen using the first-past-the-post system.[10] Through telephone calls, meetings, working dinners and networking in cities up and down Italy, Publitalia's managers were able to make around 4,000 contacts.

Marcello Dell'Utri, a long-time friend and associate of Berlusconi who was Publitalia's managing director, was credited with being the mind behind the move into politics. He and Berlusconi were looking for prospective candidates with clean records, a problem as the old political class was discredited and many businessmen had been involved in dodgy dealings of one kind or another. But probity was not the only characteristic that Berlusconi and Dell'Utri sought in potential parliamentary candidates; they also required that whoever they chose should project an image of dynamism and efficiency. During autumn 1993, Publitalia's regional managers were targeting professionally successful, locally known forty-year-old liberals.[11]

The resources of Programma Italia, Publitalia's sister-company and Fininvest's financial services subsidiary, were harnessed to Berlusconi's project as well. Programma Italia's network of financial consultants had contact with large numbers of ordinary Italians, the country's grassroots, on whose votes Berlusconi's political future would depend. After intensive training in the nuts and bolts of political organization at the beginning of November 1993, many consultants opened Forza Italia clubs. ('*Forza Italia*' – 'Go Italy' – were the words that sports fans shouted to encourage Italy's national teams.) These clubs were the foundations of Berlusconi's Forza Italia party. A national association of Forza Italia clubs was set up by a former manager of Fininvest's French television company, and the first club was inaugurated at the beginning of December 1993 in Brugherio, the town where Berlusconi had tackled his first big property project.[12]

One evening at the end of 1993, Berlusconi recounted in the autobiographical booklet *Una Storia Italiana* that he would mail in 2001 to every Italian household, his mother looked him in the eyes and told him, 'If you feel it is your duty, you must find the courage to do it.' From that moment, said his official record, she was at her son's side in his venture into politics and always ready to encourage him.[13]

It was not by chance that the political movement that he offered them was called Forza Italia, Berlusconi told viewers on 26 January

1994. With him running the country, dreams would come true: Italy would be more just, more generous to the needy, richer, happier, more modern and more efficient, a leader in Europe and the world.[14] Forza Italia would know how to fight crime and corruption with maximum determination, he assured Italians.

Berlusconi rarely missed an opportunity to vent his visceral aversion to anything not anchored on the right of the political spectrum. It was essential, he said, that the cartel of the left should be opposed. More than four years after the fall of the Berlin Wall and the collapse of communism as a political force in Europe, Forza Italia's leader continued to fight old wars and warn against non-existent threats. His vision was apocalyptic; Italy under the centre-left would be uniformly hellish. The communists had not changed, and they would ruin Italy and take away freedom. 'Our left pretends to have changed. They say that they have become liberal-democrats. But that is not true. Their people are always the same. Their mentality, their culture, their deepest convictions are the same. They do not believe in the market, private initiative, profit or the individual,' Berlusconi told viewers when he announced that he was entering politics.[15] For Forza Italia's boss, the divided world of the Iron Curtain and the Cold War was still a theme to be plugged and the centre-left remained a bogey that menaced democracy.

Election campaigning had started on 15 January when Oscar Luigi Scalfaro, Italy's president, dissolved parliament. When it was officially founded on 18 January, three days after Scalfaro's announcement of parliament's dissolution, Forza Italia was ready.[16] Indeed, it had already opened its barrage on 15 January with the first spot in a massive advertising effort to win votes. Part of the campaign aimed at brand recognition for Forza Italia and part at building up Berlusconi's image. Around 1,000 spots were transmitted on Fininvest's channels during the ten weeks that followed.[17]

ALLIES FOR GOVERNMENT

Those advertising efforts alone would not have been enough to propel Berlusconi into power, however. Forza Italia's 276 candidates stood on a populist platform of lower taxes, more privatization, less bureaucracy and better public services, but they needed allies. Forming alliances with partners of dubious origins proved the winning move for the nascent, right-wing politician in 1994.

'The principles in which we believe are the fundamental values of all the great western democracies,' began Forza Italia's charter of values. It stated that the party shared and cultivated the values of a Christian tradition and that this included tolerance towards political opponents. 'We believe in the values of our Italian culture that the whole world admires and envies us for,' claimed the charter.[18] Fine words devised to attract the votes that Berlusconi would need to win power.

Berlusconi had held talks in autumn 1993 with Mino Martinazzoli, leader of the Christian Democrat Party, and with Mario Segni, a well-known centrist politician who had been behind referenda for electoral reform, but those talks had led nowhere. At the end of 1993, Berlusconi had also made contact with Gianfranco Fini, the leader of the Movimento Sociale Italiano (the Italian Social Movement), a political party that could trace a direct line to Benito Mussolini and twenty years of fascist rule. Fini, who changed the MSI's name to Alleanza Nazionale (National Alliance) at the beginning of 1994, thought that the *Duce* was the greatest statesman of the century.[19] The National Alliance's leader had enjoyed the favour of Giorgio Almirante, the MSI's patriarch, and been groomed to take over the MSI's leadership. Almirante had worked for *La Difesa della Razza* (The Defence of the Race), an anti-Semitic publication of the fascist regime, and had also served the Republic of Salo, fascism's last bastion.[20] (Propped up by Nazi Germany, Mussolini had established the Republic of Salo in the town of the same name on the western shore of Lake Garda in northern Italy in September 1943, following the armistice between the government in Rome and the Anglo-American allies who were liberating Italy.)

Berlusconi and his advisers saw that Forza Italia's potential sources of votes overlapped with those of the National Alliance as the parties were neighbours on the political spectrum. On 13 February 1994, he and Fini announced the creation of a pact for central and southern Italy where they would run under a common banner, the Polo del

Buongoverno (Good Government Axis).[21] The agreement allowed the neo-fascists, or post-fascists as they preferred to be known, in from the political cold and brought an end to a period of over forty years during which those on the extreme right of Italian politics were treated as pariahs. The fortunes of the National Alliance's predecessors had fluctuated considerably over the years. From almost 13 per cent in 1953, the share of the vote obtained by the MSI and Italy's monarchist party, running separately, fell to a combined figure of less than 6 per cent in 1968. Their fortunes improved in 1972 when they joined forces and won almost 9 per cent, but the figure had dropped by 1987 to less than 6 per cent.[22] Thanks to Berlusconi, the National Alliance was given a kind of respectability.

While he was making overtures to Fini, Berlusconi was also deep in discussions with Umberto Bossi, the leader of the Lega Nord (Northern League), a xenophobic, secessionist party that had made headway in northern Italy. The Northern League had its origins in the late 1980s in the Lega Lombarda (Lombard League), whose cradle was in the cities of Brescia and Bergamo. The movement's initiation rites required new members to paint graffiti attacking southern Italians: 'southerners in jackets, our children in overalls' and 'southerners as doctors, our children as nurses' were two of the messages, painted in green, the party's colour, that the Lega Lombarda used to promote itself.[23] Members of the Northern League resented the large transfers of public funds for the many infrastructure works, such as roads, aqueducts, electrification schemes and schools, and incentives to industry in the south that had helped to reduce the yawning economic gap that separated it from the north. They rightly suspected that corrupt southern politicians were syphoning off part of those funds for themselves. But southerners were not the only target and the Northern League appealed to a festering streak of racism and hatred of all outsiders.

Roma Ladrona – thieving Rome, which stole northerners' hard-earned wages through taxes and wasted the money on the south and on a bloated and inefficient bureaucracy – was another rallying cry through which the Northern League's rough-spoken leader appealed to disaffected northerners. Even before *tangentopoli* exploded, exposing Milanese probity as more myth than merit and crooked businessmen and greedy politicians as part of life throughout Italy, Bossi was winning a large protest vote right across the Po Valley, from Piedmont in the west through Lombardy to the Veneto in the east, an area he vaingloriously described as a new nation called Padania. Bossi and his party attracted people who were fed up and wanted to teach a lesson to the state and thieving politicians everywhere in the country. Some of those who voted for the Northern League hoped for full secession, others for devolution and fiscal autonomy; all of them wanted to cast a protest vote.

Yet the state bureaucracy and the south, with its residual monarchist loyalties, were where Fini's party won its votes. So Bossi's denunciation of the National Alliance as fascist and the Northern League's invective against the state, southerners and the south killed any hopes that Berlusconi might have entertained of creating a triple alliance. However, two days before sealing his pact with the National Alliance, Italy's newly arrived politician had reached an agreement for northern Italy under which Forza Italia and the Northern League would run together under the banner of the Polo della Liberta (Freedom Axis).[24]

With Berlusconi on the political pitch, bringing his great personal wealth and access to the powerful medium of television, Fini and Bossi caught a whiff of power. There would have been no place for either of them on the centre-left. So Forza Italia's leader was able to put together a national coalition based on two regional pacts. His campaign promised something for everyone. It emphasized family values. It captured votes in the elections on 27 March 1994. When the ballot boxes were opened, Forza Italia was the biggest single party, edging just ahead of the Partito Democratico della Sinistra (the former Communist Party that had changed its name to the Democratic Party of the Left), with 21 per cent of the votes in the lower house.

With the memories of the mafia atrocities of 1992 still fresh and with the *tangentopoli* investigations in full swing, Italians were receptive to change. A divided centre-left, split by old rivalries and conceits and unable to present itself credibly as a clean break with the past, had passed up an opportunity to be the architect of renewal and had allowed the newcomer to win. Berlusconi's coalition took 366 of the lower chamber's 630 seats, and 156 of the 315 seats in the senate,[25] giving it a clear majority in the chamber but falling just short in the senate. Berlusconi's need for allies had ensured that Mussolini's heirs and a party in which racism has seemed a core value would be part of Italy's government.

On 16 May 1994, the new prime minister addressed parliament. Berlusconi announced that measures would be enacted during the first 100 days of government to reduce employment costs for firms, free up the labour market and create new jobs. Taxes would be reduced, incentives would be introduced to stimulate investment and privatization would be accelerated. But his first parliamentary speech did not only deal with economic matters. The government supported the work of valiant magistrates that would lead to higher standards in public life. 'It is a government of irreproachable people, keeping to irreproachable behaviour, respect for the law and to the code of ethics that regulates public life,' Berlusconi assured parliament.[26] As for his evident conflict of interest, he claimed that Italy had a robust system of guarantees and controls. Nevertheless, within four and a half months, by the end of September, an expert committee would make proposals for a bill to strengthen those guarantees and controls. Other matters were higher on Berlusconi's agenda, however, as events soon revealed.

Far from supporting the magistrature's efforts in tackling corruption, Berlusconi had his own ideas about how to improve standards in public life. His justice minister, Alfredo Biondi, a member of Forza Italia, issued a decree in July that quickly became known as the *salvaladri* (save the thieves) decree as its measures seriously weakened the powers of magistrates to deal with suspects and greatly helped criminals. Biondi's controversial decree caused outrage among ordinary Italians and threw the government into crisis, putting at risk the survival of the three-party coalition, when a senior cabinet minister, a member of the Northern League, threatened to resign.[27]

The decree gave people the right to check whether they were under investigation, a munificent act of official benevolence, said magistrates, that would be a boon to the Mafia as well as to those who thought that their involvement in *tangentopoli* might have caught the investigators' eyes.[28] There were also significant changes to the regulations that governed remand in custody. No longer would those suspected of financial crimes such as corruption, extortion, fraudulent bankruptcy, false accounting, abuse of office and illegal financing of political parties be kept in custody while being questioned.[29] This was what *salvaladri* meant. Indeed, during the seven days that passed between the decree being signed and it being voted down in parliament, almost 3,000 people were released from jail,[30] among them large numbers of businessmen, politicians and public officials who were being held in preventive detention on corruption charges. Extradition procedures for many suspected of having been involved in corruption came abruptly to a halt.

In 1993 and 1994, Italians objected strongly to the idea that those who had been corrupt should get away with their crimes. Opinion polls showed that three quarters of the population considered the decree to be wrong and only one in seven supported Berlusconi on it.[31] There were demonstrations in Milan in favour of the *mani pulite* magistrates who had resigned when the decree was issued. The parties in the coalition knew fully the risks that they were running. Only sixteen months before, the government, at that time headed by a Socialist, had nearly fallen when it tried to enact legislation that would have pardoned most of the culprits in the corruption scandals. Whatever the prime minister thought about the public's views, he was compelled to take account of the strength of feeling in the Northern League. The decree was withdrawn, but Berlusconi had shown where he stood on the question of ethics in public life.

Walking arm-in-arm in the gardens of the villa in Arcore and beaming broadly for photographers, Berlusconi and Bossi patched up their differences and the summer crisis passed. But the difficulty of keeping a fractious coalition together returned when the budget for 1995, which Berlusconi had planned to use as a vehicle for reforming the crumbling state pensions system, came under discussion in September 1994. Berlusconi wanted to show that he was in charge and capable of running a nation's economy, and that rigour would be applied where he believed it was needed, even though the firm hand of government would inevitably bring a clash with the trade unions. The result was that Italy's workers rose up in mass, packing the *piazze* across the country with around 5 million angry demonstrators on 14 October.[32] The crowd that turned out to hear the trade union leaders in Rome's Piazza San Giovanni on 12 November was estimated to have been 1.5 million strong. Bossi thought that measures to reform the pensions system should have been excluded from the budget. As in the case of the *salvaladri* decree, the proposals for pensions were unpopular and Bossi risked the erosion of his electorate if the Northern League continued to be part of Berlusconi's government.

With social strife soaring and his government tottering, Berlusconi suffered another heavy blow to his image and self-esteem that autumn. On 21 November, he was in Naples hosting a United Nations summit on crime when the news broke that he was being investigated by the *mani pulite* magistrates and that charges of corruption were possible.[33] News of *mani pulite*'s interest in him had leaked and been published in a leading daily newspaper, although investigations subsequently cleared the prosecutors' office of the leak. That the news had got out was clearly against *mani pulite*'s interests and some magistrates believed that Berlusconi's own staff, sensing the opportunity for propaganda and mischief-making, had fed the scoop to the newspaper. Berlusconi certainly exploited the fracas, claiming that it was evidence that he was the victim of political persecution by a biased, left-wing magistrature.[34]

Revelations about corruption in politics and business had already tarnished Italy's image on the international stage. The episode in Naples helped ensure that its politicians continued to cut poor figures when probity was at issue. Berlusconi did not remain as prime minister for much longer, although corruption investigations were not the reason. Bossi's loyalties had shifted; he withdrew the Northern League from the government in December 1994 and brought it down. Berlusconi complained bitterly in his resignation speech to parliament about how Bossi had stretched his and the whole government's patience for seven months.[35]

Although his first experience as a politician brought the rewards of leading a government, an exceptional start, Berlusconi's record in office was poor. His brief spell of government in 1994 was a failure. He claimed to be a businessman who favoured reducing the role of the state, but the only progess that his government made in privatization was to float a state-owned insurance company. Moreover, the credit for this went to the previous government which had taken the decision and prepared the ground. Italian workers had no reason to thank Berlusconi, unemployment rising to well over 11 per cent in 1994.

Even so, Berlusconi had left his mark: using money from his own pocket he renovated and furnished the prime minister's offices in Palazzo Chigi where official visitors were met. Interior decoration was a hobby of his and he prided himself on looking after every detail from the furniture to paintings, framed photographs, lighting and flowers, about which, he said, he was an expert.[36]

'From the start, Bill Clinton, Helmut Kohl, François Mitterrand and Boris Yeltsin understood that their Italian interlocutors were different from their predecessors,' claimed Berlusconi's official record.[37] His team were determined statesmen, it claimed, punctilious and long-sighted. But this glowing analysis was wide of the mark. Chanceries of embassies in Rome prepared ministers in their home capitals for the meetings that they would have to have with the post-fascist politicians that Berlusconi had appointed to his cabinet. And diplomats busily drafted biographical notes on this little-known political newcomer, describing the Italian prime minister's business empire, the glaring conflict of interest that arose from his ownership of a media empire and what the *mani pulite* magistrates were doing.

Berlusconi had not done much for Italy and the Italians while he was prime minister but the balance sheet was positive for himself. He had created a major political force and made his presence felt. Moreover, he had learned a valuable lesson about how to keep coalitions of widely different interests together and a crucial lesson about sharing out parliamentary seats. In agreeing Forza Italia's alliance with the Northern League, Berlusconi had been generous. Its 21 per cent of the vote had given Berlusconi's Forza Italia party and two minor allies 140 seats in the lower chamber. Yet, even though it had only just over 8 per cent of the popular vote, the Northern League had swept up 117 seats and had the power to hold the government to ransom. Moreover, the Northern League had 60 seats in the senate against the 47 of Forza Italia.[38] Berlusconi would not make such concessions to allies again.

After the unceasing ructions of Berlusconi's spell in power, the arrival of a government of technocrats headed by Lamberto Dini, who had been a non-party treasury minister in Berlusconi's cabinet, brought a welcome steady hand to government. Dini came from the prestigious Bank of Italy where he had been general manager. His cabinet contrasted sharply with the government of squabbling politicians that Berlusconi had headed. By keeping his job at the treasury ministry, as well as taking on the prime ministership, Dini maintained continuity in economic policy. He governed well for a year.[39] Thanks to his conciliatory skills and willingness to discuss matters rather than issue orders, he was able to convince the trade unions of the urgent need to reform the state pensions system, something that Berlusconi had found impossible when he was in power.

Dini's administration ended with parliamentary elections in April 1996 in which Berlusconi was handicapped by not having an alliance in northern Italy. After the Northern League had brought about the collapse of his government at the end of 1994, Berlusconi could not credibly offer a repeat of that year's Polo della Liberta, even if Bossi had been willing to join forces again. Forza Italia and its allies thus found themselves facing not just the centre-left grouping around the Ulivo (Olive Tree) alliance in northern Italy but also candidates put up by the Northern League itself.

The result was a defeat for Berlusconi and the right. Contesting the elections on its own, the Northern League won over 10 per cent of the votes and collected 59 seats in the lower chamber and 27 in the senate: ditching Berlusconi and the post-fascists had paid dividends. Forza Italia alone won just under 21 per cent of the votes and counted 123 deputies and 47 senators in its ranks. Berlusconi's new Polo della Liberta could call on 264 deputies and 117 senators, many fewer than the Ulivo and the far-left Partito Rifondazione Comunista (unreformed communists) together could muster.[40] The elections did not offer a rapid return to office for the *cavaliere* from Arcore, who had clearly failed when in government to convince the voters of his worth. For Berlusconi in April 1996, a long period beckoned as head of the parliamentary opposition.

FALLING FOUL OF THE BOSS

Despite his great wealth and the propaganda pumped out by his three television channels, Italy's richest man, a captain of industry, political leader and aspiring statesman faced the irksome role of playing second fiddle. He would be away from centre stage, deprived of photo-opportunities with the leaders of other nations and prevented from mixing with those international figures with whom he could pretend matey, back-slapping friendship. 'He imagines that he can solve the world's problems with a pat on the shoulder,' commented Vittorio Dotti, 'and he considers himself a natural leader.'[41] Dotti knew Berlusconi well, having worked closely with him for fifteen years as Fininvest's corporate lawyer. Beneath the smiles, he said, Berlusconi was very hard, very determined. Berlusconi's self-esteem was such that he believed he was more than just the best man in Italy: he was the best in the world. It was a personal affront if anyone crossed him; that was behaviour he would not tolerate. Dotti said that he was a man who stored up rancour.

The lawyer would discover that vengeful side of Berlusconi's character towards the end of 1995. When Berlusconi set up Forza Italia, he wanted trusted associates from his business empire to follow him in his new venture. Dotti had always been interested in politics and was an obvious candidate. He was elected to parliament in 1994 where he became deputy speaker in the lower house, as well as heading Forza Italia's parliamentary group. He became a public figure, appearing on television, being interviewed in newspapers and presenting an image of moderation and reason. Forza Italia was something completely new in Italian politics and Dotti was proud to be part of it. One of the party's doves, he believed that Berlusconi's grand project was based on the ideology of efficiency. Above all, they were in government to get good things done, thought Dotti, and to do them well.

Dotti's experience as a member of parliament was short-lived. It came to a traumatic and bitter end when his partner, Stefania Ariosto, was questioned by the Guardia di Finanza financial police in February 1995 in connection with some bearer savings books that Berlusconi had lent to Dotti for an advance on his professional fees.[42] Sickened by the rottenness of the Rome milieu in which she moved, she decided to reveal what she knew about the corruption of judges in the Italian capital. *Teste Omega* (witness Omega), as she was first known, told *mani pulite*'s magistrates that one of those involved in this corruption was the Rome lawyer Cesare Previti.

Previti was more than just a lawyer, as we have seen. He was a close friend of Berlusconi and a member of parliament, and had been defence minister in Berlusconi's short-lived administration. When Previti was brought to trial in 2000 charged with judicial corruption, defence counsel tried to portray Ariosto as a liar and a schemer. Her accusations were aimed at damaging Previti's political career and furthering that of Dotti, suggested the defence. In court in June 2003 as a defendant in that same case of judicial corruption, in a declaration not made under oath and not subject to questioning, Berlusconi himself went to great lengths to smear Ariosto. 'Mrs Ariosto has lied about everything. There is not one circumstance in her accusations that has subsequently been confirmed as truthful,' he claimed.[43] She had completely invented her story, he alleged. The court found differently and accepted that she had spoken the truth.

Addressing the court eleven days before Berlusconi made his declaration, the advocate representing the state as a damaged civil co-plaintiff had already dismissed as risible the notion that Ariosto and Dotti had plotted Previti's downfall. Such a scheme would have caused the ruin of both Ariosto and Dotti, he said. Indeed, that is what happened. 'Dotti, who had headed Forza Italia's group, not only ceased to be that but was not put forward at the next parliamentary elections, nor at any other elections,' noted the advocate.[44]

The abrupt fall from grace did not finish with Dotti's exclusion from Forza Italia, however. Berlusconi's group had been his main client ever since his relationship with Fininvest had started in 1980 with negotiations to buy a bankrupt property company. Although those negotiations were not successful, they were the beginning of fifteen busy years for Dotti. As Berlusconi's group expanded vertiginously, Dotti had handled important, visible legal affairs, from the purchases of the Retequattro and Italia 1 television channels to those of the AC Milan football club, Mondadori and Mediolanum.[45] Now that work dried up.

Dotti's legal chambers in central Milan were on the tenth floor of the Martini tower, one of those mid-1950s buildings that added gloss to the city's name and elegance to its skyline. On a clear day, the landscape windows gave Dotti and his visitors magnificent views of the Alps where the snow-covered Monte Rosa stood out. They were also directly in front of the entrance to the Galleria Vittorio Emanuele, the vast arcade that led from the square outside the cathedral to the Piazza della Scala. This was the very heart of Milan, the place where *tangentopoli* beat strongest. Above the porticos in that square were the offices where Bettino Craxi, the corrupt Socialist prime minister, friend and supporter of Berlusconi, had collected bribes. As we have seen earlier, Berlusconi's corporate empire had a secret offshore part that included a Jersey-based company called All Iberian which was used as a transit treasury for clandestine operations and it was from here that Berlusconi's group had paid 23 billion lire into offshore accounts controlled by Craxi between 1991 and 1992.[46]

Dotti and Ariosto's lives were turned upside down by the corruption scandal, but though Dotti's old associates tried to pressure him to turn against Stefania Ariosto, he never did. 'In all conscience, however, I just could not say that she was mad or a liar,' he said.[47]

As to Ariosto herself, she was harassed and hounded in court by the defence's lawyers, and outside the court she was threatened, made the target of a vicious smear campaign by some sections of the press and her property was damaged. She fought back by bringing and winning libel actions against the smearers.[48] Two days before Christmas 1995, a few months after she began telling the magistrates what she had seen and heard, she opened a fancily wrapped parcel that had just been delivered to her home in Milan. It contained a cruel and gruesome gift: a skinned rabbit with its throat cut and dripping blood. But years later, even after Previti and the corrupt judges had been found guilty and sentenced, this witness to the grossest acts of corruption ever uncovered in Italy, her nerves shot by the violence of the reaction to her testimony, still lived in a permanent state of fear.

STRENGTHENING THE PARTY

Forza Italia's leader had achieved an important result in winning the election in March 1994, within months of launching his party, and the outcome of the parliamentary elections two years later, in April 1996, was also impressive. Forza Italia seemed to have planted its roots firmly. Indeed, as the conservative splinter parties that had sprouted from the collapse of the Christian Democrat Party ran separately in 1996, Forza Italia's achievement was as great then as it had been in 1994. Although his coalition had lost the election, Berlusconi's party effectively increased its share of the vote. Yet, although it gained ground, that was not enough. It needed to create a solid foundation for the future and to change from being a political party improvised from within Berlusconi's business empire and based on the resources of his companies. Forza Italia needed an organization more like that of the political parties with which it was competing.

The weaknesses of a party that owed its existence mainly to one man's idea, determination and money showed up soon during the parliament of 1994 to 1996. Many people who had responded to Berlusconi's call and flocked to the Forza Italia clubs at the end of 1993 and beginning of 1994 thought that their efforts deserved greater recognition. Fininvest's owner had exploited their enthusiasm and they felt excluded from the fruits of victory. They wanted their voices to be heard, believed that it was their party, not just Berlusconi's, and that it suffered from being undemocratic. The grass-roots was not alone in thinking that something was missing. Some newly elected members of parliament were also dissatisfied by the command exerted by former managers from the Fininvest group.

Forza Italia suffered from a lack of structure and an absence of democratic rules. The party's governing presidential committee was effectively an extension of Fininvest's management. The power that the people at the top of Forza Italia enjoyed did not require additional formalization and legitimation. They knew Berlusconi well and he knew them, as they came mostly from a common corporate past and shared a common corporate culture.[49] In September 1994, Berlusconi appointed Previti, then defence minister and one of his closest intimates, as the party's national coordinator.

Previti was a political hawk perched well to the right on the political spectrum. He had grown up in Rome during a period when nostalgia for the past and carrying the flag for Almirante's neo-fascists was fashionable among a certain middle class. Previti was someone unlikely to open up Berlusconi's party and allow the membership a voice. Forza Italia had started as a top-down organization, with the president running the show and making the decisions that counted, and it continued to be so after Previti became its national coordinator. In autumn 1994, Previti said that all party officers would be elected, but the organization and command under which the party operated at that time would remain in place until well after the electoral defeat in April 1996. Forza Italia's members had to wait until the beginning of 1997 for the chance to have a greater say in the party.

The guidelines for Forza Italia's structure revealed by Berlusconi in summer 1995 merely underlined its autocratic nature. Party officials would continue to be appointed from above, regional officers would continue to be Berlusconi's satraps and grassroots participation in running the party would be discouraged. Berlusconi was forced to reconsider this approach after the parliamentary elections in April 1996. In January 1997, Forza Italia announced a new statute. Changes in the new statute were introduced later that year and by the party's first national conference in April 1998.[50]

That Forza Italia aimed to be an all-embracing political movement was clear from the opening words of the new statute. Berlusconi had erected a big tent with room for almost everyone. Its roots were in democratic liberalism and Catholic liberalism, the party claimed, as well as in European secular and reformative traditions. Berlusconi and his party's thinkers and bigwigs were out to capture votes from all quarters. Forza Italia's statute claimed that its policies would aim at universal values of justice, and that the party was committed to a modern market economy.

Despite the local structure the statute gave to the party and the voice the membership would apparently enjoy in the party's affairs, Forza Italia would continue to be tightly controlled from the centre and the top. The party's chairman would appoint the regional co-ordinators, key figures in party management, and the regional coordinators would appoint five members of the regional committees and nominate deputies. Although the national administrator, another key figure in the party's hierarchy, would be elected by the national council, his nomination would come from the chairman's committee. This committee, of which the national administrator would be a member, would include six members appointed by the chairman, as well as other members who owed their positions, directly or indirectly, to the chairman. Even after the drafting of a statute that aimed to add democracy to the movement, Forza Italia continued to belong to Berlusconi. He owned it and was in charge.

RIGHT AND LEFT

Forza Italia's leader was able to assert at its first national conference in April 1998, held on the outskirts of Milan, that the party, described by some observers as a plastic, virtual or company party, existed in flesh and bone. There were no doubts about that. Forza Italia had garnered almost 8 million votes in the parliamentary elections two years before.

More than 3,000 members of Forza Italia were at the conference and heard Berlusconi's diatribes against the centre-left. Forza Italia's leader spoke about his party's distant roots; his political preferences lay well to the right. Forza Italia held the post-fascist National Alliance and its leader in high esteem. The two parties were more than simply allies, they were friends. Berlusconi had attended the National Alliance's conference in Verona to express his affection for its leader, Gianfranco Fini. The post-fascist party did not need a licence of legitimacy, affirmed Forza Italia's leader, because it had been given full approval by the votes that it had received from millions of Italians.[51]

When he was campaigning in local elections in November 1998, Berlusconi said that he had learned that for ordinary people one concern stood out above all others: Italians begged him to save them from the communists, the red menace that he had never tired of warning them against.[52] Italy's centre-left politicians, he said, were in thrall to a religion that was nothing other than the conquest of power, the management of power and the strengthening of their grip on it.[53] A big brother, a big boss that wanted to control and dominate society, the centre-left sought to impose an all-embracing state, claimed Berlusconi.[54]

Celebrating the tenth anniversary of the fall of the Berlin Wall at the end of 1999, Forza Italia's leader described the wall he saw separating Italy from its European partners, from real democracy, justice, a true rule of law, economic liberty and real freedom.[55] For him, the centre-left government that was in office threatened to reduce Italy to the conditions that the people of Eastern Europe had suffered under the yoke of communism. Berlusconi had by then been tied for almost six years to the heirs of fascism.

Those to the left of Berlusconi and his political allies stood for decline, an authoritarian and invasive state, higher taxes and higher unemployment; in one word, the other side's policies brought poverty. 'With us there is growth, freedom, initiative,' Berlusconi told a meeting of Forza Italia in Verona in May 1999.[56] Certainly, beating this drum often and loudly found a large and receptive audience and won votes, but there was little doubt about the sincerity of Berlusconi's intense contempt for his political opponents and their policies.

IN THE WILDERNESS

The centre-left was not alone in being a target for the businessman-turned-politician. Berlusconi used Forza Italia's first conference to launch fierce attacks on the magistrature and the rule of law. He said that magistrates in Milan were to blame for the death of all Italy's small political parties: the Liberal Party, the Social Democrat Party, the Republican Party and the Socialist Party.[57] Like the larger Christian Democrat Party and the Communist Party, those small parties had stolen from the public purse and been deeply and criminally corrupt, although Berlusconi did not mention this. Forza Italia's leader also complained about how he and his business had been investigated by prosecutors in Palermo, saying bitterly that such investigations were politically motivated. Three and a half years after the affair in Naples, Berlusconi reminded Forza Italia's first congress in April 1998 of the shame to which he had been subjected at the United Nations summit. It was, he said, something that had discredited the prime minister and the government.

The centre-left had been in office for two years when Forza Italia's first national conference was held and the legislature had a further three years to run, but Berlusconi was already gearing up for a major effort to win over the electorate. Shortly before the national conference, he had addressed a gathering of Forza Italia's women supporters in San Remo. This had been the chance to show how much he was adored by his female voters, women who saw him as the ideal husband, ideal son, perfect son-in-law; the perfect salesman tried constantly to be in tune with what the target of his pitch was feeling. An embrace for every one of you, the populist leader told his admirers. Berlusconi's heart was full of emotion for the hugs, he said, for the kisses and for the handshakes that had been given him.[58] Despite the suffering, so many sacrifices and so much work, he called on the Forza Italia women to continue the struggle to defend the future of their children, grandchildren and freedom.

As with the women of Forza Italia, so at every meeting with his supporters, Berlusconi always gave a sentimental charge to what he said. He chose his words to create a tight emotional bond with his audience. 'Thank you from my heart,' Berlusconi told Forza Italia's white-haired ranks of senior citizens when he addressed their first national meeting in Rome on 27 February 1999.[59] The lives of the members of his audience, he said, had been filled with work and struggle but much satisfaction also. Though they were all over sixty they still had battles to win and ideals to fight for.

'Let's let out the boy or girl that we have inside us because we are young in body and, I believe, we are young in spirit,' Berlusconi urged Forza Italia's senior citizens.[60] Five years later, in February 2004, Umberto Scapagnini, Berlusconi's doctor, a specialist in the problems of ageing, said that Berlusconi's physical age was fifty-five, which was twelve years less than his real age. Scapagnini, who followed Berlusconi politically and was mayor of Catania in Sicily, said that the party's leader was genetically exceptional. 'He has a truly extraordinary brain, of an intelligence beyond the norm that allows him to forecast how things will turn out.'[61] Berlusconi, who had had a face-lift during the preceding Christmas break, was technically almost immortal, said his doctor. Addressing Forza Italia's senior citizens in February 1999, Berlusconi had predicted, 'Medicine, biology and surgery have worked miracles, and will work even more in the future.'[62]

He told his elderly audience that he wanted them to contribute wisdom, patience and prudence to the party. He expected other things from Forza Italia's younger members, he said at their national conference in Rome in December 1999. It was important, he urged, that they should have objectives in work and in politics, and always have 'sun in their pockets' to bring out at the right moment and give with a smile to everyone, above all to those dear to them. He had built a model city safe for children and had had the good fortune to raise his own children well. He had created a group and trained a team of managers. He would have liked to have passed to his audience some of the experience that he had gained in all the adventures he had had. 'An affectionate embrace for all of you and a prayer, an order, to keep me in your hearts,' he said at the end of his speech.[63]

Berlusconi campaigned busily in 1999. As well as addressing conferences of the party's pensioners and of its young members, he spoke at two other big events aimed at capturing attention in 1999. One was in May when Berlusconi spoke to a gathering in Verona, in a day of protest for Forza Italia against taxes and the excesses of taxation, and against fiscal, regulatory and bureaucratic oppression. Fiscal pressure in Italy was the highest in Europe, Berlusconi told his followers, and the Italian state spent more than one half of the product, labour and annual sacrifice of them all. These matters were close to his heart and his cry against the unjust taxman was heard over a satellite-link in over 100 Italian cities. In July 1998, a court in Milan had already found that companies belonging to Berlusconi had bribed officers of Italy's Guardia di Finanza tax police to go easy when undertaking tax inspections. And in November 2001, the supreme court would confirm that a Fininvest manager and two members of the Guardia di Finanza were guilty of corruption and that Massimo Berruti, the former officer of the Guardia di Finanza who, as we have seen earlier, became one of Berlusconi's lawyers and a member of parliament, was guilty of aiding and abetting the crime. 'We went into politics because we were scared, at a certain moment, that a concept might prevail of man, society and the state that was different from ours,' Berlusconi explained to his audience in May 1999.[64]

Security was the other issue that Berlusconi emphasized in 1999. Freedom from fear was the right of every citizen, he said. Like taxes, public safety was an issue on which the words of Forza Italia's leader could strike a chord with many Italians. The majority of them, he claimed, thought that delinquency and crime were Italy's biggest problems. Two thirds of Italians believed that crime was worryingly on the increase and that going out in the evening was dangerous. Many thought that immigrants were to blame for the fact that Italy's cities had become the theatre for every possible crime imaginable. Illegal immigrants were a big concern, said Berlusconi, as they changed their names or gave false ones and could slip out of the authorities' net and keep committing crimes.

Part of the problem was that the centre-left government, then in office, was soft on crime and had underestimated the issue. Not only that, said Berlusconi, the centre-left had exploited and transformed the struggle against the Mafia into a fight against political adversaries. In October 1999, on Security Day, as Forza Italia billed the event, Berlusconi explained how he would tackle crime when he became prime minister. He indicated that the magistrature and defenders of justice were in his sights as much as the criminals that worried the Italian man-in-the-street, and perhaps even more so. Wrapped in words that might reassure the broad mass of the electorate, Berlusconi's message disturbed those Italians who cared about the independent administration of justice.

FINANCIAL SECURITY FOR FININVEST

During the six years of *la traversata del deserto* (literally, crossing the desert) Berlusconi had been able to deal with the difficulties in his business empire. Indeed, by the time he embarked on Forza Italia's campaign in 1999, the serious financial problems at Fininvest had been solved and he was free from the worries that had beset his heavily indebted group during the first half of the 1990s. Fininvest had been in poor financial shape as building up the television business in Italy, making an unsuccessful football club successful (although not profitable), acquiring a big publishing group, developing financial services and expanding abroad had been expensive. Moreover, an important acquisition had turned out to be a costly failure. This was Standa, the large Italian supermarket chain that was bought in 1988.

The reason behind Fininvest's decision to buy Standa, a significant shift from its media businesses, was that it would give Berlusconi's group a strategic lever for expansion. Television advertising would bring customers into the stores, financial services would be marketed through retail outlets, shops would increase their sales and profits, and the group would prosper. Far from working out that way, Standa ran up heavy losses and was eventually sold in 1998. But it had served another purpose at a critical time; the day-by-day flow of cash through the tills of its shops had provided financial oxygen to the gasping Fininvest group in the early 1990s.

By expanding Fininvest so ambitiously, Berlusconi had dangerously overstretched his group. Combined with the *tangentopoli* scandals, the collapse of the political parties, and the crisis in the economy and Italy's public sector accounts this threatened to sink his whole enterprise. Berlusconi's decision to establish his own political party and enter politics was one lifebelt. Another came from the decision to widen ownership to outsiders. Berlusconi took his first step in this direction in 1994 when Fininvest spun off its television and advertising assets into a new, wholly-owned subsidiary called Mediaset.

Berlusconi made the next step, a rights issue of Mediaset's shares worth 1,800 billion lire (just over £650 million or $1 billion at the time), in July the following year. The equity was to be taken up by three new shareholders who together would acquire almost one fifth of Mediaset, whose indebtedness then amounted to about 2 billion lire. With a 10 per cent interest, the biggest of the three strategic partners was to be Germany's Kirch group, that would subsequently be put into receivership and dismantled by creditors in 2002, the others being South Africa's Rembrandt group, through a 6 per cent stake held by its Netherlands Nethold subsidiary, and the Saudi prince

Alwaleed Bin Talal, who agreed to buy just over 4 per cent. These newcomers wanted guarantees to prevent Fininvest and its owner from doing what they wanted with Mediaset. They were given them, Kirch being allowed two directors and the other two new shareholders a further two between them in a board of twenty-one members. Provisions were drawn up to prevent Berlusconi from making investments and selling assets as he pleased, and strict limits were placed on transactions between Berlusconi's companies.[65]

Berlusconi and his advisers had considered the sale of the whole of Fininvest but negotiations with Rupert Murdoch, a global media baron, had come to nothing, partly because of the taxes that would have been incurred by selling. The big stumbling block would, however, have been the transfer of a strategic national company to foreign ownership, said Berlusconi, who had received many letters from viewers asking him not to sell out to foreigners. To have sold the business to Murdoch would have betrayed those Italians who had voted in his favour in a referendum on television, said Berlusconi, so he kept control.[66] There were to be two further steps to secure his group's financial safety: the recruitment of institutional investors as shareholders and Mediaset's flotation on Milan's stock market at the beginning of July 1996. Fininvest's stake in Mediaset had been reduced to 71 per cent when the television company's shares were offered to the public.[67]

Berlusconi blitzed the nation's screens with an advertising campaign. On sale were 288 million shares. As earlier rights issues had already reinforced Mediaset's balance sheet, less than half of the shares being sold in the flotation were new shares whose revenues would go to the company to strengthen its capital base. Berlusconi used the opportunity to raise cash for Fininvest, and thus for himself, by offering 145 million shares for sale from Fininvest's own stake in Mediaset. Mediaset would receive around 990 billion lire (about £350 million or $550 million) and Berlusconi would get about the same.[68]

Four of Mediaset's twenty-one directors were caught up in judicial proceedings at the time of the flotation and four pages of the prospectus dealt with legal problems; the company could not exclude the possibility that Mediaset's share price might be affected by their eventual adverse outcome or by the attention of the media to those matters. Another acknowledged risk was the impact of technological change in the television sector. Most of the attention in the section of the prospectus dealing with risks focused, however, on the regulatory framework within which television companies operated in Italy. Mediaset's accounts were based on the assumption that it would be able to continue broadcasting on three television channels, despite a ruling of the constitutional court in December 1994 that limited the number of national channels that a single owner could possess to one quarter of the total in Italy. On the grounds of pluralism, the court disapproved in principle of allowing a single owner to have one quarter of national channels but left it to parliament to find a remedy for the matter. The politicians had two choices: either to reduce the number of channels held by one owner or to increase the number of national channels.

Between the ruling of the constitutional court and the public offering of Mediaset's shares, Italians had voted in referenda concerning the television sector. Unsurprisingly, Mediaset had exploited its resources to drum up the vote in its favour and Italians had rejected a proposal to abolish the law that permitted one owner to possess more than one national television channel. The results of the referenda also allowed advertising breaks in films and plays, and the ownership of advertising businesses by television groups. That type of endorsement was a marvellous fillip to Berlusconi personally and to Mediaset's value.

Mediaset had been adding media glitter to Milan's stock market for almost five years when Berlusconi won the elections in May 2001. The price of its shares had risen and fallen according to the current feelings on broadcasting regulation in Italy and with the boom and bust in telecommunications, media and technology stocks. The politicians had done nothing. Italy had been governed by a centre-left coalition for five years but it had been a mere spectator in the field of television broadcasting and had allowed Canale 5, Italia 1 and Retequattro to continue unscathed within Mediaset. Fininvest and Berlusconi still owned just under one half of the company and he had used it relentlessly to promote his political ends.

BACK IN POWER

Slick marketing paid off. A glib and consummate salesman, Silvio Berlusconi captured many Italian hearts, minds and votes when he signed a mock contract with his fellow citizens. An election campaign was reaching its climax in spring 2001 when Berlusconi, the leader of the opposition, flourished his pen and put it to that contract in front of millions of television viewers. It was drawn up on lined, wide-margined paper, just like that used by Italian lawyers and notaries for their legal documents, and on it Silvio Berlusconi, 'leader of Forza Italia and the Casa delle Liberta [House of Freedoms, as Berlusconi called his coalition], acting in full agreement with all the coalition's allies', made a commitment. Should his coalition win the election, it would achieve five aims during the next five years.[69]

Taxes would be drastically cut, said Berlusconi. Incomes of less than 22 million lire (then about £7,000 or $11,000) would be exempt, the rate on incomes up to 200 million lire would be slashed to 23 per cent, while incomes above that figure would be taxed at a modest 33 per cent. Gift and inheritance taxes would be abolished. Italy's monthly minimum pension would rise to 1 million lire (about £320 or $500). Under the Casa delle Liberta, its leader confidently claimed, the unemployment rate would be halved and at least 1.5 million new jobs created. Concrete would be poured as legislation and administrative efficiency opened building sites in a massive programme of public works. Italians would feel and be safer; Berlusconi's contract assured them that crime would fall sharply.[70]

Such were the rosy prospects for the *bel paese* under the right-wing coalition that Berlusconi promised during a popular chat-show on RAI 1, the main state television channel. He enjoyed several advantages over his centre-left opponent, Francesco Rutelli, particularly in his access to channels of communication with the electorate. The face of Forza Italia's leader, Italy's richest man, seemed everywhere, beaming and promising from roadside posters across the country. Occasionally Rutelli's photogenic features popped up, but hoardings carrying his face were far outnumbered by those of Berlusconi.

The imbalance in media power had the greatest impact, however, in the election campaigns on Italy's television channels. There RAI and Mediaset, Berlusconi's own television company, both with three channels, dominated the market with shares of around 45 per cent each. During the two-month run-up to the election, Mediaset was heavily biased towards its owner. Broadcasting monitors in Pavia and Rome that kept a close eye on which politicians appeared on television, and measured how much time each was given to explain his programme, found that Mediaset's channels splurged over 1,400 minutes of air-time on Berlusconi, compared with the less than 900 minutes that Rutelli was allowed to put his case across. Unsurprisingly, during the five years from 1996 to 2001 when the centre-left coalition governed Italy, they had already been busy in their owner's cause. Yet, even the state television company favoured the opposition candidate over the government's man. Between 10 March and 11 May 2001, RAI's channels gave Berlusconi 465 minutes, an advantage of 5 per cent over Rutelli. Moreover, Berlusconi's allies enjoyed far more time on state television than did those of Rutelli.[71] In Italy's parliamentary election, there was an unequal contest on the television sets in the country's living rooms and kitchens.

Despite all this, the centre-left mainly had itself to blame for being beaten at the polls on 13 May 2001. During five years of prudent economic management, centre-left administrations had cut inflation from 4 per cent to 2.7 per cent and knocked the country's parlous public-sector accounts into shape, slimming the budget deficit from 7 per cent to under 2 per cent. Above all, they had deftly managed the lira's entry into the euro, Europe's single currency, an enormous and unexpected success that disproved many predictions that Italy was not ready for such a big step. Yet they had failed to capitalize on these solid achievements. Another reason why the centre-left was defeated lay in its incomprehensible failure while in office to enact legislation on television broadcasting aimed at preventing bias and manipulation, trimming Berlusconi's huge unfair advantage and tackling the gross conflict of interest in which his media empire entangled him. Moreover, thanks to the personal vanities of its leaders and their readiness to stab each other in the back, the centre-left presented a divided front that contrasted sharply with the cohesion that helped Berlusconi's coalition to victory. They seemed to seek defeat.

Indeed, when the votes were counted, Berlusconi's House of

Freedoms had won just under 46 per cent of the vote for the lower house of parliament against just under 44 per cent for the Ulivo (Olive Tree) in the first-past-the-post system. For the upper house, the voters gave Berlusconi's right-wing coalition an advantage of more than 3 percentage points over Rutelli's centre-left. The voting figures, however, obscured a far heavier defeat for the centre-left in parliament. Italy's complex electoral system, combining first-past-the-post with proportional representation, awarded Berlusconi and his allies a total of 368 seats in the lower house. The Ulivo won only 247. The election's outcome was equally harsh on the centre-left in the upper house, where it could call on just 128 senators against the 176 who packed the benches on the government's side.[72] After being out of power for six years, Berlusconi was back in grand style, with an apparently impregnable parliamentary majority.

In June he made his first speech to the new parliament in Rome and spoke about respect for the rules and of a tradition shared and accepted by all Italians. In the programme that Forza Italia had offered the electorate in its campaign in spring 2001, Berlusconi's party had affirmed a commitment to protect human and civil rights. Now he told the lower chamber, 'We are here to attempt a second great work of modernization of our extraordinary country.'[73]

BLOODSHED IN GENOA

Genoa, on Italy's northwest coast, was a city of bankers and merchants in the Middle Ages. It had enjoyed a glorious era as a maritime republic between the eleventh and fourteenth centuries and, following a period in decline, had returned to independence and prominence in the early sixteenth century, dominating the Tyrrhenian Sea and extending its influence to North Africa, the Aegean, the Crimea and Syria. For Silvio Berlusconi, freshly returned to power and again Italy's prime minister, the city of Genoa presented a grand opportunity just one month after he had taken office to show the world that he was back in political business and again in charge of Italy. In Genoa in July 2001 Italy was to host a meeting of the G8 group of the world's seven great economic powers plus Russia.

Berlusconi took a personal interest in the city's appearance. It had to look good for George W. Bush, Vladimir Putin and the Italian prime minister's other powerful guests. Genoa had the grubby charm that went with container depots, huge oil tanks, high-rise social housing and elevated highways cutting through the city's heart. Like the citizens of Naples, Palermo and other ports around the Mediterranean, people in Genoa hung their washing on lines strung between windows and balconies, so the dreary apartment blocks above the city and the rundown buildings close to the old centre of town were usually decorated with assorted bed linen, shirts and underwear of all colours and sizes. Drying washing was an eyesore, however, and clashed with Berlusconi's notions of smartness and public order, and even perhaps risked raising contemptuous comments from the visitors. Genoa's citizens would be encouraged to keep their washing indoors until the visitors had left.

Italy's prime minister did not leave matters to chance and paid special attention to his guests, always careful about detail and alert to the personal touch. He had been scrupulous about this when he was a captain of industry. The Christmas dinner that he held at Arcore on 23 December of every year for his group's most important managers and their wives was one such example of Berlusconi's meticulous ways. 'I personally dealt with the purchase of jewellery for each *signora*, with an attention that came from my perfectionist character. With help from a computer, over the years I gave the ear-rings, the bracelet, the necklace and the brooch, avoiding repetition and choosing the type of jewellery to build up a complete set,' Berlusconi recounted to a court in Milan.[74]

As with jewellery for his managers' wives in Arcore, so in Genoa, where security had to be very tight to ensure that his guests were safe, attention to detail was paramount. Anti-globalization activists would not be allowed to wreck the show that Berlusconi wanted to choreograph for the world's leaders. At least, that was the plan. If the plan also aimed for a peaceful event, however, it failed badly. Berlusconi, the other politicians and their regiments of advisers and bag-carriers were stuck in a tightly guarded ghetto while the city became off-limits as Italy's police forces flexed their muscles and ran amok, filling the air with tear gas, wielding batons, cracking skulls and shedding blood.

There had been trouble with demonstrators earlier in the year in Naples at a global forum on the encouragement of democracy and development through the internet, when the centre-left predecessor to Berlusconi's right-wing government was in office. On 27 April, two weeks before Berlusconi won the elections that would take him to power, Amnesty International had written to Enzo Bianco, the internal affairs minister in the centre-left government, about the use of excessive force by law officers in Naples.

Independent of any government, political persuasion or religious creed, Amnesty International did not support or oppose any government or political system. It was and is concerned only with the impartial protection of human rights, neither supporting nor opposing the views of victims. It had written to Bianco to ask for an independent commission of inquiry into police tactics and behaviour in Naples. Investigations needed to be prompt, thorough and impartial because only that way could the reputations of law enforcement officers subject to unfounded accusations be protected and the interests of genuine victims of ill-treatment be safeguarded.

Well-documented allegations offered a disturbing picture of widespread abuses and violations of international human rights in Naples by members of the state police, *carabinieri* military police and the Guardia di Finanza. A video used as evidence against a man charged with violently resisting police officers 'records him lying on the ground while *carabinieri* officers kick him and inflict blows to his head and body using a truncheon and rifle butt,' said Amnesty International's letter to Bianco.[75] A doctor reported that his son and daughter were among a group of young people who had been gratuitously assaulted. His daughter had tried to lodge a complaint with the police. 'However, she was detained along with others from the group who were also trying to make a complaint, and transferred to a police station where they were, inter alia, strip-searched and photographed,' said the letter. The victims of brutality by Italy's law enforcers apparently included schoolchildren, the elderly, the physically disabled and journalists who were covering the events.

On 10 July 2001, Amnesty International wrote to Claudio Scajola, Bianco's successor at the internal affairs ministry. The organization expressed disappointment at Bianco's reply refusing to set up an independent commission to undertake a comprehensive investigation into what had happened in Naples in March. It also raised questions about allegations of use of excessive force by police on 6 July when a ship left Naples for Genoa, where it was to be used as an accommodation vessel for the G8 summit. Again there had been accusations of gratuitous police violence. Amnesty International sought confirmation that Scajola had opened an administrative investigation into the incidents in the port of Naples.

Concerns mounted about what might happen to innocent demonstrators and passers-by in Genoa. Amnesty International urged Berlusconi's government to ensure that law enforcement officers in the city would exercise maximum self-restraint in dealing with demonstrators, that they should be aware of and act at all times in accordance with international human rights and standards. These included the right to freedom of expression, to free assembly and not to be subject to arbitrary arrest or detention. The rights of those held in police custody should also be respected.

Those concerns and reminders about policing in a democracy went unheeded. The G8 summit Berlusconi hosted in Genoa turned out a bloody fiasco. On 31 July, Amnesty International wrote to Berlusconi, drawing his attention to its letter to Scajola. It had received numerous reports and allegations of the violation of human rights in Genoa. The list was long: forcible deportation, gratuitous violence, indiscriminate assaults, arbitrary and illegal arrest, verbal abuse, threats of an obscene sexual nature, deprivation of food, water and sleep, threats of death and rape, and denial of access to lawyers and consular officials.

Newspaper pictures and reports and television news footage showing police apparently out of control and on the rampage gave credibility to the accusations. An absence of badges made it difficult to identify the Italian law enforcement officers who might have been involved. In its letter to Berlusconi, Amnesty International expressed its deep concern about the conduct of law enforcement and prison officers in Genoa, and about the circumstances in which a demonstrator was fatally shot by a twenty-year-old *carabiniere* who was doing his obligatory military service in that force.

'Maltreatment and torture is not a new problem in Italy,' said

Marco Bertotto, chairman of Amnesty International's Italian section, speaking one year after the violence.[76] By this time, Amnesty International was no longer referring to allegations or accusations but to a dramatic series of human rights violations in Genoa. Neither Berlusconi nor his interior minister had replied to Amnesty International's letters of 10 and 31 July 2001 but there were well-documented reports of aggression by agents of the forces of order against non-violent demonstrators and against journalists and health workers clearly identified as such. The large number of victims and the level of force used on demonstrators was one reason for public concern, another was the planting of false evidence to justify the aggression by the police forces.

Almost two years after the summit, magistrates in Genoa closed the cases that had been opened against demonstrators for resisting arrest. The violence had been the other way. There had been acts of gratuitous brutality by the police forces against peaceful demonstrators, concluded magistrates in September 2003, after their investigations of police suspected of that brutality.[77] Yet, Berlusconi's government gave no sign of regret that it had grossly mishandled the summit, or that the violence the police forces meted out was shameful and to be expected in a fascist dictatorship rather than a major western democracy. Many foreigners who were aware of Italians' shared and accepted traditions and the protection of human rights about which Berlusconi and his Forza Italia party had bragged, returned home from Genoa bemused and wondering why Italy called itself the *bel paese*. In Genoa, and in how they dealt with its aftermath, Berlusconi's government showed the world that Italy had another, ugly, side and that the government itself was in fact indifferent to human rights.

ON THE WORLD STAGE

Yet, the poor impression of Italy and its right-wing government that the violence in Genoa made on many foreigners did not deter Berlusconi from travelling abroad; indeed his enthusiasm for foreign affairs was quite undampened. Meeting the leaders of other countries gave him the chance to escape some of the drudgery and criticism that went with his government's attempts to tackle pressing problems at home such as the economy and labour reform. He enjoyed being in the international spotlight and presenting himself to Italians as an important figure in global politics.

When he formed his government after the elections in May 2001, he had appointed Renato Ruggiero as foreign minister. An internationally well-known retired career diplomat, Ruggiero had held a senior position with the European Union in Brussels, been a trade minister in Rome and headed the World Trade Organisation. He possessed the right credentials to strengthen the administration that Berlusconi had put together, bringing experience, gravitas and genuine skill to the foreign minister's job, and his appointment had been supported by Italy's president who was anxious to see Italy well represented abroad.

However, Ruggiero was a technocrat, without the party affiliations of the rest of the cabinet, and he was on a different wavelength from a government in which some members were deeply sceptical about the European Union and others had various extremist political leanings. Moreover, Italy's prime minister preferred to shine in person rather than in the reflected light of others. So at the beginning of January 2002 Ruggiero was forced out, and Berlusconi stepped promptly in, adding the foreign minister's portfolio to that of prime minister. The glad-handing effusiveness that he took to the summits of heads of governments would now be deployed in foreign ministers' meetings as well.

Italians were told that Berlusconi would carry this double burden only for a short time, just long enough to shake up the ministry. Italian diplomats would learn from a successful businessman how to carry out their business in a businesslike way; those tasked with selling Italy would learn a trick or two about how real salesmen did their jobs. Italy's representatives abroad would have to proffer hands that were firmly dry, and definitely not sweaty, and they would have to keep garlic from their plates and off their breath – garlic was a particular aversion of Berlusconi.[78]

The months passed and at the beginning of July 2002 Berlusconi said that he would leave the foreign minister's job by the end of that month.[79] Eventually, in mid-November, he named his successor. Meanwhile, he had travelled the international stage for almost a year in his dual role, including a visit to Tripoli in October to meet Muammar Gadaffy. 'You are a real super-professional,' said Berlusconi, admitting that he was an amateur compared with the Libyan dictator.[80]

Improvisation stamped the prime minister's efforts as a statesman. He had been in Moscow to meet Vladimir Putin, Russia's president, shortly before visiting Libya. In the Russian capital, Berlusconi had gone along with Putin's views on Saddam Hussein, the Iraqi leader. 'Nobody can have the aim of regime change. International law does not allow it,' said Berlusconi. As for the role of the United Nations in dealing with the crisis in Iraq, he said that there was 'no alternative to two resolutions, given the position of China, France and Russia'.[81] Yet, one month earlier as the guest of George W. Bush at Camp David, Berlusconi had expressed a different view. 'A second resolution of the Security Council as France asks would be a nonsense,' he had affirmed.[82] Italy was a loyal and faithful ally of the United States; Berlusconi and Bush had been in full agreement on Iraq. 'Today with Putin because we are in Moscow, yesterday with Bush because the doors to the woody retreat of Camp David had been opened,' commented Italy's daily business newspaper.[83] Berlusconi tried to have a foot in every camp and keep everyone happy but it was an impossible exercise.

Led by the ever-smiling Silvio Berlusconi, Italy was an erratic ally. Soon after he had backtracked on Iraq in Moscow, a meeting in November in Prague of the Euro-Atlantic Partnership Council, which brought together the members of Nato and other non-Nato European countries, provided another reminder of Italian fickleness. Leonid Kuchma, the Ukrainian president, had gatecrashed a Nato dinner in the Czech capital the day before. He was an unwelcome visitor to this gathering because Ukraine was suspected of having sold high-performance anti-aircraft radar to Iraq. To avoid the embarrassment of seating Kuchma next to the United Kingdom's prime minister, Tony Blair, and just one place from the president of the United States of America, French was the language used for the seating plan. The United Kingdom was called Royaume Uni and the USA was called

Etats Unis – and Ukraine was nowhere near either of them.[84] Kuchma was not wanted but Berlusconi met cordially with him in Prague and invited him to visit Rome the following week.

Italy lacked that firmness of political purpose that allies sought in each other. Membership of Nato had been a pillar of the country's foreign and defence policy for decades and this continued under Berlusconi. Yet, Italy was a second-division power militarily; many Italians were and are glad about this. Mussolini's adventures and braggadocio had left a national legacy of doubt about armies and navies and helped to build a strong pacifist constituency. Moreover, the Roman Catholic Church's teaching and the pope's weekly exhortations for the peaceful resolution of disputes were listened to.

Colourful banners supporting the peace movement adorned countless windows and balconies up and down the country, and 2 million people poured into Rome in February 2003 to demonstrate against the use of force in Iraq. Opinion polls showed that about three quarters of Italians opposed military intervention there.[85] A hawk, Italy's prime minister was out of tune with his country on the use of force but, despite his posturing, Italy did not send troops to fight alongside the American and British soldiers who invaded Iraq. Berlusconi attacked the people and the parties of the centre-left who opposed military action. 'It is hard to stomach the fact that the flags of peace are often outnumbered by red flags representing anything other than tolerance, respect for human rights, democracy and peace,' he said.[86] Somebody had suggested that communism's flags were red, he said, because they were marked by the blood of 100 million innocent victims. 'Flying them alongside the flags of peace really is a curse on peace,' said Berlusconi.[87]

Article 11 of the constitution states, 'Italy repudiates war, an offence to the freedom of other people, as a means of resolving international controversies.' Perhaps the words of Italy's president to remind him of this in mid-March 2003 and the huge swell of anti-war sentiment among Italians dissuaded him from leaping to America's side. War and militarism did not win votes in Italy and domestic politics played a part in keeping Italian soldiers out of the invasion of Iraq. Berlusconi had been astute; he could win points by his posturing beside Bush, safe in the knowledge that Italian troops would not be involved. Sadly, after Bush had declared fighting in Iraq to be over and Italy had sent forces on a peace-keeping mission, nineteen Italian lives were lost in November 2003 when a suicide bomber crashed a lorry into a base that the *carabinieri* military police had set up in Nassiriyah.

Though a major economic force – one of Europe's four biggest economies – and a member of the G8, Italy spent reluctantly on defence. The *Libro Bianco* (White Book) presented by Berlusconi's defence minister at the end of 2001, the first such broad-ranging review since 1985, revealed how much Italian defence spending lagged behind that of its partners. Defence would cost about 1 per cent of Italy's gross domestic product in 2002. Britain by contrast spent 2.5 per cent of its GDP on defence and America much more, around 4 per cent; even Germany outdid Italy.[88] Nevertheless, both before Berlusconi won power and after, Italian forces performed creditably in operations in different parts of the world. They had been involved in the First Gulf War and in peace-keeping in Lebanon. At the end of 2002, Italy had more than 7,000 soldiers serving in the Balkans and Italian troops were part of a United Nations' mission in Ethiopia and Eritrea. The defence minister told a parliamentary commission in December 2002 that an Italian contingent of about 1,000 soldiers was planned for operations in Afghanistan.

Italy's armed forces were put at a serious disadvantage by the modest resources within which they had to operate; its air force's contribution to Nato included the long-obsolete F-104 Starfighter.[89] Although Berlusconi appeared eager to play a central figure on the global stage, Italy could not transfer its economic weight into the foreign-policy ring without massive investment in defence. Belt-tightening and budget difficulties meant, however, that the funds that might have given Italy a louder voice were not available. Berlusconi was not backed by an arsenal fitting for someone of his ambitions.

BERLUSCONI'S EU PRESIDENCY

Defence was, however, only one factor that defined how Italy was seen beyond its borders. A large part of the western world's media was critical of Berlusconi both before and after he won power: his legal problems were well known; his extensive television and publishing interests created a huge conflict of interest that he had never seemed inclined to resolve; his government was responsible for bespoke laws to tackle his legal problems and help his business empire; and his attacks on the magistrature were self-serving and aimed at undermining Italy's criminal justice system. Many foreign observers found the political ties that Berlusconi had formed with the post-fascist National Alliance and the xenophobic Northern League hard to digest. Some thought that he was unfit to govern Italy and, when Italy took over the presidency of the European Union in July 2003, believed that he was unfit to lead Europe.[90]

Some thought Berlusconi was gaffe-prone, others that he just wanted to show he was above the rules of diplomatic etiquette and that protocol did not apply to him; yet others felt that his down-to-earth vulgarity merely revealed that he had a sympathetic, human touch. His sally in the European Parliament in Strasbourg at the beginning of the Italian presidency was too much for many, however. Members of the European Parliament were flabbergasted when the Italian prime minister likened Martin Schulz, a German social-democrat member, to a Nazi concentration camp guard.[91] Such a comment coming from the mouth of the prime minister of the country that gave the world fascism – a politician whose allies included the heirs to those very fascists – seemed outrageous, at the very least. Berlusconi had committed more than a gaffe; he had been deeply and gratuitously offensive and confirmed the fears about his suitability as a leader.[92] An apology was demanded but refused.[93] And when Germany's chancellor Gerhard Schroeder decided to cancel a three-week holiday in Italy, Berlusconi said that he was sorry for him.[94]

Italy's presidency of the European Union got off to a bad start with the diplomatic incident in Strasbourg. It got worse when Berlusconi hosted Vladimir Putin in Rome in November 2003 and neglected to present the European Union's position on Chechnya to the Russian leader. Berlusconi intervened at a press conference when a French journalist asked the Russian leader about the violation of human rights in Chechnya. Putin had been slandered, said Berlusconi, and was the victim of media misinformation. The truth, claimed

Berlusconi, was that there were realities both in Italy and outside that were often distorted by the press.[95] Chechnya and the affair of a Russian businessman who had been arrested at Putin's behest were such cases. The governments of Italy's European partners were furious: the European Union's grave concern about Chechnya and that businessman had been clearly spelt out but Berlusconi had not expressed it.[96] His failure to present Putin with the EU's position drew criticism from the commission in Brussels. EU foreign ministers complained to their Italian counterpart about Berlusconi's behaviour and the European Parliament voted a motion of censure. The plutocratic Italian politician who had made his name as a businessman preferred to curry favour with a Russian leader who had made his mark as a successful operative in the secret service of a communist state.

Italian centrist members of the European Parliament were dismayed by the shame that Berlusconi had brought on the country during his presidency of the European Union's council of ministers. At a summit of the European Union's leaders in Brussels in December 2003, when attempts to reach agreement on a constitution ground to a halt, he had tried to break the ice with some light-hearted banter. 'Gerhard, you have experience with wives, give us some advice on how to treat women,' Berlusconi said to the four-times-married German chancellor.[97] Just over a year earlier, at a press conference in Rome with Denmark's prime minister, Anders Fogh Rasmussen, he had joked about rumours of his wife's relationship with a former mayor of Venice, Massimo Cacciari, a bearded philosophy professor. 'Rasmussen is the most handsome prime minister in Europe. I am thinking of introducing him to my wife because he is even more handsome than Cacciari.'[98]

But it was not just the gaffes that did the damage. Berlusconi was a failure as a manager. He had simply failed to organize the Italian term, said Mario Segni, and had not prepared a fall-back position in the event of failure to win an accord on a European constitution. A former Christian Democrat politician with whom Berlusconi had spoken about a possible alliance ten years before, Segni wondered why the Italian prime minister had not realized that he would have great difficulty in reaching such an accord.[99] Ciriaco De Mita, a former Christian Democrat prime minister and once head of his party, was scathing about Berlusconi's ability as a politician. Based on broad smiles, firm handshakes and hearty embraces, Berlusconi's approach could only work where he alone took the decisions and was able to impose his will. 'This approach was doomed to fail where his interlocutors had their own interests that were at stake,' observed De Mita.[100]

On 16 December 2003, with the end of the Italian presidency drawing close, Berlusconi was once again in Strasbourg for a session of the European Parliament, a moment for a review of performance and an inventory of the results of the Italian presidency. If the previous six months had had any redeeming features, however, few could find them. When a visibly tense Italian prime minister walked into a crowded press room at around 12.40 p.m., the rigid smile into which he had clamped his jaws spoke clearly of the strain that he had been under during the morning's session in the parliament's chamber. Berlusconi had found himself under fire not just from members of parliament on the political left but also from centrist representatives. It was hard to escape the conclusion that the Italian presidency had been a personal failure, said Graham Watson, a British liberal democrat who headed the European liberal democrat group in Strasbourg.[101]

For someone accustomed to praise at home, and who described his six months of leading Europe as a success, such fierce public criticism and scorn abroad would have been a bruising and burning experience. During nine and a half years as a member of the parliament, the British politician had never experienced such a badly prepared presidency. 'Most presidencies present their programmes weeks before they are due to start,' said Watson, 'but Berlusconi's presidency had already begun when it presented its programme, and then only in Italian.'[102] Watson had met Berlusconi in Rome at the end of June, a few days before the Italian presidency was due to begin, and had been placed next to him at dinner. Affairs of state and the European presidency had seemed far from Berlusconi's mind that evening. 'At the beginning he kept insisting that all journalists and judges were hardline communists,' remembered Watson, 'and then he spent the rest of the evening telling jokes like an insurance salesman.'[103] Watson came away from the encounter thinking that the Italian prime minister might have been out of his depth.

The Italian presidency had highlighted Berlusconi's lack of diplomatic skills, noted Watson, and had wasted six months. 'Berlusconi failed to smooth over differences and find a compromise on the European constitution; he conspired to undermine the rules of the economic and stability pact that joins the countries who participate in the euro single currency rather than ensure respect for them; he gave great offence by cancelling an important meeting of the European Union with the Canadian government; he ignored values that Europeans hold dear,' said Watson.[104]

The British liberal democrat was not alone in his scathing verdict on the Italian presidency. Jill Evans, a Welsh member of the European Parliament, was very encouraged by the remarks of the Irish prime minister who took over the presidency from Berlusconi. 'The depth and breadth of Ireland's priorities for its leadership of the EU came as a breath of fresh air after the arrogance and bullying that characterized Berlusconi's approach to the job,' she said.[105] 'None of the other leaders blamed Mr Berlusconi in public, but among themselves many were fuming,' said a report on the BBC News.[106] That report quoted Chris Patten, the EU's external affairs commissioner, who had described the Brussels summit as 'a fiasco but not a disaster'.

Yet, foreign politicians had put aside their scruples when dealing with Berlusconi's government, particularly in the wake of the terrorist attacks by al-Qaeda in America on 11 September 2001. Any ally was welcome, whatever doubts were harboured about political or other credentials. If George W. Bush felt anything about Berlusconi, perhaps it was the affinity of one businessman for another and for the way that, like Bush himself, Berlusconi had surrounded himself with cronies. That two right-wing leaders should hit it off was understandable, but that Tony Blair, Britain's Labour prime minister, was on close and cordial terms with Berlusconi raised eyebrows among democrats in Britain who wondered how it was possible that a centre-left leader could be so cosy with someone so patently far to the right. Writing in the *Guardian*, Martin Jacques, a visting fellow at the London School of Economics, said of Berlusconi, 'He is not just another right-wing politician; he represents the greatest challenge to democracy anywhere in Europe.'[107]

Perhaps Blair, with his freakish need to control, saw something to admire in Berlusconi's tight grip on the Italian media. Robin Cook, the foreign minister in Blair's first administration, certainly thought that Berlusconi was 'a curious partner for a leader of the Labour Party who had shot to prominence on the commitment to be tough on crime'.[108] There were others like Cook. One was Anna Lindh, Sweden's foreign minister, who was murdered in September 2003. She had been outspoken in her criticism of Berlusconi and thought that members of the European Parliament had a right to ask critical questions without being treated in the way that Berlusconi had treated Schulz. 'If we had an elected chairman of the European Council, we would not have had Mr Berlusconi as chairman,' she said.[109] But realpolitik had become paramount, and Berlusconi's ministers were not ostracized in foreign capitals, despite the words and actions of Berlusconi's governing coalition.

As well as the few foreign politicians who were willing to express their concern, there were groups of people outside Italy who were unwilling to forget the sinister alliance that Berlusconi had gladly forged with Mussolini's heirs in 1994 and continued ever since. When Gianfranco Fini, the National Alliance's leader and Berlusconi's deputy as prime minister, travelled to Britain, the British Anti-Nazi League protested at his presence. But even Fini, sitting beside Berlusconi in Strasbourg, had looked shocked when he attacked Schulz.

AT THE EXTREME RIGHT

Forza Nuova (New Force), an extremist party headed by Roberto Fiore and even further to the right of the political spectrum than the National Alliance, was founded in September 1997. Fini and the National Alliance were sometimes actually the target of Forza Nuova, a party that claimed to be the only force that fought for fatherland, family and the social state. At their meetings, members of the Forza Nuova raised their right arms in the fascist salute. They also shouted the words that had rung across Italy's *piazze* during the two black decades of fascism: *Duce! Duce!* One evening, they gathered in Piazza Santi Apostoli in central Rome, barely 100 yards from Piazza

Venezia, and the palace where Mussolini had his offices and from whose balcony he had harangued the crowds beneath. Mario Borghezio was on the platform that evening to address the Forza Nuova rally. Borghezio was a member of parliament of the xenophobic and secessionist Northern League, a partner in Berlusconi's governing coalition to which the prime minister had allocated three ministerial posts. The Northern League used racism to catch votes. 'I do not tolerate this attempt of globalization to bastardize our blood,' said Borghezio.[110] The Northern League wanted the government to tackle clandestine immigration with an iron fist.

To the delight of the political right, the Northern League's leader, Umberto Bossi, and Gianfranco Fini had drafted a law that aimed to hit immigrants hard. The Bossi–Fini Law went some way to appease the Forza Nuova. The two politicians and their followers wanted to forget that Italy, as recently as the 1970s, had itself been a nation of economic migrants who, shabbily dressed and loaded down with string-tied cartons, packed the trains that headed north towards Germany, Switzerland and jobs.

Supporters of racial intolerance were encouraged by Berlusconi's government. Probably, few members of the racist Forza Nuova knew that soldiers from Asia and Africa serving with the allied armies during the Second World War had played an important part in liberating Italy from Nazi-Fascism, and had fought valiantly beside Italian soldiers in the tremendous battles in the spring of 1944 around Monte Cassino. It was, moreover, the French North African soldiers who had swung the battle on the Germans' defensive Gustav line. There were two Moroccan divisions and one Algerian in the four-division-strong French Expeditionary Corps. The Moroccans were Goums, hardy mountain fighters. It was these troops who advanced spectacularly across the roadless Aurunci mountains that the defenders had thought impassable.[111] By the end of the war, there were 300,000 Moroccans in the French army. Just south of Cassino, outside the town of Venafro, a French military cemetery held the graves of more than 3,000 soldiers, many Muslim, who helped to free Italy from Nazi-Fascist dictatorship, and the political and religious persecution that went with it.

Berlusconi had his own ideas about Islam. 'The west must be

aware of the superiority of its civilization,' he said.[112] Western civilization, he added, had given rise to widespread wellbeing and respect for human, religious and political rights that did not exist in Islamic countries. 'The west is bound to continue conquering other people as it has conquered the communist world and a part of Islam,' he told journalists in Berlin at the end of September 2001.[113] When other western leaders were trying to avoid inflaming relations between religions and civilizations, Italy's prime minister had made his thoughts clear. He later said that he had been misinterpreted,[114] but misinterpretation by the media was Berlusconi's excuse for his gaffes on other occasions also.

Guy Verhofstadt, Belgium's prime minister, who held the European Union's rotating presidency at the time, said, 'I cannot believe that he said such derogatory things about Islam.' Louis Michel, Belgium's foreign minister, who was leading a European delegation in Cairo, described Berlusconi's words as 'unacceptable'.[115]

A FALTERING ECONOMY

As his second administration moved into its third year, in the spring of 2003, Berlusconi continued to be caught up in the whirl of foreign affairs and was still kept busy with bespoke legislation that seemed to aim at resolving the legal difficulties that beset him and Cesare Previti. Indeed the problems of the economy had taken second place to those other matters. In 2002, Italy's gross domestic product grew by only 0.4 per cent which was less than half the average for the euro-zone and less than a quarter of Britain's growth. A similarly disappointing result marked 2003. Industrial output actually fell by 1.4 per cent in 2002 and the figure for 2003 looked equally poor. Moreover, Italy's unemployment stuck stubbornly around 9 per cent in the three years 2001 to 2003.[116] The Italian economy was in trouble but the government in Rome had other things on its mind.

Italy had been fortunate to squeeze the lira into the euro as its stock of public-sector debt was almost double the 60 per cent of gross domestic product that had been set as the ceiling for a currency to qualify for membership of Europe's single currency. Prudent financial management by the centre-left government between 1996 and 2001 had, however, convinced Italy's partners to relax the rules and allow the lira in. But these improvements came to a halt under Berlusconi and the politician who had been so successful as a businessman was unable to work his magic on the state's accounts.

In April 2001, Italy's richest man had promised Italians lower taxes on families, work and business, and that less bureaucracy and less waste of public funds would give rise to higher growth, more jobs and more resources for investment. Yet, the budgets that Berlusconi's government presented satisfied few people, and even Confindustria, the employers' confederation that was once a firm ally of Berlusconi, turned against him. Up and down Italy, mayors and regional authorities of all parties squealed as they had to bear heavy cuts in public spending.[117] These meant Italians would have to pay higher charges for local transport, refuse collection, health services and medicines.

When Berlusconi became prime minister in 2001, he and his economic team said they were looking forward to annual economic growth of 3 per cent. Against all the signs that this was a vain expectation, the government was persistently optimistic but two years later was finally forced to admit that economic growth would be well below 1 per cent. This lower figure had serious implications for the budget deficit and public-sector debt. The public-sector borrowing requirement had been 1.7 per cent in 1999 and 1.8 per cent in the following year but in 2001, after Berlusconi took over the country's economic management, it increased to 2.6 per cent. While it fell to 2.3 per cent in 2002, [118] Berlusconi's government had been compelled to adopt one-off measures such as tax and foreign exchange amnesties to achieve this modest result. Moreover, the challenge of balancing the state's books would continue to weigh heavily.

Berlusconi also failed to get to grips with Italy's generous and expensive state pension system when he returned to power. The cost of pensions was becoming unsustainable, absorbing almost 15 per cent of Italy's GDP, but trimming benefits would be bound to be unpopular and lose votes. The government headed by Dini between 1995 and 1996 had made changes to the pension system and the effect of these was due to be reviewed after five years in 2001, just when Berlusconi won the parliamentary elections.[119] There was a way around this conundrum, he thought. He declared that state pensions were a European problem which meant that a solution had to be found and imposed by the European Union.[120] If the European Union set the rules, Berlusconi could pass the buck and dodge the anger of discontented Italians.

Although he claimed to be a market-liberal, Berlusconi's economic philosophy was closer to paternalistic intervention. After all, he had been a big beneficiary of a system in which highly placed political friends bestowed largesse on chums and their businesses. Legislation offering opportunities for personal gain would be enacted. Despite the prime minister's words, rolling back the frontiers of the state was not a priority and the programme of privatization came to a halt when Berlusconi won power.

Under Dini's administration and the centre-left governments that followed between 1996 and 2001, Italy overtook Britain as Europe's leading privatizer. ENI, the large oil, gas and chemicals group, was floated in autumn 1995 and the treasury ministry sold further tranches of its shares in 1996 and 1997. In autumn 1999, Italy achieved the world's largest-ever flotation when it sold shares in Enel, the giant electricity corporation, and raised revenues of about 18 billion euros.[121] Privatization took toll highways, banks, airports and telecommunications out of the state's hands and into private ownership, raising about 155,000 billion lire (about 78 billion euros) between 1996 and 2000.[122] Before winning the elections in 2001, Berlusconi's coalition made a commitment. 'State-owned assets like Enel and ENI will definitely be sold completely and the state will give up control.'[123] Yet three years later the treasury ministry still kept a firm grip on these assets.

As in other spheres, so in Italy's economic management Berlusconi's character was on display. Problems would be overcome by optimism and a broad smile. He was someone who wanted to be liked so, however tough the problems, harsh remedies were out of the question. There was even speculation that the government would get involved with individual companies if they ran into difficulties. The National Alliance was strongly inclined towards intervention; it believed that certain industries and companies were strategic and the government should keep control of them. The Northern League was keen to lay its hands on private charitable foundations that owned important stakes in banks. Berlusconi's government had little real enthusiasm for the disciplines of the market.

DEALINGS WITH THE MEDIA

Those concerned about democracy in Italy were less worried about the government's industrial policy than its meddling with the media. The biggest cause of concern was Berlusconi himself who after winning power effectively added control of the two main channels of the state television's three channels to a media empire that already included the country's three large commercial channels and about 45 per cent of the national television audience. On becoming Italian prime minister again in 2001, Berlusconi seemed determined to take a much firmer hold over the 45 per cent or so of national television broadcasting that RAI represented than he had done when he was prime minister in 1994.

He definitely would not brook criticism from RAI. He had had a handful of annoying experiences that involved the television channels of the state broadcaster and was determined there should be no repeats. Early in 2001, Marco Travaglio, a journalist who had written a book about the origins of Berlusconi's fortune, was a guest on a satirical programme hosted by Daniele Luttazzi and they conjectured at length about Berlusconi's early years in business. Enzo Biagi, the 82-year-old doyen of Italian journalism, had invited Roberto Benigni to appear on his current affairs programme *Il Fatto* (The Fact) just before the parliamentary elections in 2001 and elicited a masterful performance from the film actor and director that raised smiles at Berlusconi's expense. Michele Santoro had hosted a current affairs programme named *Sciuscia* (shoe-shine, the call of Neapolitan urchins offering boot-shines to American servicemen after the Second World War) that had often dug embarrassingly deep into official and political business.

In April 2002, speaking at a press conference in Sofia, the Bulgarian capital, Berlusconi sent an aggressive open message that left no room for interpretation. He expected the management of RAI to deal with the three television journalists who presented the programmes in which he had been criticized. 'Paid with public money, the three journalists have made a criminal use of public television,' stated Berlusconi, 'and I believe that RAI's new management has a definite duty to stop that happening.'[124] Biagi expressed surprise that someone who had three television channels of his own, and declared and devoted friends in the other, state-owned, channels, did not already have sufficient means to defend himself. 'Does he not think that in democracy even the opponents, who do not have his resources, should have the opportunity to show their dissent?' asked Biagi.[125] Indeed, there were figures that supported Biagi's concern that Berlusconi had devoted friends in state television: RAI's television news programmes seemed biased in favour of government parties. On TG1, the news on RAI's first channel, they were given 70 per cent of the total 'voice time' allowed to politicians in 2003, against the 28 per cent allotted to parties of the opposition, while on TG2, the second channel's news services, government parties got 71 per cent and the opposition only 26 per cent. Only on TG3 was the total time shared equitably between government and opposition; 53 per cent for parties of the former and 44 per cent for parties belonging to the latter.[126]

The contracts of the three broadcasters were not renewed and Berlusconi had got his way at RAI, but not without causing an upheaval. Two directors resigned in protest against what they considered to be manipulation of news and current affairs programmes and a strategy of weakening RAI in order to favour Berlusconi's Mediaset business. Then calls by Carlo Azeglio Ciampi, Italy's president, for pluralism of information fell on deaf ears as the government drove legislation through parliament at the end of 2003 that aimed to entrench Mediaset more deeply and enrich the prime minister's media group still further. Urgently needed because Mediaset had to get round the constitutional court's requirement that Retequattro should cease terrestrial broadcasting before the year ended, a bill called the Legge Gasparri, after the minister responsible for it, was given priority. It passed through parliament in the autumn but Ciampi refused to sign it into law, referring it back to the government for changes. The bill failed to ensure that Italians would have a variety of sources for their news, noted Ciampi, and it risked creating a dominant position in television, threatened the advertising revenues that print media needed for survival and failed to set a suitable timetable for the shift from analogue to digital broadcasting. Whatever the reasons for Ciampi's doubts, Berlusconi was unconcerned. 'I have not read the observations and I will not read them,' he said about the document that Ciampi's experts had written to explain why the president had blocked the bill.[127] The president had referred back the Legge Gasparri, claimed Berlusconi, because he had been put under pressure by newspaper owners.[128]

After Ciampi's firm stand on 15 December, Mediaset's need became even more urgent. Something had to be done quickly to safeguard Retequattro and Berlusconi, the channel's owner, signed a decree just before Christmas that would keep it on the air. As for a conflict of interest, affirmed the Italian prime minister, such a notion was an invention.[129] However, while most Italians were unconcerned that the Legge Gasparri would allow Mediaset to broaden its advertising base and open the way for Berlusconi to expand in newspapers, elsewhere in Europe there was growing concern about the Italian tycoon's media power. 'Berlusconi does not follow the rules of democracy. Europe must not remain a spectator and must take steps to intervene through European-wide regulations,' said Graham Watson, leader of the liberal democrat group in the European Parliament.[130]

RAI was a fierce political battleground under Berlusconi, as it had been under earlier governments. Factions in his governing coalition fought each other over appointments at the state broadcaster and over how it should be organized. Italy's prime minister wanted to ensure that critical journalists and presenters within RAI would be firmly gagged. Such critics were, in any case, few in number, as most presenters and journalists at the state television service did their best to give the prime minister favourable coverage and his government an easy ride. Berlusconi had made plain what he expected; careful selectiveness in reporting of the news, bias and servility in interviews with government politicians became the watchwords.

Much news-reporting, in print as well as on television, became self-censored as the Italian media bent before the wind. Journalists working for leading Italian newspapers spoke of heavy pressure. Some Italians thought that their best hopes of news being fairly and fully reported lay with the foreign press and its attention to events in their country, even though Berlusconi's government leaned on foreign journalists as well.

Towards the end of 2002, Reporters without Borders, a public interest association established to defend press freedom and the right to information, published the first worldwide press freedom index. All the European Union's fifteen members scored well, except for Italy which was ranked fortieth and worse even than countries such as Costa Rica in fifteenth position and Benin in twenty-first place. Reporters without Borders considered that the best countries for press freedom were Finland, Iceland, The Netherlands, Norway and Denmark. Italy slipped to fifty-third place in 2003.

'Diversity of news is not guaranteed in Italy, the only major western democracy where most of the broadcasting media, both privately and publicly owned, are directly or indirectly in the hands of the government,' said the organization in its annual report on Italy in May 2003.[131] 'Numerous attacks on press freedom occurred during the year, especially the censorship of five TV programmes and the increasing number of searches of newspaper offices and journalists' homes on the pretext of fighting terrorism. Courts also contravened United Nations standards by sentencing two journalists to prison for media offences,' said the report. One week before the publication of this report, Reporters without Borders had published a special investigation into the conflict of interest triggered by Berlusconi's repeated meddling in the management of RAI and the dismissal of two journalists. 'Berlusconi's intervention in the appointment of the RAI's new board, regardless of the constitutional rules, and his vitriolic atacks on RAI journalists are inappropriate and unacceptable from someone in his position,' said the report of the investigation.[132]

Some Italians, worried about the threat to democracy that Berlusconi posed, thought that international pressure would help. But few believed that there would be a repeat of sanctions like those that the European Union imposed on Austria after Jorg Haider's extremist right-wing Freedom Party entered a ruling coalition in 2000. Yet the pressure on journalists who criticized the government was an ominous sign not just for Italy but for the whole of Europe. Promising legal action against a protester in the Milan court building who called him a *buffone* (clown) and shouted that the prime minister should be tried as any normal citizen, Berlusconi showed that he thought that the usual rules of politics in a democracy did not apply to him.[133] Being a target for heckling and verbal abuse is part of being a public figure but Berlusconi did not understand that. Less than a fortnight after the protest in Milan, members of the public in Bari heckled Berlusconi. He responded with another threat. 'In the past twenty days, wherever I've gone, there have been organized demonstrators shouting insults. This is not acceptable in a civilized country. I don't believe I'm illiberal, but if this climate does not stop I will issue legal proceedings against those who attack the institutional office I hold,' he said.[134] Berlusconi's reaction to criticism was in keeping with a vain and authoritarian streak and he could afford teams of lawyers to intimidate opponents into silence.

His past, clouded with opaque dealings and unanswered questions, should have warned Italians about how he might try to smother freedom of expression. He had, moreover, been a member of the secretive P2 masonic lodge which, as we have seen, had manoeuvred sinisterly to take effective control of *Corriere della Sera* at the beginning of the 1980s. The P2's *piano di rinascita democratica* (plan of democratic rebirth) was no such thing – it sought to control public opinion. It was perhaps no coincidence that Berlusconi wanted to bring *Corriere della Sera* into his empire and that in May 2003 the editor of the newspaper, whose reports of trials in which Berlusconi and Previti were defendants had increasingly been an irritant, resigned after being put under great pressure by government supporters.[135] Writing soon after the incident in the Milan court, Giuliana Quattromini, a Neapolitan lawyer, observed that journalists were in the front line for receiving writs. The threat of them discouraged criticism and the government counted on the effectiveness of such discouragement. 'These writs are becoming the rope on which Italian democracy will hang itself. The prime minister and his close allies have means of information, economic resources and platoons of lawyers in quantities that allow them to sue hundreds of people every day,' she said.[136] Where information could not be managed or the means of information bought, those involved in informing the public would be pressured into keeping in line. Berlusconi's money, media muscle and political power made an alarming combination.

5

Law

SAVE THE THIEVES

A successful businessman, Silvio Berlusconi had been clever at practical politics, but he had much to learn about the art of politics in government when he had his first taste of parliamentary power in May 1994. The leader of the right-wing coalition thought that he could do without the lessons of history when he tried to push through legislation that would have relaxed the law for people involved in crimes of corruption.

Just one year before Berlusconi won power, Giuliano Amato of the Socialist Party showed how plans could go badly awry even for an astute and experienced politician. Not for nothing was Amato, a member of parliament from 1983, treasury minister from 1987 to 1989 and prime minister between 1992 and 1993, known as *Dottor Sottile* (Doctor Subtle). He had studied constitutional law at the Law School of Columbia University in New York before teaching the subject at universities in Italy.[1] Yet, even a skilful operator like Amato was capable of serious misjudgement when it came to dealing with the vexed questions of graft and corrupt politicians, and of passing laws to tackle them.

Just before Christmas 1992, Bettino Craxi, the Socialist Party's leader, had been served with a notice that he was under investigation for various corruption-related crimes. Then, over the next three months, the government lost five ministers who found themselves caught in the investigators' relentless digging.[2] The pressure on Amato to find a way to fend off the magistrates and stop political heads from rolling increased sharply. Early in March 1993, as magistrates in

Milan dug deeper into the midden of *tangentopoli*, Amato and his minister of justice concocted a scheme that aimed at a political solution to the scandal.

Italy's president, Oscar Luigi Scalfaro, had put forward an idea that contained the kernel of what one of the *mani pulite* team had suggested in July 1992. Those who had been corrupt might be amnestied, said Scalfaro, provided they told the whole truth about their corrupt behaviour, gave back the money they had misappropriated and retired for good from public life. Scalfaro was adamant that there should be no place in public life for bent politicians and crooked businessmen but Amato and his cabinet turned a deaf ear. They saw things differently and drafted a package of decrees that decriminalized illegal political financing and downgraded it to an administrative offence. The package also allowed plea-bargaining for the crimes of bribery and extortion and enabled corrupt businessmen to avoid prison.

Italians, however, were not yet ready to forgive the good-for-little politicians and businessmen who had shamelessly colluded to raid the public purse and steal huge amounts of money. They were also angered by the claim of Amato and his minister of justice that the government had done no more than prepare decrees that would put into law what the team of magistrates of *mani pulite* wanted. The politicians had a brazen cheek to claim that the measures they had prepared enjoyed the magistrates' seal of approval. That was plainly untrue. Those decrees had not been asked for, wanted or approved by *mani pulite*, Francesco Saverio Borrelli, the team's head, fired back in an immediate riposte.[3] Amato had misread public feelings and mishandled the situation.

A technocratic administration comprising ministers with competence specific to their ministerial posts and having no declared allegiance to political parties took over in April 1993 after Amato's government resigned following a referendum on the electoral system, but it did not attempt to tackle the question of corruption. That was left to the government that followed, the administration formed by Berlusconi after parliamentary elections in March 1994. History offered a lesson but, just sixteen months later, the new prime minister ignored it. He had cleverly timed his legislation on corruption to coincide with the summer holidays and an international football championship, but even those distractions did not stop many Italians from loudly voicing their anger and opposition when Berlusconi and his minister of justice issued the decree that became known as the *salvaladri* (save the thieves) decree.

The *mani pulite* team in Milan understood immediately what the decree meant. Although it had to be ratified by parliament within sixty days in order to have the permanent effectiveness of law, the decree had become effective on 14 July, the very day that it was signed. Borrelli thought that it was ironic that the walls of San Vittore and Opera (two prisons in Milan) should have been breached on the anniversary of the storming of the Bastille in 1789.[4] The head of the anti-corruption team expressed surprise that the government seemed more concerned about damaging existing laws and procedures that allowed the magistrates to work efficiently and effectively than about introducing measures to tackle corruption. Borrelli's team were up in arms and one of them read a statement that evening on television saying that they had asked to be transferred from anti-corruption cases to other work; it was quite simply a matter of conscience for them. The *mani pulite* team was not alone in its indignation and hundreds of Milanese gathered outside the court building to protest against Berlusconi's decree and to support the magistrates.

Berlusconi would handle such matters very differently the next time he was in power. First, however, he would need a larger and more solid majority than the one that had failed to push through the *salvaladri* decree. He won such a majority in the elections in May 2001 which secured him a firm parliamentary base from which to launch an assault on the criminal code. But a firm parliamentary base alone was not enough. His laws had to be prepared by professionals and he needed to place the right people in the right parliamentary commissions. What better way for Berlusconi to organize this matter than by getting his own lawyers, who had amassed considerable experience through defending him in court on various charges of corruption and other white-collar crime, selected as candidates, elected to parliament and then appointed to those commissions? Stuffing parliamentary commissions with trusted legal counsel was an obvious strategy to ensure that laws on criminal justice could be tailored to personal needs.

A PARLIAMENTARY LEGAL TEAM

Forza Italia's thirteen representatives among the judicial affairs commission's membership of forty-four reflected its position as the largest party in parliament. One of them was Gaetano Pecorella. A criminal lawyer born in Milan in 1938, Pecorella had been chairman of the criminal bar association in his home city. His name was on the judgements of courts in Milan where he defended Berlusconi against charges of bribing judges. He entered parliament's lower house in June 1998 to replace a deputy who had resigned and, as a member of his client's Forza Italia party, was elected for a constituency in Milan in 2001, winning almost 55 per cent of the votes.[5] When parliament assembled, Pecorella became chairman of the lower house's second commission, the commission that dealt with justice.

Niccolo Ghedini was Pecorella's junior by over twenty years. Born in Padua, in northeast Italy, Ghedini was also a criminal lawyer. Like Pecorella, he too was defending Berlusconi in cases in Milan; again like Pecorella, he belonged to his client's political party. He had also stood for parliament in May 2001 and been elected for the Este constituency of the Veneto region, taking almost 48 per cent of the votes cast.[6] Alongside Pecorella on the bench in Milan courtrooms to defend Berlusconi against criminal charges, Ghedini found himself not simply Pecorella's parliamentary colleague in Forza Italia's ranks but also a member of the judicial affairs commission. Antonino Mormino, a criminal lawyer from Palermo who had made a reputation defending *mafiosi*, was another of Forza Italia's members on the commission.

Michele Saponara, a criminal lawyer who practised in Milan, was also a member of Forza Italia. He was elected to parliament in 1996 and re-elected in 2001 for Milanese constituencies. Saponara defended Berlusconi's friend Cesare Previti against charges of bribing judges and had led Forza Italia's representatives in the judicial affairs commission during the 13th legislature, from 1996 to 2001, when Berlusconi had been in opposition.[7] After re-election, he became Forza Italia's leader in the constitutional affairs commission, a key post for implementing Berlusconi's strategy, as the work of the constitutional affairs and judicial affairs commissions often went hand-in-hand. Saponara was also a member of the lower house's small legislation committee where the chairman was Enzo Trantino, a Sicilian lawyer involved in the defence of Marcello Dell'Utri, who had been on trial in Palermo since 1997, facing charges of association with the Mafia, a trial expected to end in autumn 2004.

There was some concern that a conflict of interest was created by the presence of these lawyers both in parliament and on key parliamentary commissions. Was it possible for them to be independent when drafting legislation and voting on it? And even if they were not involved and did not vote, their very presence in parliament and on parliamentary commissions meant that they exerted pressure. After all, they were defending the prime minister, who also happened to be the country's richest man, and two close friends of his against criminal charges, and as defence lawyers they had a duty to do whatever was best for their clients. That did not necessarily coincide with what was best for the country.

'In strictly legal terms,' said Franzo Grande Stevens, 'there is no conflict of interest.'[8] He thought that the lawyers' dual role was inopportune, however, and that ethical standards were jeopardized. It was strange that a lawyer defending Berlusconi knew that the minister of justice had decided to transfer a judge from the panel of three judges while the president of the panel and the prosecutors in the trial were themselves in the dark about that decision; the lawyer had then used that information to try to stop the trial from going ahead.[9] Moreover, defence lawyers who were members of parliament could use their own parliamentary duties as a reason to have hearings suspended or cancelled. The courts were powerless to deal with such behaviour. 'These lawyers went to parliament in the interests of a wealthy client, the prime minister, who pays them and got them elected,' said Grande Stevens.[10] The real issue, he believed, was that the lawyers sacrificed the public interest to that of the client. 'Certainly the behaviour of some lawyers gives the law a bad name,' he commented.[11]

There were lawyers who disliked the way that fellow members of the legal profession were using parliament to advance the causes of their clients, which obviously ran contrary to the principle that everyone should be equal before the law. But no law prohibited

Berlusconi's lawyers from behaving as they did; neither were they prevented by rules or standards. The incompatibility of the two roles – lawyer and member of parliament – badly damaged the profession's reputation, said Carlo Smuraglia, a leading jurist.[12] He thought that if self-regulation was ineffective and if lawyers were insensitive to the issue, legislation should be enacted to prevent the kind of situation into which Berlusconi and his lawyers had plunged parliament and the judicial system. Any such legislation would have to wait, however, until Berlusconi and his team of lawyers-turned-parliamentarians had completed their business and Berlusconi's right-wing alliance was no longer in power.

FALSE ACCOUNTING

A question facing the prime minister and his cabal of criminal lawyers in May 2001 was what priority to attach to the various legal issues they wanted parliament to tackle. They decided that false accounting would head the list, and at the end of September, less than three weeks after the terrorist attacks in America, they completed their first move. Berlusconi and his legal team had decided to scrap existing legislation on false accounting and replace it with a law that was far, far softer.

Pecorella was one of the two members of parliament who sponsored the law at the beginning of July. It passed rapidly through parliament and was published in the official gazette just three months later. The law radically altered what a company's directors could do without risking prison. False accounting was downgraded as a crime. The maximum penalty was lowered from five to four years' imprisonment where companies listed on the stock market were concerned and to three years for non-listed companies. Investigators would no longer be able to use telephone taps on people suspected of the crime. Moreover, the statute of limitations, the deadline before which those accused of false accounting had to be tried and sentenced, arrived much sooner under the new law than before. False accounting would become statute-barred after seven years in cases involving listed companies, rather than fifteen, and after just four and a half years in cases involving non-listed firms.[13]

The reason why Berlusconi and his lawyers were eager to down-grade the crime of false accounting was simple and clear. Narrowly, the prime minister had a strong personal interest: among the legal difficulties he had faced when he stood for election in May 2001 were charges of false accounting. Indeed, Italy's prime minister had been found guilty by a court of first instance in 1997 in a case concerning the purchase of Medusa, a film production company, in an operation that had allowed 10 billion lire of black funds to be generated. The sentence of sixteen months' imprisonment that was passed on Berlusconi, who had claimed not to have known about the illicit transaction, would later be overturned on appeal and the supreme court would subsequently confirm the acquittal by the appeal court.[14]

The outstanding cases in May 2001 concerned the purchase of a footballer by the AC Milan soccer club, Fininvest holding company, Fininvest group accounts and a subsidiary charge of false accounting in connection with the SME case.[15] As we have seen earlier, Berlusconi was acquitted in the case concerning the footballer because, after the enactment of the legislation on false accounting, the crime of which he was accused had become statute-barred. While the statute of limitations had also been applied by courts of first instance to acquit Berlusconi in the other outstanding cases, prosecutors had been given leave to appeal and the appeals were still awaited in spring 2004.

If Berlusconi's situation was helped by the changes in the statute of limitations, it may also have been improved by a change in how false accounting in non-listed firms could be legally pursued. Under the new law, magistrates could take action against directors only when shareholders or creditors laid complaints. Pursuing false accounting on the basis of complaints by shareholders would be like pursuing theft thanks to complaints by the thief, said one magistrate.[16] The law sponsored by Berlusconi's lawyer Pecorella also set quantitative hurdles below which false accounting would not be punishable. Directors would henceforth be able to falsify their companies' accounts by as much as 5 per cent of pre-tax profits or 10 per cent of net assets without putting themselves at risk.

Looked at more broadly, much of the work of the *mani pulite* magistrates in Milan was triggered by their investigation of this crime. False accounting had been the key with which the anti-corruption team had been able to unlock many of the secrets of bribery, extortion and other criminal behaviour that linked companies to public officials and politicians.

Some leaders in Italy's financial world were dismayed by the law. In the aftermath of the terrorist attacks in America, and with huge corporate scandals breaking, there was growing concern about hidden financial transactions. Just when the world was demanding more transparency about how money was moved and how corporations managed their affairs, Berlusconi's government made sure that Italian firms would be providing far less.

Companies in Italy had, in any case, long enjoyed a poor reputation for accounting probity. Their books were notoriously unreliable and jokes abounded about how they kept several sets of accounting records: one for the taxman, another to comply with civil code requirements and yet another for the banks. The owner's own accounts were expected to be somewhere near the truth. The law that the government rushed on to the statute book seemed to confirm that accounting in Italy was little more than a charade; one news magazine thought that the law would shame even the voters of a banana republic.[17]

Until the mid-1990s, Italy's financial and industrial concerns had a poor image abroad. There had been some big corporate scandals and *tangentopoli* had shown that Italy was rotten from top to bottom. Yet, by the end of the 1990s, after memories of these scandals had receded and the sound economic policies of centre-left administrations had produced results, the country's reputation had improved. Berlusconi's government did more than just dash hopes for further progress. In the matter of company accounts, falsity was back in fashion and honesty something for mugs. Enjoying an official nod towards false accounts, Italian firms would find it hard to resist the temptation to fall back on their bad old habit of cooking the books.[18] The law that the prime minister and his lawyers conjured up showed that Italy had not really changed.

'The image of Italian business has been damaged by the new law. We had a hard job to improve our reputation for transparency and now we are back to square one,' said Salvatore Bragantini,[19] who had been a member of the Commissione Nazionale per le Societa e la Borsa (Consob, Italy's companies and stock market watchdog) between

1996 and 2001. Tacit government encouragement of dishonesty would carry a price. 'The new law on false accounting will cause a higher cost of capital for Italian companies,' Bragantini noted.[20] Investors were willing to accept lower yields on bonds if they felt confident that management was straight and that transactions were correctly disclosed. The erosion of trust would mean that companies would have to pay more for funds that they borrowed. Honest Italian companies would suffer because competitors who cheated would benefit from the distortion of competition that false accounting bred. 'If my company plays by the rules but your company does not, then you are competing unfairly. Berlusconi's government spouts about the benefits of competition but then forgets that a firm has an unfair competitive edge when it falsifies its accounts,' said Bragantini.[21]

Another part of the price of the law on false accounting would be lower investment. Even before Berlusconi came to power, central and local government had had great difficulty in persuading foreign companies to build new factories in Italy. The law on false accounting added to the problem. 'Foreign companies are more likely to have to keep to stricter rules,' noted Bragantini.[22] What honest foreign company would want to put money into a country where false accounting enjoyed official endorsement?

Indeed, the figures for inward direct investment into Italy showed how unattractive the country was to foreign investors. The Bank of Italy noted in 2001 that foreign direct investment into the country had stagnated since the 1980s and that Italy was low in the international league for attracting investment from abroad. In 2002, the stock of overseas direct investment in Italy amounted to about $130 billion, compared with about $700 billion in Britain, about $500 billion in Germany and about $430 billion in France. Even Spain, a smaller country and only a recent member of the European Union, could boast a stock of overseas direct investment that was higher than Italy's.[23]

INTERNATIONAL JUDICIAL ASSISTANCE

Much of the corruption the *mani pulite* team investigated involved companies and bank accounts outside Italy and many secrets had been locked up abroad. For help in exposing these secrets the Italian magistrates made requests for international judicial assistance, called *rogatorie*, to their counterparts in other countries. Little wonder that neutralizing the *rogatorie* seemed important after Berlusconi won power and installed his lawyers in parliament.

Italy and Switzerland had reached an agreement in September 1998 that completed the European convention on judicial assistance and the Swiss ratified it soon after but it still had to be ratified by Italy and procedures put in place for its implementation. After the government took office, Berlusconi and his lawyers wasted no time, moving quickly to make crucial amendments to the agreement and slipping these changes into the legislation that ratified and put the agreement into effect. Marcello Dell'Utri was among the signatories of amendments that appeared to aim at sinking the trials in Milan in which Italy's prime minister and his friend Cesare Previti faced charges of bribing judges. (The fourth section of Milan's criminal court would, on 27 April 2004, find Dell'Utri guilty of attempted extortion and sentence him to two years' imprisonment, against which he would appeal.[24])

Under the amendments, to which Dell'Utri was a signatory, evidence from abroad would not be admissible unless documents were originals, or were authenticated as originals with official stamps on every document. Moreover, defendants would not even have to raise objections for documents that failed to satisfy these new requirements to be ruled inadmissible. The changes did not stop there. The new rules would apply to cases already underway, whatever stage trials had reached.[25]

The centre-left administration that preceded Berlusconi's government had been slow, absent-minded or inefficient and had left the agreement among the unfinished business of the 13th legislature. Not surprisingly, the Swiss authorities were upset about the way in which the agreement they had reached with Italy's government in 1998 was being wrecked by Berlusconi's administration. As everyone knew, the originals of bank statements in Swiss banks were stored in computers, on hard disks, and what was printed were copies. As for requiring an official stamp on each and every piece of paper, that was patently nothing other than a scheme to ensure evidence was ruled inadmissible in Italian courts. It seemed that with this one law, Berlusconi and Previti would leap clear of their menacing legal predicaments in Milan.

The speed and timing of the legislation on the *rogatorie* were most unusual. Work started in the senate on 3 August and the bill was given final approval on 3 October 2001.[26] Tackling economic problems was far, far less important and the war against global terrorism ranked much, much lower on the Italian government's agenda. Nothing was more urgent than this bill. That surprised outsiders and some Italians too. Parliament's foreign affairs and judicial affairs commissions started discussing the *rogatorie* bill exactly one week after the Twin Towers in New York had been struck and destroyed. With the world reeling from shock, some people thought that judicial cooperation between western countries needed to be strengthened. Instead, Berlusconi's government sought to weaken it.

However much he hurried the bill through parliament, Berlusconi alone could not put it into effect. Italy's president, Carlo Azeglio Ciampi, had to sign the bill and it had to be published in the official gazette in order to become law. Seemingly indifferent to the uproar that the legislation had caused and to how Italy's reputation had been sullied, Ciampi signed the bill on the day it landed on his desk. Approved on Wednesday 3 October, signed by Berlusconi on the following day and by Ciampi on Friday 5 October, it was rushed into the official gazette on Saturday 6 October and became effective from Monday 8 October. Usually the pace of the Italian legislature and bureaucracy was very much slower. Italy was urgently engaged, it seemed, in enacting laws that would hamper the fight against global terrorism and cross-border crime. Some Italians thought that it was far from coincidental that a hearing in the Milan court of the case involving Cesare Previti had been scheduled for Tuesday 9 October.[27]

Switzerland made its displeasure known by freezing the post-ratification procedures for the treaty. Carla Del Ponte, the Swiss chief prosecutor at the international criminal court in The Hague, had worked closely with anti-Mafia magistrates in Palermo and with the anti-corruption team in Milan. With her practical experience of cross-border work, she knew the *rogatorie* question well. Moreover, she had helped to prepare the bilateral treaty with Italy. Switzerland wanted the accord to speed up cooperation and make it more efficient but Italy had different ideas. She was shocked. What the government had done was discouraging, she said.[28]

Italian magistrates were disturbed but neither discouraged nor deterred. The law on the *rogatorie* affected cases in courts throughout Italy and prosecutors in one of these cases considered that the new law was unconstitutional and appealed against it to the supreme court. To the government's fury, the prosecutors won their appeal and the supreme court's judgement, filed on 8 March 2002, was subsequently upheld by the constitutional court. (The constitutional court is Italy's highest court and is called on to rule in cases concerning the constitutional legitimacy of laws and to settle conflicts that arise between functions of the state.) Normal international practice would continue to determine the admissibility of evidence in Italy, rather than legislation invented by Italian members of parliament seeking to save the skin of important colleagues. A letter signed by a foreign magistrate to accompany documents sent from abroad would continue to be sufficient to guarantee the authenticity of those documents. The attempts to use legislation to sabotage international judicial assistance and the acquisition of evidence abroad failed.

Neither did magistrates in Milan let the law on false accounting go unchallenged. One year after the law's approval, in September 2002, Gherardo Colombo raised an objection that it was contrary to European law. As a member of the European Union, Italy was required to abide by European law, he argued, and article 6 of the directive issued by the European Council of Ministers on 9 March 1968 required member states to set appropriate penalties where firms failed to publish balance sheets and profit and loss accounts. 'If appropriate penalties should be laid down for failing to publish accounts, there is an even greater case for them where published accounts are false,' wrote Colombo, pleading his case.[29] Prosecutors thought that there were other flaws in Berlusconi's law on false accounting. The *mani pulite* team had presented a sufficient argument for the court in Milan to rule that the subsidiary charge of false accounting that Berlusconi faced in the SME case should be referred to the European Court of Justice, where in spring 2004 the appeal was still waiting to be heard.

By putting legislation on false accounting and international judicial assistance at the top of his government's agenda, Berlusconi showed what he considered were the most important matters for his administration. When it failed to deliver what was expected, the prime minister and his team of criminal lawyers conjured up another ploy. This was called the Cirami Law, named after its sponsor, Melchiorre Cirami, a senator in one of Forza Italia's ally-parties in the House of Freedoms coalition.

ANOTHER BESPOKE LAW

Cirami was born in Raffadali, a small town in the depths of the southern Sicilian countryside, about ten miles northwest of Agrigento. He had begun a career in the magistrature in Canicatti and worked there in 1970 and 1971 before moving to the court in Agrigento. He was elected to parliament in 1996 and re-elected in 2001, on both occasions for constituencies in the province of Agrigento.[30] When Cirami was a magistrate, he had been involved in various controversial decisions that had upset environmentalists. Cirami was little known outside the southernmost part of Sicily, but he made a name for himself throughout the country during Berlusconi's second administration.

Both Previti and Berlusconi had made it clear that they thought they would not receive fair treatment in Milan's court and sought to get their trials transferred elsewhere.[31] Many people suspected, however, that a change of jurisdiction was not the only reason why Previti and his leader wanted the hearings shifted. Once moved, the trials would probably have to start again from the beginning. New courts would bring new opportunities for procedural gambits, different judges would want to review the evidence, and the inevitable delays would bring the statute of limitations closer, as well as allow time for other laws to be passed.

Cirami's bill proposed that a defendant should have the right to challenge the court on the grounds of legitimate suspicion if they thought the court might be prejudiced. According to the bill's supporters, there was a legislative vacuum concerning legitimate suspicion that needed to be filled and the senator's bill would fill it. Not so, claimed the opposition, countering that an earlier reform of the code of criminal procedure had deliberately omitted the question of legitimate suspicion. Whatever the jostling between government and opposition, however, Cirami presented his bill on 9 July 2002 and it was first discussed during the afternoon sitting of the senate's judicial affairs commission on 18 July.[32]

The senate's speaker, who occupied an institutional position second only to Italy's president and was supposed to be above party politics, decided that the matter was urgent and fixed schedules to push the bill through quickly. Although the summer holidays had begun, many Italians took to the streets to show their disapproval of what Cirami was doing to help Berlusconi and Previti. Demonstrations were held outside parliament and the courts to contest a bill that the demonstrators believed was just another bespoke measure to tackle the prime minister's personal legal problems and those of his close friend. This view was reinforced when defendants in the judicial corruption trials in Milan sent sick-notes to get hearings postponed, an action seemingly aimed at dragging out proceedings until after the bill had obtained parliamentary approval.[33]

On the afternoon of 24 July, Senator Rita Levi Montalcini addressed the judicial affairs commission of parliament's upper house.[34] Levi Montalcini was a figure of great authority and integrity. A brilliant medical scientist, she was awarded the Nobel Prize in 1986 for her work on the nerve growth factor. Because she was a Jew, she had been compelled by Italy's racial laws to leave her university post in 1938. She lived clandestinely in Florence during 1943 and 1944, helped the Anglo-American allies in the liberation of the city and worked with their forces as a volunteer doctor. She was appointed life-senator in August 2001 and sat with the non-aligned senators.[35] Levi Montalcini was ninety-three years old when she spoke against the Cirami bill. Some members of the right-wing coalition thought that she made a pathetic sight, just an old lady talking of something she knew nothing about, and they loudly made their views known. Certainly Levi Montalcini was politically far from the post-fascists and the members of Forza Italia, but she represented an important part of Italian society concerned that Berlusconi's coalition was dragging the country into a moral morass.

Unusually, the senate's afternoon sitting at which the eminent scientist spoke worked through that night, the first of a series of night sittings that caused tempers to fray.[36] Opposition senators complained that the government was breaking parliamentary rules and using undemocratic tricks. The government was rushing to get the bill into law, said Stefano Passigli, an opposition senator, because it was scared that the constitutional court, which had been asked by the appeal court for a ruling on the question of legitimate suspicion, would not deliver what Berlusconi wanted. 'The suggestion that Cirami's bill will fill a legislative vacuum,' said Passigli, 'is an enormous and knowing lie, obsessively repeated to cover the truth that it is the exploitation of legislative power in the private interests of the prime minister and Previti to escape from the trials in Milan.'[37]

The opposition lost its first battle, however, when Cirami's bill won approval in the senate on the afternoon of 1 August.[38] It then had to be discussed in the lower house. Such was the urgency to propel it rapidly through parliament that Pecorella spoke about the possibility of reopening for a special holiday session in mid-August. But it was not the job of the prime minister's lawyer to set parliamentary schedules. That belonged to the chambers' speakers, and the speaker of the lower house said that the matter could wait until September.

Government politicians had not been alone in busying themselves with Cirami's bill during the summer break. People dismayed at what Berlusconi was doing planned a demonstration for 14 September, a day of peaceful protest in defence of moral values. Neither the trade unions nor the political parties of the opposition were involved. Instead it was staged by the *girotondi* (literally, ring-a-ring-a-roses), a broad-based civil society pressure group that had previously organized demonstrations outside parliament and courts in various cities. Rome's Piazza San Giovanni overflowed with demonstrators waving flags and banners of every type. The turn-out was a surprise; some estimates put the figure at one million.

Grandparents pushed babies in prams. Parents carried children on their shoulders. Very young, young, middle-aged and elderly Italians carried their concerns about what was happening to the justice system in Italy to Piazza San Giovanni. Workers, intellectuals and ordinary middle-class people heard speeches, but not from politicians. Rita Borsellino, the sister of the right-wing prosecutor murdered by the Mafia, told the crowds that people had been silent too long. The playwright and Nobel Prize-winner Dario Fo was there with his actress wife, Franca Rame.

Nanni Moretti, the film director and a driving force behind the *girotondi*, organized the speakers and the music. Some big names of Italian rock music were on-stage and film-makers Francesco Rosi and Liliana Cavani were among the crowd. Ettore Scola filmed the happening and so did Pasquale Squitieri, once a senator with the National Alliance, one of Berlusconi's allies in the House of Freedoms coalition. 'A popular demonstration is not only legitimate but also desirable,' said Squitieri.[39] He thought the event was marvellous. Vittorio Dotti turned up. For fifteen years Berlusconi's lawyer at Fininvest, Dotti was not on the political left and had once been Forza Italia's leader in parliament's lower house. He was in Piazza San Giovanni, he said, 'to help stop the devastation of justice'.[40]

All to no avail. Pecorella pressed on. He told the lower house's joint commission on the morning of the demonstration that he was at peace with his conscience. To avoid further conflict, he would not vote on the bill, but that was rather an empty gesture as his vote was not needed to ensure its approval.[41] On 10 October, the day the lower house voted on the bill, one politician of the centre-left asked who had drafted the bill and its amendments. He wanted to establish what margin of independence members of parliament on the government's side would possess from someone 'who looked after his interests by means of laws that ought to serve the country and not himself'.[42]

Filippo Mancuso was an eighty-year-old former magistrate who had been minister of justice in 1995. A Sicilian from Palermo, he had been elected to the lower house in the ranks of Forza Italia for constituencies in the city in 1996 and 2001. Mancuso thought that Previti was putting pressure on Berlusconi to get Cirami's bill through parliament and he wrote a long document saying why, but the speaker refused to allow it to be filed in the lower house's official record.[43] That Pecorella had threatened the dissolution of parliament if the bill were not approved was also a sign that his client and his client's friend were extremely anxious that the bill should be approved quickly.[44]

Apart from the many ordinary Italians who were angered by Cirami's bill, and the centre-left opposition in parliament that was trying to block the measure, experts at the Consiglio Superiore della Magistratura (CSM, the magistrature's governing body) also entered the fray. This body had an institutional duty to give its view on bills concerning judicial affairs and one of the CSM's own commissions wrote a report after the senate had approved the bill, but while it was still under discussion in the lower house.[45] This commission pointed to several problems. Every trial had its natural jurisdiction, it said, and moving trials from their natural jurisdictions gave rise to fundamental constitutional issues. The commission was worried that the lack of precise terms of reference for legitimate suspicion would help organized crime. There would be a sharp increase in the number of applications by defendants. The suspension of trials while objections concerning legitimate suspicion were heard would lead to the lengthening of trials and run counter to the constitutional principle that trials should be of a reasonable duration. The commission saw difficulties for judges in jurisdictions to which trials were transferred in deciding on the admissibility of evidence already presented. Where cases involved more than one defendant, warned the commission, there would be opportunities for abuse by defendants. Finally, transferring cases between jurisdictions would create problems of credibility and undermine confidence in the system.

The commission wanted the full body of the CSM to approve a document that formalized these concerns but the government wanted to gag the experts who knew how it was tampering with the country's legal system and the damage that this tampering might do. Five of the CSM's members had been appointed by Berlusconi's House of Freedoms coalition and, claiming that the CSM was trying to extend its powers, they abandoned the council's meeting so that there was no quorum. The result of their withdrawal was that the CSM was not able to discuss or vote on the document.[46]

Cirami's bill continued to make its way inexorably through parliament, although not without encountering obstacles. Despite its importance and all the attention that it had been given, the bill contained errors which had to be corrected through amendments. When the senate had its final vote about twenty senators on the government's benches were filmed pressing the voting buttons of absent colleagues. Some of them just did not care that they were seen when they cheated, others glanced around furtively and tried to hide their hands beneath newspapers. The whole shabby business of railroading Cirami's bill on to the statute book could be summed up in the government senators' behaviour. Despite evidence of what seemed to many to be disgraceful conduct, the speaker of the senate ruled that parliamentary procedures had been properly observed.[47]

From the senate, the bill passed back to the lower house. There, on 5 November 2002, just under two weeks after the marathon in the senate was completed, Cirami's bill overcame its last parliamentary hurdle. Its final version had been agreed beforehand with the Italian president's office. On the following day, the film director Nanni Moretti led some *girotondini* in a candle-lit vigil around the president's Quirinale Palace in a last-ditch effort to persuade Carlo Azeglio Ciampi not to sign the bill. The *girotondini* made their point but the Italian president put his signature to the bill on 7 November.[48] That same night the law was published in the official gazette and became effective.

Meanwhile, a presiding judge in Milan had done everything he could to avoid being accused of bias against Previti and a group of co-defendants. This was the trial that started on 11 May 2000, described earlier, in which the defendants were charged with the corruption of judges to swing a decision concerning the Mondadori publishing house in Berlusconi's favour and a decision concerning the bankrupt IMI-SIR chemicals group in favour of its owner. In mid-September 2002, the presiding judge said that, before retiring to consider the evidence and reach a verdict, he would suspend the trial and await the decision of the constitutional court on the question of legitimate suspicion.[49]

In March 2002, Previti and Berlusconi had asked that the trial in which they were accused of bribing judges, in the case involving the SME food conglomerate, be transferred from Milan to another jurisdiction. The grounds on which they had made their application were that the court in Milan was not impartial and that the situation in the city prevented the trial from being conducted in the atmosphere of calm that was necessary. During the preceding eight years, said the pleading prepared by Berlusconi's lawyers, the politician, members of his family, and companies and staff of his Fininvest group had been involved in sixty criminal proceedings. During that period they had had to engage almost 100 lawyers and over thirty consultants in their defence.[50]

At the end of May 2002, the supreme court, the highest level of appeal in a criminal case, decided that it could not rule on the question. It passed to the constitutional court, the court responsible for ruling on the constitutional legitimacy of legislation, the responsibility for deciding whether or not the defendants were right in arguing that there was a legislative vacuum on legitimate suspicion. Just ten days after the Cirami Law was enacted, the constitutional court said that there had been no such legislative vacuum. There had, in effect, been no need for Cirami's law, but the judgement arrived too late.

The question of transferring the trials from Milan still needed to be settled, however. Responsibility for dealing with this controversial matter fell to the supreme court which would decide in accordance with the Cirami Law. On 28 January 2003, the supreme court announced that the defendants did not have grounds for suspecting that they would not have fair trials in Milan. There was no legitimate suspicion to justify transferring the trials to another jurisdiction and the situation in Milan did not justify such a transfer. The prosecutors had not exerted improper pressure to sway judges or witnesses and the judges' impartiality was therefore not in question. The trials would remain in Milan. The costs of the case, said the supreme court, would be borne by the appellants – but that, of course, would not be a problem for Italy's richest man.

Gaetano Pecorella, Berlusconi's lawyer and the man who chaired the judicial affairs commission in parliament's lower house, commented specifically on the court's ruling: 'It is difficult to still trust the magistrature after the sequence of events that border on the unreal and bizarre.'[51] Berlusconi and Pecorella had steamrollered parliament and hustled the House of Freedoms coalition to obtain approval for the Cirami Law but the judges found the subsequent legal arguments wholly empty. Italy's prime minister and his lawyers lost their case in court.

Judges in Italy's supreme court had shown their independence and determination not to be cowed by a defendant's wealth, political position or power over the media. Berlusconi had severe words for them. Sitting in his study in Arcore, he recorded a message almost six minutes long that was handed to journalists.[52] Italy's prime minister did not want to answer questions but merely to state his views.

Berlusconi said he was above being judged by the courts and that only parliament had the right to judge him. 'In a liberal democracy, the people and their representatives govern, not those who have succeeded in competitive examinations and put on robes. Their function is to apply the law,' he said. In Italy, he complained, 'a left-wing Jacobinic' magistrature was persecuting him.

LOOKING FOR IMMUNITY

Until the moment the supreme court delivered its judgement, Berlusconi had been confident that the Cirami Law would be enough, the court would find in his and Previti's favour and the trials would be shifted from Milan.[53] His confidence had been misplaced. With the supreme court's decision, the assault on criminal law that Berlusconi and his lawyers had launched in parliament was repulsed. Legislation on false accounting, international judicial assistance and legitimate suspicion had not been enough to ward off the prosecutors and the judges.

Parliamentary immunity still offered an escape from the judiciary's attentions, however. This solution to Berlusconi's legal problems had always been a possibility and government minds started to turn to it in July 2002 when Forza Italia seemed ready to launch a blitz to force legislation through parliament.[54] The central point of the draft legislation would be the suspension of criminal proceedings against members of parliament until their parliamentary mandates ended.

Italy's constitution states that members of parliament cannot be prosecuted for their opinions or for how they vote in the course of their parliamentary duties – a right that lies at the heart of any democracy. However, parliamentary immunity in Italy had once gone way beyond that, members of the parliament in Rome being far more privileged and enjoying a broad immunity that they often seemed ready to abuse. Before 1993, members of parliament could not be subject to criminal proceedings, neither could they be arrested, deprived of personal freedom or searched without the authorization of the chamber of parliament to which they belonged. The only exceptions were cases where politicians had been caught red-handed committing crimes for which arrest was mandatory. Parliament's authorization had also been needed for the arrest of members even after appeal processes had been exhausted and verdicts of guilt definitively confirmed.[55] When called to authorize proceedings, arrest or search, however, the parliamentary pals had usually stuck together in arrogant disregard for the notion of the equality of all citizens.

After the crimes of *tangentopoli* were exposed, and with the whole political system tottering, even politicians recognized that such generosity towards corrupt colleagues had to come to an end, not least because almost 200 members of parliament had been caught in the nets of the anti-corruption magistrates. In April 1993, the lower house had refused all four requests made by magistrates in Milan to initiate proceedings against Bettino Craxi, the leader of the Socialist Party, and his parliamentary immunity had not been lifted. The accusations against him, claimed Craxi, were part of a political plot;[56] a similar refrain would later be taken up loudly by Berlusconi and members of Forza Italia. Nevertheless, conditions were ripe in 1993 to tackle the vexed question of how far members of parliament should be allowed to escape retribution for their crimes.

Under Carlo Azeglio Ciampi, parliament changed the constitution in October that year. Although members still could not be arrested or searched without parliament's authorization except in cases where they were caught *in flagrante*, magistrates would no longer need parliamentary authorization to start proceedings. Moreover, magistrates would no longer need parliament's authorization to arrest members once definitive prison sentences had been passed. This big advance in helping the magistrature tackle crooked politicians was weakened, however, by a new area for immunity that the politicians had slipped in: magistrates would need parliament's authorization before intercepting correspondence or tapping telephone conversations,[57] limitations that would later handicap the forces of law in cases in which criminals or suspected criminals contacted members of parliament.

Some people were aghast when rumours began circulating early in the administration that Berlusconi formed after winning the parliamentary election in May 2001 about legislation to widen again the immunity of members of parliament. Changes to the constitution's treatment of parliamentary immunity, which had been approved almost unanimously by parliament and had been greeted by ordinary Italians as a decisive step in applying the fundamental principle of the equality of all citizens before the law, were almost the only remaining positive result of the efforts of the prosecutors of the *mani pulite* team, said the state prosecutor in Milan in July 2002.[58] Widening politicians' immunity would be a step backwards towards a situation in which some citizens were more equal than others.

When the end of Cesare Previti's trial in the IMI-SIR and Lodo Mondadori cases in Milan was in sight and legislative ploys such as the law on international judicial assistance and the Cirami Law on legitimate suspicion had turned out insufficient to help his defence, members on the government's benches again started talking about immunity. Some in Forza Italia's ranks thought that the government should have brought in legislation in the summer of 2001, immediately after Berlusconi's resounding victory at the polls. But it was not too late, even in 2003, to pass a decree, using a vote of confidence if necessary, to suspend criminal proceedings against members of parliament.[59]

During the senate's heated debate of the Cirami bill in the summer of 2002, one member of the opposition asked why the government had not taken up his suggestion of a law to offer immunity to the prime minister and to ten people of the prime minister's choosing. This would at least have put everything out in the open and parliament would not then have been suspected of passing bespoke laws to favour individuals.[60] Instead, in June 2003, on the eve of Italy assuming the presidency of the European Union, with the prosecutors in the SME trial close to winding up the case against Berlusconi and calling for him to be sentenced to a long term in jail, parliament had thrown a lifebelt to the businessman-turned-politician, rushing through a law that suspended trial proceedings against him and effectively granting him immunity by suspending his trial while he held office.[61]

The law was immediately contested in the court as unconstitutional and civil society groups such as the *girotondi* and *libertà e giustizia*, demanded a referendum for its abrogation. It concerned five high state offices: the president of the republic, the speaker of the senate, the speaker of the chamber of deputies, the president of the constitutional court and the president of the council of ministers, as the Italian prime minister is called. Opponents argued that parliament had approved the law solely for the benefit of the fifth: the prime minister, Silvio Berlusconi.

At the end of January 2003, after the appeal court had ruled that there were no grounds for changing the jurisdiction of the trial in which Berlusconi was accused of bribing judges, he had complained that those who governed elsewhere in the world enjoyed 'immunity and guarantees that put them beyond the risk of political persecution by magistrates'.[62] Almost five months later, after the enactment of the immunity law, he said that this law at last aligned Italy with other European countries.[63] But he had spoken too soon. On 13 January 2004, the constitutional court ruled that the law violated two articles of the constitution: it violated Berlusconi's constitutional right to defend himself in court against the charges that the prosecutors had made and it violated the equality that all Italians should enjoy before the law. The prime minister's trial in the SME case would restart in the spring.

6

Complicity

SUCCESS IN SICILY

Crushing victories came no larger and Berlusconi's House of Freedoms coalition's trouncing of the centre-left in Sicily at the parliamentary elections in May 2001 left no room for equivocation. Berlusconi and his allies had achieved a clean sweep by taking all 61 seats of the 61 first-past-the-post seats contested on the island, 41 for parliament's lower house in Rome and 20 for the senate.[1] Such a resounding result raised questions about how far the Mafia might have helped. After all, the island's economy was almost completely under the Mafia's control, which would have allowed it considerable political leverage. Moreover, there was talk of a market in votes in 2001, and when the diocese of Cefalu, a coastal town about 50 miles east of Palermo, undertook a survey, it found that many people said that they had been offered jobs or money in exchange for votes.[2]

Sicily had proved the most fruitful region in Forza Italia's campaign in spring 2001. By winning almost 37 per cent of the votes cast for candidates standing for the lower house it became the island's biggest party.[3] That Forza Italia was open to infiltration by the Mafia was hardly a surprise. Indeed, a leading member of the association behind Berlusconi's political movement had recognized that awkward fact well before the party's election success in 2001. After the parliamentary elections in 1994, the party did not deny that some of its clubs, the grassroots foundations on which Forza Italia had been built, might have been infiltrated by members of the old guard who hoped to be politically recycled. Infiltration might even have been achieved by people close to mafia organizations who were seeking to make contact with the new political movement.[4]

There were even greater concerns. On 22 July 1998, the state prosecutor in Caltanissetta had set in motion an investigation of Berlusconi and Marcello Dell'Utri for 'aggravated complicity' in slaughter, opening the way for the two men who had founded Forza Italia to be investigated on suspicion of commissioning the murders of Falcone and Borsellino and their escorts in Palermo in 1992. The state prosecutor's decision to put the names of Berlusconi and Dell'Utri on the register of people under investigation was triggered by the depositions of Salvatore Cancemi, a *mafioso* who had given himself up to the *carabinieri* in July 1993 and had decided to cooperate with the authorities. Cancemi had told them about 'the involvement of "important people" in the decision to eliminate Falcone and Borsellino as part of a broader strategy of terror by Cosa Nostra, as well as the relations, first managed by Vittorio Mangano and then by Salvatore Riina, with top people of the Fininvest business group', noted the judgement handed down on 3 May 2002 by Giovanbattista Tona, a judge responsible for preliminary investigations in Caltanissetta.[5] Mangano had been employed by Berlusconi himself at his villa in Arcore near Milan and Riina was the Mafia's boss of bosses. As the regent of an important *mandamento* in the centre of Palermo, the Porta Nuova district in the area of the cathedral and the parliament building of Sicily's regional government, Cancemi had been Mangano's boss. The prosecutor also took account of statements by four other *mafiosi*; those by Tullio Cannella and Gioacchino La Barbera concerning contacts between Cosa Nostra and northern businessmen, and those by Gioacchino Pennino and Angelo Siino concerning persons with an interest in killing two magistrates who had become very knowledgeable about relationships between the Mafia and business.[6]

Arrested in July 1995, Cannella quickly decided to become a *pentito* and began to cooperate with the authorities later the same month. He had never formally been initiated into Cosa Nostra, said the judgement of the third trial of the magistrate's killers in Caltanissetta, the trial known as Borsellino Ter, but even so he was a *mafioso*, and one who was politically well connected too. 'Cannella had had relations with eminent mafia figures from when, still a youth, he had started to attend the local headquarters of the Christian Democrat Party in the Brancaccio-Ciaculli district where he lived. He had been the party's district deputy-secretary and had successfully taken part in elections for the district council,' the judgement of the Borsellino Ter trial noted on 9 December 1999.[7] A grim district of densely packed high-rise apartment blocks, scruffy workshops and commercial storage buildings on the eastern edge of Palermo, Brancaccio, and its mafia family, had long enjoyed particular notoriety. Cannella knew the bosses, had their trust and had fronted for Pino Greco and Michele Graviano, two top *mafiosi* in Brancaccio, by putting assets owned by the two men in his name to avoid their confiscation, said the court's judgement.

In May and June 1993, Cannella had hidden Leoluca Bagarella, a leading *mafioso* from Corleone who was then on the run. As a businessman with an unblemished police record, Cannella had been an ideal front-man for promoting the Mafia's political schemes. Towards the end of 1993, the court noted, Bagarella had given him the job of setting up a political movement to seek Sicilian independence and financed him to do it. The party was to be called Sicilia Libera. 'It was to be the presentable interface of Cosa Nostra in its relations with national political leaders from whom the Mafia intended to obtain a significant slackening of the authorities' efforts against them and an easing of the laws and administrative measures used to combat them,' said the judgement of the Borsellino Ter trial.[8] Given the job of pushing ahead with this scheme, Cannella had contacted mafia bosses in Catania, in the east of Sicily, and Trapani, in the southwest, to encourage them to back the movement and put forward candidates for election. 'Cannella's efforts in this project came to a halt around December 1993 and January 1994 when Bagarella told Cannella that the forthcoming creation of the Forza Italia party made the Sicilian independence party redundant,' said the court's judgement.[9] Indeed, as future parliamentary elections would show, Forza Italia was destined to become the driving force in Sicilian politics. One of the first Sicilian Forza Italia clubs was inaugurated in a huge hotel overlooking the sea in Brancaccio, the San Paolo Palace, which its owner, a front for the Graviano brothers, had made available to the party's new members.

Two and a half years after the assize court had delivered its verdict in the Borsellino Ter trial, judge Tona in Caltanissetta, who was overseeing the preliminary investigations into Berlusconi and Dell'Utri, noted that, while there had been sufficient proof that Cosa Nostra had first supported Sicilia Libera and then switched its allegiance to Forza Italia, evidence about the existence of earlier agreements between Bagarella and the promoters of Forza Italia was vague.[10] If there had been stronger evidence of such agreements, this 'would have been significant in supporting the accusations at the root of the investigations', noted Tona. However, people connected with the Mafia had been in contact with companies in the Fininvest group and Tona said that these contacts might offer scope for further investigations. 'These proven relations between companies in the Fininvest group and people in various positions linked to Cosa Nostra lent plausibility to depositions, made by various mafia witnesses who were cooperating with the authorities, that Berlusconi and Dell'Utri were considered easily contactable by the criminal organization,' said Tona's judgement.[11]

One of the people from whom the magistrates obtained evidence was Ezio Cartotto, a journalist who had worked with Dell'Utri and helped him draw up plans for a new political party. Cartotto had got to know Dell'Utri during the 1970s, when he had met him at conferences of the Christian Democrat Party, among other places. At Dell'Utri's request, Cartotto had on various occasions since 1981 prepared seminars on political matters for staff in firms belonging to Fininvest, a job that became particularly hectic after September 1992. Giving evidence to magistrates in Caltanissetta on 16 July 1999, Cartotto said, 'In reality, Dell'Utri pointed out to me the need to identify new political reference points for the Fininvest group as the traditional ones were no longer enough.'[12] But Dell'Utri and Fininvest were not alone in searching for new patrons, and their political initiatives, aimed at gathering consensus around formations not opposed to the group, would have aroused Cosa Nostra's interest had they known about it. The Mafia also urgently needed to create new political contacts to replace those of the existing political order who had let them down and whose power was, in any case, being eroded by corruption investigations in Milan.

Berlusconi's employment of Mangano as stable-boss and factotum at Arcore between 1973 and 1974 was a matter that interested magistrates. Cancemi told magistrates that Riina had decided to manage the alleged contacts with Dell'Utri and Berlusconi directly. In February 1994 and April 1998, both times in reply to the questions of magistrates from Caltanissetta, Cancemi said that around the end of 1990 Riina had instructed him to order Mangano, a subordinate in the *mandamento* that Cancemi headed, to step aside so that Riina himself would be directly involved in the alleged relationship with Berlusconi and Dell'Utri. Tona's judgement referred to Cancemi's deposition to the Caltanissetta magistrates on 29 January 1998 when he had spoken of how he had met Riina at a party following the murder of Falcone. Cancemi told the magistrates that Riina had said, 'I am prepared to bet, we don't have to worry, I have Dell'Utri and Berlusconi in the palm of my hand and this is good for all Cosa Nostra.'[13]

A police report of 18 February 1994 documented relations between Dell'Utri and his brother Alberto with exponents of the Mafia, noted Tona's judgement.[14] Further investigations had shown that Dell'Utri had had contact with 'leading figures in Palermo who had later been subject to investigation for crimes connected with Cosa Nostra's activities'.[15] Indeed, when the state prosecutor in Caltanissetta put the names of Berlusconi and Dell'Utri into the register of people under investigation, Dell'Utri was already on trial in Palermo, charged with aiding and abetting the Mafia. The anti-Mafia team in Palermo had asked for him to be sent for trial on 26 October 1996. They said that Dell'Utri had participated personally in meetings with leaders of Cosa Nostra and that he had not only maintained continuous relationships with numerous leading *mafiosi* but had also helped *mafiosi* who were on the run from the police. Backing the prosecutors' case were numerous transcripts of questionings of witnesses and hearings, analyses of telephone traffic, court sentences and bank documents, as well as eight of Dell'Utri's own diaries from the years 1984 to 1993.[16] The request for Dell'Utri's indictment was signed by the chief prosecutor, Gian Carlo Caselli, the man who had arrived in Palermo in the aftermath of the horrific murders of Falcone and Borsellino to give backbone to the battle against the Mafia.

Mangano told the magistrates in June 1996 that Dell'Utri and Gaetano Cina, an important *mafioso* of the Malaspina family, had suggested the job that he took at Berlusconi's villa in Arcore.[17] Mangano had been sentenced to ten years' imprisonment in the 1980s for drug-trafficking, but that did not end his relationship with Dell'Utri. Berlusconi's former employee was back in jail again in 1995, however, and was sentenced to fifteen years' imprisonment in 1999, again for drug-trafficking, and to a further fifteen years for extortion in 2000. Just three days before he died of cancer in July 2000, a court in Palermo gave him a life sentence for the murder of an elderly district boss in 1995.[18] Questioned in July 1996, Dell'Utri said that he did not know that Cina and Mangano were *uomini d'onore*, an assertion that some Sicilians found hard to believe.

In presenting their case against Dell'Utri, the prosecutors offered insights into how the Mafia had sought to infiltrate the activities of Forza Italia. Gianfranco Micciche had worked for Fininvest's Publitalia subsidiary in Sicily for ten years before getting involved in Berlusconi's political party. He had been elected to parliament for a Sicilian constituency in 1994 and was then appointed a junior minister in the transport ministry in Berlusconi's first administration. Re-elected in 1996 and 2001, again for constituencies in Sicily, he was appointed deputy economics and finance minister in Berlusconi's second administration. Micciche was Dell'Utri's *alter ego* in Sicily, said the prosecutors, and was acquainted with people close to the Brancaccio mafia family in Palermo. Establishing the political party happened rapidly, Micciche told prosecutors, explaining Forza Italia's beginnings in Sicily. At the outset the party's organizers were unaware of the risks, he claimed. 'Then, little by little, we realized that we did not like some of the members as they were people about whom there was a lot of speculation,' he said.[19]

Hard as some politicians in Sicily may have tried to avoid being tainted, Cosa Nostra did its utmost to encroach into the world of politics. What the Christian Democrat Party had found before, so Forza Italia discovered in the 1990s. On 20 January 2003, giving evidence to a court in Palermo in Dell'Utri's trial for association with the Mafia, the *pentito* Antonino Giuffre said that Cosa Nostra was delighted when Forza Italia was established. Towards the end of

1993, word had started to circulate about plans to set up a new party, he told the court. Speaking quietly and slowly on a video-link from a secret location, Giuffre, who had been a member of Cosa Nostra's governing provincial *commissione* since 1983, said that Cosa Nostra was always on the lookout for anything that might be of help and for new personalities of importance. Provenzano had given orders that votes should be cast for Forza Italia, he said; the mafia boss knew Italian politicians were for sale.[20] Giuffre said he did not ask Provenzano what political guarantees might have been given in exchange for the Mafia's support. Such questions were not asked in Cosa Nostra, he told the court, but the Mafia certainly expected an easing of the authorities' efforts against them.

Although Giuffre had qualified as an agricultural technician and had taught the subject at a specialist institute in Palermo, it nevertheless came as a surprise when Domenico Gozzo, a member of the team of magistrates prosecuting Dell'Utri, asked the *pentito* to tell the court about mutual symbiosis. 'It is an agricultural term concerning the plants of beans, peas and pulses that absorb nitrogen thanks to bacteria that live in the roots; these bacteria give the plants the nitrogen that they need to live. We can easily draw a parallel with the business world. I guarantee the safety of the businessman and receive an economic return. And as well as getting assurance about his own economic interests, the businessman puts me in touch with his friends who are influential in areas where I might have need,' explained Giuffre. Gozzo wanted to know whether there might be political parallels. Indeed there were, said Giuffre. When he had guaranteed the election of a provincial or regional councillor, he had expected to receive economic or other favours in return.[21]

While the case in Palermo continued, Giovanbattista Tona, the judge in Caltanissetta, had ruled almost nine months before Giuffre gave evidence against Dell'Utri that the investigations into Berlusconi and his friend should be closed. Borsellino had not been murdered as a vendetta but as a precautionary measure, the Mafia's aims being to bring pressure on government politicians who had taken action against it and to encourage potential political interlocutors to come forward. People like Borsellino, who would have discouraged any kind of rapprochement to Cosa Nostra, had to be eliminated, but the two founders of Forza Italia were not accomplices in those terrible crimes in 1992. Tona said that 'the changing and slippery divulgations made by Cancemi and his constant tendency to play down his own role in crimes impaired his evidence'.[22] Moreover, the declarations made by other *pentiti* were insufficiently reliable and the magistrate responsible for the investigations into the possible involvement of Berlusconi and Dell'Utri had decided that his inquiries had not turned up the evidence needed to take the matter further. He asked Tona to close the case.

In Sicily, politics and the Mafia were insidiously entwined. Yet, as prosecutors recognized, proving the connections between the Mafia and politicians and demonstrating beyond doubt that those connections had effectively aided Cosa Nostra was far from easy. Winning cases where the defendants were politicians was very hard. There was a huge challenge in obtaining solid evidence that stood up in court, explained Gozzo. In cases of murder, there were weapons, perhaps traces of blood and so on, but where political complicity with Cosa Nostra was concerned the prosecutors were dealing with agreements between politicians and *mafiosi*. 'While there may be compromising photographs showing politicians in bad company, there are definitely no written contracts,' he said.[23] Complicity with the Mafia was a tough crime to prove. Prosecutors in Palermo said that the body of evidence that they had presented in trials of politicians was ten to twenty times greater than that presented in cases they had successfully brought against common *mafiosi*.

'Politics is to the Mafia as water to the fish,' said Gozzo.[24] That is how a *mafioso* who had decided to cooperate with the authorities had described the relationship. Fish needed water, otherwise they died. Sicily often suffered drought but the Mafia had never lacked what it needed. Fish and water, plants and bacteria or whatever the analogy, Cosa Nostra could always count on willing political accomplices.

A MAFIA POLITICIAN

Vito Ciancimino, mayor of Palermo in 1970, gained the dubious distinction of being the first Italian politician to be found guilty of association with the Mafia. He died on 19 November 2002 in his apartment in Rome, but there was no mystery about his death: an autopsy revealed that he had died from natural causes, struck down by a heart attack while he slept. Although the church of San Michele Arcangelo in Palermo was packed for his funeral service, no political leaders were there to hear the priest say that the dead man had done much that was good for others.[25] The dead *mafioso* politician was not from the Sicilian capital; his birthplace was the notorious mafia town of Corleone, the stronghold of bosses such as Luciano Leggio, Salvatore Riina and Bernardo Provenzano. Ciancimino's father had emigrated from Corleone to New York in 1910 but returned to his home town to open a barber's shop where the young Vito would sometimes help. After the Second World War the family moved to Palermo, although Vito Ciancimino did not finally change his official residence from Corleone to the Sicilian capital until 1963. During the 1980s Ciancimino had twice been convicted for offences arising from the management of contracts by Palermo's city council.[26] When he died, the 78-year-old was under house arrest; the supreme court had confirmed a thirteen-year jail sentence in November 2001 but for reasons of age and health he was not in prison.

As much as anyone, Ciancimino came to represent the alliance in which Italian politicans and members of the Mafia worked hand-in-hand. Immediately after his election to the city council in 1956, in the ranks of the dominant Christian Democrat Party, he had become chairman of the municipal board. That post allowed him to do favours for his *mafiosi* associates. Ciancimino's big chance arrived three years later, in July 1959, when he became chairman of public works. Taking over from Salvo Lima, who had become mayor and would be murdered in March 1992 by disgruntled *mafiosi*, Ciancimino held the post for five years.

Ciancimino and Lima were a formidable pair. They seized the chance between 1959 and 1964 to allow myriad construction schemes in their city, opening the door to a frenzy of building speculation, fuelled by the approval of 4,000 building licences, that would soon be called 'the sack of Palermo'. Art Nouveau villas were demolished, gardens became construction sites, large groves of orange and lemon trees were grubbed up and the western part of the Sicilian capital was submerged under cement as ten- and twelve-storey apartment blocks sprang up. The church in Palermo where Ciancimino's funeral was celebrated was in the middle of the area of urban depredation for which he had been responsible. Most of the building licences were issued by Ciancimino and Lima to three pensioners of modest means who had previously had nothing to do with real estate development and who were clearly fronting for the Mafia.[27]

Details of how Palermo was ravaged by the Mafia and the crooked politicians who acted as its willing accomplices continued to emerge over the next forty years. The largest sequestration and confiscation ordered by the city's court, of various cases from the mid-1990s onwards, removed assets estimated to be worth well over 2,000 billion lire (about £650 million or $1 billion) from Vincenzo Piazza, a *mafioso* belonging to the Uditore family.[28] Easy finance from large Sicilian banks, advance notice of land to be scheduled for development and contracts to let buildings to the public authorities even before the first cement had been poured all helped Piazza's property empire to grow. The city, provincial and regional authorities paid him large sums for the offices they rented from his group, and Palermo was unique among Italian local governments in renting schools – more than fifty – from the Mafia.[29] Cosa Nostra laundered dirty money from illegal activities such as drug-trafficking through Piazza and then made clean revenues from leasing properties to the authorities. He had property from one side of the city to the other, his hand reaching everywhere, even as far as the apartment where Giovanni Falcone had lived. When they sought Piazza's arrest and the sequestration of his assets, the magistrates knew where to point their fingers: Piazza owed his steady rise in the property world to 'his membership of the Mafia and to the unconditional and self-interested support he was given by high-ranking representatives of Palermo's public administration, particularly Vito Ciancimino'.[30]

Ciancimino was indicted in 1984 and expelled from the Christian Democrat Party, but he continued to exert great influence in Sicilian politics. Almost ten years later, at the beginning of the 1990s, he was still a puppet-master who pulled the strings and a politician whose name would always be linked to the most ferocious mafia family. Despite Ciancimino's powerful mafia connections, however, some people had been willing to speak out against him. He sued for defamation two Sicilian journalists who had said that the property speculation that had ruined large areas of Palermo had been managed by the Mafia and that Ciancimino had been party to it. In 1974, a judge threw the case out. What had happened in Palermo, said the judge, coupled to Ciancimino's behaviour, justified belief that the law had been violated and that the Mafia had profited greatly from those violations.[31] The journalists had been correct in saying that Ciancimino had colluded with Cosa Nostra.

A CASE OF MALADMINISTRATION

That same year, 1974, the Teatro Massimo shut its doors. Nobody expected Palermo's opera house would remain closed for almost a quarter of a century. In no other Italian city, not even Milan with its La Scala, did local people so much look on the opera house as their city's civic symbol. For the Sicilian capital, however, the Teatro Massimo was just that. The architect was Giovanni Battista Basile, who was born in Palermo and worked extensively there in the second half of the nineteenth century. Verdi's opera *Falstaff* inaugurated the theatre's opening in 1897. The 1950s and 1960s were a golden age when the world's greatest singers and conductors travelled to Palermo to perform in the city's opera house, but the Teatro Massimo was high on operatic itineraries from the day it opened.

'The theatre was closed at a particularly black moment in the city's history. The sack of Palermo had reached its peak, the city had been devastated and its architectural heritage destroyed. Then, soon after the theatre closed, the Mafia started an offensive that continued throughout the 1970s and 1980s and only ended with the terrible slaughter of 1992. People who lived in Palermo knew that for a long time the city's streets, squares and crossroads were grimly remembered by the names of those the Mafia had killed there,' recalled Francesco Giambrone, Teatro Massimo's *sovrintendente* (director) between 1999 and 2002.[32]

After a fire burned down a cinema in Turin in northwest Italy, the government had tightened the regulations and many theatres and cinemas had closed temporarily to make the alterations needed to satisfy the new regulations. Installing and improving safety equipment in Palermo's opera house should have taken only six months. Few in the city believed that the six-month closure would actually be enough, but nobody expected that the Teatro Massimo would remain closed for twenty-three years.

Urban blight worsened during that period. More people deserted the historic centre and ugly suburbs spread to take them. Little was done to repair the damage that the centre had suffered from bombardment during the Second World War. Churches closed, monuments decayed and the city's old heart became a dangerous no-man's land where few ventured after dark. And there in the centre of it stood the Teatro Massimo, its neo-classical façade and dome sticking out above the metal sheeting that clad the iron railings around the building. The theatre was shut but it could not be hidden.

Palermo's city fathers spent hundreds of billions of lire on work done in the theatre while it was closed. Some of that work was damaging, some of it simply useless. Whatever the case, the empty theatre just kept devouring money. There was no scheme, no plan, no project. When the Teatro Massimo had been shut for twenty years, people started to ask what had been done so far, what still needed to be done, and when the theatre would open again. They discovered that those responsible for the works did not have drawings of the theatre or know how it was built. 'I cannot say whether the Mafia was involved or not, but there were obviously powerful economic interests in play, powerful interests for keeping the theatre shut,' said Giambrone.[33] The theatre's *sovrintendente* avoided blaming complicity between the city's authorities and the Mafia but 'powerful economic interests' had only one meaning in Sicily.

CHRISTIAN DEMOCRAT COMPLICITY

By the time the Teatro Massimo reopened in 1997 – thanks in large measure to the civic spirit and drive of Leoluca Orlando, the mayor, who had abandoned the Christian Democrat Party in protest several years earlier to form his own party, La Rete (the network) – the landscape of Italian politics had changed dramatically. The Christian Democrat Party, winning almost 39 nine per cent of the vote at the parliamentary elections in 1972, had been the biggest party in Italy by a long stretch.[34] Twenty-five years later, blown apart by the corruption scandals that had erupted in 1992, the party itself no longer existed but had splintered into several minor parties. In May 2001, the party that won most votes nationally was Berlusconi's Forza Italia, which took just under 30 per cent.[35]

Nowhere was the upheaval felt more than in Sicily. Throughout the 1970s and most of the 1980s, the Christian Democrat Party dominated the island's government and public affairs. Salvo Lima, the mayor of Palermo with whom Vito Ciancimino had worked closely, became an important figure in the party. Unlike Ciancimino, who remained a local politician, Lima graduated to national and European politics. He was elected to the parliament in Rome in 1968 but never forgot his home constituency and that he owed his position in Rome to his strength in Sicily.

In the early 1960s, he teamed up with Giulio Andreotti, who later served seven times as Italy's prime minister. Drawing on Lima's vote-gathering in Sicily, Andreotti was able to boost his position in the Christian Democrat Party. It was an arrangement that suited both politicians; Andreotti needed more votes in the party in order to be more powerful and Lima wanted the skilful Roman on his side. Before Lima gave his support, Andreotti's strength had been in Lazio, the region around Rome, but Andreotti had then been able to count on only 2 per cent of party members. After the Sicilian alliance, Andreotti's faction in the Christian Democrat Party accounted for between 13 and 17 per cent and the wily politician became a major force within his party.[36]

Yet, Lima did not climb as far up the national tree as he had hoped and expected; he was too closely linked to the Mafia. He was someone *in odore di mafia*, someone who smelled of the Mafia. His appointment as junior minister in the budget ministry in 1974, where Andreotti was then the minister, caused a stir. A leading economist resigned in protest from the national economic planning committee, writing to the *Corriere della Sera*, Italy's daily newspaper of record, to point out that Lima's management of Palermo's affairs had repeatedly attracted the attention of the judiciary. Evidence gathered by investigating magistrates had been so strong that, on four occasions, even parliament's lower house had authorized the judiciary to initiate proceedings against Lima.[37] He was too powerful and too dangerous for doubts about him to cause his downfall, but the Sicilian politician never rose above the bottom rung of the ministerial ladder.

Behind Lima and the Christian Democrat Party in Sicily were the Salvo cousins, who derived enormous power from their concession for tax-farming on the island. Antonino and Ignazio Salvo collected taxes on behalf of the government and were well rewarded for the job. Their cut was 10 per cent of the money they collected, three times the average figure for similar businesses elsewhere in Italy.[38] Moreover, they held these tax revenues for months before transferring them to the government. The business was splendidly lucrative for the Salvo cousins who not only carved out a huge slice of the taxes for themselves but got extra income from the interest on what they had collected. Political influence went hand-in-hand with economic power and the Salvo cousins were the puppet-masters of Sicilian politics. By controlling between one half and two thirds of the Christian Democrat representatives in the Sicilian assembly in Palermo they had the power to make or break the regional government.[39]

The Salvo cousins had been deeply involved with Cosa Nostra, said a court in Palermo in October 1999. A *mafioso* who was cooperating with the prosecutors had told the court that the pair had participated in planning the murder of the head of the investigative office in Palermo in 1983.[40] But the Salvo cousins' ties to the Mafia had been known for many years. According to the prosecutors in the first maxi-trial of *mafiosi* that began in February 1986 and concerned 475 defendants, the Salvo cousins had provided a political-financial-mafia nexus around which the Christian Democrat Party in Sicily turned.

Comfortable cohabitation between the Christian Democrat Party and the Mafia became bumpy after the maxi-trials in the second half of the 1980s which ended with lengthy prison sentences for hundreds of *mafiosi*. The Mafia had thought that its powerful political accomplices allowed it to be above the law, dodge trials and escape lightly when found guilty. With the first maxi-trial underway in Palermo, Cosa Nostra showed its displeasure when parliamentary elections

9 Legal leaders
(*above*) Chief prosecutors.
Francesco Saverio Borrelli (anti-
corruption (*left*)) and Gian Carlo
Caselli (anti-Mafia (*right*)).
(*right*) Franzo Grande Stevens,
chairman of the Italian bar, who
said that telling the truth should
be everyone's duty and practice.

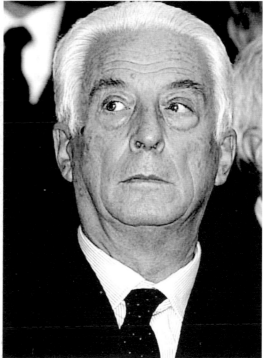

10 & 11 On the side of
justice
(*above*) The Capaci exit,
where Falcone died in May
1992.
(*left*) Anti-Mafia
magistrates Giovanni
Falcone (*left*) and Paolo
Borsellino (*right*).
(*bottom*) Via D'Amelio,
where Borsellino died in
July 1992.

(*above left*) Anna Maria Palma, who prosecuted Borsellino's killers. (*above right*) Domenico Gozzo (*left*) and Antonio Ingroia (*right*), who prosecuted Dell'Utri. (*right*) Ilda Boccassini (*left*), who prosecuted Berlusconi and Previti, and Armando Spataro (*right*), who prosecuted terrorists. (*below right*) *Mani pulite*. Gherardo Colombo (*left*), Antonio Di Pietro (*centre*) and Piercamillo Davigo (*right*), Milan, June 1993.

12 & 13 Italians gathered in Rome to demonstrate against the Cirami Law, September 2002

(*left*) 'We want just justice. Berlusconi–Previti bandits in Italy, outlaws in Europe.'

(*below*) 'Shame! Crooks out of parliament and the senate.'

(*bottom*) 'I have a legitimate suspicion that Berlusconi, Previti and chums are guilty.'

(*right*) 'Berlusconi's justice – an infinite disgrace.'
(*below*) 'I have a legitimate suspicion that Previti and Berlusconi are *mafiosi*???'; 'President Pera, Berlusconi's servant' (as the senate's speaker, Marcello Pera held Italy's second highest state office).

La GIUSTIZIA

DI BERLUSCONI
UNA VERGOGNA

INFINITA

PRESIDENTE PERA

SERVO DI

BERLUSCONI

HO UN LEGITTIMO
SOSPETTO
-PREVITI-
-BERLUSCONI-
SONO MAFIOSI???

14 Close to the heart
(*above*) Presenting new players for AC Milan's line-up.
(*below*) Presenting Mediaset, his television company, with friend and colleague
Fedele Confalonieri (*left*) and finance director Ubaldo Livolsi (*right*).

15 Multiple images
(*above*) Magazine posters.
(*below*) Making the news.

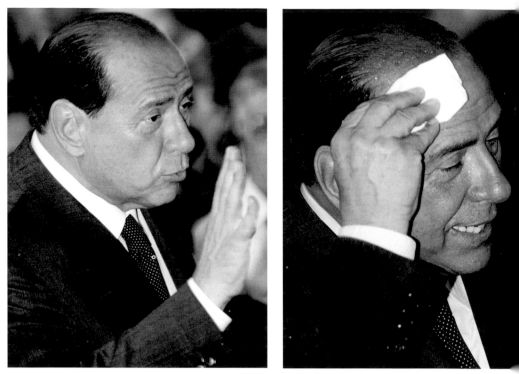

16 On trial for judicial corruption and allowed to lie, untroubled by questions, Berlusconi makes a 'spontaneous declaration' in a Milanese court, June 2003.

were held in 1987. With a handful of exceptions, it had always backed candidates of the Christian Democrat Party, but this time the Mafia decided to drum up the vote for the Socialist Party and the small Radical Party.

These two parties had shown themselves friendlier than the Christian Democrats. They had campaigned for a referendum to be held on the magistrature, with the aim of clipping its wings, reducing the law's effectiveness and strengthening the position of defendants in court. These were just the kind of proposals that the Mafia wanted to hear, and mafia bosses and their underlings gave orders as to where votes should go.[41] The election went very well for Bettino Craxi's Socialist Party in Sicily, its share of the vote in Palermo leaping from under 10 per cent to over 16 per cent, and the Radical Party also gained significantly.[42] The big loser was the Christian Democrat Party which had badly let down its mafia electorate and was punished at the ballot box for doing so.

On 30 January 1992, when the supreme court delivered its verdict on the appeals of the *mafiosi* convicted in the maxi-trial, the Mafia knew that its friends in politics had been unable to keep their word. They had not come up with legislation to reduce the penalties or make life easier for *mafiosi* who were behind bars, and interfering with the court's deliberations had also been beyond them. By murdering Salvo Lima in March 1992, the Mafia showed its frustration and anger and settled an outstanding account.

The Christian Democrat Party was not alone in letting down the Mafia, however. The Socialist Party would prove a great disappointment too. Named as minister of justice in February 1991, Claudio Martelli, a leading figure in the party, appointed Giovanni Falcone to head the ministry's penal affairs, an appointment that was for the Mafia not just a betrayal by the Socialist Party but also a very serious threat. According to the Mafia, Falcone had been responsible for preventing its traditional political allies from intervening to obtain a favourable outcome from the court that was hearing the appeals against the maxi-trial's verdicts.

With the breaking of the *tangentopoli* corruption scandals in Milan in February 1992, the political system within which the Mafia had moved so confidently began to fall rapidly apart. Parliamentary

elections at the beginning of April 1992 showed a sharp weakening
of public support for the parties that had long governed Italy. A political earthquake had hit the country and the murders of Falcone in
May and Borsellino two months later amplified the shock.

VILLABATE AND CACCAMO

Villabate, a town on the coast about five miles east of Palermo, has a
special place in mafia history. It won that special place in February
1893 when killers stabbed to death an aristocratic politician in a
carriage of a train travelling along the coastal railway line between
Termini Imerese, a town about 20 miles east of Palermo, and the
Sicilian capital.[43] Emanuele Notarbartolo di San Giovanni had been
mayor of Palermo from 1873 to 1876 and then been appointed general manager of the Banco di Sicilia, the island's biggest bank, where
he worked until 1890. He had a reputation as a capable banker and
administrator and was known as a person of irreproachable moral
standing.[44] Notarbartolo became the Mafia's first *cadavere eccellente*
(excellent cadaver or illustrious victim). His two killers belonged to
the mafia clan in Villabate and the person who commissioned them
was a leading politician in Palermo who had business interests and
close contacts with the Mafia in Caccamo, a town a few miles inland
from Termini Imerese.[45]

Notarbartolo's murder was just the beginning; a century later the
Mafia in Villabate and Caccamo was still making news. When the
provincial headquarters of the *carabinieri* military police in Palermo
announced a big operation on 9 June 1998 they called it Caccamo/
Nettuno.[46] Orders had been given to arrest seventeen men suspected
of association with the Mafia, money-laundering, extortion, drug-
trafficking, corruption, aggravated interference with competitive tenders and the violation of bankruptcy laws. Top of the list was
Antonino Mandala, a businessman who had been Forza Italia's chairman in Villabate. The second name was Antonino Giuffre, described
as the boss of the *mandamento* of Caccamo, a mafia district centred
on the small town of Caccamo and embracing the families of Cosa
Nostra in Caccamo itself and another eight towns and villages east of

the Sicilian capital. These included Termini Imerese, where the coastal plain had been turned into a large industrial estate. Long sought by the police, Giuffre was on the run from the law at the time and would eventually be captured in the countryside near Caccamo almost four years later.

The *carabinieri*'s announcement carried an eighteenth name, that of Gaspare Giudice, whose arrest, because he was a member of parliament, had to be requested through the justice ministry in Rome. Giudice had been born in 1943 in Canicatti in the southern Sicilian province of Agrigento and had fought 1996's parliamentary elections in the island's seventh electoral college. His constituency for the chamber of deputies was Bagheria, a town on the coast between Palermo and Termini Imerese where the Mafia was deeply entrenched, and the 39,000 votes that he was given were well over 50 per cent of the total cast.[47] He stood for election in the ranks of Silvio Berlusconi's Forza Italia and as the party's deputy regional coordinator between 1995 and 1998 was an important cog in Forza Italia's Sicilian machine.

The investigations, whose results were announced in June 1998, sprang from leads obtained during an earlier operation called *Venerdi Nero* (Black Friday) that had allowed the *carabinieri* to smash a ferocious band of killers run by the bosses of the *mandamenti* of Caccamo and Villabate. The investigators had spent two years gathering evidence using a wide range of devices and methods: telephone taps, tails, bugs, satellite intercepts, filmed observation and checks on bank accounts and assets held in Italy and abroad. They had looked closely at public-sector contracts and business relationships in the area.[48] Penetrating the Mafia in Caccamo and Villabate had been difficult, said the *carabinieri*, but they had been able to find evidence of illicit activities from the first half of the 1980s onwards.

Gaspare Giudice was on the *carabinieri*'s list but he desperately wanted to stay out of jail and, as he appealed to the chamber of deputies, the lower house of parliament in Rome, his voice was breaking with emotion.[49] He told his fellow members of parliament that he had never had anything to do with the Mafia. He knew, he said, that he did not deserve to go to jail. Giudice's plea was heard: on 16 July 1998, the chamber of deputies voted to overturn the decision of a parliamentary commission that had ruled in favour of the Palermo magistrates' request that the police be allowed to arrest him.[50] Giudice's problems were not over, however. Parliament's vote did not put a stop to the matter and, less than a year after the lower house had blocked the magistrates' request, a judge in Palermo sent Giudice for trial.[51] Renato Grillo, the judge responsible for the preliminary investigations, had decided that there was sufficient evidence to indict the Forza Italia deputy on charges of association with the Mafia, fraudulent bankruptcy and money-laundering. The judgement that Grillo handed down on 15 April 1999 did not mean remand in jail for Giudice who because of parliament's ruling would not be arrested and remained free. Fifteen other people, including Mandala and Giuffre, were also sent for trial and the Caccamo/Nettuno case, although drawing to an end, was still being heard in a Palermo court in spring 2004.

A person trusted by the bosses of the *mandamenti*, said the prosecutors when they presented their case, Guidice had used his position as an employee of Sicilcassa, a large Sicilian bank, to undertake operations to launder money obtained from crime.[52] Giudice had been the manager of Sicilcassa's Termini Imerese Alta branch from 1980 until 1985. He had been arrested in May 1986 and suspended by the bank from the beginning of 1988 until October 1992. His arrest had arisen in connection with a scheme through which Italy's tax authorities had been defrauded, but a court had subsequently dismissed the charges against him.

In 1996, ten years after Giudice had been arrested on suspicion of tax fraud, a *mafioso* called Salvatore Barbagallo who had decided to cooperate with the authorities mentioned Giudice's name while being questioned about the activities of Giuseppe Panzeca, regent of the Caccamo *mandamento*. Barbagallo, who had been the driver of Lorenzo Di Gesu, another leading *mafioso* from Caccamo, told the magistrates that Di Gesu had used Giudice to launder money for the Mafia. Barbagallo had gone twice a month to Sicilcassa's branch at Termini Imerese Alta, said the magistrates, carrying large sums of cash, as much as 50 million lire a trip, that Giudice either changed into notes of different denominations or deposited in bearer passbooks with the names of flowers. When investigators checked documents at the bank, they found accounts called 'dahlia', 'daisy', 'petal' and 'tulip', and operations like those that Barbagallo had described. Barbagallo told the magistrates that soon after his initiation into Cosa Nostra, at the end of 1982, Di Gesu had introduced Giudice as *la stessa cosa* (the same thing).[53] This was the Mafia's way of identifying one of their own.

Cassa Centrale di Risparmio Vittorio Emanuele per le Province Siciliane, to give Sicilcassa its full name, was the second largest bank in Sicily. A public-sector bank where the politicians' words were those that counted, and with around 300 branches, it was well entrenched throughout the island. But its strong market position did not save it from failure; overmanned, badly managed and infiltrated by the Mafia, Sicilcassa was ignominiously mired in losses and bad loans. In one of Italy's biggest banking crashes, the Bank of Italy put Sicilcassa into liquidation in September 1997.

In June 1997, Sicilcassa's general manager was questioned by the magistrates in connection with the Caccamo/Nettuno investigations. After Giudice's election to parliament in 1996, Sicilcassa had received a court order placing a lien on one fifth of his salary because, said the court order, Giudice had failed to honour a debt of 50 million lire. The general manager became curious and made inquiries about the employee who had been in Forza Italia's parliamentary ranks for just over a year. He learned that Giudice had had problems with another debt and had been arrested for allegedly helping the Mafia. Sicilcassa's general manager also learned that Giudice's daughter and estranged wife were named as guarantors of a group of companies controlled by Giuseppe Panzeca, who would become one of Giudice's co-defendants after their indictment in April 1999. He discovered that the bank's loan to that group had turned sour and the bank was one step away from legal action. The general manager soon passed the files to the bank's lawyers, a move that irritated Giudice, who wrote to his former employer to complain.[54]

The head of Sicilcassa's legal department, who had been aware that Panzeca was implicated in judicial proceedings, told the magistrates that when the matter was brought to his attention he had realized it was rather delicate. An expert consultant from the Bank of Italy had dug into Sicilcassa's records and concluded that the department that kept loans under observation had shown minimal concern for the bank's interests. Finding the drafts of letters sent by Panzeca to the bank in Sicilcassa's own files was definitely not normal practice and suggested close ties of complicity between the parties that were certainly not to Sicilcassa's benefit. The senior politician of Forza Italia had managed all the bank's dealings with the troubled Panzeca group although this was not part of his job.

Barbagallo first mentioned Giudice's name to the investigators in May 1996, just one month after the parliamentary elections had been held. One former associate told the magistrates that Giudice owed his election to the support of *mafiosi* such as Panzeca and Mandala, and to members of various mafia families who collected votes in the constituency.[55] Between the end of 1994 and mid-1995, after a bloody conflict between mafia families in Villabate, Mandala moved to the top of the *mandamento*. Thanks to this, he had become a very important figure in the main political and business circles in Villabate and Palermo.

Mandala had officially resigned from the chairmanship of Forza Italia in Villabate, following his son's arrest in connection with murders in the town. The magistrates and investigators were sure, however, that he still exerted great political influence. 'Let's not forget, Gaspare, that you have duties to your constituency,' said Mandala, in a telephone conversation with Giudice that the *carabinieri* had tapped.[56] Mandala complained that the member of parliament who sat in Forza Italia's ranks was not doing enough. Perhaps Giudice had indeed been pushing things ahead, said Mandala, but he could not see the results. There were people who expected clear signs and wanted facts, he added.

That the judge overseeing the preliminary investigations had found sufficient grounds to send Giudice for trial did not bring an end to the politician's parliamentary career. Instead, in April 2001, two years after the judge decided that he should stand trial, Giudice was again campaigning for election to the chamber of deputies. This time he was a candidate in Sicily's 13th electoral college, the Villagrazia district of the island's capital. The constituency lay in Palermo's hinterland, an area between Villabate and Monreale, a town known for a solid mafia presence as well as the cathedral's twelfth- and thirteenth-century mosaics. He was successful against four other candidates on the ballot paper and won over half of the votes cast.[57] Returned to parliament, Giudice was a deputy in Rome while on trial for serious crimes in Palermo.

MAKING A GARDEN

'The world has a dream: to copy Palermo,' proclaimed giant hoardings in the Sicilian capital. A sense of civic pride surrounded the conference on transnational organized crime that the United Nations held in Palermo in December 2000. Fourteen heads of state, ministers from more than 100 countries and the United Nations' secretary-general Kofi Annan were there. Before the conference closed, three quarters of the world's nations had signed a convention aimed at fighting the Mafia in its many global forms.

Palermo's authorities had made a great effort to ensure their city looked its best. They spruced up public buildings and transformed the main square from squalor to elegance, cleaning the marble pavilion that stood there and installing pinpoint lights that sparkled underfoot in the square's broad pavements. A large new garden had been specially created on the sea-front promenade, across the road from the old Kalsa district where Falcone and Borsellino were born and had grown up. A brown oval plaque hung at the entrance. On it were the words: '*Città di Palermo – 2000 – Giardino delle Nazioni Unite*'.

One year later, the triumphal avenue flanked with columns that led from the road to the sea was a reminder of how the grand conference's fine intentions had soon been forgotten. The column's metal bases had rusted and lamps beside the avenue had been broken. A torn card told passers-by not to walk over the seeded lawns, but few people were around to take notice. Instead, the garden – now a bumpy patch of weeds that rain turned to mud – was home to packs of stray dogs. Two years after the conference, the oval plaque had been defaced with one word: *vergogna* (shame).

Behind the garden's decline from civic jewel to urban blight lay a familiar story of general indifference and official maladministration. Public money had been wasted and there had been oversights in managing the tender for the garden. One of the two firms that presented the joint winning bid had submitted false certificates and the firm beaten in the bidding had issued a writ seeking substantial damages for the cost of tendering, lost profits and the damage to its image resulting from failure to win the contract.[58]

Two months after the conference, the city authorities annulled the contract but by then work had been done and the firms wanted to be paid. They had officially handed over the garden to the authorities in May 2001, six months after the conference. But there had been mistakes in making the garden: the ground had not been properly prepared, the watering system had not been up to scratch and the type of seed had been wrong for Palermo's climate and the seaside site. By August, the garden was a complete ruin, said the city council.[59]

Palermo's city authorities had been in a tangle ever since they signed the contract. Changes in the administration had been an extra complication. In the year that followed the conference, between the end of 2000 and the end of 2001, Palermo had been headed first by one mayor, then by a special commissioner and finally by another mayor of a different political colour from the first. Independent experts had been called in, many meetings held and lawyers kept busy. Eventually, in March 2002, fifteen months after the conference, the city council announced that the dispute with the firms that had won the contract had been settled. They had decided to accept 900,000 euros to close the matter.[60] In November 2002, the city authorities awarded a contract to a consortium of three firms to do the work again. The United Nations' conference on global organized crime had faded into the past but the saga of Palermo's United Nations' garden dragged on. Not just wasteful and costly for the taxpayer, such messy bureaucratic situations in Sicily could offer fertile conditions for the Mafia to flourish.

LIVING WITH THE MAFIA

Piero Grasso, Palermo's chief prosecutor, was a speaker at the conference in December 2000. Before returning to the role of prosecutor, he had sat as a judge during the maxi-trial, which he described as a fine moment in the battle against the Mafia. Grasso told the conference that this battle had to aim at severing the Mafia's relations with the contaminated sectors of civil society and the institutions. An important, but often neglected, part of strategy was the defence of the legal and political system against infiltration and conditioning by the Mafia.

The authorities needed to crack down hard on every lapse in the public administration, revoking licences and building permits, and cancelling contracts and sub-contracts wherever there was mafia involvement. Municipal or provincial councils had to be dissolved where they had links with the Mafia or had been infiltrated by collusive administrators. Grasso said that severe penalties had to be imposed where money was offered in return for votes or where obstacles were erected to obstruct the free exercise of the vote. 'There should be,' said Grasso, 'a limitation on the rights to be candidates at elections of persons committed for trial on grave charges.'[61]

Grasso's predecessor in Palermo was Gian Carlo Caselli, who had volunteered for the job after Falcone and Borsellino had been murdered. He worked in the Sicilian capital from 1993 to 1999, having transferred from his home city of Turin in northwest Italy. He gave up his personal freedom, living in military barracks and being closely escorted wherever he went. The state could not afford another atrocity like those in which magistrates and their escorts had been slaughtered in Sicily. During Caselli's seven very hard years in Palermo, the magistrates investigated almost 9,000 people suspected of being in or connected to the Mafia and won indictments against over 3,000 of them.

Important results were obtained, as the 251 life sentences passed or confirmed by the courts in the Sicilian capital's judicial district in 2000 and 2001 showed. Yet, during that two-year period not one *imputato eccellente* (illustrious defendant, such as a politician or leading businessman) was found guilty. 'How can we explain this huge difference?' asked Caselli.[62] Was it possible that the prosecutors were skilful and efficient against common *mafiosi*, he wondered, but incapable and inefficient against *imputati eccellenti*? Or perhaps the burden of proof changed or proof was objectively much harder to find?

'For more than 100 years,' said Caselli, 'the Mafia has been the

Mafia insofar as it could always count on political collusion.'[63] Caselli thought that an important part of an anti-Mafia strategy ought to lie in excluding people with mafia ties from positions of influence and power. 'Politicians who are in league with the Mafia must be isolated, above all politically. This has not always happened here,' he said.[64] The Mafia had survived and prospered not just because it was a band of dangerous gangsters, he added, but because it was a band of dangerous gangsters who could rely on political support and alliances. Such alliances were in the Mafia's genes and it was in those alliances that the authorities needed to intervene. Italy had to put the Mafia and its supporters in quarantine. Instead, rather than combating the Mafia with every possible weapon, Berlusconi's government seemed to acquiesce in the inevitability of the Mafia's presence.

When he formed his government in June 2001, Berlusconi appointed Pietro Lunardi as transport minister, the minister responsible for public works. A businessman with substantial interests in the construction industry, Lunardi soon made his presence known. 'The Mafia and the Camorra have always been around; alas, they are there and we must live with this reality,' he remarked at the end of August 2001. At the beginning of October, he said, 'We are forced to live with the Mafia as with other realities, like for example the 7,000 killed on the roads.'[65] In October 2002, when seated opposite Caselli at a ceremonial lunch at a research centre near Turin, where the senior magistrate had recently been appointed state prosecutor, Lunardi had the opportunity to argue his case.[66] Living with the Mafia was, however, far from Caselli's way of tackling it. Indeed, the prosecutor called the minister's opinion a gaffe.[67]

Lunardi's remarks were startling because the Mafia was more deeply involved in construction and public works than any other sector of the legitimate economy. These were areas in which it could cement and exploit political ties, make substantial illicit gains and strengthen its control on the ground. Infiltration by Cosa Nostra into public works contracts was a matter that greatly worried the Direzione Nazionale Antimafia (DNA, the national anti-Mafia body) in Rome. The DNA's concern was such that, in 2001, it established a separate department to keep an eye on public works. Two magistrates appointed to the new department said that what they had found led to an unavoidable conclusion: the authorities needed to do much more to equip themselves with the tools for countering mafia infiltration. The problems were everywhere, they said in their report, from tendering procedures to materials supply and plant-hire. Public works was mafia business in the year 2000 and had been so for decades. The Mafia's tight political links and solid ties with business and the world of finance were nowhere stronger or more evident.

During the 1980s, the Mafia had moved away from a crude, parasitic method of making money from public works: the extortion of cash from firms that were engaged in construction projects. Instead it had developed an integrated, vertical control over the sector that allowed it to grip public works in Sicily tightly in its tentacles. Angelo Siino headed a group of small construction firms; he gave his name to the method through which the Mafia took charge and was called the Mafia's minister for public works. He was close to the Brusca mafia family of San Giuseppe Jato, a large town about 20 miles south of Palermo. Siino was a member of the Oriente masonic lodge in the Sicilian capital and had established good relations with important politicians and local government officials.[68]

Siino had the advantage of expert knowledge of the complex and obscure rules of public works tendering, understood only by bureaucrats and firms in the system, and he offered it and his network of contacts to Salvatore Riina, Cosa Nostra's boss. Siino's idea was that firms should take turns to win contracts and that they needed to collude in the tendering process through which the firm that offered the largest discount on the base price won the job. Under normal, competitive market conditions, discounts were higher than 20 per cent. Siino rigged the market so that the discounts in Sicily were well under 5 per cent, yielding the Mafia fat profits. He became the Mafia's business representative, organized agreements between firms and would later be convicted of mafia crimes, a sentence of eight years' imprisonment being confirmed by the supreme court on 12 April 1997. By the second half of the 1980s, the system had spread beyond Palermo.

Local government officials and politicians worked hand-in-hand with the Mafia to rig the bidding or set the conditions for tendering so that only firms with mafia ties could participate. They also played their part in organizing the finance and ensuring the payment of works. Forming temporary consortia allowed more of them to benefit. Winning firms paid off their mafia contacts, who then paid the appropriate mafia families and the collusive politicians and officials. From managing the tendering process, the Mafia's control then extended to choosing sub-contractors – suppliers of materials and plant-hire firms – from among the local Mafia where the works were undertaken. Those that got in the way were quickly and firmly dissuaded by threats of violence or by violence itself.

'The system worked in a manner that made the Mafia barely visible,' said the anti-Mafia authorities.[69] Cosa Nostra had established a cohabitation that was protected by a climate of silence, born not only of intimidation but also of common interests. Everyone had learned to live with the Mafia. The advice of the minister of transport in Berlusconi's government had already been heeded.

Entrenched throughout Sicily, the system did not collapse with Siino's arrest and his decision, in August 1997, to cooperate with the prosecutors.[70] The Mafia continued to hold public works in a firm grip. In a report published at the end of 2001, the DNA noted that investigations in Catania in eastern Sicily had identified politicians whom businessmen and members of the Santapaolo clan had used in order to win valuable public-sector contracts.[71] 'Public works contracts are under Cosa Nostra's full and total control. There is not one kind of business, whether it be the supply of plant or materials or labour, that is not subject to mafia approval,' said Anna Maria Palma, speaking about the situation in the province of Agrigento in the south of the island.[72] Indeed, the massive flow of funds for infrastructure projects, promised by Rome and by the European Union in Brussels, made the sector still more appetizing to Cosa Nostra.

Probably no project caught the Mafia's eye more than the proposed bridge over the Strait of Messina. The idea of joining Sicily to mainland Italy had been discussed for many years. There had originally been talk of building a tunnel but a bridge spanning the two miles between Calabria and Sicily was chosen when Berlusconi's government made its decision and work was expected to start in 2005. The towers that would carry the cables to support the planned suspension bridge would rise to about 1,200 feet. The cost of building the bridge was estimated at almost 5 billion euros (about £3.3 billion or $5 billion). And if everything went to plan, traffic would start to flow in 2011.[73]

Controversy surrounded the project. The volume of traffic would never be enough to justify it and the tolls would never cover the bridge's financing costs, let alone repay the debt that would be incurred in construction. Some studies pointed to the movement of tectonic plates, others to the serious seismic risk in that part of Italy. The Sicilian city of Messina had been razed by an earthquake in 1908 and the coastlines on the opposite sides of the strait had shifted significantly then. Some Italians were worried about the impact that the bridge would have on the local environment. Others said that Sicily had more urgent need of other infrastructural projects. Many pointed to the power of the Mafia on both sides of the strait. They did not have to point far. Improvements to the highway running north to Naples from Reggio Calabria, across the strait from Messina, started at the end of 1997. Not only was progress delayed by myriad difficulties but, five years after the work began, anti-Mafia investigators were busy digging into infiltration by the 'Ndrangheta, the Calabria region's Mafia, into the highway's upgrading project.

According to investigators, the construction materials used for building the highway had not been as specified in the contracts, but that should have been no surprise. The DNA had noted in 2001 that people knew, and it had been proved in court, that the production and supply of inert materials were controlled by mafia organizations; the licensing regime for this industry had never been subject to regulations suitable for tackling the risks of mafia infiltration. 'If it is true, for example, that 1,100,000 tonnes of cement will be needed for the bridge over the Strait of Messina, the impact on mafia organizations is easily imaginable,' warned the DNA.[74] Palermo's Cosa Nostra had colonized the province of Messina. Interlocking interests, alliances and family ties at the highest levels of institutional life showed a tendency to condition political, social, economic, judicial, cultural and academic life there.[75]

Everywhere the Mafia was a problem. There was mass illegality in the province of Agrigento, where people were even more determined than other Sicilians to show that ownership of land and property carried an absolute right to build how, when and where the owner wanted. Everyone had a blatant disregard for planning laws and the whole of Agrigento's political class seemed to be caught up in this illegality. A politician once told Ignazio De Francisci, who had been appointed chief prosecutor in the city in the summer of 1999, that planning abuse had marked politics in Agrigento for fifty years and that this was just something they had to live with.[76] The prosecutor had discovered local administrations polluted by crime and many town councils had found themselves involved in criminal proceedings or being investigated over tendering procedures for public works.

GIULIO ANDREOTTI

From Agrigento in the most southerly part of Sicily to Palermo and Messina in the north, and on the mainland from Reggio Calabria to Naples, magistrates faced similar challenges. In the countryside, small towns or large cities, whether tackling the Camorra in the region of Campania around Naples, the *Sacra Corona Unita* in the heel region of Puglia, the *'Ndrangheta* in Calabria or Cosa Nostra in Sicily, investigators and the judiciary everywhere in the *mezzogiorno* were up against mafia infiltration and administrative and political complicity. Yet, in 2004, just as twelve years earlier when Falcone and Borsellino were murdered, the investigators and the judiciary who were fighting the Mafia received scant support from politicians.

Giulio Andreotti was the victim of justice gone mad, claimed Silvio Berlusconi in November 2002 when the appeal court in Perugia sentenced the seven-times former prime minister to twenty-four years in prison for complicity in murder – a sentence that would be quashed by the supreme court in October 2003. 'Politicized sections of the judiciary have sought to change the course of political democracy and rewrite Italian history,' Berlusconi said.[77]

A historian and expert on the Mafia, Nicola Tranfaglia, took a different view. Writing after Andreotti was acquitted in October 1999 by a court in Palermo, where he had faced charges of association with the Mafia, Tranfaglia was less concerned with the politician's judicial and penal responsibilities than with his historical and political responsibilities. In 1945, at the age of twenty-six, Andreotti had been a member of the post-war national assembly. Two years later, he had been appointed to his first government post, a junior ministership in the cabinet, and he was never away from positions of power after that. Andreotti formed the first of his seven administrations in February 1972, having built a solid alliance with Salvo Lima and being able to call on a smoothly running Sicilian connection. Tranfaglia said that Andreotti bore heavy responsibility for what had happened in Italy. He and his fellow political leaders over many decades had failed to fight the Mafia with the determination that was needed and Tranfaglia thought that the veteran Christian Democrat politician deserved to be kept at a distance.

'Politicians and the public should treat with greater prudence, even distrust, the person who headed a political faction in Sicily that was heavily polluted by Cosa Nostra and who had for a long time close relationships with people like Michele Sindona, Salvo Lima, Ignazio and Nino Salvo,' said Tranfaglia about Andreotti.[78] Andreotti said that he had not known the Salvos but the court thought this was not true. 'The assertion of the defendant that he had had no relationship with the Salvo cousins was unequivocally contradicted by the evidence,' stated the court's judgement in October 1999.[79] At a convivial gathering at a hotel in Sicily in June 1979, Andreotti had spoken repeatedly with Antonino Salvo in a way that led others present to be convinced that the two already knew each other. Andreotti gave a silver tray as a wedding gift to Antonino Salvo's oldest daughter. In 1983, he inquired after the health of a friend and business partner of the Salvo cousins. Ignazio Salvo's diary for 1984 contained an entry with Andreotti's telephone number. On various trips in Sicily, Andreotti used the car that Antonino Salvo had lent to Salvo Lima.[80] Yet, the court decided that, although the Salvo cousins had told various *mafiosi* that they were friends of Andreotti and that they could ask for favours from the politician, this was insufficient evidence that Andreotti had been willing to play a part in their criminal schemes. Neither cousin was able to testify in Andreotti's trial as mafia gunmen had murdered Ignazio Salvo in September 1992 and his cousin Antonino had died of cancer.

The prosecutors in Palermo appealed against the lower court's verdict and in May 2003, three and a half years after the lower court had found Andreotti not guilty, the appeal court confirmed that verdict. However, in the judgement that it filed on 25 July 2003, the appeal court gave some comfort to the prosecutors. The judges noted that the statute of limitations had already become effective for any offence of criminal association that had been committed before the spring of 1980. Far from absolving Andreotti, as the lower court had done, the appeal court found evidence to support the prosecution's case that there had been criminal association by the former prime minister until then. 'The authentic, stable and friendly openness towards *mafiosi* did not continue beyond the spring of 1980,' said the appeal court.[81] For these judges, Andreotti's faction in the Christian Democrat Party had benefited from his amicable and direct relations with Lima and the Salvo cousins and the former prime minister had been grateful for the electoral support of *mafiosi*.[82] Andreotti would appeal to the supreme court against the appeal court's judgement but the supreme court had still not given its judgement in spring 2004.

Another of Andreotti's severe critics was Nando Dalla Chiesa, a centre-left senator whose father, General Carlo Alberto Dalla Chiesa, the prefect of Palermo, had been murdered in August 1982. In November 2003, Dalla Chiesa attended a sitting of the senate in which Andreotti claimed that he had been the victim of a plot. Dalla Chiesa was angered by the way Andreotti, elevated to life-senator in 1991 because he had 'brought honour to his motherland by his great achievements in the social, scientific, artistic and literary fields',[83] and members of Berlusconi's coalition had turned parliament into a forum for debating the judgements of criminal courts and by what had been said to whitewash Andreotti. Dalla Chiesa remembered how he had heard the news of his father's murder by a mafia gunman, and he recalled his father's diary and the desperate letter that his father had written to the prime minister. Members of Andreotti's faction were up to their necks in mafia business and were the most polluted political family in the place, the general had confided in his writings. Once asked why he had not attended the general's funeral, Andreotti said he preferred baptisms. Andreotti told his supporters after Dalla Chiesa's murder that people spoke badly of Sicily's

Christian Democrats because they were strong. The Christian Democrat leader thought that the myth of the *carabiniere* general sent to his death in Palermo needed to be deconstructed.[84] Twenty years after General Dalla Chiesa died serving his country, Andreotti was alive and giving his view of history.

Nando Dalla Chiesa was not alone in being offended by what Andreotti had said to his fellow senators. The elderly politician whose power-base had depended so heavily on his Sicilian allies had been untruthful, said a group of anti-Mafia magistrates, and this had damaged their reputations. Writing to the president and vice-president of the magistrature's governing body, the magistrates said that Andreotti's declarations needed to be quickly rectified.[85] The evidence that had been heard in trials showed that Andreotti's claims about the origins of investigations concerning him were baseless; what Andreotti had said was 'completely detached from reality'. The doubt that the life-senator had seemed to express regarding the transcript of the deposition of a *collaboratore di giustizia* was 'wholly without foundation'. On the matter of part of the testimony of this *collaboratore di giustizia*, Andreotti's claim to the senate was 'just not true'.

That Italian public opinion failed to condemn the friendships and relationships between politicians and *mafiosi* was due partly to a large segment of the country's media, the television networks and newspapers that had once danced to the tune of the Christian Democrat Party and their allies in government and then did so with the political parties that made up Berlusconi's governing coalition. Indeed, Andreotti did not need rehabilitation after his trial for association with the Mafia, despite what it had revealed. He was a welcome guest on television chat-shows and journalists eagerly asked him what he thought about every possible subject under the sun. He continued to be praised and revered as a great statesman by politicians and many Italians. In celebration of Andreotti's eighty-fifth birthday, the Pontificia Universita Lateranense awarded him an *honoris causa* degree in civil and canon law.[86] Maybe some admired Andreotti for the way he had been able to tread the line so carefully or were fascinated by his consummate skills in political manoeuvring. And perhaps, as the Mafia taught, figures of power just had to be respected. No harm would be done in fawning to them.

When the votes were counted after the parliamentary elections of 1994, it was clear that the support given to Andreotti's Christian Democrat Party in Sicily had shifted to Berlusconi's Forza Italia. The evidence in mafia investigations and trials confirmed this. Some people considered that such a political inheritance was an embarrassment but it underpinned the crushing victory of Berlusconi's House of Freedoms coalition in May 2001.

As we have seen earlier, Piero Grasso, the chief prosecutor in Palermo, believed there should be a limitation on the rights to be candidates at elections of persons committed to trial on grave charges. On 8 June 2004, prosecutors of Grasso's anti-Mafia team asked a court in Palermo to find Marcello Dell'Utri guilty of association with the Mafia and to sentence him to eleven years' imprisonment.[87] Even so, on 15 June, just one week later and less than two months after a court in Milan had found Dell'Utri guilty of attempted extortion and sentenced him to two years' imprisonment, the speaker of the senate, a member of Berlusconi's Forza Italia party, nominated his party colleague and fellow-senator to be a delegate to the Council of Europe.[88] One of the Council of Europe's functions is judicial; it is responsible for electing judges to the European Court of Human Rights. On trial on grave charges in Palermo, Dell'Utri would be able to vote in Strasbourg on important international judicial appointments.

7

Justice

BERLUSCONI IN COURT

Crowds of photographers, journalists and television crews were milling in the corridor outside the courtroom two hours before the hearing was due to start. A scrum that big would have boosted even a film star's ego. There was neither glamour and glitter nor the gore of violent crime in prospect, however – just a matter of white-collar wrongdoing.

It was Monday 5 May 2003 and Silvio Berlusconi, Italy's prime minister, was expected to appear before a panel of three judges in the first section of Milan's criminal court. Taped to the door were details of the trial that was underway: case 879 of 2000 in the court's register. For the prosecution, the case was number 11749; it had begun in 1997. Nine defendants faced charges of judicial corruption and heading the list of defendants was Berlusconi himself.[1]

The journalists wanted to hear what the prime minister had to say and were keen to find good places in the courtroom. When the door was opened, the quickest rushed straight for the cage, the place in which dangerous defendants, such as terrorists and *mafiosi*, were securely penned at hearings. Behind the steel bars, the press people were beside the prosecution's bench and close to the desk where Berlusconi was expected to stand. They were also near the dais where the judges would sit, the inscription on the wall behind them proclaiming *La Legge è Uguale per Tutti*.[2] Fine words in Italian and in English: everyone is equal before the law. With Italy's prime minister, and the country's richest man, on trial on a serious criminal charge, this was a reassuring message.

As the few public benches and the cage filled, television crews set up their tripods and photographers squatted close to the defendants' desk, it was plain that the authorities had underestimated interest in the hearing. There was not enough space. The presiding judge ordered the courtroom to be cleared and *carabinieri* military police and members of the prison guard service tried to enforce the ruling.[3] Reluctant to yield the places that they had secured, and wondering whether this was a ploy to get the matter heard in camera, away from the public eye and ear, some journalists held their ground.

Then the presiding judge announced that the hearing had been transferred to a much larger courtroom used by the assize court for appeals. This courtroom was different in another way. When Berlusconi addressed the judges, no longer would he have to face, right before his eyes, the inscription *La Legge è Uguale per Tutti*. The wall behind the judges was decorated with a mosaic but there were no words, nothing to remind the prime minister that everyone was equal before the law.[4] That affirmation of how justice worked in a democracy was missing.

Berlusconi had decided to make a spontaneous declaration – his right as a defendant – and he was allowed to speak without interruption. As evidence, the value of his declaration was slight; he did not speak under oath. The procedures for the spontaneous declaration did not allow prosecutors and lawyers for co-plaintiffs to cross-examine him and the judges could not intervene. As a propaganda device, its value was rather greater. Berlusconi enjoyed a free rein and exploited his loquacity to speak for almost an hour without notes. He was already in full flow by the time many journalists and photographers were able to get into the new courtroom and they did not hear him say that he had taken no interest in the matter until about three weeks before the hearing. Indeed, he had read the indictment, issued more than three years earlier, only during a meeting with his lawyers on the evening before the hearing.[5] The indictment, based on articles 81, 110, 319, 319ter and 321 of the criminal code, accused Berlusconi of acts of judicial corruption.

'He asked me to get directly involved,' Berlusconi said, describing to the court how in 1985 his friend Bettino Craxi, who was then prime minister, had asked him to lend a hand in interfering with a business deal, the planned privatization of a food group.[6] The year before Craxi was given this help, he had promulgated controversial decrees that legalized Berlusconi's television operations. Giving his version of how a state holding corporation had attempted to sell its food group, called SME, Berlusconi claimed that his intervention had brought huge financial benefits for Italy.

Few at the hearing in the court in Milan were surprised that Berlusconi stepped around the question of the monies that the prosecutors said had found a way into the accounts of judges in Rome. He avoided mentioning the involvement of the secret, offshore part of his Fininvest business empire in a complex series of payments to lawyers who, the prosecution said, had given money to judges. (Cesare Previti had told the court that the money he had received was in payment for professional services.) Instead, Berlusconi underlined his important position as the country's prime minister and the great prestige that went with this. Not only did he have heavy commitments as head of the Italian government, but since the beginning of 2003, he had been one of the trio of prime ministers representing the European club, which comprised the heads of government of the countries holding the current, incoming and outgoing presidencies of the European Union. At the beginning of July 2003, Italy would itself take on the presidency for six months. He would have to visit at least twenty-five countries and his busy schedule already included seventy-six trips abroad.[7] The court would have to bear this in mind, he reminded the judges, in fixing hearings in the case as he would want to be present at all those that involved him.

Berlusconi had appeared at a hearing just over two weeks before he made his spontaneous declaration. Then he had been too busy to wait while a court-appointed lawyer was found for one of his fellow defendants. Berlusconi had not stayed long, but he had ceased to be contumacious just by being present at one hearing and, by recognizing the court's summons, had acquired the right to be present at all hearings. And this gave him the right to claim just impediment to get hearings postponed. His duties as prime minister were exactly the kind of impediment that he would be able to use to obstruct progress in the trial. As prime minister and president of the council of ministers of the European Union, moreover, he was able to summon up commitments more or less as he pleased.

The first hearing in Berlusconi's trial in Milan had been in March 2000, more than three years before he made his first attendance at a hearing of the case. During that period the court had held only 102 hearings, an average of less than forty a year, and the one at which Berlusconi made his spontaneous declaration took the total to 103.[8] The court had set a calendar in which there would be twenty-seven hearings during the three months that remained before the summer break in 2003, a leisurely pace of about two hearings a week that was threatened with being brought to a complete halt by Berlusconi's absence. Those figures alone said something about what was wrong with the criminal justice system in Italy. The rate at which trials progressed was very slow and it could be made even slower by the advantage that money and power could buy.

That a major trial like the SME case was part-heard, meaning that there was no day-after-day continuity of hearings, was something that judges and lawyers in Britain or America thought most strange. How were the panel of judges in Milan, the prosecutors and, not least, the defence counsel and those whom they were defending able to focus on the case if it was forever stopping and starting? Involving a very serious crime and important people, here was a case that deserved the closest and most scrupulous attention and needed a verdict sooner rather than later.

The country had a right to know whether its prime minister had bribed judges, as the prosecution claimed, or not, as Berlusconi asserted. And with Berlusconi holding the presidency of the European Union, the citizens in Italy's fourteen partner countries also had the right to know. It was unlikely that the Danes, Swedes, Germans, Britons and citizens of the other countries of the European Union would feel comfortable being represented by someone who had bribed judges. Many people already thought that it was wrong that the presidency should be held by a prime minister who was on trial for such a grave crime.

Such a case needed to be heard without delay. That the trial had progressed at a rhythm of less than three hearings a month was unusual, even wrong; at least many outsiders thought so. That the prime minister and the lawyers and former judges who were his co-defendants seemed to be party to monkeying with the court's programme added to the unease. Playing for time, dragging cases out until the statute of limitations kicked in, was a strategy open to wealthy and powerful defendants.

SLOW JUSTICE

Dilatory justice was usually harmful for ordinary Italians who found themselves in the dock, however. Most defendants wanted to get their trials over quickly because they did not want to have to worry for years about their outcome. The slowness of the Italian justice system was notorious and had often been criticized by international bodies, yet Italy's constitution was clear on how trials were to be conducted. As well as guaranteeing parity between defence and prosecution in front of impartial judges, the constitution guaranteed that trials would be of a reasonable duration.

The figures from Milan's criminal court for the year to 30 June 2001 showed how serious the problem of delay was. The sheer volume of work faced by examining magistrates, prosecutors and judges in the Lombard capital and the surrounding district was enormous. At the beginning of that year, judges responsible for preliminary investigations and hearings had a backlog of over 31,000 criminal cases in which the defendant was known. More than 103,000 new cases landed on their desks during the year, but they were able to deal only with 85,000. When the year ended, the backlog stood at more than 49,000. Almost 12,000 of the cases they dealt with were brought to an end because of the statute of limitations.[9] The criminal justice system had simply run out of time even before cases reached trial.

Matters were not much better one year later. When the chief prosecutor in Milan made his annual report in January 2003, the statistics showed that the eleven courts that made up the judicial district for which the Lombard capital was responsible continued to have difficulty in keeping up. The number of new criminal cases where the defendants were known was 10,000 fewer during the year to 30 June 2002, but the backlog in the hands of the judges for preliminary investigations fell by only 6,000 to 43,000.[10] The application of the statute of limitations was the reason for the closure of more than one fifth of the total of 68,000 criminal cases closed by judges responsible for preliminary investigations.[11]

If the figures were bad in Milan, nationally they were even worse. Criminal justice in Italy seemed to be sinking under an awesome weight of numbers. There were over 3.25 million criminal cases with prosecutors at the end of the 2002 judicial year. Almost 2 million were in the hands of judges for preliminary investigations and 311,000 were in the course of being tried in criminal courts. And at the same time, appeal courts up and down the country were grappling with 106,000 criminal cases and a further 28,000 were before the supreme court. The number of outstanding cases had grown significantly between 2001 and 2002.[12]

Although justice had speeded up a little, Italian criminal cases continued to be lengthy affairs. On average, prosecution departments spent around thirteen months investigating cases and preparing them for trial. The next phase was also a slow business, a further nine months in the hands of judges who would decide on whether cases should go for trial. For those that did, defendants could look forward to another nine months during which their cases would be heard. Appeals in criminal cases lasted nearly a year and a half on average.[13] So the time from when a case got underway with the prosecutors until the appeal court delivered its verdict amounted to about four years.

The fact that Italy's criminal justice system was overloaded and worked at snail's pace served the purposes of many criminals as eight out of ten crimes went unpunished. It also served some defendants, but it was a bad and harmful system for most people who had stepped on to the wrong side of the law, been caught and faced trial. Between 1996 and 2001, the centre-left government then in office tried to put things in order, superficially at least. However, the administration meddled mindlessly with the criminal justice system, and far from bringing efficiency, fairness and a faster justice system, legislation during those five years simply made matters worse. Vittorio Grevi, a national figure in criminal law and head of the department in the law faculty of Pavia University, who would later become a trenchant critic of the way that Berlusconi's right-wing government set about undermining Italy's criminal justice system, was severe in his public speeches and writing about what the preceding centre-left administration had done.[14] He thought that the law modifying the article of the constitution dealing with criminal justice, which began the centre-left's initiatives in that field towards the end of 1999, was misguided and damaging.

With no sense of irony, the politicians called the law the *giusto processo*: fair trial. Grevi was suspicious of the unusual speed with which politicians from left to right across the spectrum joined forces to rush through a crucial change in the constitution and left no time for considering the implications or consulting legal experts. He wondered what lay behind such a suspect political alliance, what secret agreements the government and opposition parties might have reached, and in what areas. The flouting of the spirit of an article of the constitution that required a double reading of bills that changed the constitution itself was wholly wrong.[15] The founders of the Italian republic wanted legislators to allow a period for genuine reflection before making changes to the constitution, but the 1996–2001 parliament knew better.

That the politicians should have called the legislation, which sprang from a conflict between parliament and the constitutional court and was parliament's way of showing who ruled,[16] the *giusto processo* was a cunning and outrageous piece of arrogance. After all, who would speak against a bill that was called the fair trial? People without a solid legal background did not feel competent to criticize it and few lawyers made their views known.[17]

In essence, the *giusto processo* dealt with the admissibility of evidence and the right to silence of both defendants and witnesses. It was detailed and specific, inappropriately so for an article in the constitution, and badly worded. It swung the balance heavily in favour of defendants, noted Grevi, without offering the least nod towards the victims of crime and the defence of their interests in criminal trials.[18] Although the bill's supporters claimed that it was modelled on the European convention for human rights, their claims were off the mark. Italy's fair trial law was lopsided and lacked the checks and balances that the drafters had felt necessary for the European convention.

The *giusto processo* began a period of intense activity in the last two years of the 1996–2001 parliament. The centre-left government seemed particularly keen on tinkering with the criminal justice system in the run-up to the elections in May 2001, a period of six months during which five important pieces of legislation reached the statute book. Given the fierce antagonism between the government and Berlusconi's right-wing opposition, the convergence and consensus that these laws enjoyed was surprising.[19] That the laws were drafted in the offices of the political parties rather than coming from the justice ministry meant that political compromise, rather than technical considerations needed to improve the system, was the overriding factor.

Not only did the 1996–2001 parliament enact laws that further hobbled a criminal justice system that was already limping badly, but it inexplicably left some critical issues untackled. One of these was agreement with Switzerland on judicial assistance that would have speeded up many trials, a particularly surprising failure in the light of the government's declared aim of cutting trial times. When in office, Italy's centre-left also failed to bring in new corporate and bankruptcy laws. It did not tackle defence counsel's rights to deploy a range of objections, or to bring these rights into line with the new procedures that had been introduced for trials, nor did it enact measures to support the principle that penalties should be effective.

Instead, the frenzied activity that marked the centre-left's work inflicted considerable damage, multiplying formal guarantees, compromising the need for justice to be quicker and hitting the rights of the victims of crime.[20] The legacy was a mess. The Carotti Law passed in December 1999 originally aimed at revising rules in the criminal code concerned with trials presided by a single judge, but the changes that parliament approved added to incompatibility between judges, creating difficulties for those undertaking investigations and significantly lengthening trials. Typical of the trouble that the centre-left government brought on itself and on the criminal justice system was the matter of shortened trial procedures. Politicians woke up only when the law concerning these procedures was in place, and they then learned that it was flawed and that new legislation was urgently needed to block the loopholes.[21] Parliament had unwittingly eased remand in custody and abolished life sentences.

Another item in the catalogue of legislative errors was rules, enacted in February 2001, that seemed more likely to deter criminals from cooperating with the prosecutors than to encourage them to do so. Two months earlier, parliament had passed a law giving defence counsel the right to undertake investigations, allowing a freedom of action in this area that prosecutors did not enjoy.[22] Above all, this was a law that would help wealthy and powerful defendants and big-time criminals.

A MOVEMENT FOR JUSTICE

For twenty-two years between 1976 and 1998, Armando Spataro was a prosecutor who gladly went verbal blow-for-blow against defendants and their counsel, the kind of man to have on your side in a dark alley in a dangerous part of town. Spataro stood no nonsense and his smile carried a barely veiled hint of menace. He kept trim by training for marathon races and running competitively throughout the world. He had entered the magistrature in 1975 and had received a hard schooling when he arrived in Milan the following year, young, inexperienced and full of ideals. He had been assigned to investigations and trials at the toughest, most dangerous end of the criminal spectrum: kidnapping, Mafia and terrorism. There was nothing petty or white-collar about Spataro's cases.

Until 1985, Spataro tackled the extremist splinter groups that, for over a decade, had spread terror in Italy's big cities, particularly Milan where, in the worst periods of tension, streets were soon deserted in the evening after shops and offices shut. The Brigate Rosse (Red Brigades) and Prima Linea (Front Line) were the best-known left-wing terrorist groups; others were Comitati Comunisti Rivoluzionari (Revolutionary Communist Committees), Proletari Armati per il Comunismo (Armed Proletarians for Communism) and the Brigata 28 Marzo (28th March Brigade). Spataro prepared forty-six cases for trial in that period, trials that often involved large numbers of defendants. In one case alone he prosecuted 207 people accused of various crimes related to political terrorism by extremist left-wing groups, 152 in another and fifty-six in a third.

'I gave absolutely no quarter when I prosecuted those cases and they called me a fascist then,' he remembered.[23] He had reason to be relentless. Two people in the Milanese magistrature to whom he was close and who had acted as his mentors had been gunned down by left-wing terrorists: Emilio Alessandrini in 1979 and Guido Galli in 1980. For the Red Brigades and the like, and for their sympathizers, Spataro was a lackey of a capitalist state and an oppressor of the working class.

Less than twenty years later he would be a target of hate for Berlusconi's media, who called him a *toga rossa* (red robe, a term of abuse for prosecutors dealing with cases involving politicians). Being a *toga rossa* really meant being prepared to stand up and fight for the principle of legality, said Spataro.[24] What interested him above all was seeing justice done and getting it done efficiently. In 1988, after his friend Falcone had been passed over to lead the anti-Mafia pool in Palermo following Caponnetto's departure, he and Falcone and a group of like-minded magistrates set up an association called Movimento per la Giustizia (Movement for Justice) with a platform of efficiency and an emphasis on ethics.

He was elected to the Consiglio Superiore della Magistratura (CSM, the magistrature's governing body) in 1998 and served on it for four years. In his office and the council chamber at the CSM in Rome, he heard the worries of colleagues in courts up and down the country. He watched, horrified, as the centre-left government wreaked havoc through its disastrous programme of legislation and was greatly concerned about the direction in which the criminal justice system was being headed. Spataro had never been a political activist but he was pulled into the defensive front line for his profession and, even more, for the country's criminal justice system. And against his own wishes, he found himself dragged into the political arena.[25] After Berlusconi's coalition won power in May 2001, he thought that what the right-wing government did was wrong and spoke his mind, but he had also found himself at odds with the centre-left government and warned loudly that its package of laws on justice would have a devastating impact on criminal trials.

In 2000, he was a member of a delegation of the CSM that travelled to Strasbourg to talk to judges at Europe's Court of Human Rights, a body that had often passed adverse judgements on Italy's criminal justice system. The judges in the French city were surprised by 1999's so-called *giusto processo* law. It was a poor effort that fell short of ensuring fair trials for defendants as well as creating considerable problems for prosecutors. Despite the claims of Italian politicians, the Court of Human Rights had not sought the changes in Italy's constitution that the law introduced. Indeed, the *giusto processo* probably made appeals to the court in Strasbourg more likely. 'They told us that no country in the world was as generous as Italy in providing defendants with such a level of guarantees,' said Spataro.[26] But for ordinary defendants these guarantees were often more a matter of formality than reality, guarantees that existed on paper rather than in practice.

JUSTICE – INQUISITORIAL TO ADVERSARIAL

Even before the centre-left government put its hands to the task, nobody with good intentions towards the criminal justice system denied that it needed a radical overhaul. The huge backlog of cases and the desperately slow pace of justice were convincing evidence of the need well before the 1996–2001 parliament. The legacy of the centre-left government was, however, a system of selective guarantees for the few that were not available to the vast majority of people who found themselves caught up in the machinery of Italian justice. For neighbourhood drug dealers, illegal immigrants and the like, penalties were stiffer and the prison doors swung open easily to take them in. Instead, for those with money, the rules written by the centre-left government provided ways to avoid being tried or, if on trial, to drag out cases so that the statute of limitations would arrive before the verdict and the sentence.

Until the end of the Second World War and the fall of fascism, Italy's criminal trial system was modelled on inquisitorial lines, the continental European scheme that was strongly influenced by the Roman Catholic Church. The aim of the examining magistrates, who searched for proof, took all the decisions about the case and generally ran the trial, was to discover the absolute truth.[27] Defendants were completely in the magistrates' hands and were not allowed the presence of counsel when questioned. The relationship between magistrates and defendants evolved into a kind of psychological engagement in which, as well as seeking the facts, magistrates also sought an admission of guilt. In mitigation of the magistrates' power, however, defendants were not obliged to reply to questions or to tell the truth if they did answer. Criminal trials were more written affairs than oral and magistrates had to provide written judgements in which, to justify their decisions, the facts were fully described. These judgements were a blessing for defendants as they often gave grounds for appeal.

Italy's post-war republican constitution contained elements that contradicted the inquisitorial model of the criminal trial. In attempts to iron out the creases, parliament passed legislative measures and the constitutional court took decisions that moved the criminal trial system away from its inquisitorial origins, restricting the powers of examining magistrates and giving more scope to the defence. Change by evolution did not achieve the desired results but, while it was soon clear that major reform was urgently needed, legislative lethargy obstructed progress and the government set about it only in 1988.[28] It made changes that became effective in October of the following year but botched the job badly.

The alternative to the inquisitorial model was the adversarial model like that used by courts in Britain and America, with prosecution and defence as adversaries offering evidence and examining and cross-examining witnesses to convince impartial judges and juries of the merit of their case, and to win conviction or discharge for the defendants.

Although 1988's legislation drew heavily on the adversarial model, parliament lacked the courage to ditch the old inquisitorial system completely.[29] So Italy was given a hybrid encumbered with contradictions such as the right of defendants to lie when giving evidence and defence counsel's right to advise clients to tell lies. The guarantees of the adversarial model were simply added to those that the inquisitorial model offered defendants.

A feature of the Italian criminal justice system that left some outsiders bemused was the guarantee enshrined in the constitution that defendants were not considered guilty until judgement by the very highest court of appeal was given.[30] Slow justice was one factor that postponed that day. Another factor was the layers of judgement through which a defendant might pass. After the various reforms and changes, there were a total of four. The first arrived after the prosecutor's request for indictment. This was the preliminary hearing which followed the period of up to two years that magistrates were allowed to complete their investigations. Next came the court of first instance, then the appeal court and finally the supreme court. And the supreme court had the power to refer cases back to the appeal court for retrial. According to the constitution, the defendant was guilty only when the supreme court finally ruled so. As we have seen earlier, these levels of appeal allowed the lawyers of wealthy defendants to play for time, spinning out cases until the statute of limitations applied.

Moreover, for the average defendant, the pace at which trials were conducted, with cases being allocated perhaps one or two hearings a week, made a mockery of the constitution's rule that the law should ensure a reasonable duration for criminal trials.[31] That clearly did not happen. And it also made a mockery of the requirement that courts should judge cases on the oral evidence placed before them. The lapse of time between a crime being committed and the trial of those accused of committing it was such that witnesses generally needed notes or reports to remember what had happened.

Trials were quicker if defendants opted for fast-track procedures in which the examination and cross-examination of witnesses was bypassed, and after which the prosecution's right to appeal was restricted, procedures advisable where defendants were sure that the cases against them would be dismissed. Fast-track was also a smart choice for defendants who felt certain that they would be found guilty, as it reduced prison terms by one third.[32]

PLEA-BARGAINING

Cerro Maggiore is a little-known town in the Milanese hinterland. About 15 miles northwest of the city and close to the highway that leads to Malpensa airport, the town won a footnote in Italian history books soon after the Second World War. As the war drew to an end, Italian partisans were active in the foothills of the Alps and controlled the valleys and roads running from the Piedmontese and Lombard plain to Switzerland. It was on one such road, on the western shore of Lake Como and towards the lake's northern end and the border with Switzerland, that a group of partisans captured Benito Mussolini as he tried to flee the country. After being sentenced to death by a field tribunal, the fascist *Duce* was shot near the small lakeside town of Dongo on the afternoon of 28 April 1945.[33] The partisans then took his corpse to Milan and strung it up, along with that of his mistress, Claretta Pettaci, and other fascist leaders, in Piazzale Loreto in the centre of the city.

After a day of being spat at and otherwise abused by the crowds in Piazzale Loreto, Mussolini's body was taken to the coroner's department at the city's university and from there to a numbered grave in the cemetery at Musocco, a district in the north of Milan. One night in April of the following year, the body was removed from this grave by a small group of fascist loyalists and moved to the Valtellina valley in the mountains east of Lake Como. The corpse's peregrinations continued with sojourns in the church of Sant'Angelo in Milan and the Certosa of Pavia. Before reaching its final destination in Predappio, Mussolini's birthplace in the Emilia Romagna region about 125 miles southeast of Milan, the *Duce*'s body was buried in Cerro Maggiore.[34]

Fifty years after Mussolini's body found a temporary resting place there, the town was in the news once more. Yet again the notoriety concerned a hole in the ground, but this time a rather bigger one: a former quarry that had been put to use as a waste disposal site. The notoriety arose from the corruption that surrounded the business of managing the site, the fact that Silvio Berlusconi's younger brother Paolo was involved and that the authorities collected a record settlement from Paolo Berlusconi to close the case that the prosecutors had brought against him. Between 1991 and 1996, a company called Simec, in which Paolo Berlusconi was the main shareholder, had the contract to manage the site to which refuse was taken from throughout the province of Milan. According to the magistrates, Simec and its owners made enormous profits by fraudulently overcharging the city's waste-collection board for its services.[35] The magistrates had gathered evidence that the real costs incurred by Simec were much lower than those claimed by the company, which had camouflaged its crime through an absence of controls and accounts. Far from using the surplus to provide a better service, that surplus was milked for the personal enrichment of Simec's shareholders and people linked to them.[36]

By paying 38 million euros to Italy's tax authorities, Paolo Berlusconi had already settled a tax case against the company,[37] but he still faced trial for corruption and misappropriation. In May 2002, a few months after settling the tax matter and facing imprisonment for one year and nine months, including the penalty arising from a sentence for another crime, he agreed to pay 49 million euros in damages to the authorities that had been cheated.[38] Antonio Di Pietro, one of the *mani pulite* magistrates who had gone after the white-collar criminals who had turned Milan into bribesville in the 1980s and 1990s, had been involved in the case at the beginning of the investigations. He noted that the amount the state had been able to get from the Berlusconi family through its efforts in the Cerro Maggiore case more than covered all the costs incurred during a decade by the anti-corruption team.[39]

Fast-track procedures allowed defendants one way to escape from the obstacle course of criminal justice. Paolo Berlusconi used another route to avoid even being sent for trial. He took advantage of a procedure called *patteggiamento*, the Italian equivalent of plea-bargaining, reaching an agreement to pay that massive financial settlement on the eve of a preliminary hearing at which the magistrates intended to seek an indictment. He was able to make his pact with them because the penalty for the offences for which he was being investigated did not exceed two years' imprisonment, allowing for mitigating circumstances that might have reduced the penalty in the event of a guilty verdict.[40]

Offering defendants various carrots, including a reduction of up to one third of the prison sentences that they would otherwise have received, *patteggiamento* also gave some relief to Italy's overstretched criminal justice system by reducing the courts' workloads. Of around 3,000 people whom the *mani pulite*'s team asked to be sent for trial during the decade after *tangentopoli* broke, more than 500 settled with plea bargains during the preliminary investigations and a further 340 had agreements with the prosecutors sealed by judges in the courts of first instance. *Patteggiamento* was inappropriate for defendants who were sure to be found innocent and unattractive to defendants in sight of salvation by the statute of limitations.[41] The supreme court had ruled that a *patteggiamento* judgement was not the same as a verdict of guilty, but no defendant who expected to be found innocent would opt for it. In legal circles, there were few doubts about what *patteggiamento* meant. 'It is an admission of guilt,' said Spataro, 'otherwise there would be no point to it.'[42]

THE MAGISTRATURE

Reaching agreements with the magistrature was the last thing that Silvio Berlusconi seemed to want. 'A cancer to be cut out'[43] – that was how he described magistrates whom he accused of using judicial power for political ends. The Italian prime minister made this remark in an interview with the French newspaper *Le Figaro* shortly before Italy took over the rotating presidency of the European Union at the beginning of July 2003, and he repeated it a few weeks later on French radio.

Reality was very different, however, from the bleak picture of a prejudiced Italian magistrature that Berlusconi painted for French readers and listeners. The 8,500 men and women[44] who sat on the judges' benches, investigated crimes and prepared cases for trial, or served as prosecutors in Italy's courts were really, politically speaking, nothing more, nor less, than a mirror of Italy itself, with allegiances or preferences running from the right, across the centre to the left of the spectrum. Memberships of the four main associations to which magistrates (both judges, who made up about three quarters of the total number, and examining magistrates and prosecutors, who accounted for the remaining quarter) belonged revealed an absence of political homogeneity. Unita per la Costituzione, a centrist association, enjoyed the support of about one third of magistrates, against one quarter who supported the progressive, leftist Magistratura

Democratica. Around one sixth sided with Spataro's non-aligned Movimento per la Giustizia and a little less than that supported the conservative, rightist Magistratura Independente.[45] Perhaps one in ten of Italian magistrates belonged to no association at all, not even to the Associazione Nazionale Magistrati (ANM, national magistrates' association) within which all four associations worked together. Established at the beginning of the twentieth century by a group of young magistrates seeking better working conditions and a more independent magistrature, the ANM was dissolved under fascism. It was resurrected after the Second World War; the four associations were the result of the different ways magistrates thought about society and the law and of the factions that had formed within the ANM.

So Italy's magistrates were far from being the band of left-wing extremists Berlusconi and members of his government mendaciously sought to depict. Even Magistratura Democratica, towards whose members the stream of venom seemed particularly directed, stood and worked for ideas with which no democrat could disagree. This association believed in respect for the principles of the democratic rule of law, the protection of the rights of minorities and the weaker members of society, the judiciary's independence, the transparency of the justice system and the encouragement of a democratic judicial culture.[46] As the Consiglio Superiore della Magistratura (CSM) firmly noted, there was nothing to suggest that the influence of political preferences or membership of associations or political parties compromised a magistrate's impartiality. It was not party membership that undermined judicial impartiality, said the CSM, but the individual magistrate's inability to prevent his own political views from influencing his judgement.[47]

Indeed, the principles to which Magistratura Democratica held were not a monopoly of that association. The other three associations held them as well and all were quick to close ranks when under political attack. After Berlusconi's virulent outpourings on the European stage against his country's magistrature, the ANM sprang to defend its name. It was deeply disturbed that the prime minister had decided to take his attacks on Italian judges and prosecutors abroad. Berlusconi had followed up his description of the Italian magistrature as cancerous with an accusation that magistrates abused their position in order to attack him and his political supporters.[48] That kind of allegation cast doubts on the magistrature's impartiality, noted Associazione Nazionale Magistrati, and created serious concern elsewhere in Europe about the violation of the separation of powers.[49]

Italy's constitution laid down clearly where and how the judiciary fitted into the post-war scheme of things. It would be autonomous and independent of every other power, stated the constitution, and would be governed by the CSM which would decide on judicial appointments, transfers, promotions and discipline, though initiating disciplinary action also lay within the competence of the minister of justice. Only the CSM could move a magistrate from one court to another or suspend a magistrate from service. The CSM would be presided over by Italy's head of state, said the constitution. There were to be two members, the president and chief prosecutor of the supreme court, who would automatically sit on the body thanks to the posts they held. The thirty other members would be elected, two thirds by the magistrates themselves and the remaining third by parliament in a procedure of proportional representation that would give the opposition a voice in the CSM.[50] Following legislation introduced by Berlusconi's government and approved in March 2002, the number of the CSM's elected members was reduced to twenty-four. When a new CSM met at the beginning of August 2002 for the first time at the start of its four-year term, five of the eight members parliament had elected were there because of the votes of members of parliament belonging to Berlusconi's coalition. That number was sufficient to ensure that they could obstruct the CSM's workings by withdrawing from sessions so that the council lacked a quorum.

Those five showed their political colours when the CSM elected its vice-president, the person to whom the responsibility fell for overseeing the CSM's day-to-day business, Italy's president being a figurehead for the organization and not its active head. Virginio Rognoni was almost seventy-eight when he obtained twenty-one votes of the twenty-six that were cast, and was eminently qualified for the task he faced. He had taught law at Pavia University and had served in parliament for over a quarter of a century, until 1994, heading at different times the justice, home affairs and defence ministries.[51] His candidature won unanimous approval from among the magistrates left to right, as well as getting the votes of three councillors chosen by parliament, of whom Rognoni himself was one. Rognoni's election was strongly opposed by the councillors who owed their places on the CSM to Berlusconi's coalition. Rognoni's election was a vote against the government, said Roberto Castelli, the minister of justice, and he would keep this in mind.[52]

In fact, the choice of Rognoni was a vote against the politicization of the CSM that Berlusconi's government sought and a clear statement in support of an independent magistrature. There was no place for party loyalties in the CSM, said Rognoni, as its role was the self-government of the magistrature that Italy's constitution stipulated. The CSM would fulfil its responsibilities of guarding the autonomy and independence of the magistrature as a whole and the dignity of individual magistrates, he promised.[53] With the government determined to whip the magistrature into line and seemingly intent on undermining the rule of law, Rognoni's words amounted to a political statement.

Certainly, the hard-pushed magistrature would have wished to have been spared the incessant sniping from Berlusconi's government. Judges and prosecutors already faced enormous problems without always having politicians on their backs. They were criticized for being inefficient, yet one reason for the huge backlog of cases was the fact that, despite the workload, the number of magistrates in service was substantially smaller than the number needed. In 2003, there was a shortfall of over 8 per cent on the numbers that there should have been.[54] Another reason was the duty of magistrates, laid down in the constitution, to take action when informed of possible criminal offences.[55] In addition, judges and prosecutors were forced to make do with administrative and other support services that were wholly insufficient for the demands being made on the system. In October 2001, in a report to parliament on the state of justice in Italy, the CSM placed the blame for the inefficiency of the criminal justice system squarely on the politicians – the 1996–2001 parliament and the centre-left government then in office being especially culpable. Italy's politicians enacted legislation affecting justice but failed to vote the resources that were needed for the system to work efficiently. The constitution stated that any law which meant new or increased expenditure by the state should indicate where the financial cover would be found. That had not happened in the case of the many changes in the justice system.[56] Not only had reforms been badly thought through, they had not been costed, and money had not been found to cover the costs.

Berlusconi's government eagerly grasped parliament's own failings as a stick with which to beat the magistrature. The court in Milan where he was on trial for bribing judges was a favourite target. Inspectors from the ministry of justice who undertook an inspection there in 2003 found much to criticize in terms of inefficiency, back-logs and delays in the judicial process. Yet, the fault lay with the ministry itself, said a former chief prosecutor at the court. For two years, he had drawn the ministry's attention to a serious shortage of administrative staff.[57] But instead of allowing recruitment, cuts had been made. If it had been difficult before, with the arrival of Berlusconi's government in 2001 the situation in the court in Milan worsened. The former chief prosecutor was ignored: it served what seemed to be the government's aim of undermining the magistrature's credibility to make the court struggle with insufficient staff and inadequate equipment. The government's first priority was to reduce taxes, so state expenditure had to be cut and the justice system would be the first to feel the knife, the minister told Spataro.[58]

Even worse would be in store for the judiciary, however, if the government had its way. Berlusconi wanted to bring the magistrates to heel and under political control. His government initially talked about a separation of functions in the magistrature, even though such a clear separation of functions already existed between *magistrati giudicanti* (judges) and *magistrati requirenti/inquirenti* (prosecutors and investigating magistrates). There was a single magistrature but the functions were clearly different and separate. Then the government began to speak about imposing separate career paths, a move that would lead to a barrier between the two arms of the judiciary and open the way to bringing prosecutors under governmental control; a bill introducing the changes overcame its first parliamentary hurdle in January 2004. Try to imagine the justice minister allowing the prosecution of the prime minister, suggested Spataro a year before the enactment of a law that gave Berlusconi immunity from trial while in office.[59]

Indeed, immunity from trial was not enough, as the justice ministry showed when it moved, in July 2003, to obstruct the investigations that magistrates in Milan had initiated into transactions involving film rights that had been carried out by companies in Berlusconi's media group.[60] The ministry's action in blocking the judicial assistance that the Italian magistrates sought from the American authorities seemed like an abuse of office and raised a question about the separation of powers. Yet only six months earlier, when welcoming a group of young recruits to the magistrature, Carlo Azeglio Ciampi, Italy's head of state, acting in his role as the CSM's president, had emphasized just how important the separation of powers was. 'The principle of the division of powers constitutes the very essence of democracy and defence for the proper working of the state's institutions,' said Ciampi.[61] He added that it was fundamental to the nation's civil and democratic life.

The right-wing government had very different ideas about how justice should be allowed to function, however. Berlusconi even floated the notion that prosecutors should be elected by popular vote, effectively turning them into servants of the governing party. Under such a scheme, candidates with access to the media or enjoying substantial financial backing would have enormous advantages over those who were less fortunate, and great opportunities would arise for the perversion of justice. Although just an idea, Berlusconi's proposal got an immediate and loud reaction. On 9 July 2003, Magistratura Democratica expressed its concerns vigorously; elected prosecutors would open the way for the government to decide which crimes to pursue or not to pursue. Countries where there were elected prosecutors had strong systems of checks and balances and had cast-iron rules about institutional propriety, said the magistrates' association, whereas those conditions simply did not exist in Italy. Equality before the law would become an even emptier expression as Italians would find themselves exposed to the initiatives of political prosecutors. Magistratura Democratica advised its members: 'Keep calm, stay indignant.'[62]

When the founders of the Italian republic drafted their country's constitution in 1947, the Second World War was a recent memory and so were twenty years of fascist dictatorship. This constitution sought to build a system of criminal justice on a truly democratic foundation, something totally different from the previous regime in which the exercise of justice had been abused through limitations on rights and pressures on the magistrature. The constitution paid particular attention to preventing such abuses happening again, said the CSM, and the magistrature's independence and autonomy were fundamental to achieving this.[63] With its schemes for reforming the judiciary, Berlusconi's government wanted to turn the clock back to a period when Italian justice was not justice at all, but merely the crude exercise of power.

8

Betrayal

IN MEMORIAM

After the deaths of Falcone and Borsellino, the airport at Punta Raisi was renamed Falcone–Borsellino. Fifteen yards of crimson-painted guardrail mark the place where Giovanni Falcone died on the highway and an olive tree was planted at the spot where Paolo Borsellino was murdered. The magistrates' names are also engraved on a monumental grey stone wall curving round a small *piazza* behind Palermo's massive court building, together with those of another nine Sicilian magistrates murdered by the Mafia during two decades of terrible bloodshed. Many open spaces in the Sicilian capital are filled with the noise of children playing but that *piazza* is a sombre place, occupied by armed *carabinieri* and a few dogs that occasionally stir from lazing in the sun. It is called Piazza della Memoria, remembrance square.

Any judgement on Italy's magistrature should keep in mind the magistrates who were murdered because they were doing their duty, said Luciano Violante, a former chairman of parliament's anti-Mafia commission and once a magistrate himself.[1] But, intolerant of magistrates who did their jobs, the government headed by Silvio Berlusconi seemed to want to forget Falcone and Borsellino. On 19 July 2002, ten years after the massacre in Via D'Amelio, Berlusconi avoided mention of the Mafia in a brief message he sent to the ceremony in memory of the deaths of Borsellino and his escort. Almost two months before, the speaker of the senate and the minister responsible for the postal service were in Palermo for a gathering to mark the murders at Capaci. Neither the justice minister nor the home affairs minister was there. The official commemorations were vacuous, thought Rita, Paolo Borsellino's sister.[2] She had the impression that certain participants showed up only because they felt they must and were glad when the business was over.

On 4 September 2002, Italy remembered another public servant killed in the line of duty in Palermo. General Carlo Alberto Dalla Chiesa, his wife and escort had been killed by a mafia gunman twenty years before. Piero Grasso, Palermo's chief prosecutor, used the occasion to warn about the risks and dangers that the government's legislation was putting in the way of the magistrature. Representatives of the state and the government were in the city to remember the murder of Dalla Chiesa, who had been Palermo's prefect for only a few months before being killed. The speaker of parliament's lower house looked worried when Grasso spoke, the home affairs minister kept his eyes down and the minister for regional affairs, a Sicilian, drummed his fingers.[3] Members of Berlusconi's coalition appeared uneasy when reminded that public servants had given their lives while serving a state whose criminal justice system the government was doing its best to undermine.

With twenty-four magistrates murdered in the space of twenty years, Italy was not a normal country, said Piercamillo Davigo. Those things did not happen in normal countries; the forces of order were not blown up in civilized countries.[4] The murders of Falcone, Borsellino and their escorts extended the long trail of blood that marked the sacrifices made by Italian magistrates, law officers and lawyers. But those sacrifices had been forgotten by the government and that forgetfulness was a betrayal of their service.

TWO VICTIMS OF RED TERRORISM

Berlusconi's cases and laws cast shadows over Italy's legal profession, but there were many lawyers to whom values were important. They remembered their fellow lawyers who had died serving their profession and their country. Murdered by left-wing terrorists of the Red Brigades on 28 April 1977, Fulvio Croce, chairman of the Turin bar and a lawyer of integrity and courage, was one of them. Croce was returning to his chambers in mid-afternoon and had reached the entrance lobby when a voice behind him called, '*Avvocato*.'[5] As he turned, the killer shot him.

The chambers of Franzo Grande Stevens, in the heart of Turin's legal district, were close to where Croce was murdered. Like the other lawyers who hurried to their colleague's chambers when they heard that Croce had been shot, Grande Stevens felt deep sorrow and great indignation. That sadness did not lessen over the years and not a day passed, a longcase clock ticking quietly in the corner of his office, without Grande Stevens glancing at the photograph of Croce that he kept by his desk.[6]

For Croce, the defence of Red Brigades' terrorists was a matter of duty and loyalty to professional principles, although obeying the call of duty would cost him his life. He was murdered for not turning away from the unwelcome task that had fallen to him one year earlier. The terrorists had contested the court's right to try them, claiming that it was part of a capitalist system whose overthrow they sought, and had withdrawn the briefs to their lawyers. They would not accept defence lawyers appointed by the court, they said threateningly. Nevertheless, with Croce leading, the members of Turin's bar council took on the defence.

Turin's court held the first trial of the leaders of the terrorist group. That extreme left-wing terrorists found fertile ground in the Piedmont capital in Italy's northwest corner was unsurprising. An industrial city, Turin had been a magnet for large waves of migrant workers from Italy's *mezzogiorno* after the Second World War and harsh factory conditions and grim apartment blocks helped alienate the immigrants and their children.

The first capital of a united Italy was a city of contrasts. On one side, the elegant cafés in the porticos of Piazza Castello and Piazza San Carlo, the centre's baroque buildings, the luxurious Del Cambio restaurant, plush crimson velvet, gilded mirrors and the favourite dining place of Camillo Cavour, one of Italy's founding fathers. On the other, the drab high-rise apartment blocks in the city's outskirts and *cintura* ring of satellite towns. On one side, an intensely Catholic city whose cathedral housed the *Sacra Sindone* (Holy Shroud); on the other, an increasing number in a working class who embraced left-wing ideals and atheism.

Croce chose eight of the bar council's members to defend the Red Brigades' leaders who were on trial. Grande Stevens and a colleague were assigned the defence of Renato Curcio, the *capo storico* (historic chief) of the terrorist band, and another three of the accused. Despite the objections and threats, said Grande Stevens, we decided to have a conference with the defendants in the prison in which they were being held. The meeting was icy and ended with Curcio's warning that the two lawyers' lives were at risk if they did not refuse the brief.

Grande Stevens and his colleague told the bar council what the terrorists had said. The threat of death hung over those responsible for the defence but Croce was not dissuaded. Italian law required that defendants should be defended and the lawyers' code required that a proper defence should be made. This experience, a major criminal trial fraught with difficulties and dangers, was far beyond what Croce and Grande Stevens had ever expected to encounter. Neither had had anything to do with criminal law; that was another part of the profession and not their business. The chairman of Turin's bar council was a successful civil lawyer and so too was Grande Stevens, who later stamped his name at the top of corporate law in Italy.

Under steady guidance from Croce, the defence lawyers decided their strategy. They would not put up a superficial defence, nor would they claim extenuating factors for the crimes because the defendants did not in any way want to do so. The lawyers would raise objections to the least infringement of the rules that guaranteed fair trial and they would fight for the defendants' right to defend themselves, as that was what the Red Brigades' leaders wanted to do. 'We defended seriously in that trial,' said Grande Stevens many years later, 'although there were politicians who asked us not to, with the aim of getting the accused found guilty as quickly as possible.'[7]

Tension was palpable when, on 7 June 1976, Grande Stevens rose and presented the defence's case. One of the band, who was nicknamed Granny Mao, embraced Grande Stevens when he had finished, telling him he had given the performance of a real lawyer. In a way that was typical of him, Croce lowered the tension by saying loudly that Grande Stevens had made a conquest. Beneath the humour, however, Croce knew the risks he was running. He told a few of us that he thought he was always being followed, remembered Grande Stevens, but he carried on undeterred.

The worst of the *anni di piombo*, the years of lead, when fringe left-wing groups turned to the gun to target those they saw as class-enemies, and extremists on the right used bombs to sow slaughter among innocent bystanders, were still to come when Croce was murdered in 1977. Turin was only one centre where left-wing terrorism had taken root in the mid-1970s. Another was Milan, the capital of neighbouring Lombardy, whose streets were also stained by episodes in which good people were killed because of the work they did.

Viale Umbria is one of the busy inner ring roads that circle Milan's historic centre. At around 8.15 on the morning of 29 January 1979, an armed band murdered Emilio Alessandrini while his car was stopped at one of the road's busy intersections. The victim, a young and highly regarded prosecutor, worked in the Palazzo di Giustizia court building, less than a mile from the scene of the crime. As he usually did, Alessandrini had just taken his nine-year-old son Marco to the Ottolini-Belgioioso elementary school, a block away from that intersection.[8]

Only two months before, Alessandrini had been assigned a new case. A large team of inspectors from the central bank's supervisory service had been busy for about six months digging into Roberto Calvi's Banco Ambrosiano, completing their job in mid-November. After a committee of experts at the central bank decided that there was a *prima facie* case of foreign exchange violations against the Banco Ambrosiano's chairman, the supervisory service's report was passed to the magistrature in Milan. The case was given to Alessandrini, who had made his name taking on terrorist groups but was also an expert in financial crime.

Alessandrini had investigated the massacre at a branch of the Banca Nazionale dell'Agricoltura in Piazza Fontana, near Milan's cathedral, where a bomb had exploded in December 1969 and killed and injured many customers. That crime had been committed by right-wing terrorists as part of a strategy of terror aimed at ratcheting up political tension in Italy. Some of Alessandrini's colleagues were worried that this line of investigation into his murder, including the possibility that deviant, extreme right-wing members of the secret services were involved in the killing, might be ignored.[9] They had good reason for concern because, only two years after Alessandrini was murdered, magistrates from Milan uncovered Calvi's membership of the subversive P2 masonic lodge, where brother masons included many military people and rightwingers.

The investigations confirmed, however, that Alessandrini had been killed by an extreme left-wing terrorist group called Prima Linea (Front Line). A statement from Front Line said that they had shot the prosecutor because he was one of the magistrates who, through his personal standing and professionalism, had done most to give credibility to the criminal justice system. 'The proletariat's real enemies are democratic and reformist magistrates,' said the Front Line. The *anni di piombo* was a crazy season of crazy ideology, said Armando Spataro, a young colleague of Alessandrini at the time. He recalled many years later, 'It just seemed impossible that an organization that described itself as being of the left, even if it did aim to overthrow the state, could target someone like Emilio, a person so committed to progress and democracy.'[10]

Spataro had arrived in Milan in September 1976, fresh from training for the prosecutor's job, and in June 1977 he had been assigned the task of prosecuting the hard core of leaders of the Red Brigades in the trial that had been transferred from Turin. The chief prosecutor preferred not to expose his senior and better-known staff to the risks of tackling the Red Brigades in court and turned to this recently qualified but promising young prosecutor. 'I felt honoured and obviously accepted the job,' said Spataro. Alessandrini was also assigned to the trial and accompanied his younger colleague into the courtroom where he discreetly took a place some way from the prosecutors' table.

He saw an altercation between Spataro and the defence lawyers whose briefs had been withdrawn by the terrorists in a tactical ploy, but who were nevertheless seeking to confer privately with the defendants. They warned Spataro that they would tell the Red Brigades' leaders that the prosecutor had refused the conference they sought. They had not recognized Spataro but there was no doubt about the barely veiled threat; the Red Brigades killed prosecutors. 'Perhaps you would like my name?' Spataro asked them as he wrote it on a piece of paper. 'Emilio approached me. He wondered if I had often played at being a prosecutor when I was a boy,' Spataro remembered.[11] He had learned it from his father, he told Alessandrini, being rewarded with a pat on his shoulder as the older prosecutor turned with a smile to leave the courtroom.

Spataro and Alessandrini were neighbours in an apartment block near Milan's court building. When Spataro heard about the shooting of his colleague, he was quickly at the scene. He found Alessandrini's orange Renault 5 blocking the traffic, surrounded by policemen, the door open and his colleague's body slumped over the steering wheel. He had got to know Alessandrini during the two years he had been in Milan and this older colleague had always been helpful, as he was to all young magistrates. 'Those who knew him, loved him,' said Spataro.[12] A quarter of a century later, many still had photographs of the murdered prosecutor on their office desks or at home. A bust of Alessandrini had been placed in the Palazzo di Giustizia.

MORE MURDER IN MILAN

Giorgio Ambrosoli, the lawyer responsible for the liquidation of Michele Sindona's Banca Privata Italiana, knew Milan's court well. He was there on the morning of 11 July 1979. About twelve hours later, after dinner and an evening spent with friends, he was murdered by a mafia gunman outside his apartment[13] in a side-street close to Santa Maria delle Grazie, the church where Leonardo painted his fresco of the Last Supper. Ambrosoli had had an appointment at the Palazzo di Giustizia to assist American prosecutors with their investigations into Sindona's crimes. It was the last of three days of hearings. Guido Viola, the Milan prosecutor with whom Ambrosoli had worked for five years on the Banca Privata Italiana's liquidation, was there and so also were Sindona's lawyers and interpreters.

Early in the liquidation, Ambrosoli realized that the job would be dangerous. More than four years before, in February 1975, when he was about to submit to the court his findings regarding the bank's liabilities, he had written to his wife, Annalori. Without doubt he would pay a very high price for the assignment, he had told her, but he knew this before accepting it and did not complain. He was aware that he had enemies but this was a unique opportunity for him to do something for his country. He wrote, 'Whatever happens, however, you know what you must do and I am sure that you will know how to manage very well. You will have to bring up the children and teach them to respect the values in which we have believed . . . You will cope very well, I am certain, because you are very good and because each of the children is better than the other . . . It will be a hard life for you, but you are such a good woman that you will always manage, and you will always do what is right, whatever the cost.'[14]

Most people think of heroes as soldiers or perhaps even as working-class people, said Corrado Stajano, a writer who described Ambrosoli as a middle-class hero.[15] The letter the lawyer wrote to his wife expressed their middle-class values. Stajano spent ten years digging into the case and peering into the dark tunnel down which Ambrosoli plunged in September 1974 when he accepted the task of liquidating Sindona's bankrupt banking business. The book Stajano wrote, *Un Eroe Borghese* (A Middle-class Hero), described the events in which Ambrosoli became caught up, the drama of the betrayal of a good man by Italian politicians and a corrupt and cynical class of bankers and businessmen that ended with his murder.

As the assignment moved forward, Ambrosoli found himself increasingly isolated. From 1977 onwards there were threats and intimidation as Sindona rallied his political supporters and mafia friends. In New York in December 1973, Giulio Andreotti, many times Italy's prime minister, had described Sindona as the saviour of the lira. Ambrosoli had allies at the Palazzo di Giustizia, where relations with Viola and Ovilio Urbisci, the investigating magistrate on the case, were excellent, but they were not enough. 'It seemed clear that blood would be shed,' said Silvio Novembre, an investigator who worked closely with Ambrosoli on the liquidation.[16] Like Ambrosoli, he too was threatened.

Three days after Ambrosoli was gunned down, his funeral was held in the church of San Vittore. Nobody from the government was there nor anyone from the local authorities. Paolo Baffi, the Bank of Italy's governor, was present, as were Viola, Urbisci and other members of the Milanese magistrature.[17] Some people described

Ambrosoli as introverted and unsociable, but that was just shyness. He was very generous, said Novembre. The investigator still felt a burning sense of outrage more than twenty years after attending Ambrosoli's funeral. 'It is so wrong that the state allows its best and most trusty servants to be killed. Ambrosoli paid for his honesty and his principles with his life.'[18]

Giorgio Ambrosoli was an honest and determined lawyer. A plaque commemorating him was fixed to the wall outside the Milanese bar council's offices on the first floor of the Palazzo di Giustizia, a reminder to the city's lawyers of the values on which so many Milanese turned their backs during the years of *tangentopoli*, and continued to keep them turned even after the dirt and the enormity of the corruption had been exposed.

The Mafia murdered Ambrosoli. Like his colleague Alessandrini, Guido Galli was shot and killed in Milan by left-wing terrorists. He had gone home for lunch from the Palazzo di Giustizia on 19 March 1980 as it was his son's name-day, San Giuseppe, which was also Father's Day for Italians. Spataro remembered accompanying Galli home with his escort, as he often did, because Galli did not have any protection.[19] Galli was due to lecture that afternoon at the city's university, a short distance from the court, and the two prosecutors had planned to meet again later.

Spataro was waiting in his office when the telephone rang just before 5 p.m. It was the head of the Digos, Italy's state security body. Something terrible had happened. Dashing from his office, Spataro ran to the university. There were just two *carabinieri* captains and an official at the scene when he arrived. 'They tried to keep me away,' said Spataro, 'because they knew what Guido meant to me; he was not only my teacher but the elder brother I never had.' Galli was lying on the ground, a copy of the criminal code less than a yard away. In his address book was a note saying that should anything happen to him, Spataro should be called.[20] Galli left five children. Two of them became magistrates and Spataro was their mentor when they started, just as their father had befriended and supported him at the end of the 1970s, not long after he began working in the magistrature.

Although he was a prosecutor when he was murdered, Galli was an examining magistrate when Spataro met him in September 1978 after arresting Corrado Alunni, a left-wing terrorist, in a city hideout that turned out to be a huge armoury stocked with around forty pistols and machine guns, as well as bombs and explosives. The role of examining magistrate on the case, the first major Milanese investigation into terrorism, was assigned to Galli. During the next fifteen months, the two worked closely together, questioning people in Milan and the neighbouring provinces of Bergamo and Varese. They travelled to Bologna and Rome. Spataro remembered those investigations well. 'We met magistrates who were glad to pass their investigations to us and policemen who had discovered and written everything without any recognition from magistrates who were scared or incompetent. We found that we had the best criminal police in the world,' he said.[21] In collecting evidence, Galli and Spataro had discovered a country of contrasts, of courage and cowardice.

The case of Alunni was a lesson about courage for Piercamillo Davigo. In the panic of the terrorist campaign, the only people who seemed to keep their heads were magistrates; Italy's politicians were in a complete funk. But even in the magistrature there were people who had decided that discretion was the better part of valour. Not only were juries hard to put together because of the great risks, but some judges themselves shied away from duty, changing jobs or moving cities.

Others displayed steely determination, moral backbone and brave resolution. They set examples that would shine throughout the dark period of terrorism and mafia violence and later be beacons of firmness and probity in the face of the assault on justice that Berlusconi's coalition launched. 'The president of the eighth criminal section was at home with a leg in plaster, but he returned to preside over Alunni's trial,' recalled Davigo.[22] That judge was Francesco Saverio Borrelli who later headed the anti-corruption team. Davigo was also struck by the decision of a colleague in Milan's civil court, immediately after the murder of Emilio Alessandrini, to apply for a transfer to the criminal prosecution department. Killers had to know there would always be magistrates ready to take the place of murdered colleagues.

Galli's death came as an awful shock. Gherardo Colombo had spoken to him late in the morning of 19 March, reminding him of an important meeting that evening. He was an exceptional person from every point of view, said Colombo, who had got to know Galli before he entered the magistrature. Colombo had spent three months training in the third criminal section when Galli was its presiding judge. 'His standards cost him his life. If he had been a mediocre judicial bureaucrat, as some were in our department, he would not have run any risk,' said Colombo.[23]

Galli was the third magistrate to be murdered in the space of four days. 'We were convinced in the investigating magistrates' department that we would all be murdered,' recalled Colombo of that grim period.[24] 'The first thing to give sense to Galli's martyrdom was the request by Elena Paciotti, and other colleagues of the civil judiciary after her, to be transferred to the investigating magistrates' department,' he added.[25]

It had been a terrorist murder that had taken Galli to the prosecutors' department. After the Red Brigades had murdered his friend Girolamo Tartaglione, Galli had asked to be transferred to the prosecutors' department where expertise in terrorist crimes was valued. The chief prosecutor was glad to welcome such a capable and respected recruit, but ashamed that he could not offer the kind of conditions that Galli's seniority and experience merited. Galli had joined the prosecutor's department to be an assistant like the others, however, just to work with those who were engaged in the struggle against terrorism.

The year that Galli was gunned down outside Milan's university was terrible for the Italian magistrature. Not only did left-wing terrorists seem to get the upper hand, but judges, prosecutors and investigating magistrates faced enemies on other fronts as well. One of these adversaries lay in Rome, where the government and members of parliament, even after the murder of Aldo Moro, a former prime minister, and his escort in 1978, seemed incapable of giving the firm support that the magistrature merited. Another adversary was the moral cowardice of a large part of Italy's managerial class, where the corruption that would later surface through the discovery of the infamous P2 masonic lodge and the *tangentopoli* scandal was already working its corrosive effects. The magistrature was almost alone in Milan, as it was in Sicily where the Mafia, opposed by weak or compliant politicians and to widespread public indifference, continued to kill servants of the state.

MURDER BY THE MAFIA

Like Galli in Milan, Gaetano Costa, the chief prosecutor in Palermo, was alone when he was murdered in the late afternoon of 6 August 1980. He was walking the short distance that separated his home from the Palazzo di Giustizia to tidy up papers in his office there before going on holiday the following day.

Up Via Cavour, past the Bank of Italy's large regional head office, Costa had almost reached Piazza Verdi and the Teatro Massimo opera house. He had paused at a newsagents and book stall to choose a book when a white car drew up at the kerb and a man got out carrying a newspaper, a pistol hidden beneath. The mafia murderer fired, ensured that Costa was dead with a *coup de grâce* and got back into the car. The vehicle was found afterwards; it had been set alight in a small square behind the baroque church of San Domenico, close to the Vucciria market. There were no witnesses.

> Gaetano Costa, prosecutor of the republic, fell here,
> treacherously assassinated on 6 August 1980.
> The city placed this stone to express its abhorrence
> of the crime and to inspire civic virtues.[26]

Remembered by a plaque on the wall of a branch of UniCredito Italiano, Gaetano Costa had taken up the post in Palermo in July 1978, moving from Caltanissetta in central Sicily. A year later, he was caught up in the investigations into the murder of Boris Giuliano, the city's deputy chief of police. Only two months had passed before a colleague was murdered. Cesare Terranova had been in the prosecution service in Marsala where he had earned a good name as a magistrate and had returned to the magistrature to head the team of examining magistrates in Palermo after serving a term in parliament.

Rita Bartoli Costa, the chief prosecutor's wife, had called on Giovanna Terranova then and learned of the disgust that Terranova had felt at having shaken 'hands that were not clean' when people offered their condolences at her husband's funeral.[27] Less than a year later, Bartoli Costa would herself experience the bitter grief of widowhood and receive the meaningless, murmured condolences of politicians and officials for whom her husband's murder had been a cause for secret celebration.

Captain Emanuele Basile died on 5 May 1980, shot while returning to his quarters in the station of the *carabinieri* military police in Monreale. Basile was with his wife and was holding their three-year-old daughter in his arms. They were returning from an evening of festivities for Monreale's feast of the Holy Crucifix when three men came up from behind and shot him. It was a miracle that the baby was unhurt.

The killing of Basile was to lead to Costa's own murder. At the time of his death, the *carabiniere* captain was working on a major investigation into drug-trafficking and murder that had been started by Giuliano. In the days after Basile was killed, the chief of police in Palermo had arrested fifty-five people involved in the trafficking and Costa was asked to validate the arrest warrants. Costa's deputy did not attend the meeting at which the warrants were discussed and the two assistant prosecutors involved in the case declined to sign, and let everyone know that they had refused to put their names to the warrants. Promptly, decisively and calmly, said the chief prosecutor's widow, he alone had validated the arrest warrants – and had signed his own death sentence in doing so.[28]

Palermo's chief prosecutor was isolated and an easy target for the Mafia. The organization of escorts was inadequate. Costa was entitled to an armour-plated car with a driver and one policeman as bodyguard in the same car. But the driver went off duty at 2 p.m., after accompanying the prosecutor home. On the day he was murdered, Costa was alone in Via Cavour. Yet, the police had decided that they would escort him the following day during the journey to the port of Milazzo. From there he would have been escorted by the *carabinieri* to the island of Vulcano where he and his wife had planned to spend their holidays.

ESCORTS

Croce, Alessandrini, Ambrosoli, Galli and Costa were vulnerable; walking back to chambers or court after lunch, doing the school-run, returning home after an evening with friends, outside the university. None had had escorts. When Falcone and Borsellino travelled, they moved in armoured cars with escorts in front and behind. Yet both had been murdered and eight members of their escorts had died with them. And the policeman who was guarding Dalla Chiesa was also murdered when the Mafia killed the prefect of Palermo and his wife. When the Mafia set its mind to murder, it almost never failed. The question of escorts was a vexed one. The state had a duty to protect its servants, but how far did that responsibility extend?

The question forced itself back into the news a year after Berlusconi returned to power. On 19 March 2002, in the centre of Bologna, Marco Biagi was shot and killed by terrorists. A university professor of labour law who was working as a consultant to the minister of labour and had helped draft controversial legislation, Biagi had just arrived outside his home, having cycled from the railway station. There had been warning signs, not least in an earlier murder. In May 1999, Massimo D'Antona, a law professor in Rome, had been shot and killed in Via Salaria, opposite university buildings near the Villa Torlonia. The scene of the crime was less than ten minutes' walk from the ministry of labour where D'Antona was a consultant to the minister, a centre-left politician at that time.

Biagi had been threatened and he knew he was a target. He had been given an escort but it had later been taken away. In its first reaction to the murder, the home affairs ministry, which controlled the police and oversaw the question of escorts, said that the decision to remove Biagi's escort did not require disciplinary action or imply legal responsibility. Nobody was to blame. Quite simply, the system had slipped up, Claudio Scajola, the home affairs minister, told parliament one month after Biagi's murder.[29] Noting Scajola's remarks, the lawyer acting for the dead professor's widow said that the Biagi family did not want to interfere with the magistrature's investigations in Bologna into eventual acts of omission that might have been factors in Biagi's murder.[30] Less than four months later, both the police chief and the prefect of Bologna were placed under investigation although that was subsequently closed without further action.

Meanwhile, Scajola had been forced to resign after making disparaging remarks about the dead professor and his work. 'He was a pain in the arse who wanted his consultancy contract renewed,' said Scajola. 'In Bologna they killed Biagi who was without protection, but if there had been an escort there would have been three dead,' observed the minister.[31] He subsequently admitted that his comments had been offensive and apologized. Scajola thought Biagi a 'pain in the arse', but people wanting escorts could be a nuisance to the authorities who provided them. Not long before Costa was murdered, his wife had asked the police chief to station men at the end of their road because Costa returned home late in the evening, alone and in the dark. The police chief, she found, neither cared nor understood.[32]

In fact, Berlusconi's government had laid down its policy in September 2001, six months before Biagi's murder, when Scajola's ministry issued a circular that addressed the question of escorts and ordered that the resources allocated to them should be reduced by at least 30 per cent. The circular caused great concern in the magistrature, particularly among magistrates working on cases involving the Mafia.[33] Just over a month after it was issued, the Consiglio Superiore della Magistratura asked the justice minister to raise with the appropriate authorities the question of the reductions in the escorts of magistrates at risk.

The CSM was particularly worried about magistrates working in Reggio Calabria and Palermo. The magistrature's governing body noted how important personal safety was for ensuring that magistrates were impartial and independent. Two days after Biagi was murdered, the CSM reviewed the work that an internal commission had undertaken since October, the month after the circular was issued. The commission took issue with the home affairs ministry; it had done a bad job. 'The concerns raised by the heads of the judiciary in Reggio Calabria and Palermo were well-founded,' said the CSM.[34] Many magistrates, particularly judges, had been left with no protection whatsoever. For others, the level of protection had been reduced. The home affairs ministry's decision to replace non-uniformed escorts with uniformed personnel was inopportune. It increased the risk by bringing attention to the fact that someone was being escorted. In addition, the number of armour-plated cars in the livery of the various police forces was way below what was needed, making the escort service risky and exposing personnel to grave danger.

The home affairs ministry was wrong in how it decided who was at risk. One of the magistrates who gave evidence to the CSM had noted that all those involved in dealing with certain types of crime were exposed to danger, not just the investigating magistrates but everyone including the president of the court and the judges who tried the cases and handed down the sentences. The Mafia did not warn who it intended to attack.[35] Moreover, measures of protection were needed not only for magistrates whose current work put them at risk but also for those who had previously been involved in that kind of work. As long as the Mafia in its various regional forms remained so powerful the state would need to provide protection; that would be more likely to require greater resources than less.

Cutting costs was certainly a reason for the government's decision to reduce the escorts of magistrates, but the aggression that members of Berlusconi's coalition directed against the magistrature led to suspicions that there was an unspoken reason behind the cuts and that the government also wanted to use the issue as a way to whip the magistrates into line. One of the people affected was Ilda Boccassini, a prosecutor in Milan involved in the two cases of the corruption of Rome judges in which the defendants included Italy's prime minister himself and his former defence minister, Cesare Previti. A friend of Giovanni Falcone, Boccassini had asked for and obtained a transfer to Caltanissetta to help the investigation and prosecution of Falcone's murderers and had returned to Milan in 1995 to work with the *mani pulite* anti-corruption team.

Police forces should be used as escorts only when and where strictly necessary, said Francesco Saverio Borrelli, Milan's former chief prosecutor, and it would be wholly wrong to seek an escort as an ego-trip to boost self-esteem. 'I believe that the ministry's circular was right. What was wrong was how it was applied,' Borrelli observed.[36] Of course the cuts in escorts had been made across the board, but the decision to cut Boccassini's escort was mistaken because she had been and continued to be particularly exposed to danger. 'Naturally nobody wants to say that the home affairs minister or the prime minister or any other politician wants Ilda Boccassini hurt,' said Borrelli, 'but the decision to cut her escort certainly contained a little lesson to cut her down to size.'[37]

Gherardo Colombo, Boccassini's colleague on the judge-bribing cases, was also affected by the reductions in escorts. Like Boccassini, he received anonymous, abusive and threatening letters. But these were not an indicator of risk or danger and they had to be ignored. 'There would be an almighty fuss if they shot me, Borrelli or Boccassini. You take precautions, but you need to be fatalistic about these things,' said Colombo.[38] Magistrates who dealt with the Mafia lived in a different environment and the risks they ran were greater.

INSPECTIONS

The reduction, denial or removal of escorts to magistrates at risk was only one instrument of pressure on the magistrature to which Berlusconi's government resorted after taking office in 2001. It had other well-tried means to hand. One was 'inspections', which invariably disrupted the magistrates' work, as had happened in 1994 when Alfredo Biondi, the justice minister in the government that Berlusconi headed at the time, initiated an inspection of the *mani pulite* team.

The minister of justice could require the ministry's inspectorate to undertake special inspections beyond its routine work of periodically checking the efficiency of Italy's courts. Such non-routine inspections could be triggered by complaints from the public or they could be set in motion directly by the minister on his own initiative and, indirectly, by the prime minister. 'Problems arise from inspections instigated by people who want to obstruct the course of justice,' said Spataro in August 2002.[39] The system offered great opportunities for mischief-making, and unscrupulous lawyers and politicians exploited them.

In the autumn of 1994, Biondi instructed inspectors to undertake a detailed investigation into how the *mani pulite* magistrates in Milan had been doing their jobs.[40] The minister sought evidence of misconduct that would have allowed him to ask the CSM to take disciplinary action or something that would show that circumstances in Milan were incompatible with justice. Behind Biondi's move was a set of complaints, the complainants including Berlusconi and his friend and colleague Fedele Confalonieri, Fininvest's chairman. Another complaint concerned the remand in custody of a Fininvest manager.

Milan's bar council had also complained. 'The bar council had invited its members to tell the inspectors about things they thought were wrong in our investigations. It was an invitation to make accusations against us,' said Gherardo Colombo.[41] *Tangentopoli* became a rich and extendable seam of briefs for the lawyers.

That the inspection yielded nothing was due to Borrelli's determination.[42] When the chief prosecutor asked the inspectors for their mandate, he found that the ministry had botched it. Whatever the minister thought, his ministry was not allowed to send inspectors on wide-ranging fishing expeditions and the mandate with which the inspectors swooped on the prosecutors' offices in Milan was simply worthless. The inspectors should have been given precise and specific instructions, to check whether a certain judge was always late for his court, for example, or whether a certain magistrate used foul or threatening language when questioning suspects. The CSM backed Borrelli with an important ruling. Borrelli had had a duty to ask about the scope of the mandate within which Biondi's inspectors would work. Inspections that were not impartial or were incorrectly formulated would be stopped.

In any event, inspectors were not allowed to concern themselves with how prosecutors or judges dealt with their cases. Inspectors were not allowed to ask why a magistrate spoke to a particular witness and not to another, or why a judge made a particular ruling. 'Neither the minister of justice nor the CSM may investigate the work of magistrates within the cases they handle. The justice system itself provides the guarantees and remedies for mistakes made by prosecutors and judges,' Spataro pointed out.[43]

Biondi's inspection of *mani pulite* ended with a long report from his inspectors that fully absolved the Milanese magistrates. As well as noting the magistrates' great commitment and professional skills, the inspectors reported on the harmonious working relationships and the spirit of sacrifice demonstrated by the anti-corruption team.[44] Like the judges in London's High Court, Biondi's inspectors could find no justification whatsoever for the accusations of political persecution and misconduct levelled at the magistrates by Berlusconi and Confalonieri. They were investigating crimes and suspected crimes, and prosecuting those suspected of having committed them. However inconvenient and embarrassing to wealthy and powerful people this might be, the magistrates were simply doing their jobs.

However, that report, delivered in March 1995, was not the end of the business. *Tangentopoli* was then three years old and Italy's politicians, across the spectrum, had begun to seek revenge. 'The political class had kept its tail between its legs and its head low for a long time. Then it started to rebel against the magistrates,' said Borrelli.[45] There was more trouble over inspections in 1995, during the technocratic administration formed by Lamberto Dini after Berlusconi fell from power. Filippo Mancuso, Dini's elderly justice minister who later became a member of parliament for Berlusconi's Forza Italia party, decided that Biondi's inspectors were young, ingenuous and had not done the inspection properly. Moreover, alleged Mancuso, the inspectors had been terrorized by the hostility of the magistrates in Milan. The inspectors protested, threatened to resign *en masse* and were sacked by Mancuso.[46] After the CSM and the senate approved motions supporting the inspectors and the magistrature, Mancuso's inspection was suspended, and his inspectors' resignations and their sackings were withdrawn.

Inspections of Italy's magistrature were useful, however, for people on trial or under threat of it. Inspections disrupted the criminal justice system. The vast majority of complaints against the magistrature were vexatious and were judged so after being investigated. Inspections were generally a wasteful drain on resources. Because of the need to prepare, to put together documents, to recall what had been done and how things had happened, inspections always absorbed a lot of time.

Not only that; there was also the issue of intimidation. Not everyone in the magistrature had the experience or mental armour to cope with intimidatory inspections, said Colombo, and the arrival of inspectors could be a message to magistrates that they should toe the line.[47] Colombo had not personally been influenced by the arrival of inspectors or the threat of inspections. In almost thirty years of service, he had been in tougher situations than those that inspections brought and he thought that the fact of having been conscientious and competent would always be sufficient defence against the most demanding inspectors.

Disciplinary procedures were another arm that politicians could wield in their war of attrition against magistrates who showed signs of being inconveniently independent. One was started by Mancuso and targeted Borrelli and Piercamillo Davigo as well as Colombo. In this case, the charge was that of intimidation of the justice ministry's inspectors. 'This disciplinary action was closed with no action against the prosecutors,' said Colombo, who by 2002 had been subjected to three disciplinary actions.[48] The first two had been closed in the initial stages, without being sent for trial. In the third, he was tried in 1999 by the CSM, the body responsible for disciplinary matters. The centre-left government at the time had taken umbrage over a newspaper interview that Colombo had given. The justice minister raised several disciplinary issues when he initiated the action but Colombo was found innocent.

Another method open to those who wished to sabotage the criminal justice system was to lodge complaints of criminal offences against magistrates. The ploy used by the lawyers defending the *mafiosi* who had murdered Borsellino was often used against the anti-corruption team in Milan. Like his colleagues in *mani pulite*, Davigo had to deal with a series of such measures. Initially, he was indignant but then he began to treat them with the detachment they deserved. 'I faced thirty-six complaints of criminal behaviour in the court in Brescia. All were dismissed,' said Davigo, with a wry smile.[49] Despite the fact that the charges were dismissed, just having to tackle a constant barrage of criminal accusations was an enormous drain on magistrates' time and energy.

In July 2003, Colombo and Boccassini found themselves the subject of investigations by the court in Brescia. They had been accused of abuse of office by a group linked to Forza Italia called Comitato Nazionale per la Giustizia (National Committee for Justice) in a clear attempt to derail the trial in Milan in which they were prosecuting Cesare Previti on charges of judicial corruption. That attempt failed, however, when magistrates in Brescia ruled four months later that the accusation was groundless.[50]

Antonio Di Pietro, the prosecutor who as much as any personified the *mani pulite* team in the eyes of the Italian public, found himself the target of ferocious criminal intrigue. He was accused of various acts of corruption. Like his former colleagues, he was investigated by the magistrates in Brescia, but the charges were shown to have absolutely no foundation and the judge ruled that there had been no crime. 'On 18 February 1999, the judge for preliminary investigations in Brescia recognized the inconsistency of the prosecution's case and once again found me innocent of every charge, rejecting the request to send me for trial,' said Di Pietro.[51]

Di Pietro's judicial calvary in Brescia lasted for over four years as he fought to show the falsity of the evidence and testimony put up against him. Behind the denigration and accusations, he said, was a three-fold objective: to damage his reputation of complete integrity as a magistrate, to throw doubts over *mani pulite* and de-legitimize its work, and to torpedo his entry into politics. Between 1995 and 1998, he had been subjected to orchestrated and cunning salvos of criminal investigations. Despite this, he had always shown respect for the due process of law. 'For years, I attended hearings in the Brescia court at a cost of enormous personal suffering,' said Di Pietro.[52]

Yet another ploy used by those wanting to subvert Italy's criminal justice system was to slander or libel members of the magistrature involved in tricky cases. The prosecutors of the *mani pulite* team were obliged to issue writs to defend themselves against defamation. 'I had never been slandered or libelled in the sixteen years before 1994. This changed when I began prosecuting people accused of the crime of corruption,' said Davigo.[53] Behind the vicious campaigns of slander and libel was the multiple aim of smearing the prosecutors in the eyes of the public, absorbing their energies, distracting and discouraging them, and undermining their work in court.

VERBAL ASSAULT

The bodies of Falcone, Borsellino and their escorts had been laid to rest for barely two years when the magistrature's efforts began to be mauled. Sacrifices had been forgotten and magistrates were forced to fend off vicious verbal assaults by politicians and sections of the media, and to face shameful attempts to prevent them from doing their job.

Biondi's decree in 1994, during Berlusconi's first administration, was the turning point, recalled Davigo. Tired of being on the defensive over corruption, politicians thought the time had come to reassert themselves. 'I started to be violently attacked,' said Davigo.[54] His membership of Magistratura Indipendente, which placed him on the most conservative wing of a generally conservative profession, added irony to the fact that those attacks originated mainly on the right of the political spectrum, spearheaded by Berlusconi's Forza Italia party whose influence over the media gave opponents of the criminal justice system an advantage over the institutions responsible for bringing law-breakers to book.

Campaigns to undermine the institutions responsible for administering the law and to attack the prosecutors and judges worried the magistrature's governing body and it responded quickly when politicians and their allies in the media launched their attacks. On 1 December 1994, it passed a resolution expressing its concern. The CSM had a firm institutional duty to protect its members against denigratory and defamatory attacks, it said, defence by the CSM being the right of every judge and prosecutor. Magistrates should not have to deal personally with denigration and defamation. 'The council must be the body that authoritatively and publicly re-establishes the image of magistrates who are unjustly attacked, assaulted or treated with contempt,' recalled the CSM when it returned to this issue in July 1998.[55] The CSM had to speak out again less than a year and a half later; it approved almost unanimously another resolution that emphasized its concern in December 1999. Two lay, non-magistrature members of the CSM, political nominees appointed by Berlusconi's Polo della Liberta coalition which at that time formed the parliamentary opposition, voted against the resolution.

Between the end of 1994 and the end of 1999 there had been an alarming widening of the attacks. The assault had originally been directed mainly at the prosecuting arm of the magistrature, in itself an extremely serious and insidious matter. But by 1999 the attacks were also being made against magistrates whose role was that of judging cases. 'There is a real danger that these attacks may influence the judicial function, the judge being scared of finding himself exposed to campaigns of denigration because of sentences that he has passed on powerful public or private figures,' said the CSM.[56] This would gravely prejudice the correct and impartial application of justice.

As for the charge that magistrates exercised justice without being impartial and on the basis of political prejudice, such an allegation was wholly unacceptable. Borrelli's view on this subject was characteristically forthright. 'Prosecutors work with the evidence that they are given or uncover,' he said.[57] They did not invent evidence or crimes, neither did they close their eyes to them.

The CSM warned, 'It is one of the gravest accusations that can be made against a magistrate and, at the same time, one of the most destructive for the credibility and prestige of the judiciary, as it threatens to undermine citizens' trust in justice.'[58] To avoid an erosion of the public's trust in the magistrature's impartiality, the job required the highest professional standards and total observance of ethical standards. Italy's magistrates did not object to criticism, even harsh criticism, or to having their decisions subjected to close scrutiny and control by public opinion. This formed part of democracy and the rule of law.

What happened after the mid-1990s, however, went far beyond criticism. Politicians and parts of the media had put together highly organized campaigns of personal insults aimed at magistrates who had been responsible for disagreeable decisions. They had exploited their criticism of the magistrature in order to justify their refusal to submit to the judicial process. Yet the judicial process was a guarantee of the principle of legality and the equality of all citizens before the law.

The magistrature's governing body's words at the end of 1999 went unheard. The CSM was given still more cause for concern when Berlusconi returned to power in 2001. It called a special meeting on 27 November 2001 to address once again the deeply disturbing issue of the attacks on prosecutors and judges. Spataro expressed his grave concern to fellow councillors. 'The entire justice system is being subjected to an all-round offensive from well-defined sectors of Italian politics,' he said.[59] The thrust of the strategy of government politicians was to erode the magistrature's independence. 'Magistrates, identified by name, have been attacked or praised depending on their decisions,' Spataro told the CSM.[60] Berlusconi's parliamentarians were using the classic technique of hitting some magistrates to teach all of them that they would be better off falling into line than stepping out of it.

The aggression directed at the magistrature arose solely in connection with a certain kind of person on trial, the *eccellenti*, the illustrious defendants who were powerful or rich, noted Spataro. 'These attacks have a character that is peculiarly Italian, typical of democratically less developed systems,' he said.[61] Heads of state and government, ministers and senior members of the state bureaucracy had been put on trial in America, France, Germany and Spain. Elsewhere the respect towards the justice system of those on trial or under investigation was there for everyone to see. The disdain for legal institutions shown by Berlusconi and members of his coalition was unique among western countries.

Addressing the CSM at the end of November 2001, Spataro gave some examples of the attacks that the magistrature had endured in the preceding months. Earlier that month while on an official trip to Granada in Spain, a country racked by a real civil war in the 1930s, Berlusconi accused Italian magistrates of having fomented a civil war over recent years. He told his Spanish audience that Italy's judges wanted to overturn the system. That same day, Gaetano Pecorella, the lawyer who combined the job of defending Berlusconi in Milan against charges of bribing judges with chairing parliament's judicial affairs committee, added his voice to that of his client on the question of civil wars.[62] As 2001 drew to an end, other government politicians fuelled the flames of odium against the magistrature, calling for judges to be arrested and put in prison.

Deaf to a call by Italy's president, Carlo Azeglio Ciampi, for respect of the magistrature, the senators of Berlusconi's coalition approved a motion on 5 December 2001 that disregarded the concept of the separation of powers. The motion referred to cases that were being tried and made grave accusations against 'some magistrates in various courts who have attempted and still attempt today to use their positions, and the powers that the constitution gives them, to undertake a political struggle, interfering with the country's political life by laying charges of a clearly illiberal nature'.[63] This motion followed soon after a court interpretation of the law on international judicial assistance that went against Berlusconi and Previti; it was a clear attack on the Milan court. Grande Stevens strongly criticized what the senate had done. Addressing the annual meeting of the national magistrates' association in March 2002, the doyen of the Italian bar observed that the government's politicians had acted improperly by approving the motion. Judges' decisions may be criticized and appealed against, he said, or laws can be enacted interpreting parliament's will. 'But one institutional power of the state, the legislature, must not interfere with another, the judiciary.'[64] Such a move by parliament undermined the rule of law, particularly when judges' decisions concerned parliamentarians.

A group of university law professors also took exception to the senate's motion. The prime minister's parliamentarians had used the institution of parliament to interfere with an ongoing case. The motion was a grave act of intimidation, said the law professors, because it contained a judgement on judicial decisions that were still subject to the ordinary means of appeal. The senators had 'attacked the freedom of the judges to pass judgement in the current and successive levels of trial'.[65] They had created a conflict between the powers of the state by violating the long-held principle that forbade parliament from interfering in individual trials.

Expressing their solidarity with the magistrature, the law professors remembered what Piero Calamandrei, one of the founding fathers of Italy's post-war republic, had written of a Tuscan judge who served during the two decades of Mussolini's dictatorship: 'Someone, in the early days of fascism, called him the red judge. Really, he was neither red nor grey. He just had a clear, proud conscience, and was unwilling to deny justice in order to satisfy the fascist thugs who invaded the courtrooms. He was simply a just judge. For this he was called red because, among the many sufferings that await a just judge, there is always also that of being accused, when unwilling to serve one faction, of being at the service of the opposing faction.'[66]

Being a magistrate in fascist Italy had been a thankless task for magistrates with consciences and decades later, during the *anni di piombo* of terrorism and in the fight against the Mafia, recognition of the magistrature's sacrifices was slight. While Dini's technocratic government and the centre-left administrations that followed it had shown the magistrature no favours, something far different came from Silvio Berlusconi and his right-wing allies. What distinguished their assault on the magistrature was its unrelenting ferociousness and Berlusconi's access to the media to make it. After he entered politics, the magistrature's service and duty were repaid with malevolence and abuse. The attacks on the magistrature and the undermining of the rule of law betrayed the memory of servants of the Italian state who had died upholding the law and defending the principles of justice. More than that, in its campaign of venom and mendacity, Berlusconi's coalition seemed intent on betraying the very principles on which the republic itself was founded.

Epilogue

When, as we have seen, Silvio Berlusconi was in Naples hosting a United Nations' summit on crime in November 1994, the world learned that the Italian prime minister was under investigation in connection with financial felonies. Four months earlier, while attending a meeting of leaders of the G7 countries in the same city, John Major, Britain's Conservative prime minister, had also been shaken by bad news. The head of his parliamentary party had telephoned to say that the *Sunday Times* had caused a splash with a scoop about junior ministers taking money in return for asking questions in parliament. By the end of the day, two Conservative politicians had been suspended from their jobs.[1]

That article was the beginning of a far bigger story of misconduct and corruption in British politics. It opened a season in which 'sleaze' became the word to describe the avidity of politicians in London and their willingness to ignore the ethical standards that should have governed how they behaved. Sleaze would be a factor in Major's electoral defeat two and a half years later. He was never able to shrug off the label that had been tied to his Conservative Party the weekend he was in Naples basking in the spotlight on the international stage with the leaders of the world's other big economies. In October 1994, the *Guardian*, a daily newspaper, gave its readers more details of the 'cash for questions' scandal. The minister for Northern Ireland resigned at once[2] and two other ministers' heads subsequently rolled.

The outcry was such that Major announced on 25 October that a committee, to be chaired by a senior judge, Lord Nolan, a member of Britain's highest appeal court, would be set up to look into standards in public life. Its terms of reference were brief but broad; the committee was charged with examining concerns about the standards of conduct of holders of public office, including the financial and commercial arrangements in which they might have been involved. Lord Nolan's committee was asked to make recommendations 'to ensure the highest standards of propriety in public life'.[3] In six weeks of public hearings during January and February 1995 in the Central Hall Westminster, the committee heard evidence from more than 100 witnesses. It also received almost 2,000 letters and written submissions.

Three months after the committee had finished collecting its evidence, Lord Nolan presented his report to the prime minister. A few politicians in Britain had been paid as general multi-client parliamentary consultants, some had accepted hospitality without declaring an interest and a handful of ministers, on leaving office, had taken positions in companies with which they had had dealings. The scale of morally dubious behaviour was risibly small compared with the reprehensibly gross corruption in which Italian politicians and businessmen had wallowed for many years and which was being brought to light through the efforts of dedicated magistrates in the *mani pulite* team. Where money had changed hands the sums involved had been modest and measured in thousands of pounds. Not for British members of parliament and their financial sponsors the millions of pounds that had changed hands in Milan or flowed between the offshore accounts of Italian politicians and their accomplices in crime. Even so, Lord Nolan was deeply concerned. 'The erosion of public confidence in the holders of public office is a serious matter,' he said.[4] It was important to have respect for the ethical values inherent in the idea of public service.

The committee had heard the expression 'grey area' used to rationalize morally dubious behaviour. The judge was worried by the ubiquity of the expression and the implication that some people were not certain about the difference between right and wrong in public life. The solution to such moral uncertainty, he suggested, was the rejection of any course of action if there was doubt about whether it was consistent with standards of upright behaviour.[5] A degree of austerity was not only desirable, it was essential. Britain had good reason to pride itself on the standards of conduct of public servants and the threat to those standards was not great, but everything should be done to prevent them slipping. 'Experience elsewhere warns that, unless the strictest standards are maintained and where necessary restored, corruption and malpractice can become part of the way of life,' he said.[6] Perhaps the judge was thinking of Italy, probably the European country offering the most egregious example of endemic public corruption.

Lord Nolan's committee laid down a set of principles to govern the conduct of those who served the public. They included selflessness, integrity, accountability, openness and honesty.[7] Holders of public office should take decisions solely in terms of the public interest, should not place themselves under any financial or other obligation to outside individuals and should resolve conflicts between private interests and public duties in order to protect the public interest rather than their own. Holding public office brought responsibilities and duties. Submitting oneself to scrutiny was one. The public had a right to ask and to know about those who occupied public office; they should be held accountable for their actions and words.[8]

A secondary-school teacher, and parent of two teenagers, wrote to the committee to express deep disappointment that public figures appeared to escape retribution for actions and attitudes that set such a poor example to British youth. Another member of the public regretted that the principles of honesty, truth and integrity had been debased by those at the highest levels of society who should have provided examples to ordinary folk.[9] These aggrieved Britons would have had more reason for moral outrage if the disregard for probity in public life revealed by *tangentopoli* as commonplace in Italy had come to light in Britain; it showed how widely expectations about standards of conduct differed between the two countries.

One explanation for the different ways of looking at corruption might lie in the contrast between two types of Christianity. The conscience of the Roman Catholic, that can be put at ease through priestly mediation in the confessional, is perhaps less demanding than that of the Protestant, accountable directly to God. Protestantism stresses the punishment of sins more strongly than Roman Catholicism which places an emphasis on penitence and how this leads to forgiveness. Moreover, the Protestant ethic of work and thrift married better with the idea of public service than Catholic leaning to godly service and charity.[10] Yet, Pope John Paul II held clear views on crime, public figures and corruption. The day that Berlusconi wrote to *Il Foglio*, a newspaper owned by his wife, in blustering defence of his friends Cesare Previti, who had just been sentenced to eleven years' imprisonment for judicial corruption, and Bettino Craxi, the deeply corrupt former prime minister who had been Berlusconi's political patron,[11] the pope sternly addressed his weekly general audience in the vast *piazza* outside Saint Peter's basilica.

Crime, justice and leadership had been on Pope John Paul II's mind when he prepared his sermon for that audience. '*Misericordiam et judicium* – my song shall be of mercy and judgement.' The pope had based his sermon for the last Wednesday of April 2003 on Psalm 101, which he described as the programme of a king faithful to God.[12] In unremitting reproof of wrongdoing, the psalm warned that liars, those who were arrogant and the deceitful would be cast from the kingdom, slanderers would be destroyed and the wicked would be rooted out. In their every choice, said the pope, all Christians should make sure that they kept far from wickedness, but leaders had a particular duty and people with public responsibilities needed to show an implacable commitment to fighting crime. Despite the psalm's strong words, however, there was ambiguity in the pope's sermon that might have fostered an indifference in the faithful as to whether their political leaders should be straight or could be crooked. Mercy came first, said Pope John Paul II, and then judgement.[13]

Unperturbed that Berlusconi won power in May 2001 with serious criminal charges hanging over him and that his government introduced laws that allowed the prime minister to dodge the legal process for those charges, Italians were merciful. They did not judge by the standards of voters in countries in northern Europe. Those who elected Berlusconi were unconcerned that he had given false evidence when under oath in court in Verona in 1988. That he had used weasel words to avoid admitting an adulterous relationship counted little. By availing himself of the right to silence when prosecutors wanted to question him about his early business affairs, his employment of a *mafioso* and other matters, Berlusconi showed he did not care for accountability and openness. His declarations in May and June 2003 to the court in Milan where he was on trial for judicial corruption were vigorously contested by people he sought to smear, although not in court where he was allowed to speak unchallenged. Just how much was true of what the Italian prime minister had said would probably never be tested. He was not under oath and, as we have seen earlier, as a defendant he had the right to lie. Indeed, in at least one matter he did speak untruthfully. 'Not one of the judges on trial, not just Squillante but none of his colleagues, dealt with a case that in any way, directly or indirectly, concerned me personally or my companies,' Berlusconi told the court in Milan that would later find Squillante guilty of corruption.[14] Yet in May 1984 Berlusconi had appeared in front of Squillante in a matter concerning television antennae and he had been accompanied by Previti.[15] When Berlusconi left the Milan court after making his declaration on 17 June 2003, he gave his word that, whatever happened, he would be available eight days later to take up where he had left off.[16] His declarations concerning the case had ended then, however, and his return to court looked a distant prospect.

Italians had voted Berlusconi into power, but did they trust him? In 1993, before 'sleaze' became an issue in Britain, Market and Opinion Research International (MORI) had conducted an opinion poll in which they asked people there how far they trusted the members of various occupations to speak the truth. Politicians fared badly, only one person in seven trusting them to be truthful. Ministers were held in even lower regard, only one person in nine believing that those in government and responsible for running the country spoke honestly.[17] Perhaps Italians were more gullible or more trusting – or just more cynical. In whatever ways Berlusconi had made his fortune and was holding on to it, the man in the street may have reasoned that his prime minister would work similar magic as head of government to create wealth for the country as a whole. Moreover, the ordinary person may have thought that Italy's wealthiest man would not take advantage of public office to make yet more money for himself. In that respect, at least, Italians displayed a kind of trust when they voted for Berlusconi and his House of Freedoms coalition. Whether he merited the trust required for public office was another matter. The way that politicians and other public figures had been discarded for misconduct or morally dubious behaviour in countries like Britain, Germany, Sweden and Finland suggested that he would not have been elected in those countries; someone like him would not even have been acceptable as a candidate for public office.

Widespread corruption, deeply entrenched organized crime and a governing coalition more intent on bespoke legislation to help get the prime minister off his legal hooks than on beating criminals were symptoms of a nasty malady that explained why many northern Europeans were concerned that a lowering of standards to Italian levels might be infectious and were anxious that the right example should be given to the recently democratized countries in central Europe. Standards for wickedness and the moral convictions of people throughout Europe might arguably have been similar but, as Italy showed, the ways of expressing them were distinctly different. 'At least within the western world, there has been for the past two thousand years a common standard of political ethics to which people subscribe in a rough and ready way, such that they know when they have to find excuses,' said Professor Alan Ryan, the warden of New College, Oxford, talking about the question of cross-cultural judgements.[18] Italians did not generally say that they found corruption and the lies of defendants in court perfectly acceptable. Instead, they excused corruption as a necessary local practice to oil the wheels of business or, as part of the cost of democracy, to keep a choice of political parties going. Telling lies was merely what defendants were allowed to do, and did, in order to get off charges, although the official condoning of lying to courts and the notion of trust were plainly at odds.

Perhaps those who voted for Berlusconi did not trust him, any politician or any institution of the state. Indeed, *tangentopoli* had provided Italians with good reason for distrusting businessmen and politicians, particularly those who had been running the country during the 1980s and at the beginning of the 1990s. Yet in 1994 and 2001 they voted into power a man who owed a large part of his wealth and success in business to friendship with the politician who as much as any had stood for institutionalized corruption. The *cavaliere* of Arcore may have put himself forward as a new man, but he was an improbable candidate for the role and an unlikely standard-bearer for the moralization of public life in Italy. When the magistrates of the *mani pulite* team tackled corruption and the political structure crumbled, Italians were given an opportunity to cleanse the shameful impropriety that stained politics and business and to start afresh. Instead, they put Berlusconi into power.

Did that mean that Italians wanted corruption to continue, with what that implied for standards in public life? Possibly many of them did not care. In his book on the political conditions that produce the pursuit of cleaner government, Professor Robert Neild of Trinity College, Cambridge notes, '. . . public corruption harms the community as a whole rather than individuals who might quickly protest at the damage they suffer'.[19] Writing just after the outbreak of the Second World War, Piero Calamandrei was appalled by the cultural and social gangrene whose infection had spread in fascist Italy. 'Italy's tragedy is this general moral putrefaction, this indifference, this singular systematic cowardice,' he lamented.[20] Not much had changed in half a century, as the anti-corruption magistrates in Milan found when Berlusconi's politicians attacked them and Italians voted those politicians into government.

Were Italians dazzled by Berlusconi's money and mesmerized by his media power? Perhaps they were. Italian infatuation with *bella figura* (looking good) would have helped him, and his command of the media was impressive as well as insidious. Moreover, Italian history was full of powerful people who ruled for a while before being pushed aside; ordinary people knew how to bend with the wind. Or maybe Berlusconi's political victories were simply the proof of old prejudices on which he had cleverly played when he assembled a coalition that included the National Alliance and the Northern League. Many southern Italians complained of northern arrogance and many northerners believed that people in the south were parasites who lived off the northerners' hard work. Voters did not see a contradiction in a coalition where one partner fostered northern prejudices and wanted independence while another had its power base in the south and stood for an integral state. Or maybe they had understood the contradiction and hoped that their party would best the others in the coalition; in which case, trust was left outside.

Yet trust was fundamental to those voters' lives as it is to the lives of almost everyone. As Niklas Luhmann, a sociologist, observed, 'A complete absence of trust would prevent even getting up in the morning.'[21] Italians trusted that supermarkets would sell safe food, that the electricity utility would supply power to keep refrigerators working and provide light at the touch of a switch, that other drivers would keep to their side of the road and that their telephones would allow them to speak to others, and without being eavesdropped on. Like the vast majority of people, Italians needed to be able to trust others to do as others said they would and they needed others to trust them to act how they said they would. Common sense suggested that Italians should have sought ways to strengthen trust and eliminate the things that undermined it, and that they had acted perversely by not seizing the chance that the efforts of *mani pulite* offered for the renewal of public life. 'I think that deception is the real enemy of trust,' said Professor Onora O'Neill, the principal of Newnham College, Cambridge.[22] And deception on a massive scale by Italy's politicians and businessmen was what *tangentopoli* had been.

'Deception is not a minor or a marginal moral failure. Deceivers do not treat others as moral equals; they exempt themselves from obligations that they rely on others to live up to,' argued O'Neill in the Reith Lectures, a prestigious series of lectures on the radio service of the British Broadcasting Corporation named after the BBC's founder.[23] O'Neill addressed the question of trust generally. She pointed out that deception lay at the heart of many serious crimes including fraud, perjury, false accounting, slander and libel. Those who deceived were not simply making mistakes, neither were those who made commitments they had no intention of honouring nor those who cheated on their partners. 'If we want to increase trust we need to avoid deception,' she said.[24]

Certainly the enormity of the deception that was engineered in Italy by the corruptors and corrupted of the country's public life was extraordinary in several respects. The sums of money involved were huge and the spread of corruption involved politicians, officials and businessmen at all levels everywhere. Most corrosive of all was that judges were themselves involved. One of the two trials in Milan in which Cesare Previti was found guilty of corruption should have been spoken of less as the trial of Previti, the Milanese court noted when giving its judgement, and more as the trial of some judges of the appeal court in Rome who had been responsible for debasing justice into a system for private benefit.[25]

'Judicial corruption is one of the most serious crimes. Its effect is devastating,' said Oscar Luigi Scalfaro, Italy's president from 1992 until 1999 and once a magistrate himself.[26] Scalfaro had saved Italy and its justice system from a terrible fate in 1994 when he had refused Berlusconi's proposal that Previti should be appointed justice minister in the government that Berlusconi was forming after winning the elections.[27] The crimes of which Previti had been found guilty gravely wounded the right of every citizen to be treated equally before the law and seriously undermined the citizen's trust in the justice system. 'The state is dead when judges cannot be trusted because they are corrupt,' said Scalfaro.[28] Even so, it was important that Italians should know whether judges had been bribed or not and the former president was sure that people had the right to know the truth.[29] This right that Scalfaro thought important had itself, as we have seen, been put in jeopardy by the vicious smear campaign waged by Berlusconi's coalition against the magistrature, particularly against the prosecutors and judges involved in cases of judicial corruption concerning the prime minister and his friend. For two years, the two panels of three judges in the court in Milan had been the target of savage criticism and of the most infamous accusations both within and from outside the courtroom.[30]

In the Orwellian world into which Berlusconi tried to take Italy after he gained power in May 2001, those decent magistrates who laboured conscientiously to discover the facts and apply the laws were slandered rather than praised. The dishonest became trustworthy and lies became truth. Berlusconi claimed that Italy's judges and prosecutors were deranged. 'These judges are mad twice over. First, because they are politically that way, and second, because they are mad anyway. To do that job you need to be mentally disturbed, you need psychic disturbances,' he said.[31] Some Italians were deeply concerned by such intemperance. Remarks like those Berlusconi made were plainly wrong: prime ministers in democratic societies just did not say such things about the judiciary. Scalfaro thought that the attacks on the magistrature led citizens to believe that not everyone was equal before the law.[32] It was understandable that some people, not least among the besieged and battered judiciary, thought that Berlusconi's coalition was undermining the rule of law, and in so doing was threatening to pull down an essential pillar of democratic society in Italy.

The late Professor John Rawls, one of the great moral and political philosophers of the twentieth century, believed that the citizens of a well-ordered society would normally want the rule of law maintained, and that meant that they wanted the regular and impartial administration of public rules through a legal system that regulated conduct and provided the framework for cooperation within society. Just rules, said Rawls, constituted the grounds for persons to rely on one another and to object when their expectations were not met.[33] In the absence of enforceable rules, some members of society might believe that others were not doing what they should and these members might be tempted to follow that example. 'The suspicion that others are not honoring their duties and obligations is increased by the fact that, in the absence of the authoritative interpretation and enforcement of the rules, it is particularly easy to find excuses for breaking them,' wrote Rawls.[34]

The attempts by Berlusconi's coalition to intimidate the judiciary and enact legislation to limit its independence were one reason why some Italians thought that the rule of law was under threat. The bespoke laws that the government drove through parliament in Rome to help the prime minister were another reason why such Italians saw signs that respecting the rule of law did not matter to Berlusconi and his allies. Italy's criminal law was moulded to the prime minister's personal needs. More than that, he seemed to consider himself to be above the law.

Some academics might argue that Berlusconi did not violate the rule of law, which was simply determined by courts enforcing rules within a system that allowed the changing of those rules. Laws might have been made to help him and his cronies, but they were laws all the same. Viewed from this angle, Italians worried by Berlusconi's behaviour might have been justified in making a kind of moral complaint against him, rather than complaining that he was breaching the rule of law. Yet, because of the moral values inherent in the idea of legal systems, others might reason, the violation of those values destroyed the systems. These two points of view tended to converge when the tampering with legal systems became sufficiently bad. 'When a system becomes an instrument for the arbitrary imposition of the will of one or a few people for their own benefit, then it really does not seem to be a legal system at all,' observes Ryan.[35] At some point down the line that Berlusconi followed during the first three years of his second administration, the law would in effect be replaced by the manipulation of the justice system for the benefit of particular people. For many Italians, by disregarding the requirement that legislation was meant to be for the public good, in a broad sense, and not for the good of some particular specified persons, Berlusconi had passed that point soon after winning the elections in May 2001.

Berlusconi imagined that victory in parliamentary elections was sufficient to allow him to rule as he wished. He seemed to think that freedom meant the liberty to do what he liked without interference from others. He was the owner of a large business and owners of businesses, particularly large ones, could behave as they thought fit in Italy. Constitutional rules were obstacles to be got over and majorities in parliament were licences to enact whatever laws governments wanted. He had said during 2001's election campaign that he would change the constitution and he thought that a parliamentary majority gave him the right to do so. Former president Scalfaro had other ideas about what parliamentary majorities allowed governments to do, however, and acting just as they pleased was not one of them. He had been a member of the constituent assembly that drew up Italy's constitution after the Second World War, was aghast at Berlusconi's threat to change it and thought that what Berlusconi had said was itself an attack on the constitution. 'I was a member of that assembly and swore loyalty to the constitution as head of state many years later. Everyone owes absolute respect to the constitution,' said Scalfaro.[36] He believed that any scheme to use a simple parliamentary majority to force through legislation to reform the magistrature and change the justice system, matters that affected all citizens, would be an attack on democracy and an act of brutal arrogance.[37] He was not alone in thinking this. 'The principle of majority rule is a long way down the hierarchy of moral justification. A prime minister cannot simply do what he wants on the basis of having enough numbers on his side,' notes Ryan.[38]

Numbers in parliament were not the only weapon that Berlusconi had on his side. He possessed the enormous advantage of controlling the channels of information through which Italians heard the news and he exploited this advantage ruthlessly. His three Mediaset television channels had helped him win the parliamentary elections in 1994, soon after he entered politics, and from then onwards they continued to propagandize loyally for him. Even before Berlusconi won power again in 2001, the state television company had been biased in his favour; after he returned to government, its main channels became an instrument under his firm control. Public opinion could act as a brake on executive action but the concentration of media power in Berlusconi's hands prevented Italians from reaching informed opinions about what the government was doing. Careful selection of which news items to cover and the attentive slanting of presentation ensured that Berlusconi and his government were put in favourable light. On 29 September 2003, the day after Italy suffered a catastrophic nationwide electricity blackout, the prime minister commandeered all the television channels for a simultaneous broadcast, but not to explain why the lights had gone out.[39] Instead he beat the drum for plans to reform the state pensions system, bashed the trade unions and exhorted support for his government.

That the prime minister had hijacked the airwaves for little more than a personal appeal did not seem unusual to many Italians, for whom family mattered and the pursuit of self-interest was understandable while the broader community and common good counted far less. Indeed, in his rise to economic and political power, Berlusconi was helped by widespread indifference towards rules, civil society and the state, and by a weak democracy that lacked the checks and balances to rein back people like him and to absorb bumps and shocks and the strains of extremism. Perhaps that was because the relatively young modern Italian state had always suffered from a strong sensation of not enjoying public moral consensus. Much had militated against the construction of a robust democracy. The absence of a solid and efficient civil service was a huge handicap,[40] and historically many sharp divides had split the country: radicals against conservatives; capitalism against socialism; industrial society, which arrived late, against agrarian society; absentee landlords against agricultural labourers; clericalism against anti-clericalism.

So the public generally appeared unconcerned by the blatant conflicts of interest that their prime minister was never inclined to resolve. Given that Berlusconi had made a priority of his own affairs, it was hardly surprising that half-way through the parliament's term, at the end of 2003, he could point to few successes for the country. Subordinated to efforts aimed at sorting out the prime minister's legal difficulties, the government's financial, economic and industrial policies had not produced results. Berlusconi's foreign policy had been quirky and gaffe-prone. Measured against the requirements for honesty and trustworthiness, he was arguably unqualified for political office. Not least, the businessman-turned-politician had failed to live up to the promise of managing Italy's affairs competently. With people's welfare depending heavily on what prime ministers did, being efficient was a moral obligation. 'Forza Italia has brought about a great moral revolution in the country: it has brought true morality to political life and that means the morality of doing, building and achieving,' said Berlusconi.[41] Many people thought that real morality also embraced other things and, in any case, that such claims were empty and he had failed in this duty.

Being prime minister no doubt brought sacrifices. Perhaps not being free to do whatever he wanted was irksome. Perhaps heading the government tied him to some unwelcome timetables, brought him into contact with people he would have preferred not to meet, caused him to face problems he would rather have avoided and carried him to places where he did not want to go. But being in power did not only impose annoying routines and restrictions; he was able to pick some fruits of office for himself.

As his supporters tried to show him in the best possible light, some of their efforts were sheer sycophancy. There were members of Forza Italia who even thought that what they saw as their party leader's decisive efforts at unifying the world merited the Nobel Prize for peace and they began to canvass for his nomination. Berlusconi had been the driving force behind bringing Russia into Nato, they said, and no politician had worked so hard for the cause of peace in the

Middle East.[42] They could have pointed to historical precedent for the idea. After the Locarno Treaty in 1925, an accord in which Italy, Germany, France, Britain and Belgium guaranteed the frontier between France and Germany, Benito Mussolini had been suggested as a candidate for the Nobel Prize for peace.[43] The fascist leader, who claimed the honours for bringing the treaty about, loved such flattery. Eleven years later, Hitler would describe his Italian partner in the pact of steel as 'the first statesman in the world, to whom no one else could remotely be compared'.[44]

Berlusconi claimed to be a man of action and so too had Mussolini. Both men showed no understanding of the limits to what they were allowed to do; both said that they worked very long hours and paid great attention to precision and detail; both hated criticism and considered they were beyond it; both believed that the world was divided into friends and enemies. There were other similarities; an aversion to a free press was one. Italy's newspaper of record and a thorn in Mussolini's side, *Corriere della Sera*, came under pressure at the end of 1925 and its owners succumbed and sacked the liberally minded editor.[45] In 2003, when Berlusconi was in power, the pressure of writs and complaints about the newspaper's coverage of court cases and the government's performance was such that the editor resigned.[46] Berlusconi complained about an international press that criticized him and his government. Foreign newspapers and magazines, he believed, were parties to a left-inspired conspiracy and in league with the opposition in the Italian parliament. 'I do not give press conferences to the foreign press because they just use it as an opportunity to attack me,' he said.[47] Eighty years earlier, Mussolini had fumed about an 'utterly unacceptable' English press campaign that was likely to cause permanent damage to relations between the countries.[48]

Milan had been Mussolini's power base, as the city would later become for Berlusconi. Carlo Maria Martini, cardinal archbishop of Milan from 1979 to 2002, had a clear idea about power. 'Whoever has power is, in fact, inclined to use it for his own interest without concern for the interest of others. Even more than that, he is easily disposed to sacrifice the interest of others in order to win more power and maintain positions of advantage and unjustified control,' he warned.[49] During more than twenty years in the diocese he observed the worst of terrorism and corruption. Cardinal Martini was caring for the souls of the city during the period when Berlusconi's crooked friend Bettino Craxi built his centre of power there. Just as Berlusconi would later foster Craxi's rehabilitation,[50] so Craxi had been influential in launching the rehabilitation of the fascist dictator. During the 1980s, under the patronage that Craxi gave when he was prime minister, apologists for fascism put on exhibitions that highlighted fascism's originality but ignored the horrors of the dictatorship, the pain and suffering of war and the destruction and bitterness of defeat.[51] Having brought Mussolini's heirs in from the political cold and into his government, Berlusconi added his efforts to gloss over the terrible things for which fascism had been responsible. 'Mussolini did not murder anyone. Mussolini sent people on holiday to confine them,' he said.[52] Yet under Mussolini's urging fascist *squadristi* had attacked and murdered political opponents and his rise to power 'had been scarred by up to 2,000 deaths'.[53] And the killing did not stop once he was in power: among the most notorious cases were the murders of Giovanni Minzoni, a Catholic priest, in 1923 and Giacomo Matteotti, a reformist politician, in 1924.

Some historians took a different view from Berlusconi and the revisionists of history around him. To one of his recent biographers, Richard Bosworth, Mussolini was no more than an ambitious provincial intellectual who thought he could lead a state, and his legacy would be confined to the superficial. 'His propagandists declared that he was always right. However, in the most profound matters which touch on the human condition, he was, with little exception, wrong,' writes Bosworth.[54] A. J. P. Taylor was even more dismissive in his assessment of Mussolini, in his view no more than a vain, blundering boaster. 'Everything about Fascism was a fraud. The social peril from which it saved Italy was a fraud; the revolution by which it seized power was a fraud; the ability and policy of Mussolini were fraudulent; Fascist rule was corrupt, incompetent, empty,' wrote Taylor about fifteen years after the end of the Second World War and forty years after Mussolini's rise to power.[55]

The centenary in 2022 of Mussolini's fascist coup, a turning point in the twentieth century, will surely provide a moment of reflection for Italians and historians. Berlusconi's period of power will, most probably, then be over and how he was able to hoodwink people in the 1990s and early twenty-first century be better understood. Many more Italians may then ask why he was allowed to take such a grip over the media, why his enormous conflicts of interest were tolerated and why he was permitted to slander the magistrature and jeopardize institutions that were central to the proper functioning of democracy. The tycoon-turned-politician did not raise his right arm in the Roman salute or harangue crowds from a balcony in the capital's Piazza Venezia, nor did Forza Italia put small boys into uniform and make them attend weekend parades. Methods of social control had grown sophisticated during the seventy years that separated Mussolini's march on Rome from Berlusconi's getting on to the pitch. Yet, whatever might have been said then to explain and excuse the Italian anomaly called Silvio Berlusconi, his dictatorial control of Italy's channels of information posed a real and pernicious threat to democracy. It would, of course, be possible to exaggerate the comparison between Mussolini and Berlusconi, but when historians look back to how an enormously rich media mogul facing grave legal difficulties turned to politics and won power, they are unlikely to say that he brought honour to his country or that his was a period of government of which Italians could speak with pride.

Notes

Prologue

1. Harry Shindler, representative in Italy of the Italy Star Association, the association of British veterans who fought to liberate Italy between 1943 and 1945, described conditions as fine and sunny when he landed on 24 January with a party of REME engineers attached to the Sherwood Foresters infantry regiment. 'But the weather changed suddenly, conditions became atrocious and we found ourselves deep in mud' (author interview, 12/9/03).
2. C. D'Este, *Fatal Decision*, p. 123.
3. Ibid., p. 179.
4. Author interview with members of Chiarlitti's family, 19/12/02.
5. S. Berlusconi, *L'Italia che ho in mente*, p. 186. Such ideas caused offence to veterans of the Italian campaign who were still alive. 'To keep faith with the British and American soldiers who died at Anzio, we now need to defeat those who want to rewrite history,' said Harry Shindler (author interview, 29/1/03).
6. *Il Sole-24 Ore*, 5/11/02. Ciampi would later speak firmly in support of the resistance's efforts in liberating Italy. On 15 December 2003, Marcello Pera, speaker of the senate and holder of Italy's second highest state office, said that the resistance was a myth that should be abandoned and consigned to history (*Il Sole-24 Ore*, 16/12/03). Three days later, in the traditional presidential year-end address to the holders of high state office, Ciampi reminded Pera and Berlusconi who were among those present that Italy's post-war republic was founded on the values for which the resistance had fought (*Il Sole-24 Ore*, 19/12/03).
7. I Deputati e Senatori del Quattordicesimo Parlamento Repubblicano *(La Navicella)*, p. 179.
8. *La Repubblica*, 5/11/02.
9. A. Galante Garrone, *Calamandrei*, p. 267.
10. Fascism and the role of the resistance were vigorously debated at the end of 2003. Alessandra Mussolini, the dictator's granddaughter, split with the National Alliance and joined a group of fringe right-wing parties after Fini had described fascism as evil. She thought that absolute evil had occurred in Piazzale Loreto, the square in Milan where her grandfather's body was

strung up after his execution (*La Repubblica*, 19/12/03). The death of the historian Alessandro Galante Garrone on 30 October 2003 gave another impulse to the debate. A member of the resistance, Galante Garrone had entered the magistrature in 1933 and served in it for thirty years. 'I will not forget that, above all, fascism was vileness,' he had written (*Il Mite Giacobino*, p. 62). He considered the republic's constitution as something clean born from the resistance's struggle against fascism.

11. *Giù le mani dai libri di storia*, www.libertaegiustizia.it.

12. R. J. B. Bosworth, *Mussolini*, p. 232.

13. Author interview with F. Grande Stevens, 17/8/03.

14. *La Repubblica*, 12/12/02.

15. Senate records.

16. *La Navicella*, p. 832. Travaglia was one of Forza Italia's founders and headed the party's association for pensioners.

17. *Lessico Universale Italiano Vol. VIII*, p. 42 and Bosworth, *Mussolini*, p. 147.

18. *Lessico Universale Italiano Vol. VII*, p. 495.

19. Senate transcript. Sitting 457 of 31/7/03.

1. Mafia

1. R. Di Giovacchino, *Il Libro Nero della Prima Repubblica*, p. 136.

2. N. Tranfaglia, *Mafia, Politica e Affari*, p. 195.

3. P. Ginsborg, *A History of Contemporary Italy*, pp. 258, 335.

4. Ibid., pp. 111–12.

5. Tranfaglia, *Mafia*, pp. 6–7.

6. Ibid., p. 11.

7. Ibid., p. 14.

8. Ibid., p. 17.

9. Ibid., p. 20.

10. A. Stille, *Excellent Cadavers*, p. 210.

11. Court judgement, Florence assize court, second section, 6/6/98.

12. Court judgement – Capaci, Caltanissetta assize appeal court, 7/4/00.

13. Ibid.

14. Court judgement – Borsellino Ter, Caltanissetta assize court, 9/12/99.

15. Ibid. A chapter of the court's judgement deals in detail with the evidence and testimonies concerning the last period of Borsellino's life and the murder itself.

16. Author interview with A. M. Palma, 16/1/03.

17. Ibid., 17/1/03.

20. Court judgement, Florence assize court, first section, 21/1/00.

21. Court judgement, Florence assize court, second section, 6/6/98. The judgement gives great detail about the background to the crimes, how they were committed and the roles of the *mafiosi* involved.

22. Author interview with G. Chelazzi, 13/8/02.

23. Court judgement, Florence assize court, second section, 6/6/98.

24. Ibid.

25. Author interview with G. Chelazzi, 23/8/02.

26. Table (Strage del 23 maggio 1992 – Capaci) provided by prosecutor's department of Palermo court.

27. Tables (Strage del 19 luglio 1992 – Borsellino/Borsellino Bis/Borsellino Ter) provided by prosecutor's department of Palermo court.

28. Ibid.

29. Ibid.

30. Author interview with A. M. Palma, 17/1/03.

31. *La Navicella*, p. 370.

32. Author interview with A. M. Palma, 17/1/03.

33. A. M. Palma, speech in Palermo, December 2002.

34. Author interview with I. De Francisci, 5/2/03.

35. Report for 2001 of state prosecutor to Palermo's appeal court, p. 65.

36. Author interview with I. De Francisci, 5/2/03.

37. A. M. Palma, speech in Palermo, December 2002.

38. Ibid.

39. Ibid.

40. Ibid.

41. Report for 2002 of state prosecutor to Palermo's appeal court, p. 133.

42. Ibid., p. 43.

43. Direzione Nazionale Antimafia, *Relazione Annuale – Ottobre 2001*, p. 282. Silvana Saguto, a senior judge in Palermo who tries cases of the sequestration and confiscation of mafia assets, said that virtually the whole of the Sicilian economy is under the Mafia's control (author interview, 24/9/03).

44. Author interview with G. C. Caselli, 12/10/02.

45. Author interview with A. Ingroia, 15/1/02.

46. Deposition of Francesco Onorato.

47. Ibid.

48. Ibid.

49. Onorato went into hiding after murdering Lima and was helped then by D'Angelo who was still able to move about freely. 'D'Angelo soon disappeared, himself a victim of the Mafia in a *lupara bianca* (white shotgun)

killing,' said Onorato's lawyer (author interview with R. Avellone, 3/3/04).

50. Author interview with D. Gozzo, 23/1/03.

51. A Stille, *Excellent Cadavers*, pp. 129–30.

52. G. Falcone, *Interventi e Proposte*, p. 278.

53. Ibid.

54. Author interview with D. Gozzo, 23/1/03.

55. Report for 2002 of state prosecutor to Palermo's appeal court, p. 38.

56. Author's notes on court hearing.

57. Author interview with D. Gozzo, 23/1/03.

58. Author interview with A. M. Palma, 17/1/03.

59. Ibid.

60. Author interview with D. Gozzo, 23/1/03.

61. *L'Unità*, 15/12/02.

62. Court judgement, Florence assize court, second section, 6/6/98.

63. Report for 2002 of state prosecutor to Palermo's appeal court, p. 37.

64. Ibid., p. 38.

65. Ibid., p. 39.

66. Author interview with A. Ingroia, 15/1/02.

67. A. M. Palma, speech in Palermo, December 2002.

68. Ibid.

69. Author interview with A. M. Palma, 16/1/02.

2. Success

1. *Una Storia Italiana* (An Italian Story), p. 6. Berlusconi sent a glossy 128-page picture album about himself from boyhood and about his achievements as a businessman and politician to all Italian households as part of his election campaign in spring 2001. The album was printed by Mondadori, the publishing house that Berlusconi controlled.

2. Ibid.

3. Ibid., p. 6.

4. Ibid., p. 10.

5. Ibid., pp. 8–9.

6. Ibid., p. 8.

7. Ibid., p. 9.

8. Ibid.

9. Ibid., p. 10.

10. Ibid., p. 26.

11. *Chi*, 20/11/02.

12. *Una Storia Italiana*, p. 33.

13. Various, *Modern Italy, Volume Three, 1939–1960*, p. 265.
14. *Una Storia Italiana*, p. 50.
15. G. Ruggeri and M. Guarino, *Berlusconi Inchiesta sul Signor TV*, pp. 36–7.
16. Ibid., p. 39.
17. *Una Storia Italiana*, p. 51.
18. Ibid., p. 11.
19. Ibid., p. 51.
20. G. Ruggeri, *Berlusconi gli Affari del Presidente*, pp. 26–32.
21. *Una Storia Italiana*, pp. 52–3.
22. Ruggeri and Guarino, *Berlusconi Inchiesta*, p. 48.
23. L. Sisti and P. Gomez, *L'Intoccabile: Berlusconi e Cosa Nostra*, pp. 67, 167.
24. Nucleo Speciale Polizia Valutaria, letter of 28/12/79 to UIC.
25. G. Barbacetto, P. Gomez and M. Travaglio, *Mani Pulite*, pp. 251–2. (Berruti was elected to parliament's lower house in 1996 and 2001 for constituencies in the Lombardy region.)
26. UIC, letter of 11/10/79 to Nucleo Speciale Polizia Valutaria.
27. Nucleo Speciale Polizia Valutaria, letter of 28/12/79 to UIC.
28. Ibid.
29. *Una Storia Italiana*, p. 53.
30. L. Dodi, *La Storia di Arcore*, p. 99.
31. *Corriere della Sera*, 14/10/02.
32. Dodi, *La Storia*, p. 91.
33. Ibid., p. 97.
34. Ibid., p. 98.
35. Ibid., p. 94.
36. R. J. B. Bosworth, *Mussolini*, p. 143.
37. Dodi, *La Storia*, pp. 296–9.
38. Various, *La Grande Truffa*, p. 21.
39. Author interview with A. Nava, 23/7/02.
40. Ruggeri and Guarino, *Berlusconi Inchiesta*, p. 67.
41. *Una Storia Italiana*, p. 57.
42. Ibid.
43. Ibid.
44. Ibid., p. 59.
45. Ruggeri and Guarino, *Berlusconi Inchiesta*, p. 177.
46. Ibid., pp. 179–80.
47. *Una Storia Italiana*, p. 58.
48. Court transcript – SME case, Manca testimony, 28/3/01.
49. Article 77 of Italy's constitution allows the government 'in cases of extraordinary necessity and urgency' to adopt temporary measures that have

the force of law. These governmental decrees lapse 'if not converted into law within sixty days of their publication'.

50. Ruggeri and Guarino, *Berlusconi Inchiesta*, p. 223.

51. *The Europe Review*, 1991/92, p. 101.

52. Mediaset IPO Prospectus, June 1996, p. 38.

53. G. Barbacetto, P. Gomez and M. Travaglio, *Mani Pulite*, pp. 133–5. A detailed description of the ministry's frequency programme for broadcasting and the magistrates' interest in the people, inside and outside the ministry, who were involved in it is to be found in Ruggeri and Guarino, *Berlusconi Inchiesta*, pp. 227–32.

54. *Personality of the Month, August 2002*, www.adnkronos.com.

55. *Biografia di Ennio Doris*, www.bancamediolanum.com.

56. *Equity Research, Mediolanum*, Credit Suisse First Boston, 23/3/01.

57. *Equity Research, Italian Insurance*, Credit Suisse First Boston, 13/3/01.

58. UIC, letter of 11/10/79 to Nucleo Speciale Polizia Valutaria.

59. Ruggeri, *Berlusconi gli Affari*, p. 124.

60. *Una Storia Italiana*, p. 13.

61. Ibid., p. 78.

62. Ibid., pp. 11–12.

63. *Le Foto 'Proibite' del Divino Cavaliere*, 23/5/01, Dagospia.com. Bettino Craxi was one of the witnesses at the couple's civil marriage in Milan on 15 November 1990.

64. *Micromega*, 2/2003, p. 8.

65. *Una Storia Italiana*, p. 65.

66. Ibid., p. 62.

67. *L'Unità*, 6/11/02.

68. Ruggeri and Guarino, *Berlusconi Inchiesta*, p. 73.

69. Fininvest Group presentation 1999, p. 8.

70. *The Economist*, 28/4/01.

71. Direzione Investigativa Antimafia Centro Operativo Palermo, *Procedimento Penale Nr 6031/94*, Capitolo VII.

72. Ibid.

73. Ibid., Capitolo I.

74. Ibid.

75. Ibid.

76. Ibid., Capitolo II.

77. Ibid.

78. *Una Storia Italiana*, p. 47.

79. Direzione Investigativa Antimafia Centro Operativo Palermo, *Procedimento Penale Nr 6031/94*, Capitolo II.

80. Ibid.

81. Ibid., Capitolo III.
82. Ibid.
83. Ibid., Capitolo VIII.
84. Ibid.
85. Ibid.
86. Ibid.
87. Ibid.
88. Ibid.
89. Ibid., Capitolo X.
90. *The Economist*, 2/8/03.
91. Ibid., 28/4/01. Winding up the prosecution's case against Dell'Utri on 10 May 2004, Domenico Gozzo said that 17 billion lire of funding that Fininvest's Holdings received in 1977 and 1978 were of unknown origin (*La Repubblica*, 11/5/04).
92. Court transcript – Dell'Utri trial, Giuffrida testimony, 6/5/02.
93. Ibid., 7/5/02.
94. Ibid., 6/5/02.
95. Ibid., 7/5/02.
96. Ibid.
97. Ibid., 6/5/02.
98. Ibid., 7/5/02.
99. Author interview with E. Tinaglia, 18/7/03.
100. *La Repubblica*, 27/11/02.

3. Corruption

1. R v Secretary of State for the Home Department, *ex parte* Fininvest SpA and others (1997) All ER 942.
2. *The Economist*, 2/8/03.
3. R v Secretary of State for the Home Department, *ex parte* Fininvest SpA and others (1997) All ER 942.
4. Author interview with P. Davigo, 31/7/02.
5. Ibid.
6. Ibid.
7. Ibid.
8. Author interview with G. Colombo, 24/7/02.
9. Bank of Italy, *Appendix to annual report 2002*, pp. 233–4.
10. *Micromega*, 1/2002, p. 252.
11. A. Carlucci, *1992: I Primi Cento Giorni di Mani Pulite*, p. 24.
12. A. Di Pietro, *Intervista su Tangentopoli*, p. 11.

13. G. Barbacetto, P. Gomez and M. Travaglio, *Mani Pulite*, pp. 13–14.

14. A. Zambarbieri, *La Traccia dell'Uomo (Volume Primo)*, p. 142.

15. *The Economist Business Traveller's Guides – Italy*, p. 47.

16. Barbacetto, Gomez and Travaglio, *Mani Pulite*, p. 136.

17. G. Cosmacini and C. Cenedella, *I Vecchi e la Cura – Storia del Pio Albergo Trivulzio*, p. 191.

18. Barbacetto, Gomez and Travaglio, *Mani Pulite*, p. 16.

19. Author interview with G. Colombo, 24/7/02.

20. *UBS-Lugano. 633369 'Protezione'*, p. 25. This book is a publication of the court's judgement regarding the case.

21. Ibid., p. 20.

22. Court judgement, Venice appeal court, 23/10/90.

23. Ibid.

24. *The Economist*, 2/8/03.

25. *UBS-Lugano*, p. 103.

26. Author interview with G. Colombo, 24/7/02.

27. Barbacetto, Gomez and Travaglio, *Mani Pulite*, pp. 84–5.

28. Ibid., p. 87.

29. *UBS-Lugano*, pp. 41–2.

30. Court judgement, second criminal section of the supreme court, 20/4/99. With this judgement, Craxi's appeal against verdicts of guilty on counts of illicit financing of political parties and aggravated corruption in connection with the construction of Milan's underground railway reached the end of the line. On 16 April 1996, a court of first instance in Milan had sentenced the Socialist Party leader to eight years and three months' imprisonment, a fine of 150 million lire and a lifelong ban from public office. This sentence was confirmed by Milan's appeal court on 5 June 1997, but then annulled and transferred to another appeal court. The judgement of 20 April 1999 was the confirmation of Craxi's guilt. The supreme court noted the evidence that envelopes containing money from bribes had been placed in Craxi's room and that such funds were destined unquestionably for his exclusive use. This was, said the court, a lengthy matter of corruption in which 'the defendant was himself involved directly and at the highest levels'. Craxi, and his family after his death, took his case to the European Court of Human Rights which recognized in 2002 and 2003 that some rights of the Socialist Party's leader had been violated. In 2001, however, the European court had rejected the appeal against the Italian court's verdict that Craxi was guilty of corruption (*La Repubblica*, 18/7/03).

31. *UBS-Lugano*, p. 207.

32. Barbacetto, Gomez and Travaglio, *Mani Pulite*, p. 582.

33. G. Colombo, speech in Boston, 5/8/99.

34. Author interview with G. Colombo, 24/7/02.
35. Ibid.
36. G. Colombo, speech in Budapest, 26/5/98.
37. Table provided by the prosecutor's department of the Milan court.
38. *Il Sole-24 Ore*, 17/8/02.
39. R. Cornwell, *God's Banker*, p. 20.
40. Ibid., p. 50.
41. C. Stajano, *Un Eroe Borghese*, p. 235.
42. L. Tescaroli, *I Misteri dell'Addaura*, p. 126.
43. Author interview, 4/7/02.
44. Mediaset press statement, 2/7/02.
45. *The Europe Review*, 1990, p. 107.
46. Ibid., 1991/92, p. 106.
47. *La Maxitangente Enimont*, p. 143. A publication of the judgement handed down by the court that tried the Enimont case, this book is on the same pattern as *UBS-Lugano. 633369 'Protezione'*.
48. ENI IPO prospectus, p. 74.
49. Author interview with P. Davigo, 31/7/02.
50. Author interview with G. Colombo, 24/7/02.
51. Author interview with C. Smuraglia, 29/7/02.
52. Author interview with G. Pisapia, 30/7/02.
53. *Corriere della Sera*, 30/4/02.
54. Court judgement, Milan appeal court, fifth criminal section, 12/5/01.
55. Ibid.
56. Court judgement, Milan court, office of the judge for preliminary investigations, 19/6/00.
57. Ibid.
58. Ibid.
59. Court judgement, Milan appeal court, fifth criminal section, 12/5/01.
60. Court judgement, Milan court, office of the judge for preliminary investigations, 19/6/00.
61. Court judgement, Milan appeal court, fifth criminal section, 12/5/01.
62. Ibid.
63. Ibid.
64. Author interview with G. Pisapia, 30/7/02.
65. Barbacetto, Gomez and Travaglio, *Mani Pulite*, p. 466.
66. Ibid., pp. 467–8.
67. Court judgement, Milan court, office of the judge for preliminary investigations, 15/11/99.
68. Ibid.
69. *Corrotti e Corruttori*, pp. 185–95. Subtitled *The Greatest Scandal in*

the History of the Republic, this book is the publication of the judgement handed down by the criminal court presided by Paolo Carfi that tried the Lodo Mondadori and IMI-SIR cases. Carfi announced the verdict and sentenced the defendants on 29 April 2003. The written judgement giving the reasons for the verdict was made public on 6 August. The book appeared in August 2003 as a supplement to the weekly news magazine *L'Espresso*.

70. Court judgement, Milan court, office of the judge for preliminary investigations, 15/11/99.

71. Ibid.

72. Ibid.

73. *La Repubblica*, 11/5/04.

74. *Corriere della Sera*, 30/4/03.

75. *Il Sole-24 Ore*, 30/4/03.

76. *Corrotti e Corruttori*, p. 314.

77. *La Repubblica*, 30/4/03.

78. Author interview with F. Grande Stevens, 25/7/02. Copies of correspondence between Grande Stevens and Previti.

79. Court judgement, Milan court, office of the judge for preliminary investigations, 26/11/99.

80. Court transcript – SME case, 17/6/03.

81. *The Economist*, 2/8/03.

82. P. Gomez and M. Travaglio, *Lo Chiamavono Impunità*, p. 67. This book tells the history of the SME case, providing court transcripts of the prosecution's winding up and the testimonies and declarations of some of the people who gave evidence.

83. Ibid., p. 199.

84. Ibid., p. 202.

85. *Corrotti e Corruttori*, p. 334.

86. Court verdict, Milan court, first criminal section, 22/11/03. The two-page verdict was announced at the end of the trial by the court's president Luisa Ponti. The court filed its judgement giving the reasons for its verdict in March 2004.

87. Court transcript – SME case, Manca testimony, 28/3/01.

88. Ibid.

89. Author interview with G. Colombo, 24/7/02.

90. Table provided by the prosecutor's department of the Milan court.

91. Author interview with F. S. Borrelli, 29/7/02.

92. Ibid.

93. Author interview with P. Davigo, 31/7/02.

94. Author interview with G. Colombo, 24/7/02.

95. G. Colombo, *Il Vizio della Memoria*, p. 184.

96. Transparency International press statement, 28/8/02.

97. Author interview with P. Davigo, 31/7/02.

98. Ibid.

99. Ibid.

100. Author interview with F. S. Borrelli, 29/7/02.

4. Power

1. *The Economist*, 24/4/01.

2. www.CNN.com, posted 1/3/02.

3. *Una Storia Italiana*, pp. 76–7.

4. Direzione Investigativa Antimafia Centro Operativo Palermo, *Procedimento Penale Nr 6031/94*, Capitolo V.

5. E. Poli, *Forza Italia*, p. 43.

6. Author interview with V. Dotti, 26/11/02.

7. Poli, *Forza Italia*, p. 50.

8. Ibid., p. 53.

9. Ibid., p. 55.

10. Ibid.

11. Ibid.

12. Ibid., p. 46.

13. *Una Storia Italiana*, p. 10.

14. Ibid., p. 77.

15. Ibid.

16. Ibid., p. 71.

17. Poli, *Forza Italia*, p. 63.

18. *La Carta dei Valori di Forza Italia*, www.forza-italia.it.

19. R. J. B. Bosworth, *Mussolini*, p. 3.

20. Ibid., p. 422.

21. Poli, *Forza Italia*, p. 60.

22. P. Ginsborg, *A History of Contemporary Italy*, p. 442.

23. F. Tabladini, *Bossi – La Grande Illusione*, p. 13.

24. Poli, *Forza Italia*, p. 60.

25. Ibid., p. 68.

26. *Diario*, 1/11/02.

27. *Financial Times*, 18/7/94.

28. G. Barbacetto, P. Gomez and M. Travaglio, *Mani Pulite*, pp. 238–9.

29. Ibid., p. 239.

30. Ibid., p. 245.

31. *Financial Times*, 18/7/94.
32. I. Montanelli and M. Cervi, *L'Italia di Berlusconi*, p. 188.
33. Barbacetto, Gomez and Travaglio, *Mani Pulite*, pp. 283–6.
34. S. Berlusconi, *L'Italia che ho in mente*, pp. 49–50.
35. *Diario*, 1/11/02.
36. *Una Storia Italiana*, pp. 24–5.
37. Ibid., p. 88.
38. Poli, *Forza Italia*, p. 68.
39. P. Ginsborg, *Italy and its Discontents*, p. 300.
40. Poli, *Forzia Italia*, p. 110.
41. Author interview with V. Dotti, 26/11/02.
42. Author interview with S. Ariosto, 4/11/03.
43. Court transcript – SME case, 17/6/03.
44. Ibid., 6/6/03.
45. Author interview with V. Dotti, 26/11/02.
46. Report of technical consultants to Milan court, case 735/96/21, 31/5/99. (The prosecutors in Milan gave the mandate to investigate Fininvest's off-shore operations to KPMG, the large international accountancy firm.)
47. Author interview with V. Dotti, 26/11/02.
48. Author interview with S. Ariosto, 4/11/03.
49. Poli, *Forza Italia*, p. 81.
50. *Statuto di Forza Italia*, www.forza-italia.it.
51. Berlusconi, *L'Italia*, p. 65.
52. Ibid., p. 183.
53. Ibid., p. 211.
54. Ibid., p. 201.
55. Ibid., p. 81.
56. Ibid., p. 242.
57. Ibid., p. 37.
58. Ibid., p. 133.
59. Ibid., p. 171.
60. Ibid., p. 172.
61. *Corriere della Sera*, 3/2/04.
62. Berlusconi, *L'Italia*, p. 179.
63. Ibid., p. 132.
64. Ibid., p. 215.
65. Author's notes, Mediaset press conference, 20/7/95.
66. Ibid.
67. Mediaset IPO prospectus, p. 15.
68. Mediaset IPO summary prospectus, p. 14.
69. S. Berlusconi, *Contratto con gli Italiani*.

70. Ibid.

71. Ed. G. Pasquino, *Dall'Ulivo al Governo Berlusconi*, p. 127.

72. Ibid., pp. 28–9.

73. S. Berlusconi, speech to chamber of deputies, 21/6/01, www.forza-italia.it.

74. Court transcript – SME case, 17/6/03.

75. Amnesty International, letter of 27/4/01 to Enzo Bianco.

76. Amnesty International, press statement of 19/7/02.

77. *La Repubblica*, 13/9/03.

78. *Una Storia Italiana*, p. 31.

79. *Il Sole-24 Ore*, 5/7/02.

80. *La Repubblica*, 29/10/02.

81. *Corriere della Sera*, 17/10/02.

82. *La Repubblica*, 15/9/02.

83. *Il Sole-24 Ore*, 17/10/02.

84. *Financial Times*, 23/11/02.

85. *La Repubblica*, 28/3/03.

86. *Ansa*, 30/3/03.

87. Ibid.

88. *Libro Bianco*, 20/12/01.

89. Ibid. The white book noted that the air force and the navy were the forces most affected by inadequate resources.

90. *The Economist*, 10/5/03. On 1/7/03, the day that the Italian presidency started, an article by Quentin Peel in the *Financial Times* noted that Berlusconi's blatantly self-serving style of government suggested that he had little concern for the rules of good governance that the European Union demanded of all its new members. Peel added, 'There can be little doubt that, if Italy were itself applying to join the EU today, its application would be rejected if Mr Berlusconi refused to break up his own media empire.'

91. *Il Sole-24 Ore*, 3/7/03.

92. Outside Italy, the European media was unanimous in expressing outrage. In Britain, an editorial article in the *Guardian* on 4/7/03 described Berlusconi as a dangerous scoundrel and on the following day a feature article in the same newspaper called Italy's prime minister the Italian poisoner. The *Independent* on 4/7/03 thought that Berlusconi's 'joke' exposed a democratic flaw at the heart of Europe. An article in the *Observer* on 6/7/03 was titled 'From Pinocchio to Mussolini and now Berlusconi, it's a story of lies'.

93. *Financial Times*, 5/7/03.

94. *Il Sole-24 Ore*, 10/7/03.

95. *L'Unità*, 7/11/03.

96. *La Repubblica*, 18/11/03 to 22/11/03.

97. Ibid., 13/12/03.
98. Ibid., 4/10/02.
99. Author interview with M. Segni, 15/12/03.
100. Author interview with C. De Mita, 15/12/03.
101. European Liberal Democrats press release, 16/12/03.
102. Author interview with G. Watson, 16/12/03.
103. Ibid.
104. Ibid.
105. European Free Alliance press release, 14/1/04.
106. BBC News, 30/12/03.
107. *Guardian*, 5/7/03.
108. Ibid., 17/4/03.
109. *Independent*, 22/8/03.
110. *L'Unità*, 3/11/02.
111. R. Trevelyan, *Rome '44*, p. 282.
112. *La Repubblica*, 26/9/01.
113. *Corriere della Sera*, 27/9/01.
114. *Diario*, 1/11/02.
115. *La Repubblica*, 27/9/01.
116. Bank of Italy, *Economic Bulletin No. 37*, pp. a1, a2, a11.
117. *The Economist*, 7/12/02.
118. Bank of Italy, *Economic Bulletin No. 37*, p. 50.
119. *Pensions International*, September 1999.
120. *La Repubblica*, 13/4/03.
121. *Privatisation International*, December 1999.
122. Ibid., February 2001.
123. Ibid.
124. *Corriere della Sera*, 18/4/02.
125. E. Biagi, *Cose Loro & Fatti Nostri*, p. 147.
126. *L'Unità*, 11/2/04.
127. *Il Sole-24 Ore*, 17/12/03.
128. *Corriere della Sera*, 21/12/03.
129. *Il Sole-24 Ore*, 21/12/03.
130. Author interview with G. Watson, 16/12/03.
131. www.rsf.fr.
132. Ibid.
133. *La Repubblica*, 6/5/03.
134. *Financial Times*, 15/5/03.
135. *La Repubblica*, 30/5/03.
136. *L'Unità*, 7/5/03.

5. Law

1. *La Navicella*, p. 587.
2. G. Barbacetto, P. Gomez and M. Travaglio, *Mani Pulite*, p. 92.
3. F. S. Borrelli (ed. C. De Cesare), *Corruzione e Giustizia*, p. 69.
4. Ibid., p. 147.
5. *La Navicella*, p. 406.
6. Ibid., p. 259.
7. Ibid., p. 470.
8. Author interview with F. Grande Stevens, 25/7/02.
9. Ibid.
10. Ibid.
11. Ibid.
12. Author interview with C. Smuraglia, 29/7/02.
13. P. Gomez and M. Travaglio, *Bravi Ragazzi*, p. 25.
14. Barbacetto, Gomez and Travaglio, *Mani Pulite*, p. 375.
15. *The Economist*, 28/4/01.
16. Gomez and Travaglio, *Bravi Ragazzi*, p. 25.
17. *The Economist*, 9/8/01.
18. As the Italian presidency of the European Union drew to an end in December 2003, Italian finance was struck by the second major corporate crash of the year. A tomato and fruit canner called Cirio collapsed early in 2003 and then, days before Christmas, came Parmalat, a large dairy company that was a blue chip component of the Italian stock market index, to devastate the portfolios of tens of thousands of Italian small savers that were bulging with its bonds. Parmalat's outstanding paper amounted to the huge sum of around 7 billion euros (*La Repubblica*, 20/12/03), meaning that the company's collapse was proportionately worse than Enron's in America. Initiating legal action against the company on 30 December 2003, America's Securities and Exchange Commission had described the Parmalat scandal as 'one of the largest and most brazen corporate financial frauds in history' (*New York Times*, 30/12/03). In Parma as in Houston, falsified accounts were at the heart of the fraud. The law on false accounting enacted in 2001 had been a clear encouragement to the culture of crime that was shown to thrive at Parmalat, a company whose controlling shareholder was described by Milanese magistrates as 'socially dangerous and lacking the minimum sense of legality' (*L'Unità*, 31/12/03).
19. Author interview with S. Bragantini, 31/7/02.
20. Ibid.
21. Ibid.

22. Ibid.

23. www.uktradeinvest.gov.uk.

24. *Il Sole-24 Ore*, 28/4/04. A sentence of two years' imprisonment would also be passed on Dell'Utri's co-defendant who at the time of sentencing was in prison for other matters that included mafia-related offences.

25. Barbacetto, Gomez and Travaglio, *Mani Pulite*, p. 659.

26. Senate records, 371-B.

27. Barbacetto, Gomez and Travaglio, *Mani Pulite*, pp. 660–61.

28. *Micromega*, 1/2002, p. 109.

29. Prosecutor's pleadings.

30. *La Navicella*, p. 646.

31. *Il Sole-24 Ore*, 2/3/02.

32. Senate records.

33. *La Repubblica*, 21/7/02. As he had done before, the president of the court ordered that a medical check should be undertaken on the veracity of Previti's claim to be suffering from a renal disturbance. It took five hours to find a doctor in Rome willing to carry out the visit.

34. Senate records, sitting 108 of judicial affairs commission.

35. *La Navicella*, p. 734.

36. Senate transcript, sitting 111 of judicial affairs commission, 29/7/02.

37. Senate transcript, sitting 230, 1/8/02.

38. Senate act 1578.

39. *Corriere della Sera*, 15/9/02.

40. *Il Messaggero*, 15/9/02.

41. Chamber of deputies joint commission transcript, 14/9/02.

42. Chamber of deputies transcript, sitting 202.

43. Gomez and Travaglio, *Bravi Ragazzi*, pp. 364–70.

44. Chamber of deputies transcript, sitting 193. Replying to a question on the matter, the chamber's speaker said that the constitution made clear that only Italy's president had the power to dissolve parliament.

45. Document of the CSM's sixth commission.

46. *Il Sole-24 Ore*, 25/9/02.

47. *La Repubblica*, 25/10/02.

48. Gomez and Travaglio, *Bravi Ragazzi*, p. 51.

49. Ibid., p. 46.

50. *Il Sole-24 Ore*, 2/3/02.

51. Ibid., 29/1/03.

52. Ibid., 30/1/03.

53. Ibid., 29/1/03.

54. *La Repubblica*, 13/7/02.

55. Italian constitution, article 68 pre-1993.

56. P. Ginsborg, *Italy and its Discontents*, pp. 274–5.

57. Italian constitution, article 68 post-1993.

58. *La Repubblica*, 13/7/02.

59. Ibid., 13/2/03.

60. Senate transcript, 29/7/02.

61. *Il Sole-24 Ore*, 21/6/03.

62. Ibid., 30/1/03.

63. Ibid., 20/6/03.

6. Complicity

1. *La Navicella*, pp. 1070–78, 1271–90, 1408–13.

2. *La Repubblica*, 8/12/01.

3. E. Poli, *Forza Italia*, p. 144.

4. Ibid., p. 74.

5. Court judgement, Caltanissetta, office of the judge for preliminary investigations, 3/5/02. This judgement closed the investigations into Berlusconi and Dell'Utri.

6. Ibid.

7. Court judgement – Borsellino Ter, Caltanissetta assize court, 9/12/99.

8. Ibid.

9. Ibid.

10. Court judgement, Caltanissetta, office of the judge for preliminary investigations, 3/5/02.

11. Ibid.

12. Ibid.

13. Ibid.

14. Ibid.

15. Ibid.

16. Request for indictment, Palermo 4578/96.

17. Court judgement, Caltanissetta, office of the judge for preliminary investigations, 3/5/02.

18. *La Repubblica*, 23/7/00.

19. Submission by prosecutors, volume three, Palermo criminal case 4578/96.

20. Author's notes of hearing. See also court transcript.

21. Court transcript – Dell'Utri trial, 20/1/03.

22. Court judgement, Caltanissetta, office of the judge for preliminary investigations, 3/5/02.

23. Author interview with D. Gozzo, 23/1/03.

24. Ibid.

25. *La Sicilia*, 23/11/02.

26. *Il Sole 24-Ore*, 20/11/02.

27. *La Repubblica*, 20/11/02.

28. Request for remand in custody of Francesco Zummo, Palermo prosecutor's office, case 4116/99.

29. Author interview with G. Cappellano Seminara, the court-appointed administrator of the assets of the Piazza group, 19/11/03.

30. Submission by prosecutors, in support of application for remand in custody and sequestration of assets of Vincenzo Piazza, Palermo case 69/94.

31. N. Tranfaglia, *Mafia, Politica e Affari*, pp. 141–3.

32. Author interview with F. Giambrone, 18/1/03.

33. Ibid.

34. P. Ginsborg, *A History of Contemporary Italy*, p. 442.

35. Poli, *Forza Italia*, p. 144.

36. R. Minna, *Un Volto nel Processo: Andreotti Giulio*, p. 41.

37. N. Tranfaglia, *La Sentenza Andreotti*, p. 50.

38. A Stille, *Excellent Cadavers*, p. 55.

39. Minna, *Un Volto*, p. 75.

40. Tranfaglia, *La Sentenza*, pp. 45–6.

41. Court judgement – Capaci, Caltanissetta assize appeal court, 7/4/00.

42. Stille, *Excellent Cadavers*, p. 207.

43. S. Lupo, *Storia della Mafia*, p. 103.

44. Ibid.

45. Ibid., pp. 83–7.

46. Regione *Carabinieri* 'Sicilia', announcement.

47. *La Navicella*, p. 269.

48. Regione *Carabinieri* 'Sicilia', announcement.

49. *La Repubblica*, 17/7/98.

50. Ibid.

51. *Giornale di Sicilia*, 16/4/99.

52. Court judgement, Palermo, 15/4/99, office of the judge for preliminary investigations, criminal proceeding 1232/97.

53. Ibid.

54. Ibid.

55. Ibid.

56. Ibid.

57. *La Navicella*, p. 1072.

58. City of Palermo council decision, 11/3/02.

59. Ibid.

60. City of Palermo press release, 12/3/02.

61. *Edited Proceedings of the International Symposium*, p. 11.
62. Author interview with G. C. Caselli, 12/10/02.
63. Ibid.
64. Ibid.
65. L. Violante, *Il Ciclo Mafioso*, pp. 8–9 (Violante quotes an interview given by Lunardi to Cesare Buonamici, a reporter for the TG5 television channel, on 22 August 2001 and Lunardi's reply to a question by Enzo Biagi).
66. Author's notes.
67. G. Mosca, *Che Cosa è la Mafia*, p. xvi of introductory paper by G. C. Caselli and A. Ingroia.
68. Report on public works by Direzione Nazionale Antimafia, p. 5.
69. Ibid., p. 8.
70. Ed. L. Violante, *I Soldi della Mafia*, p. 334.
71. Annual report 2001 of Direzione Nazionale Antimafia, p. 208.
72. A. M. Palma, speech in Palermo, December 2002.
73. *Il Sole-24 Ore*, 26/3/03.
74. Report on public works by Direzione Nazionale Antimafia, p. 53.
75. Annual report 2001 of Direzione Nazionale Antimafia, pp. 250–51.
76. Author interview with I. De Francisci, 5/2/03.
77. *The Economist*, 23/11/02.
78. Tranfaglia, *La Sentenza*, p. 9.
79. Ibid., p. 84.
80. Ibid.
81. *Corriere della Sera*, 26/7/03.
82. *La Repubblica*, 26/7/03.
83. *La Navicella*, p. 588.
84. *L'Unità*, 7/11/03.
85. Letter to CSM signed by G. C. Caselli, G. Lo Forte, R. Scarpinato and G. Natoli.
86. *Adnkronos*, 13/1/04. The entire Roman Curia and the diplomatic corps in Rome were invited to the ceremony which was televised worldwide by the Telepace channel. It was a major event for the university which dates from the time of Pope Clemence XIV at the end of the eighteenth century and is where Pope John Paul II established an institute for studies on marriage and the family in 1981. The pope himself had approved the award to Andreotti, a person 'always inspired by Christian values'.
87. *Il Sole-24 Ore*, 9/6/04.
88. *Corriere della Sera*, 16/6/04. The title of the report said that the nomination would provide Dell'Utri with 'European immunity'. On 17 June, Britain's *Independent* wrote, 'Euro job saves Berlusconi ally from trial'.

7. Justice

1. Author's notes.
2. Ibid.
3. Ibid.
4. Ibid.
5. Ibid.
6. *Il Giornale*, 6/5/03.
7. Author's notes.
8. Author's note on information from Studio Pisapia, 9/5/03.
9. Report of Milan appeal court, inauguration of judicial year 2002, p. 299.
10. Ibid., 2003, p. 311.
11. Ibid., p. 313.
12. *Il Sole-24 Ore*, 14/1/03.
13. Ibid.
14. Author interview with V. Grevi, 4/10/02.
15. V. Grevi, *Alla Ricerca di un Processo Penale 'Giusto'*, p. 312.
16. Ibid.
17. Author interview with V. Grevi, 4/10/02.
18. Grevi, *Alla Ricerca*, p. 319.
19. Author interview with A. Spataro, 6/8/02.
20. Ibid.
21. Unpublished paper by A. Spataro.
22. Author interview with A. Spataro, 6/8/02.
23. Ibid.
24. Ibid.
25. Ibid.
26. Ibid.
27. G. Colombo and A. Dal Moro, *Come Affrontare il Processo Penale*, p. 3.
28. Ibid., p. 4.
29. Ibid., p. 5.
30. Italian constitution, article 27.
31. Ibid., article 111.
32. Colombo and Dal Moro, *Come Affrontare*, p. 152.
33. R. J. B. Bosworth, *Mussolini*, p. 33.
34. Ibid., p. 416.
35. *Corriere della Sera*, 20/4/02.
36. Ibid.
37. Ibid.

38. *La Repubblica*, 12/7/02.
39. Italia dei Valori newsletter of 23/4/02. After leaving the magistrature, Di Pietro went into politics and founded Italia dei Valori.
40. Colombo and Dal Moro, *Come Affrontare*, p. 153.
41. Ibid., p. 155.
42. Author interview with A. Spataro, 6/8/02.
43. *Il Sole-24 Ore*, 20/5/03.
44. www.csm.it, 23/7/03.
45. Author interview with Ernesto Aghina, member of CSM, 23/7/03.
46. www.magistraturademocratica.it, 23/7/03.
47. Note of CSM entitled 'Le possible forme di pressione sul giudice'.
48. *La Repubblica*, 1/7/03.
49. www.magistraturademocratica.it, website carrying ANM's note 'L'attacco ai giudici sbarca in Europa' of 5/7/03.
50. Note of CSM entitled 'Composizione'.
51. www.adnkronos.com, 1/8/02.
52. www.lapadania.com, 2/8/02.
53. www.adnkronos.com, 1/8/02.
54. www.csm.it, figures at 23/7/03.
55. Italian constitution, article 112.
56. Report of CSM entitled 'Relazione al Parlamento sullo Stato della Giustizia (2001)', pp. 37–8, 63.
57. *La Repubblica*, 14/7/03.
58. Author interview with A. Spataro, 6/8/02.
59. Ibid.
60. *Il Sole-24 Ore*, 27/7/03 to 30/7/03.
61. www.magistraturaindipendente.it, website carrying Ciampi's speech of 17/2/03.
62. www.magistraturademocratica.it, circular to members of 9/7/03.
63. Note of CSM entitled 'Le Basi dell'Indipendenza della Magistratura'.

8. Betrayal

1. Author interview with L. Violante, 19/7/02.
2. *La Repubblica*, 24/5/02.
3. *L'Unità*, 5/9/02.
4. Author's note of conference in Milan, 4/7/02.
5. F. Grande Stevens, *Vita d'un Avvocato*, p. 211.
6. Author interview with F. Grande Stevens, 25/7/02.
7. Ibid.

8. C. Stajano, *Un Eroe Borghese*, p. 191.
9. Unpublished tribute to E. Alessandrini by A. Spataro.
10. Ibid.
11. Author interview with A. Spataro, 6/8/02.
12. Unpublished tribute to E. Alessandrini by A. Spataro.
13. Stajano, *Un Eroe*, p. 8.
14. Ibid., pp. 102–3.
15. Author interview with C. Stajano, 23/7/02.
16. Author interview with S. Novembre, 25/7/02.
17. Stajano, *Un Eroe*, p. 237.
18. Author interview with S. Novembre, 25/7/02.
19. Unpublished tribute to G. Galli by A. Spataro.
20. Ibid.
21. Ibid.
22. P. Davigo, *La Giubba del Re*, p. 8.
23. G. Colombo, *Il Vizio della Memoria*, p. 33.
24. Ibid., p. 35.
25. Ibid.
26. Author's notes.
27. R. Bartoli Costa, *Una Storia Vera a Palermo*, p. 25.
28. Ibid., p. 36.
29. *Il Sole-24 Ore*, 17/4/02.
30. *La Repubblica*, 17/4/02.
31. *Corriere della Sera*, 1/7/02.
32. Bartoli Costa, *Una Storia*, p. 43.
33. Resolution of CSM, 21/3/02.
34. Ibid.
35. Ibid.
36. Author interview with F. S. Borrelli, 29/7/02.
37. Ibid.
38. Author interview with G. Colombo, 24/7/02.
39. Author interview with A. Spataro, 6/8/02.
40. G. Barbacetto, P. Gomez and M. Travaglio, *Mani Pulite*, pp. 271–2.
41. Author interview with G. Colombo, 24/7/02.
42. Barbacetto, Gomez and Travaglio, *Mani Pulite*, p. 290.
43. Author interview with A. Spataro, 6/8/02.
44. Barbacetto, Gomez and Travaglio, *Mani Pulite*, pp. 325–7.
45. Author interview with F. S. Borrelli, 29/7/02.
46. Barbacetto, Gomez and Travaglio, *Mani Pulite*, pp. 327–9.
47. Author interview with G. Colombo, 24/7/02.
48. Ibid.

49. Author interview with P. Davigo, 31/7/02.
50. *La Repubblica*, 13/11/03.
51. A. Di Pietro, *Memoria*, p. 411.
52. Ibid., p. 414.
53. Author interview with P. Davigo, 31/7/02.
54. Ibid.
55. Resolution of CSM, 9/7/98.
56. Ibid., 15/12/99.
57. Author interview with F. S. Borrelli, 29/7/02.
58. Resolution of CSM, 15/12/99.
59. Statement by A. Spataro to CSM, 27/11/01.
60. Ibid.
61. Ibid.
62. Ibid.
63. Senate motion I-00045 of 5/12/01.
64. In L. Violante, *Il Ciclo Mafioso*, p. 16.
65. Statement of university professors.
66. Ibid. The university professors had taken a passage from Calamandrei's book *Elogio dei Giudici – scritto da un avvocato* (p.xiv). Opening the judicial year in Turin on 17/1/04, Caselli quoted this passage. He also quoted Calamandrei's biographer, Galante Garrone: 'I have heard too often in the complaints against magistrates accused of being political the sentiment of intolerance towards the magistrate who is simply doing his duty conscientiously and whose sole political act is that of allegiance to the constitution' (A. Galante Garrone, *Il Mite Giacobino*, p. 46).

Epilogue

1. D. Leigh and E. Vulliamy, *Sleaze*, pp. 171–2.
2. Ibid., p. 178.
3. Committee on Standards in Public Life (Nolan Committee).
4. Nolan Report, Volume I, p. 16.
5. Ibid. Alessandro Galante Garrone was also interested in the inability of people entrusted with public positions to distinguish between right and wrong. In *Il Mite Giacobino*, he looked at the case of Gabriele Cagliari, the corrupt chairman of ENI, the state energy group, who committed suicide while remanded in custody. In a letter he wrote before taking his life, Cagliari complained about the 'supreme injustice' of the proposal that those responsible for *tangentopoli* should be excluded from all public posts and from managing companies. Galante Garrone observed, 'That the person who wrote this

was ENI's chairman at the time of the century's biggest swindle at the citizens' expense is frankly astounding. It is the sign of having lost the capacity to know what is licit and what is illicit. We must say uncompromisingly, leaving aside the question of human pity, that what Cagliari considered unjust is, for us, justice that cannot be forgone' (*Il Mite Giacobino*, p. 29).

6. Nolan Report, Volume I, p. 17.

7. Ibid., p. 14.

8. Ibid.

9. Ibid., p. 16.

10. R. Neild, *Public Corruption*, pp. 10–11. Neild also suggests that the Roman Catholics' dual claims on political loyalty, to the pope as well as to their own nation states, may also be a factor to explain why Protestants might be more conscientious in their public conduct.

11. *Il Foglio*, 1/5/03. Berlusconi wrote that 29 and 30 April 1993 had been two terrible days for Italian democracy. 'On 29 April ten years ago a man of state, Bettino Craxi, hated by the PdS and their justice party, was the subject of a secret vote in the chamber of deputies. They had to decide if the notorious Milanese magistrates' request to investigate and prosecute Craxi was vitiated by the suspicion of political persecution. In a free and secret vote, the members of parliament decided that such a suspicion existed and that Craxi should be exempted from a judicial action that was neither honest nor impartial,' Berlusconi wrote to *Il Foglio*. Crowds gathered the following day, 30 April, outside Craxi's residence in Rome, shouting insults and throwing coins. Berlusconi claimed in his letter to the newspaper that these events would lead some months later to the abolition of parliamentary immunity. He said that only the 'democratic reaction offered by the birth of Forza Italia temporarily blocked the triumph of judicial barbarity' and added that the verdict of guilty handed down on Cesare Previti showed that 'ten years later they are trying again'. 'Its aim is not justice,' said Berlusconi referring to the court, 'as the proceedings and the violence with which the Forza Italia member of parliament was pilloried demonstrated but that of striking the forces that have received a mandate to govern and renew Italy.'

12. *L'Osservatore Romano*, 1/5/03. The Vatican's newspaper referred to Psalm 100. This appears as Psalm 101 in the Book of Common Prayer. The English College in Rome noted that the numbering of psalms by the Church of Rome and the Church of England changes from Psalm 40 onwards and that there are also differences in verse numbers (information from the English College, 10/9/03).

13. Ibid.

14. Court transcript – SME case, 17/6/03.

15. Court judgement, Milan court first criminal section 22/11/03. In its lengthy written judgement in the SME case, filed in March 2004, the court noted that Roma 2, the Fininvest company that managed the transmission for Canale 5 in the Rome area, had been involved in criminal proceedings and that Berlusconi and Umberto Previti had been investigated. 'The responsibility of the investigation office of the Rome court, the matter was handled by Renato Squillante who questioned the defendant Silvio Berlusconi on 24/5/84 in the presence of his lawyer Cesare Previti,' said the Milan court's judgement.

16. www.forza-italia.it, 17/6/03.

17. Nolan Report, Volume I, p. 107.

18. Author interview with A. Ryan, 2/9/03.

19. Neild, *Public Corruption*, p. 8.

20. A. Galante Garrone, *Calamandrei*, p. 103.

21. In O. O'Neill, *A Question of Trust*, p. 4.

22. Ibid., p. 70.

23. Ibid., p. 71.

24. Ibid., p. 72.

25. *Corrotti e Corruttori*, p. 11.

26. Author interview with O. L. Scalfaro, 30/1/03.

27. *The Economist*, 28/4/01.

28. Author interview with O. L. Scalfaro, 30/1/03.

29. Ibid.

30. *Corrotti e Corruttori*, p. 11.

31. *Spectator*, 6/9/03.

32. Author interview with O. L. Scalfaro, 30/1/03.

33. J. Rawls, *A Theory of Justice*, p. 207.

34. Ibid., p. 211.

35. Author interview with A. Ryan, 2/9/03.

36. Author interview with O. L. Scalfaro, 30/1/03.

37. Ibid.

38. Author interview with A. Ryan, 2/9/03.

39. *La Repubblica*, 30/9/03.

40. Galante Garrone, *Il Mite*, pp. 54–5. Galante Garrone noted that the absence of a reliable civil service was an encouragement to political parties to take control of the state bureaucracy and assume tasks and functions that should not have been theirs.

41. www.forza-italia.it, Berlusconi's message on 28/1/03 to mark the party's first nine years.

42. *La Repubblica*, 2/9/02.

43. D. Mack Smith, *Mussolini's Roman Empire*, p. 7.

44. Ibid., p. 96.
45. R. J. B. Bosworth, *Mussolini*, p. 215.
46. *The Economist*, 7/6/03.
47. *Spectator*, 6/9/03.
48. Bosworth, *Mussolini*, p. 187.
49. C. M. Martini, *Sulla Giustizia*, p. 24.
50. *La Repubblica*, 7/12/03.
51. Bosworth, *Mussolini*, p. 424.
52. *Spectator*, 13/9/03.
53. Bosworth, *Mussolini*, p. 172.
54. Ibid., p. 428.
55. A. J. P. Taylor, *The Origins of the Second World War*, p. 85.

Bibliography

Interviews played an important part in the research for *Berlusconi's Shadow*. Some were short, lasting about an hour, while others were considerably longer, one spread over two days and two each taking a full day. Some people were interviewed more than once. A tape recorder was used for many interviews and the tapes were later transcribed into notebooks. Italian was the language used, except in one case when the interview took place in English. Another part of the original, primary research was the author's own observations of events and places which were recorded in notebooks. Secondary sources included periodicals and daily newspapers, particularly *Il Sole-24 Ore* (Italy's business daily) and *La Repubblica* (a daily newspaper of centrist opinion). *Corriere della Sera* (a long-established centrist daily) and *L'Unità* (a left-of-centre daily often covering news unreported elsewhere) were also valuable sources. Various judgements and other documents concerning court cases, such as magistrates' requests for indictment and transcripts of testimony, were of great value and were drawn on extensively. Some judgements and trial documents have been published as books in Italian, *UBS-Lugano. 633369 'Protezione'* and *Corrotti e Corruttori* being two examples. Usually *Berlusconi's Shadow* draws directly on the judgements and trial documents themselves but books are cited where these, rather than the author's own copies of the judgements and documents, have been used as sources. There is a substantial and increasing body of works concerning Silvio Berlusconi himself and the three important issues dealt with in this book – (i) corruption and the efforts of the *mani pulite* team, (ii) the Mafia and the work of the anti-Mafia magistrates, and (iii) the media – and these provided a rich mine of material for *Berlusconi's Shadow*.

Agliano, Sebastiano. *Che Cos'è Questa Sicilia?* Palermo, 1996.
Almerighi, Mario (ed.). *I Banchieri di Dio*. Rome, 2002.
Amadori, Alessandro. *Mi Consenta 2*. Milan, 2003.
Arnone, Giuseppe. *La Banda*. Palermo, 2000.
—. *Ladri*. Agrigento, 2002.
Barbacetto, Gianni. *B: Tutte le Carte del Presidente*. Milan, 2004.

Barbacetto, Gianni, Gomez, Peter and Travaglio, Marco. *Mani Pulite*. Rome, 2002.

Basile, Gaetano. *Palermo E'*. Palermo, 1998.

Bellavia, Enrico and Palazzolo, Salvo. *Falcone Borsellino Mistero di Stato*. Palermo, 2002.

—. *Voglia di Mafia*. Rome, 2004.

Berlusconi, Silvio. *L'Italia che ho in Mente*. Milan, 2000.

Biagi, Enzo. *Cose Loro & Fatti Nostri*. Milan, 2002.

Bini Smaghi, Lorenzo. *Chi ci Salva dalla Prossima Crisi Finanziaria*. Bologna, 2000.

Bocca, Giorgio. *Piccolo Cesare*. Milan, 2002.

Bonatti, Walter. *K2: La Verità*. Milan, 2003.

Bondi, Sandro (ed.). *Una Storia Italiana*. Rome, 2001.

Borelli, Francesco Saverio (De Cesare, Corrado (ed.). *Corruzione e Giustizia*. Milan, 1999.

Bosworth, R. J. B. *Mussolini*. London, 2002.

Butera, Salvatore. *L'Isola Difficile*. Catanzaro, 2000.

Butera, Salvatore and Ciaccio, Giuseppe (eds.). *Aspetti e Tendenze dell'Economia Siciliana*. Rome, 2002.

Calamandrei, Piero. *Elogio dei Giudici Scritto da un Avvocato*. Milan, 1989/1999.

Carlucci, Antonio. *1992: I Primi Cento Giorni di Mani Pulite*. Milan, 2002.

Caselli, Gian Carlo and Ingroia, Antonio. *L'Eredità Scomoda*. Milan, 2001.

—. *Mafia di Ieri, Mafia di Oggi: Ovvero Cambia, ma si Ripete* (in Mosca, Gaetano. *Che Cosa è la Mafia?*). Rome-Bari, 1949/2002.

Colombo, Gherardo. *Il Vizio della Memoria*. Milan, 1996.

Colombo, Gherardo and Dal Moro, Alessandra. *Come Affrontare il Processo Penale*. Milan, 2001.

Colombo, Gherardo and Stajano, Corrado. *Ameni Inganni*. Milan, 2000.

Corbi, Alessandro and Criscuoli, Pietro. *Berlusconate*. Rome, 2003.

Corlazzoli, Alex (ed.). *I Ragazzi di Paolo: Parole di Resistenza Civile*. Turin, 2002.

Cornwell, Rupert. *God's Banker*. London, 1983.

Cosmacini, Giorgio and Cenedella, Cristina. *I Vecchi e la Cura: Storia del Pio Albergo Trivulzio*. Rome-Bari, 1994.

Costa, Pietro and Zolo, Danilo (eds.). *Lo Stato di Diritto: Storia, Teoria, Critica*. Milan, 2002.

Costa, Rita Bartoli. *Una Storia Vera a Palermo*. Caltanissetta, 2001.

Dalla Chiesa, Nando. *La Legge Sono Io*. Naples, 2002.

Davigo, Piercamillo. *La Giubba del Re*. Rome-Bari, 1998.

Debenedetti, Franco. *Sappia la Destra*. Milan, 2001.

D'Este, Carlo. *Bitter Victory: the Battle for Sicily 1943*. London, 1989.

—. *Fatal Decision: Anzio and the Battle for Rome*. London, 1991.

Di Giovacchino, Rita. *Il Libro Nero della Prima Repubblica*. Rome, 2003.

Di Pietro, Antonio. *Intervista su Tangentopoli*. Rome-Bari, 2000.

—. *Memoria*. Milan, 1999.

Falcone, Giovanni. *Interventi e Proposte*. Milan, 1994.

Falcone, Giovanni with Padovani, Marcelle. *Cose di Cosa Nostra*. Milan, 1991.

Finley, Moses, Mack Smith, Denis and Duggan, Christopher. *A History of Sicily*. London, 1986.

Flores d'Arcais, Paolo (ed.). *No alle Leggi 'Forza Ladri'*. Rome, 2001.

—. *Resistere, Resistere, Resistere*. Rome, 2002.

—. *Pace*. Rome, 2003.

Friedman, Alan. *Il Bivio*. Milan, 1996.

Friedman, Lawrence M. *Law in America*. New York, 2002.

Fusco, Gian Carlo. *Gli Indesiderabili*. Palermo, 2003.

Galante Garrone, Alessandro. *Calamandrei*. Milan, 1987.

—. *Il Mite Giacobino*. Rome, 1994.

Galdo, Antonio. *Saranno Potenti?* Milan, 2003.

Galgano, Francesco and Grande Stevens, Franzo. *Manualetto Forense*. Padua, 2001.

Galli, Giancarlo. *Il Padrone dei Padroni: Enrico Cuccia*. Milan, 1995.

Ginsborg, Paul. *A History of Contemporary Italy: Society and Politics 1943–1988*. London, 1990.

—.*Italy and its Discontents: Family, Civil Society, State 1980–2001*. London, 2001.

—. *Berlusconi: Ambizioni Patrimoniali in una Democrazia Mediatica*. Turin, 2003.

Gomez, Peter and Travaglio, Marco. *La Repubblica delle Banane*. Rome, 2001.

—. *Lo Chiamavano Impunità*. Rome, 2003.

—. *Bravi Ragazzi*. Rome, 2003.

Grande Stevens, Franzo. *Vita d'un Avvocato*. Padua, 2000.

Grevi, Vittorio. *Alla Ricerca di un Processo Penale 'Giusto'*. Milan, 2000.

Gualtieri, Roberto. *L'8 Settembre dei Partiti*. Rome, 2003.

Guarino, Mario. *Fratello P2 1816*. Milan, 2001.

—. *Il Circo Mediatico*. Rome, 2002.

Guarnieri, Carlo and Pederzoli, Patrizia. *La Magistratura*. Rome-Bari, 2002.

Hart, H. L. A. *The Concept of Law*. Oxford, 1994.

Jannuzzi, Lino. *Il Processo del Secolo*. Milan, 2000.

Jones, Tobias. *The Dark Heart of Italy*. London, 2003.

Leigh, David and Vulliamy, Ed. *Sleaze: The Corruption of Parliament*. London, 1997.

Liddell Hart, B. H. *History of the Second World War*. London, 1970.

Lodato, Saverio. *'Ho Ucciso Giovanni Falcone'*. Milan, 1999.

—. *La Mafia ha Vinto*. Milan, 1999.

Lodato, Saverio and Grasso, Piero. *La Mafia Invisibile*. Milan, 2001.

Longrigg, Clare. *Mafia Women*. London, 1998.

Lupo, Salvatore. *Storia della Mafia*. Rome, 1996.

Maccanico, Antonio (interviewed by Mele, Marco). *Il Grande Cambiamento*. Milan, 2001.

Machiavelli (ed. Skinner, Quentin and Price, Russell). *The Prince*. Cambridge, 1988.

Mack Smith, Denis. *Mussolini's Roman Empire*. London, 1976.

Martini, Carlo Maria. *Sulla Giustizia*. Milan, 1999.

Minna, Rosario. *Un Volto nel Processo: Andreotti Giulio*. Enna, 2002.

Montanelli, Indro and Cervi, Mario. *L'Italia degli Anni di Fango (1978–1993)*. Milan, 1995.

—. *L'Italia di Berlusconi (1993–1995)*. Milan, 2001.

Monti, Giommaria. *Falcone e Borsellino: la Calunnia il Tradimento la Tragedia*. Rome, 1996.

Nania, Gioacchino. *San Giuseppe e la Mafia*. Palermo-Florence, 2000.

Neild, Robert. *Public Corruption: The Dark Side of Social Evolution*. London, 2002.

Nolan, The Lord. *Standards in Public Life – Volume 1*. London, 1995.

Oliva, Ernesto and Palazzolo, Salvo. *L'Altra Mafia*. Catanzaro, 2001.

O'Neill, Onora. *A Question of Trust*. London, 2002.

Oppo, Maria Novella. *Le TV del Padrone*. Rome, 2003.

Orlando, Leoluca. *Fighting the Mafia and Renewing Sicilian Culture*. San Francisco, 2001.

Paciotti, Elena. *Sui Magistrati*. Rome-Bari, 1999.

Pasquino, Gianfranco (ed.). *Dall'Ulivo al Governo Berlusconi*. Bologna, 2002.

Pepino, Livio (ed.). *Attacco ai Diritti: Giustizia, Lavoro, Cittadinanza sotto il Governo Berlusconi*. Rome-Bari, 2003.

Petrini, Roberto. *Il Grande Bluff: Perche non va l'Economia di Berlusconi*. Rome-Bari, 2002.

Poli, Emanuela. *Forza Italia*. Bologna, 2001.

Provvisionato, Sandro. *Segreti di Mafia*. Rome-Bari, 1994.

Rawls, John. *A Theory of Justice*. Oxford, 1999.

Riccardi, Andrea. *Pio XII e Alcide De Gasperi: una Storia Segreta*. Rome-Bari, 2003.

Robb, Peter. *Midnight in Sicily*. Sydney, 1996.

Rognoni, Carlo. *Inferno TV: Berlusconi e la Legge Gasparri*. Milan, 2003.

Rossi, Giampiero and Spina, Simone. *Lo Spaccone: l'Incredibile Storia di Umberto Bossi*. Rome, 2004.

Rossi, Salvatore. *La Politica Economica Italiana 1968–1998*. Rome-Bari, 1998.

Ruggeri, Giovanni. *Berlusconi Gli Affari del Presidente*. Milan, 1994.

Ruggeri, Giovanni and Guarino, Mario. *Berlusconi Inchiesta sul Signor TV*. Milan, 1994.

Sciascia, Leonardo. *A Futura Memoria*. Bologna, 1989/2000.

—. *Il Giorno della Civetta*. Milan, 1993/2002.

Sisti, Leo and Gomez, Peter. *L'Intoccabile: Berlusconi e Cosa Nostra*. Milan, 1997.

Stajano, Corrado. *Un Eroe Borghese*. Turin, 1991.

Sterling, Claire. *The Mafia*. London, 1990.

Stille, Alexander. *Excellent Cadavers*. London, 1995.

Sylos Labini, Paolo. *Un Paese a Civiltà Limitata*. Rome-Bari, 2001.

—. *Berlusconi e gli Anticorpi: Diario di un Cittadino Indignato*. Rome-Bari, 2003.

Tabladini, Francesco. *Bossi: la Grande Illusione*. Rome, 2003.

Taylor, A. J. P. *The Origins of the Second World War*. London, 1963.

Tescaroli, Luca. *I Misteri dell'Addaura*. Catanzaro, 2001.

Tomasi di Lampedusa, Giuseppe. *The Leopard*. London, 1960/1996.

Torrealta, Maurizio. *La Trattativa*. Rome, 2002.

Tranfaglia, Nicola. *La Sentenza Andreotti*. Cernusco (Milan), 2001.

—. *Mafia, Politica e Affari*. Rome-Bari, 2001.

—. *La Transizione Italiana: Storia di un Decennio*. Milan, 2003.

Trevelyan, Raleigh. *Rome '44*. London, 1983.

Tuccari, Francesco (ed.). *Il Governo Berlusconi*. Rome-Bari, 2002.

Tuzet, Helene. *Viaggiatori Stranieri in Sicilia nel XVII Secolo*. Palermo, 1988.

Various. *La Grande Truffa*. Milan, 1998.

Veltri, Elio. *Le Toghe Rosse*. Milan, 2002.

Veltri, Elio and Travaglio, Marco. *L'Odore dei Soldi*. Rome, 2001.

Violante, Luciano. *Il Ciclo Mafioso*. Rome-Bari, 2002.

Violante, Luciano (ed.). *Mafia e Antimafia*. Rome-Bari, 1996.

—. *Mafia e Societa Italiana*. Rome-Bari, 1997.

—. *I Soldi della Mafia*. Rome-Bari, 1998.

Zaccaria, Roberto. *La Legge Gasparri: Televisione con . . . Dono*. Rome, 2003.

Zingales, Leone. *L'Alfabetiere di Cosa Nostra*. Parma, 2001.

Court proceedings (judgements, prosecutor's summings-up, requests for indictment, trial transcripts etc.) published as books:

La Vera Storia d'Italia. Naples, 1995.

Le Mazzette della Fininvest. Milan, 1996.

UBS-Lugano. 633369 'Protezione'. Milan, 1996.

La Maxitangente Enimont. Milan, 1997.

L'Onore di Dell'Utri. Milan, 1997.

Boccassini contro Previti. Rome, 2002.

Corrotti e Corruttori. Rome, 2003.

Parliamentary report published as a book:

La Lotta alla Corruzione. Rome-Bari, 1998.

Corte d'Appello di Palermo. Relazione sull'Amministrazione della Giustizia nell'anno 2001, 12 Gennaio 2002.

Corte d'Appello di Palermo. Relazione sull'Amministrazione della Giustizia nell'anno 2002, 18 Gennaio 2003.

Corte d'Appello di Milano. Anno Giudiziario 2002 – Discorso Inaugurale, 12 Gennaio 2002.

Corte d'Appello di Milano. Anno Giudiziario 2003 – Discorso Inaugurale, 18 Gennaio 2003.

Corte d'Appello di Torino. Inaugurazione dell'Anno Giudiziario 2004, 17 Gennaio 2004.

La Costituzione della Repubblica Italiana.

Codice Penale 2002.

Consiglio Superiore della Magistratura. Relazione al Parlamento sullo Stato della Giustizia (2001).

I Deputati e Senatori del Quattordicesimo Parlamento Repubblicano (*La Navicella*). Rome, 2001.

Index

INDEX

Olivetti, 65, 85
O'Neill, Professor Onora, 284
Onorato, Francesco, 30–32, 33
Oriente Masonic lodge, 221
Orlando, Leoluca, 208
Ottawa, 34

P2 masonic lodge, 86–90, 91, 115, 172, 256, 261
Pacifico, Attilio, 102, 103, 104, 105, 106, 109, 110, 111, 112, 113, 114, 115
Paciotti, Elena, 261
Palazzo Chigi, Rome, 75, 133
Palermo
    Borsellino murdered in, 13–15
    building speculation, 205–6
    Piazza della Memoria, 251
    Teatro Massimo, 207–8
    United Nations' garden, 217–18
    work of magistrates and courts, 11–12, 15, 16–17, 25, 26, 28–9, 29–30, 32, 33, 34, 35, 36, 38, 65, 66, 67, 68, 69, 70, 72, 73, 141, 178, 184, 201, 202, 204, 210, 214, 218, 219, 224, 226, 228, 252, 262, 263, 265
    other references, 9, 23, 31, 198, 199, 203, 209, 211, 212, 216
Palina, 69–70, 71, 72, 73
Palma, Anna Maria, 15–17, 24, 25, 26, 27, 36, 39, 40, 222
Palma di Montechiaro, 17, 28
Panorama (magazine), 65
Panzeca, Giuseppe, 214, 215, 216
Paris, 42
Parmafid, 68, 70
Partito Democratico della Sinistra (Democratic Party of the Left), 81, 129
Partito Rifondazione Comunista, 134
Passigli, Stefano, 188
Patten, Chris, 162
Pavia, 149, 242
Pavilion of Contemporary Art, Milan, 19, 20
Pavoncella account, 105, 109
Pecorella, Gaetano, 177, 179, 180, 188, 189, 192, 274
Pennino, Gioacchino, 198
Peru, 92
Perugia, 224
Pescara, 57
Pettaci, Claretta, 242

Pianosa prison, 22
Piazza, Vincenzo, 206
Piazza della Memoria see Palermo
Piedmont, 129
Pillitteri, Paolo, 86–7
Pio Albergo Trivulzio see Milan
Pirelli, 42, 60
Pirelli tower, Milan, 45
Pisa, 21
Pisapia, Giuliano, 102, 107
Pius IX, Pope, 43
Po Valley, 129
Polifemo account, 114
Polo del Buongoverno (Good Government Axis), 127–8
Polo della Liberta (Freedom Axis), 129, 134, 272
Ponti, Gio, 45
Pontificia Universita Lateranense, 227
Pontine marshes, 1
Portella delle Ginestre, 9
Portofino, 59
Portugal, 92
Possa, Guido, 43
Prague, 156, 157
Predappio, 242
Previti, Cesare
    bank accounts, 105, 114
    and Casati Stampi inheritance, 52–3
    and Fininvest, 66
    and Forza Italia, 138–9
    and Grande Stevens, 111–12
    and Manca, 115
    and Metta, 106
    on trial, 102, 103, 104, 108, 109, 112, 114, 136, 172, 177, 183, 184, 186, 188, 191, 193, 195, 266, 270, 284–5
    sentence, 102, 114, 280
    other references, 79, 113, 137, 165, 187, 189, 231, 275, 281
Previti, Umberto, 66
Prima Linea (Front Line), 237, 256
Prodi, Romano, 113
Programma Italia, 59, 61, 125
Proletari Armati per il Comunismo (Armed Proletarians for Communism), 237
Protestantism, 279–80
Protezione account, 88–9
Provenzano, Bernardo, 11, 12, 13, 23, 24, 34, 37, 38, 203, 205

333